MW01133966

Making the Little Black Book

Making the Little Black Book

Inside the Working Manuscript of
Twenty-Four Hours a Day

With Commentary by Damian McElrath, D.H.E.

HAZELDEN®

Hazelden
Center City, Minnesota 55012
hazelden.org

Printed in Canada

Library of Congress Cataloging-in-Publication Data

Making the little black book : inside the working manuscript of Twenty-four hours a day.
p. cm. — (Legacy 12)
ISBN 978-1-61649-407-0
1. Twenty-four hours a day. 2. Alcoholics—Prayers and devotions. 3. Devotional calendars.
I. McElrath, Damian. II. Walker, Richmond. III. Twenty-four hours a day.
BL625.45.T843M35 2012
204'.33—dc23

2012014303

Editor's note

Alcoholics Anonymous, AA, the Big Book, the *Grapevine,* and *AA Grapevine* are registered trademarks of Alcoholics Anonymous World Services, Inc.

16 15 14 13 12   1 2 3 4 5 6

Cover design by David Spohn
Interior design and typesetting by Kinne Design

LEGACY 12

Bringing AA and Twelve Step History Alive

Hazelden's *Legacy 12* publishing initiative
enriches people's recovery with dynamic multimedia works
that use rare original-source documents to bring
Alcoholics Anonymous and Twelve Step history alive.

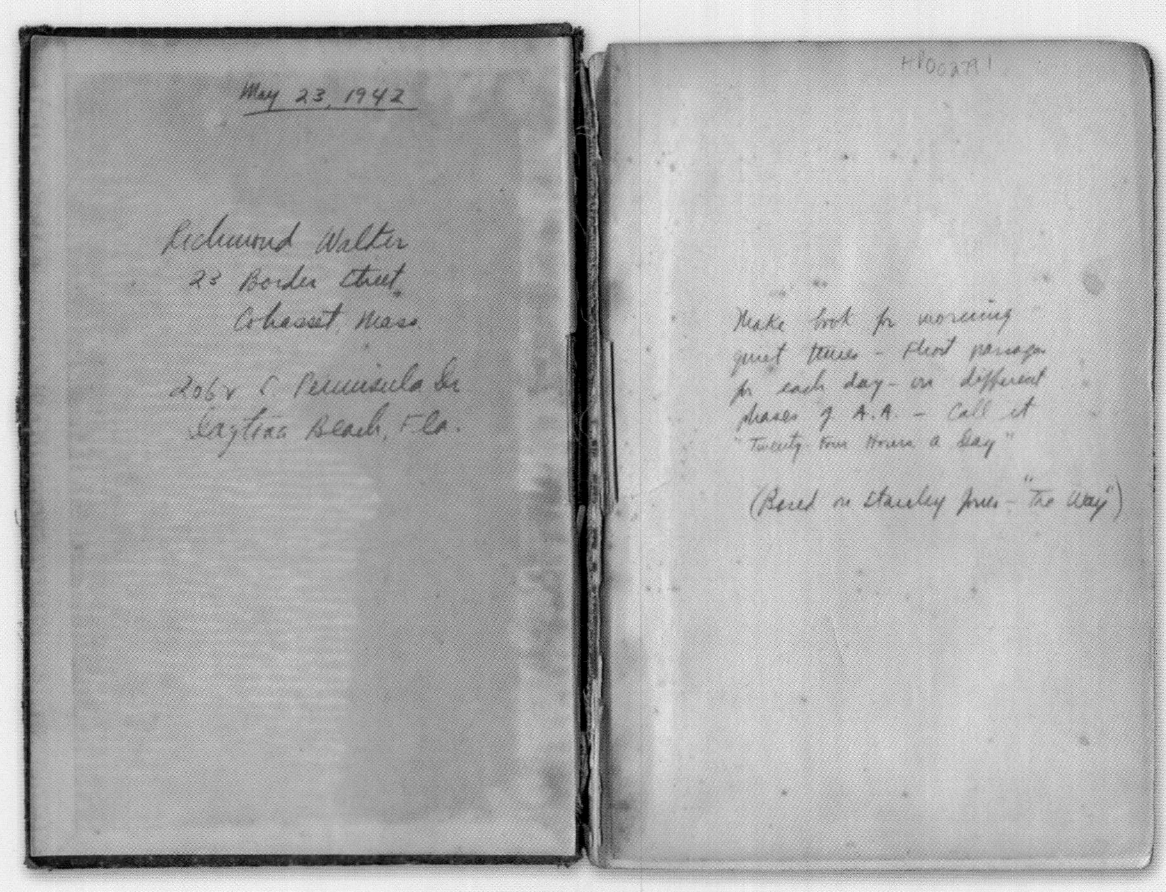

Inside the front cover of his copy of *Alcoholics Anonymous*—the Big Book—Richmond Walker made a note to himself:

MAKE BOOK FOR MORNING
QUIET TIMES–SHORT PASSAGES
FOR EACH DAY–USE DIFFERENT
PHASES OF A.A.–CALL IT
"TWENTY-FOUR HOURS A DAY"
(BASED ON STANLEY JONES—"THE WAY")

CONTENTS

Foreword xi

Three Introductory Essays by Damian McElrath

- The Genesis of a Classic 1
- The Evolution of Walker's Spirituality 25
- Sources for *Twenty-Four Hours a Day* 45

The Working Manuscript for *Twenty-Four Hours a Day* 65

The Hidden Text: The Passages Under the Taped Scraps of Paper 253

A Publishing History of *Twenty-Four Hours a Day* 261

The Richmond Walker and Patrick Butler Correspondence 269

Selected Writings by Richmond Walker 277

- A Successful Group 280
- Surrender 282
- Restitution 284
- Meditation 286
- Honesty 288
- The Cause and Cure of Alcoholism 290
- The Power to Overcome Drinking 295
- Personal Witness 297

About the Author 301

FOREWORD

The idea for *Making the Little Black Book* took root in an end-of-the-day conversation at the desk of Hazelden Publishing's editorial director in early 2011. We were discussing the unexpectedly enthusiastic response from the recovery community, the publishing world, and national media to Hazelden's 2010 release of *The Book That Started It All: The Original Working Manuscript of* Alcoholics Anonymous. We wondered that day what other iconic Twelve Step recovery books—books whose source documents would reveal their origins and history—we could bring to our readers.

Twenty-Four Hours a Day, affectionately dubbed "the Little Black Book" by generations of readers, is one of those iconic recovery books. It is handed by Twelve Step sponsors to their "sponsees" and distributed at treatment centers. Ragged, dog-eared copies protrude from old-timers' back pockets. Grateful family members place it in the caskets of departed loved ones. So, by the end of that conversation, we had a new mission: to offer readers an unprecedented inside look at the creation of Richmond Walker's *Twenty-Four Hours a Day,* the meditation book that has helped over ten million people in twenty-five countries live free and sober.

The Hazelden archives are housed in two places: in a bank vault near its treatment campus in Center City, Minnesota, where the most rare and valuable documents are kept, and in an unmarked, locked underground room on that campus. I had already retrieved from the vault Walker's original edited manuscript, submitted to then Hazelden president Pat Butler, along with copies of several letters documenting Walker's offer and Butler's acceptance of the publishing rights. But we also hoped to uncover historical documents that would provide the "look behind the curtain" that had so fascinated readers and reviewers of *The Book That Started It All.* Why had some words, sentences, and whole passages been deleted or changed? In Walker's life, where did the origins and the inspiration for the book lie?

These questions took us to the second location, the underground room that houses the historical documents, videos, audio recordings, and photographs gathered by Hazelden over its sixty-four-year history—a collection that coincidentally reflects much of the history of addiction treatment and recovery as we now know it. As we surveyed the archive, we agreed on the person ideally suited to mine it for the facts and insights we needed: Damian McElrath, former Hazelden spiritual director, professional historian, and author of our organization's official history, *Hazelden: A Spiritual Odyssey,* among other publications.

Damian accepted the task, and it was through his dogged research—reviewing published reference material, searching boxes and file folders, and going to the source, the Richmond Walker archives in Daytona Beach, Florida—that the real story could be told. Perhaps Damian's greatest find was Walker's own copy of *Alcoholics Anonymous*—the "Big Book"—featuring the margin and crib notes that now help illuminate his writings, including *Twenty-Four Hours a Day.* In the pages of the book you're about to read, Damian pursues these questions: Who was Richmond Walker? How did his early experiences shape his life and writings? What were his sources? And what was the spiritual philosophy that informed the core messages in the Little Black Book?

Since Hazelden published this book in 1954, it has helped millions worldwide find recovery from the ravages of the disease of addiction. Our treatment centers have given it to incoming patients, our publishing division has sold almost ten million copies to date, and thousands of copies have been shipped free of charge to people who otherwise could not have afforded it. The book has provided readers a rock-hard foundation for a core recovery belief: if we can get through just one day sober and clean, one day becomes two, two days four, and four days evolve into a lifetime. One grateful reader put it this way:

> Thanks so much for the Hazelden materials you sent me, especially "24 Hours." My home flooded during Hurricane Katrina and there have been many deaths and suicides . . . The materials you've sent me have helped tremendously. I am seeing a therapist through the American Red Cross and I am in a 12 Step program and attend meetings . . . Thank you for all your literature. You're helping a lot of people.
>
> — KATRINA SURVIVOR, SEPTEMBER 16, 2007

I hope these pages inspire you as they show the Little Black Book's role in unleashing the power of one-day-at-a-time living for people in recovery everywhere.

Nick Motu
Publisher, Hazelden Foundation

Richmond Walker

August 23, 1892 – March 25, 1965
Sobriety Date: May 23, 1942

"We will take no material thing with us,

but we will take with us the kind words we have said,

the kind deeds we have done,

the help we have given."

Three Introductory Essays

by Damian McElrath

The Genesis of a Classic

I still remember the first time I held *Twenty-Four Hours a Day* (which many devoted readers call the Little Black Book) in my hand. I had been a Franciscan priest for almost twenty-five years before I came to Hazelden in 1976 to take part in its yearlong clinical pastoral education program. Based at Hazelden's residential treatment center in rural Minnesota, it was a training program for clergy who wanted to learn about chemical dependency and how best to work on behalf of people afflicted with this disease. For the first quarter of my training, I was assigned to the Shoemaker Unit, named after Sam Moor Shoemaker, rector of New York's Calvary Episcopal Church, friend of Bill W., and champion and promoter of the Oxford Group, in which both Dr. Bob and Bill W. engaged. The unit supervisor asked me to do the reading for the day and handed me the Little Black Book. Thirty-five years later, I can clearly remember my thoughts and feelings upon first reading the book. My life as a Franciscan had always included meditation that encompassed the mind, our feelings or affective natures, and a prayerful resolution of some purpose for the day. Now, this Little Black Book accomplished it all in such a simple fashion. It has since become a favorite meditation manual and the perfect fulfillment of Step Eleven: "Sought through prayer and meditation to improve our conscious contact with God *as we understood Him,* praying only for knowledge of His will for us and the power to carry that out."

RICHMOND WALKER'S STORY

Much of what has been written about Richmond Walker's life is taken from the autobiographical talk that he presented to an AA group in Rutland, Vermont, in 1958, seven years before he died. It is probably the best and most accurate portrayal of his life story.[1] In this talk, he explained how, as his consumption of alcohol continually increased, he passed from the land of the living to a forsaken landscape littered with objects and shattered dreams.

Gradually, alcohol became his constant companion and remained so until May 1942, when he surrendered and left the surreal landscape of objects in favor of the firm land of relationships and real companionship. Walker's presentation to that AA group did not, however, address his most influential and enduring contribution to helping others struggling with addiction. He did not discuss the book he penned that would become one of the core guides for people in recovery, the meditation book *Twenty-Four Hours a Day.*

Early Life

"Our journey through life is a community affair—
someone has to say, 'I will be with you.'"
— Author unknown

The above sentence has particular poignancy in two principal parts of Walker's life: his thirty years of drinking and twenty-three years of sobriety. Let's begin with a look at his early life.[2]

Walker was born August 23, 1892, into a wealthy and politically active family in Massachusetts. His father, Joseph Walker, a lawyer by profession, pursued a career in politics most of his adult life, just as his own father had. Joseph served as Speaker of the House for the Massachusetts Legislature from 1905 to 1907. Richmond considered him a thoroughly honest politician, serving from a sense of duty and not for financial reward.

His mother, Caroline Richmond of Providence, Rhode Island, was the daughter of a cotton manufacturer. She met Richmond's father while he was studying at Brown University, and they married in 1888. The couple lived in Brookline, Massachusetts, where Richmond and his older brother, Joseph, were born. Rich, the recipient of his mother's maiden name, related that he always played "second fiddle" to his brother "who was older, stronger, and better loved than I." Moreover, "I was a lonesome kid who felt he was not loved enough, or appreciated enough by my mother and father. They considered me a 'problem child,' which I was." He remembers that during the first part of his life, he showed "little affection for his family." From his earliest age, Rich did not feel close to his own family, the natural community into which he had been born. As a result, he also lacked a sense of wholeness, a probable factor in how his life progressed.

Richmond Walker made it clear that in his early years, in both adolescence and early adulthood, he was a young man whose disposition was "to go it alone." At school, "I did not make close friends. I was wrapped in a cloak of reserve. There was a wall between myself and other people. I did not go halfway to make friends, and there was no love in my life. In fact 'true love' was a mystery to me. As a child I was not loved, and as a result I have never learned to truly love others. I was poorly adjusted to life, being self-contained, egocentric, immature, easily hurt and overly sensitive." [3]

Despite his social struggles, Rich was quite successful in school, both at St. George's Prep in Newport, Rhode Island, where he was captain of the football team and won a gold medal in the study of Greek, and at prestigious Williams College, where he graduated magna cum laude in 1914 after completing his coursework in three and a half years.

During his school years, Rich thought people who drank a lot were foolish. He said he avoided alcohol during this period, training as he was for the football team. He did, however, relate one drinking incident from his freshman year in college. At a fraternity initiation, he drank champagne and passed out. When he woke up, he found names written in pencil all over the front of his white shirt.

Entering the Forsaken Landscape: Walker's Drinking Years

Having finished his college coursework early, Rich Walker traveled with his best friend, Mason Garfield, through Africa and Europe for three months: February 24 to May 27, 1914. Rich's travelogue, penned almost daily, reveals that with his football days behind him, he felt free to drink and did so frequently, both on sea and on land.

In contrast to his earlier memories, his writings during this period reveal his attachment to and affection for his family, as well as their devotion to him. For example, he displayed a picture of his mother in his cabin of the ocean liner *Franconia.* In London, he purchased neckties for his father and two brothers, Joe and George, and Liberty scarves for his sisters, Catherine and Evelyn. At all the major cities of his tour, he stopped at the American Express offices to fetch his mail from home. These small touches on his part seem to contradict or at least soften what he wrote in 1958, that "as a child I was not loved." His mother met him when the *Olympia* docked in New York, and his whole family greeted him at the train station in Boston.[4]

In Walker's retelling of his life, there is a gap between finishing college and enlisting in the Army Medical Corps when the United States entered World War I. His brother George remembered that this was the period when Walker started classes at Union Theological and in the same year became engaged. However, he noted that his brother left his studies before he finished out the year and at the same time also broke his engagement.[5]

After the war, Walker went into the wool business with his brother Joe, and they lived together on Boston's Beacon Hill, where they did a lot of partying. Walker himself admitted that he became a very heavy drinker during this time. According to his brother George, "Up to that point he was idealistic and never smoked or drank. Then his animal spirits bust[ed] loose."[6]

On a blind date, Walker met Agnes Nelson in Washington, D.C., where she was working as a secretary. After some years, they decided to elope and were married in the Church of the Transfiguration—the "Little Church Around the Corner"—in New York City on May 8, 1922. He was thirty and she was twenty-eight.

Curiously, he did not tell his family about the marriage until the birth of their first child, Hilda, a year later. In Massachusetts, the couple first lived in an apartment in Brookline and then moved to a home in Chestnut Hill that was built for them by Walker's brother Joe. According to one of Agnes's friends, Roberta Manton, "They lived a very gay life around Boston where tea dancing, bath-tub gin, bear cat cars and the theatre were a way of life. Later, as he became more of an alcoholic this ended. Rich would go off without saying when or where. One weekend he went to Nantucket with a friend, both of them loaded, and he bought a house in Siasconset where, subsequently, he and his wife spent many summers. At that time that part of the island was inhabited by the 'fast set' who entertained with endless drinking parties."[7]

The partying and drinking continued for Rich, but less so for Agnes, who gave birth to three of the couple's children—Hilda, Carol, and John—while the family still lived in Chestnut Hill. Walker sold this home in 1932, during the Depression, and the family moved to Cohasset, a charming town in the South Shore area and an easy commute to Boston, where he continued to work with his brother. Moving into a new town and home signaled a new start for the family, and this was also where the couple's last child, David, was born. It was at this time that Walker promised his wife that he was through with liquor for good.

But he was unable to break his ties with the companionship that alcohol afforded, especially when the couple's oldest child, Hilda, died from spinal meningitis in the summer of 1935. It was a crushing event that intensified Walker's feelings of loneliness and isolation. He had expressed his love for his firstborn in poems that he composed on her birthdays.[8] Now he sought comfort in alcohol, and drinking became a priority for him. The promise he made his wife to stop drinking was broken time and again. He frequented the taverns around the South Shore and in Boston, where he worked. He later acknowledged that during this time, he drank more than he should have and missed the companionship of his wife and

children. During one of his layovers at the Cohasset hospital, Agnes finally had had enough and sent her lawyer to tell Walker that she would not allow him to come home.

Walker knew that his drinking wasn't fair to her or to the children and didn't blame her for throwing him out. Roberta Manton noted that throughout the period when the couple was raising four children—and losing one—Walker was drunk a good deal of the time. According to Manton, Agnes "kept the family together without complaints of any kind. Her social life was necessarily nil in a small community of economically secure people. Her children participated in the social life of the Church and schools while she remained quietly in the background."[9] The separation from his wife and children may be what led Walker to become involved with the Oxford Group, an alternative Christian movement, from 1939 to 1941. It is not clear how strong that connection was. He wrote that he neither smoked nor drank during that period.[10]

In November 1941, Walker's father died, and he encountered Agnes at the funeral. They decided to reconcile on the condition that he would never take another drink. He rejoined his family in Cohasset and recalled that he did pretty well for a while. However, in time, he was sneaking out to the corner bar after Agnes went to bed. Although she never said a thing, he knew "how she felt, and how the children felt."[11]

Surrendering and Finding Recovery

Richmond Walker took his last drink in mid-May 1942. He started with a few beers in the nearby town of Scituate, and then he went missing for a week. He came to in a Boston hotel room and somehow managed to get home, where he remained in bed for three days "suffering the tortures of hell."[12] More than thirty years had passed since his first drink in college in 1911. It had taken him that long to recognize that "liquor was poison to me" and had removed him from the land of the living. Alcohol could never end or fill the loneliness he experienced or take the place that real relationships needed to play in his life.

When Walker was strong enough to get out of bed after this final intoxication, he told his wife he would go to Alcoholics Anonymous. A friend from the Oxford Group, Evans Dick, had told him about the program a year earlier, in 1941.[13] That was also the year that an article on Alcoholics Anonymous, written by Jack Alexander, appeared in the March issue of the *Saturday Evening Post.* Its publication led to a significant increase in AA membership in the Boston area.

Although Walker told his wife that he was now ready to go to AA, he still procrastinated. A few days later, however, a friend of his called him at his office and asked him to help care for someone else who was on a drinking spree. Arriving on the scene, both men realized that they needed further help and decided to call the AA office. Jack Priest came over to the Hotel Essex to help them.[14]

The Evolution of Alcoholics Anonymous in the Boston Area

After conducting a lengthy study of the AA program, the talented but skeptical writer Jack Alexander became a convinced admirer as well as a friend and promoter of Bill Wilson, the founder of AA. His *Saturday Evening Post* article carried the positive story of AA to a large readership throughout the United States. As a result, AA enjoyed a remarkable growth. In 1941, its membership quadrupled from two thousand to eight thousand. New York soon became the single center of AA, for it was where the Big Book was published. Akron, Ohio, the birthplace of AA, now took a diminished role.

After the *Saturday Evening Post* article appeared, AA's New York office was deluged with letters from people wanting information. There were sixty-three inquiries from the Boston area. The letter writers wanted to know where they could find guidance from other AA members in the area. All of these letters were answered either by Bill Wilson himself or by Ruth Hock, his secretary. The names were then forwarded to the Jacoby Club in Boston, which in turn contacted the men who had sent the letters. It was the Jacoby Club that nurtured Boston AA during the chapter's infant years.

Until AA came to Boston, the Jacoby Club was regarded by many as the only group that seemed able to keep alcoholics sober in any large numbers. The club began as an adjunct to the social service work of the Emmanuel Club of the Emmanuel Episcopal Church in Boston, emphasizing the importance of "fellowship." The motto of the Jacoby Club was "a club for men to help themselves by helping others," stressing self-help and mutual aid. At the same time, there was an increasing emphasis on reclaiming those who were battling alcoholism and taking personal responsibility for looking after at least one other person—"a special brother." Essentially, the members of the Jacoby Club would assist the alcoholic, talking and sharing their experience with him and staying with him until he felt strong enough to help himself and then in turn help others.[15]

The first AA meetings in Boston were held irregularly in 1940, but by March 1941, about four or five alcoholics were meeting on Wednesday nights at the Jacoby Club, located at 115 Newbury Street, a few blocks from the Emmanuel Episcopal Church. As the numbers increased, the AA "club" moved from its small quarters at the Jacoby address to 306 Newbury Street.

While there, Priest invited Walker to an AA meeting. Walker went to the AA club at Newbury Street the next Wednesday, the first day of his sober journey, which lasted the rest of his life. He never looked back. He later wrote: "All we have to do is give God a chance and He can give us a new life which is so much better than the old life—that there is no comparison."[16] In the company of the fifteen other alcoholics attending the same meeting, Walker finally found that his "journey through life is indeed a community affair and that someone has to say, 'I will be with you.'" Over the next several years, while embracing the newly discovered community of AA and rediscovering the community of his family, he was also beginning a journey in "communion with" a Higher Power.

His brother George, writing a decade after Walker's death, remarked that while his brother Joe was all science and business, Rich was religious and idealistic. However, until he joined AA, Rich had never found an outlet for his aspirations. "He took to drink, I guess because of frustration and a sense of failure. In a way, I guess he was a spiritual descendent of St. Augustine."[17] Not only did both men experience a conversion, but St. Augustine's understanding of the relationship between God and humans and the theology of "merit" is hinted at in Walker's writings. Walker understood the grace of sobriety to be a free gift and not something that one could merit on one's own. His fondness for Augustine may be traced to his college days, when he was given the nickname "Gus."

WALKER'S PERIOD OF FORMATION

In the years following Walker's 1942 discovery of AA and its community, the dark clouds of isolation that had encompassed him during the decades of his drinking were replaced by a fellowship in which he found great strength, happiness, and a real purpose for his life. "Purpose" is a theme that he touches on time and again in his writings and in passages in *Twenty-Four Hours a Day.*

Between 1943 and 1948, Richmond Walker devoted his energies to three areas. The first of these was strengthening his own commitment to sobriety by engaging totally in Alcoholics Anonymous and dedicating himself to the AA Fellowship and the Twelve Steps.

At first, Walker took a backseat in most of the meetings he attended, healing from his debilitating years of continual drinking. However, it wasn't long before Walker began giving back to AA from the riches he had received, which became the second area where he focused his energy. As he gained strength and understanding, he began sharing his own story, starting with his "personal witnesses" (first and second), a practice expected of

members relatively new to the program. (Today this practice is also called "telling one's story.") His confidence restored, he became a regular speaker at meetings between 1944 and 1945 and thereafter until he died.

Walker was still living in Cohasset, an easy commute to Boston, where he continued to work and attend AA meetings. The original Boston group had regular open meetings on Wednesdays and discussion meetings on Sunday afternoons. "Rich was a regular at the Sunday meeting" and "in the discussions he most often concentrated on the spiritual side of the program, frequently quoting from the Scriptures."[18]

He gradually became recognized as a pillar of strength, first in the AA circles in Boston; then in the South Shore area, where he delivered the opening talk at the first meeting in Quincy in 1943; and finally in the AA community in Daytona Beach, Florida, which became his winter home, in the mid- to late 1940s. He was also instrumental in establishing an Intergroup, or central committee, to coordinate the AA meetings held in the Boston area, and later did the same for the South Shore groups.

During the two and a half years before he published his first book, *For Drunks Only,* Walker presented talks at AA meetings on a variety of topics dealing with the Fellowship and the Twelve Step "kit of spiritual tools," drawing upon his own recovery experience. (See "Selected Writings by Richmond Walker," page 279.) In February 1945, for example, he delivered a talk every week, clear evidence of his commitment.[19] He then edited these talks and published material from them in *For Drunks Only.* Later, these became the "A.A. Thought for the Day" for almost half of the entries in *Twenty-Four Hours a Day.*

In those early years, Walker was looked upon by his fellow AA members as a "really spiritual and humble man." One of the group members said, "From the start I believed completely in everything he said."[20] As the years passed, Walker came to assume a unique leadership position with newer members in his area, although it was not a position he consciously sought. His very quiet manner almost gave the impression of understatement when he was discussing the program.

Over the years, there was hardly anything he would not do to help someone struggling to recover. On one occasion, Walker received a phone call from a gentleman who admitted that he ought to do something about his drinking. Walker told him that since this was Friday evening, there was an open group meeting at the Unitarian church in Scituate. When the gentleman on the other end of the line asked where he could meet Walker to go to the meeting with him, Walker replied that he and his wife were going to dinner and suggested that the caller could find his own way to the church without difficulty. The caller nervously said that he couldn't picture himself walking into something like that alone.

Walker excused himself for a moment, and when he returned to the phone, he said that he had worked things out with his wife and would pick him up a little later on. The person Walker helped recalled, "I don't know whether it occurred to me at the time, but all these years later, I appreciated the kind of devotion there had to be in a man that would force him to disrupt family plans to help out a stranger . . . I am now able to help others whenever I am asked. And I cannot be sure whether all of this would have been possible if Rich W. hadn't broken his dinner date on that Friday evening."[21]

The November 17 Prayer for the Day in *Twenty-Four Hours a Day* adds perspective to Walker's unassuming nature and spirituality: "I pray that I may not desire the world's applause. I pray that I may not seek rewards for doing what I believe is right."

The years between 1942 and 1945 also provide insights into the evolution of Walker's spirituality, including his conviction of AA's effectiveness in transforming the lives of alcoholics. This aspect of his life will be discussed in more detail in the following essay, "The Evolution of Walker's Spirituality."

Walker had a particular knack for illustrating the contrast between his old self and his new self, between his old and new way of living, between life before and after AA, between the horrors of his past and the rewards of his present way of life. It was all about the importance of changed behavior, required early on by the Oxford Group and now essential to the AA way of life. His writings at this time reveal a very practical spirituality in contrast to his later writings, but they speak to both the mind and the heart.

The transformative experience that Walker found through Alcoholics Anonymous is outlined in the A.A. Thoughts for the Day between March 28 and April 1 in *Twenty-Four Hours a Day.* Walker took the material for these "Thoughts" from a presentation he gave to an AA group. In the text he wrote by hand for that presentation, Walker describes the two lives he had led: first as an alcoholic, then as a recovering person. (As Faust described it, "Two souls, alas! dwell within my breast apart.") Walker wrote that he was always impressed by the changes he saw in people after they had been in AA for a while, and he decided to take his own inventory to see how he had changed since discovering the program. This text serves as a touching portrayal of how addiction severs our relationships with our real selves, with others (family and friends), and with the God of our understanding, and how recovery helps restore these very relationships. It describes a new way of life emerging from a past way of life. What follows is a summary of Walker's description of that process.

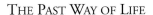

THE PAST WAY OF LIFE

Before he found AA, Walker was very selfish and wanted his way in everything. When things went wrong, he sulked like a spoiled child and usually went out and got drunk. He spent lots of money on himself and as little as possible on his wife and children. "I was all get and no give," he said.

He continued that he was very dishonest, lying to his wife about where he had been and what he had been doing. He took time off from work, feigning sickness or giving some other dishonest excuse. He could never face himself as he really was nor admit when he was wrong. He pretended that he was as good as the next fellow, although he suspected he wasn't. He admits that there was no real honesty in his alcoholic self.

He was very unloving; from the time he went away to school, he paid little attention to his mother and father, and when he was on his own, he didn't bother to keep in touch with them. Furthermore, he was unappreciative of his wife after he got married, and many a time he left her flat while he went out to have a good time. "If she didn't like it she could lump it," he said. He paid little attention to his children and never tried to understand them or "to make pals with them." He had very few friends, and he added that indeed they weren't really friends, just drinking companions, whom he used for his own pleasure. He was never ready to help them when they were in trouble; he didn't care what happened to them. "I loved nobody but myself," he said.

THE NEW WAY OF LIFE

He related that he became a different person when he came into AA, gradually becoming more *unselfish* and no longer wanting his own way in everything. When things went wrong and he didn't get what he wanted, he no longer sulked or went out to get drunk. He now tried not to waste money on himself and was happy when his wife had enough money to spend on herself and the children. He now realized that the greatest pleasure in life was in giving and not getting.

He was becoming more *honest.* He no longer had to lie to his wife and finally arrived at the point where he did not want to. He enjoyed talking with her in the evening about his day and about plans for the future. He arrived at work on time and sought to earn what he was paid. He faced himself as he really was and admitted that he had to rely on God to help him do the right thing. He finally realized that a dishonest man is only half alive because of his fear of being found out. He now discovered what it meant to be really alive and to face the world honestly and without fear.

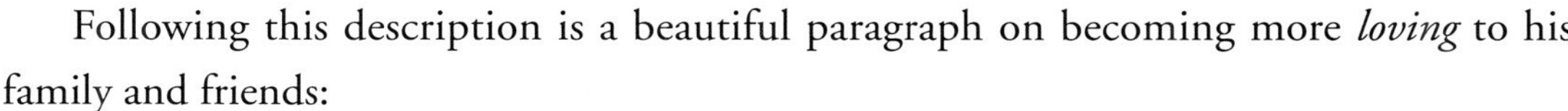

Following this description is a beautiful paragraph on becoming more *loving* to his family and friends:

> My mother is lonely since my father died, and I go out to her house Tuesday nights to have supper and play gin rummy with her. I am more appreciative of my wife, and I'm tremendously grateful to her for putting up with me all these years. I enjoy talking with her in the evening, and I enjoy tucking my youngest boy into bed and saying prayers with him. I feel that the friends that I have found in AA are real friends. I know they are always ready to help me and I want to help them if I can. For the first time in my life, I really care about other people. So I am very grateful to AA for showing me the way, not only to stop drinking but to find a better way of living.[22]

That passage is an excellent example of what this sentence from the Big Book (page 58) means: "Our stories disclose in a general way what we used to be like, what happened, and what we are like now."

As we shall see, Walker's sobriety was grounded in the God of his understanding, as was his spirituality. "I believe sobriety is a free gift of God. . . . The grace of God does for us what we cannot do for ourselves. . . . It's a matter of surrender—we admit that we are licked." If anyone was having difficulty with this program, Walker stressed that all he had to do was stop trying and get down on his knees. God will then make him a free gift of the strength to stay sober.[23]

Writing It Down

The third focus of Walker's life during the mid- to late 1940s developed when he moved to Daytona Beach, Florida, for the winters. At meetings, he would read some thoughts from slips of paper or index cards to serve as points of meditation. Some of the members of the Daytona Beach Club encouraged him to put these thoughts and meditations in book form so that so other AA members could benefit from the readings. Walker agreed and spent the years between 1946 and 1948 compiling his thoughts for publication.

We can only speculate that the readings the Daytona members were referring to were passages from *For Drunks Only* (published in 1945) or a set of sixty-five notepapers called *Thoughts,* now at the Daytona Archives—or perhaps both. (It is curious that about these "Thoughts" Walker wrote: "Do not misuse the ideas written on these slips."[24]) In any case, the Daytona people's interest prompted Walker to begin collecting the material for what became *Twenty-Four Hours a Day.* He spent the next two and a half years composing his spiritual manual.

His wife wrote that Walker "spent months on research, reading and studying many publications on Alcoholism (including the Big Book, of course), and worked on the manuscript of 'Twenty-Four Hours a Day.' . . . I believe I sent a typed manuscript of his work to Hazelden, soon after Rich's death."[25] These materials will be examined in the essay "Sources for *Twenty-Four Hours a Day.*"

PUBLISHING AND DISTRIBUTING *TWENTY-FOUR HOURS A DAY*

In 1948, Walker finished writing the A.A. Thoughts for the Day and editing the Meditations for the Day. Through the help of a friend, he was able to have it typeset and printed at the county courthouse at a reasonable price so that he could sell copies for $1.50. The book was distributed from Walker's home, and it wasn't long before orders were coming in from all over the country, wherever AA had been establishing itself. Some AA members in that early period of growth maintained that they got sober on two books: the Big Book and *Twenty-Four Hours a Day.*

AA General Services

Walker sold the self-published book for years and donated the profits to his local AA group. By 1953, the book had sold out a third printing of 14,000 copies with a steady request of about 600 orders a month. Walker was unable to keep up with the demand and wrote to the AA General Service Office asking whether AA Publishing, Inc. would assume the publication and distribution of *Twenty-Four Hours a Day* and keep any resulting income. It had simply become too much for one man, even with the occasional help of Daytona Club members.

As orders for the book continued to pile up toward the last quarter of 1953, Walker started sending a form letter to would-be buyers. Re-dated each month, the letter told them that it was sold out and urged them to write to the AA General Service Office (in particular Helen B.) to express their wish to have AA publish the book.[26] It was not a very subtle maneuver and may not have sat very well with the New York office, which received seventy-two letters from thirty-two states and seven provinces supporting Walker's request. (About the same time, the Daytona Club donated $2,000 to the General Service Office, which was strapped for money.)

Helen B., the New York secretary, responded to Walker's original letter. She wrote that his request would be discussed at the general conference the following year (1954), when the delegates would consider whether "AA should depart from a purely textbook program (publication of the Big Book and the recent *Twelve Steps and Twelve Traditions*), by printing non–text book literature, such as the '24 Hour Book of Meditation.'" She noted that the question before the delegates was not referring only to Walker's book, but concerned the possibility of AA Publishing entering an entirely different field.[27]

Twenty Four Hours A Day

P. O. BOX 2170
DAYTONA BEACH, FLORIDA

March , 1954

Gentlemen:

We received your letter of ____________, ordering _____ copies of our book: "Twenty-Four Hours A Day," also your check for $__________, for which we thank you.

As we have temporarily discontinued publishing this book, we are returning your check herewith.

The rights to the publication of our book have been offered to the A. A. Publishing Company in New York. This matter will come before the next General Service Conference in New York next April.

We will re-publish our book only if the Conference does not recommend that it be taken over by the A. A. Publishing Company.

If the book should be taken over, the A. A. Publishing Company will supply you with these books.

We would appreciate your writing to: Helen Brown, Secretary of the Conference, at the Alcoholic Foundation, P. O. Box 459 Grand Central Annex, New York 17, N. Y., expressing your desire to obtain these books from the A. A. Publishing Company.

We also suggest that you write to your delegate to the General Service Conference, asking him to approve this action.

Thanking you for your interest and cooperation and with best wishes, we are

Sincerely yours,

TWENTY-FOUR HOURS A DAY

By______________________
Richmond Walker

(Treasurer - Florida State Committee)

In support of his proposal, Walker thought of publishing a piece in the next issue of the AA periodical known as the *Grapevine,* reiterating that the large demand for *Twenty-Four Hours a Day* coming from all over the country was becoming too much for one man to handle. He scribbled some notes to the effect that he would like to see the profits go to AA Publishing and in all probability there would be a big demand for the book if assumed by AA Publishing, Inc.

Another letter written by Helen B. sheds light on what was happening behind the scenes at this time. Dated March 31, 1954, the letter was addressed to Charles B. and explains that the April Conference had to consider two points: first, that if Walker's offer were to be accepted, a precedent would be set and the Conference would then have to deal with the problem of more books being sent for Conference approval; and second, "also, some members consider the book as having religious overtones (which is contrary to textbook materials)."[28] (This second point was not included in the Conference report.) Helen's letter also confirmed that the General Service Office had received seventy-two letters in support of AA publishing Walker's book, many of them explaining that Walker had asked them to write on his behalf.[29]

Apparently this reference to the "religious overtones" of *Twenty-Four Hours a Day* did not remain confidential and was already being discussed in some AA circles. Walker received a personal letter from someone regarding the conversation occurring about the "book's explicit religiosity."

The Conference Report (April 1954) indicated that the delegates "felt it unwise to set a precedent in the case of this 'booklet' lest it open a floodgate of similar requests." The resolution *not to publish* was accepted. Of particular interest is that the delegate from Florida "said it was the consensus of his group and of his area that the proposal (to publish the book) not be accepted."[30] This position of the "Florida area" added a whole new dimension to the decision and how it had evolved.

Walker reacted to this decision with understandable anger, particularly to the intimations about the book's "religious overtones" as the principal reason why it should not be accepted. Walker had already written to the chair of the literature committee on February 18, 1954, expressing his dismay at New York's squeamish secularism. In her book *The Language of the Heart,* Trysh Travis writes: "Throwing the committee's language back in its face, he scoffed at the notion that the book's '*religious overtones*' might provoke '*misinterpretation and misunderstanding*' of AA's ecumenism, arguing that 'there is no mention of religion in the whole book, for instance, the word 'Christ' or 'Jesus' is never mentioned, nor is it ever advised

that we go to *church*. Where then is the *religion*?" Travis further remarks that to Walker, "the book's injunctions to prayer and surrender, and its quotations from and allusions to the Christian Bible indicated only that we have a spiritual program."[31] In the next couple of years, against those who seemed to be overlooking AA's spirituality, Walker would emphasize time and again that AA was indeed a spiritual program.

Glenn Chesnut, editor of the Hindsfoot Foundation, believes we should not conclude that New York's refusal to publish Walker's book was due to spiritual reasons, when money was another factor. While some did indeed regard Walker's book as too religious, there were also economic and practical reasons for not publishing it. New York had just published *Twelve Steps and Twelve Traditions* at great expense and was anxious about how it would sell. Another volume, *The Little Red Book,* was also in circulation, offering readers a brief guide to the Twelve Steps. Published in 1946 by Ed Webster and Barry Collins, it had been endorsed by Dr. Bob. Now, it seemed, the possible competition between *Twelve Steps and Twelve Traditions* and *The Little Red Book* did not need a further competitor in what had come to be known as "the Little Black Book"— that is, *Twenty-Four Hours a Day.*[32]

During the controversy, Walker had been busy composing *The Seven Points of Alcoholics Anonymous,* which was a welcome distraction. He self-published it in 1955.

Twenty-Four Hours a Day Comes to Hazelden

In 1952, Patrick Butler, the new president of Hazelden, had already come across the Little Black Book. He recalled that he did not realize the high esteem the little volume had assumed in people's lives until he went to an Irish wake. "In Catholic wakes, quite often you will see entwined in the hands of the deceased a rosary or a prayer book therein. In this particular case, I was startled to see the *Twenty-Four Hours a Day* book in his hands. So you are able to see in what high esteem a great many people held that book. And it has been a great aid to a great many people—particularly a lot of loners all over the world."[33]

Months before the General Conference decided not to publish *Twenty-Four Hours a Day,* Patrick Butler had already written to Walker on February 10, 1954, about Hazelden's interest in publishing the book. Walker had responded that should the Conference decide against it, he would consider accepting Butler's offer. And so it happened that at the very beginning of May 1954, Butler wrote that the Board of Hazelden had accepted Walker's proposal to publish his book.[34] (See "The Richmond Walker and Patrick Butler Correspondence" on page 271.)

Walker then sent his notebook containing information about where the book had been shipped and comments about the book from AA members around the country. It also contained seven hundred unsolicited endorsements regarding the book. Walker also let Butler know that on May 24, he had received a letter from Ed Webster of *The Little Red Book* offering to take over Walker's book. When he wrote Webster that he had already given it to the Hazelden Foundation, Webster had written in response that "it was in good hands."[35]

It was publicly announced that on June 1, Hazelden would take over the publication, sale, and distribution of the Little Black Book. While the contents would be the same, the cover and binding "would be of better quality and more attractive." For a while the little "black" book became the little "green" book. When Walker wrote to Butler that he felt nostalgic about the black cover, Butler ordered a further change back to the original.

Five thousand more copies were sold when it was released in 1954, eighty thousand by 1959, seven million by 1990, and well over 8.2 million as of this writing. Including translated editions, worldwide sales to date exceed 9.7 million. As a result of this book, Hazelden would eventually become the leading publisher of educational materials on addiction prevention, treatment, and recovery.

Walker and Butler kept up their correspondence for a few more years, not only about business, but also about their personal lives.

On April 28, 1958, Walker wrote to Butler concerning *Twenty-Four Hours a Day:* "Although I only compiled the book, I am naturally very pleased at its wide acceptance, even in places outside of AA." He continued, "If we can do something that will benefit just one person fifty years from now, it is worthwhile. I imagine not too many people who have not found the way of life, that we alcoholics have found, leave anything to posterity when they die, that will outlive their tombstone."[36]

A FULL LIFE

Today, Richmond Walker is remembered for the many contributions he made to the literature of recovery and for his dedication to AA. Yet there was more to Walker's life than the consumption of alcohol and the addictive self that dominated for the better part of three decades. Much more important was the recovery that allowed his real self to emerge. Though the sources are few, they reveal another very important side of Walker— a loving, caring, and gifted person as well as a person dedicated to AA.

He was a loving father. When his children were small, they thought that their daddy was sick a lot. Once he was sober, they knew he loved them, and they loved him.[37] He was not a demonstrative person, but his daughter Carol wrote that her father was a "wonderful, gentle and sensitive person and I loved him very much."[38]

She described him as being extremely gentle with her, as well as with the other children, and never losing his temper. She recalls fondly that when her mother and two brothers were escaping the winter at their home in Florida, she and her father would take the train to Boston, have lunch at Filene's, and then go to a movie.

Holidays were always pleasant. On the Fourth of July, her father would purchase bags of fireworks. The Roman candles would be carefully shot over the harbor across from their Cohasset home. Walker would carve a huge pumpkin on Halloween, and on Thanksgiving he would carve the turkey, making sure the children got the portion they asked for.

When Carol's daughter, Pamela, was twelve, she wrote about her grandfather as her "favorite character" in an essay for class. She considered him "the greatest man alive." Since he read quite a bit, she said of him, "My grandfather was very smart." At this time (around 1963), Walker was bald on the top of his head with gray hairs slicked neatly down in the back. He wore glasses and had a "bristling grey mustache that tickled you when he kissed you," Pamela wrote. "His face was shaped like an oval. He looked very intelligent and he was too. He was tall and had a large build. He always looked neat and clean."[39]

Walker was very good at oil painting as a hobby and painted scenes from the beaches on the South Shore and other settings that appealed to him. His talents as a writer extended beyond his dissertations on alcoholism and recovery. He liked to write poetry during and after his drinking days. His poems covered a variety of subjects; of these, two are of particular interest. "Not Enough" depicts the growth of a new life from an old one. "Twenty-Five Years" was written on his twenty-fifth wedding anniversary and tells of a certain serenity that had entered that marriage despite his past behavior.

Not Enough

To *understand* is not enough
To drink and dull the understanding
And fill the mind with lesser thoughts
Is not enough
I must think sustaining thoughts
And learn to live with <u>Honesty.</u>

To *feel* is not enough
To drink to block all feeling
But to feel remorse and pain
Is not enough
I must carry good things within my heart
And live with Purity.

To *hear* is not enough
To live and stop all hearing
But sense only the agonies of life
Is not enough
I must give wherever need appears
And learn to live Unselfishly.

To *reach* is not enough
To live and forget the reaching
And grasp the lesser things
Is not enough
I must see some Heaven in all mankind
And learn to live with Love.

To *believe* is not enough
To live and depend too much on self
And leave that faith untested
Is not enough
I must seek harmony with all good
And learn to live with *God.*[40]

Richmond and Agnes Walker celebrated the twenty-fifth anniversary of their marriage after he reached five years of sobriety. The couple had had some rocky times together, and it is a wonder that the marriage survived. This is what he wrote:

Twenty-Five Years

Twenty-five years ago today
We plighted our troth in the usual way
With minister quoting from chapter and verse,
We took each other for better or worse.

We started off in a carefree way—
Kind of childish it seems today—
A small apartment off a main street
We kept to ourselves, small and neat.

Then children coming to bless our home,
We moved about and began to roam.
Oh yes, there were times of trouble
When life seemed like a broken bubble.
Times of sunshine and times of rain
We parted and came together again.

The years have gone with halting paces
With uneven spots and rough in places.

But time has smoothed the uneven way
Till a certain peace has come today.
This year it seems fine to be alive
And the prospects are good for the next twenty-five.[41]

May 8, 1947.

Richmond Walker continued to write and speak to the very end of his life. In 1962, he spoke at the nineteenth anniversary of the founding of the Quincy Group, and copies remain of three talks he gave at Ormond Beach, a neighbor to the Daytona Club, during the last two years of his life.

Throughout the remainder of his life, Walker never failed to attend meetings, where he either listened or gave a talk. On May 22, 1959, he wrote, "Tonight my wife and I are going to an AA meeting in Quincy which I helped to start in 1943. Sunday I have a date for the Malden AA, Thursday a '65 Club AA meeting at Court Square, Boston. So you see I never take a vacation from AA."[42]

In his later years, Walker was well known in the Daytona Beach community. He became a deacon in the Community Church presided over by Mr. Gordon Poteat, but later joined the Unity Church because its minister was a member of AA. He served there until his death.

Poteat wrote that Walker had settled in Daytona Beach because of the presence of a strong AA community. Whenever he came across individual problems with his parishioners related to drinking, he knew that he could call upon Walker night or day and he would drop everything and come to his aid.

Walker regularly attended AA meetings in several locations, remaining active in Daytona as well as in the South Shore while in Cohasset. "He also helped create a Rehabilitation Center for those who were trying to escape the chains of habitual drinking," wrote Poteat.[43]

The year before he died, he gave a talk at the Ormond Beach AA Club on February 9, 1964. He said he believed that an AA member is happiest

> [w]hen he crosses over from the dark side of the street to the sunny side; when he opens his mind to all the good things in life; when he does not strain to be good, but simply accepts all the good which constantly surrounds him; when he appreciates the fact that by choosing the good, he has been restored to sanity; when he realizes that by changing his thinking he can change his life; when he knows that the more he can grow spiritually—the more he tries to live a good life, the farther away he is from taking a drink; when he is convinced that the Higher Power wished only good for him.[44]

Walker's papers also contain articles published in the *Grapevine*. Among them was one that he wrote the month before he died, entitled "No Cure for Alcoholism" (February 25, 1965).[45]

Richmond Walker died in his sleep on March 25, 1965, after almost twenty-three years of sobriety dedicated to helping others. He was buried in Cohasset next to his daughter Hilda, who had died in 1935. Poteat wrote that "he will be greatly missed by those who knew him and who were helped by his dedicated service. Now that he has died the name of this anonymous Good Samaritan should be known and remembered."[46]

• • •

Notes

1. I have investigated two principal archives while researching this essay: the Hazelden archives in Minnesota and the Richmond Walker archive in Florida.

   At Hazelden, the Pittman Archive (hereafter referred to as "Hazelden I") is a large repository of books and other materials on topics related to alcoholism, collected by the late William Pittman, writer and a scholar of early AA history. Housed at Hazelden's Center City campus, the Pittman Archive includes a variety of documents and other materials related to Walker's life and writings. (The originals of some of these materials are located in the Daytona Beach Archives noted below.) Also housed at Hazelden (and hereafter referred to as "Hazelden II") is a more focused collection of materials gathered around 1977, apparently for a biography of Richmond Walker. My thanks to Hazelden librarian Barbara Weiner for her valuable help in locating these two collections, and for directing me to a grant from the AA Heckman Endowed Fellowship to pursue research at the Daytona Beach Archives, the second main repository for materials on Richmond Walker.

   At noted in the text, Walker had a second home in Florida, where he was also very active in AA. The Volusia County Intergroup office at South Daytona Beach holds a collection of Walker's writings and other papers in four volumes (hereafter referred to as "Daytona Beach Archives"). I am grateful to both Carolyn Carlisle and David Withee for their generous time and guidance in pointing out details that I may otherwise have missed.

2. The most complete works on Richmond Walker's life and writing to this point have been presented by Glenn Chesnut, editor of the Hindsfoot Foundation, whose publications address alcoholism treatment and recovery. Chesnut's essay and commentary on the talk that Walker gave at Rutland, Vermont, in 1958 is one of the primary sources for Walker's life. See the full text of Walker's talk in the fiftieth anniversary edition of *Twenty-Four Hours a Day* (Center City, MN: Hazelden, 2004). See also Hindsfoot Foundation, AA Historical Materials, Part I, Richmond Walker; and Glenn Chesnut, chapter 5, "Practicing the Presence of God: Richmond Walker's 24-Hour Book" in *The Higher Power of the Twelve-Step Program: For Believers & Non-Believers* (New York: Authors Choice Press, 2001), 115–29. His section on Walker's spirituality is culled from meditations in *Twenty-Four Hours a Day.*

3. Walker's talk in Rutland, Vermont, 1958, Hazelden II.

4. Travelogue/journal, 1914. (Discovered by Glenn Chesnut, a copy of which was sent to the Daytona Beach Archives.)

5. George Walker to Roberta Manton, September 22, 1977, Hazelden II.

6. Ibid.

7. Roberta Manton to John McHale, November 16, 1977, Hazelden II.

8. It is difficult to determine with any precision the exact chronology of events from this time forward until his recovery in May 1942. There are two sources: The Rutland talk of 1958, in which he was looking back a decade and a half, and Walker's 1943 testimonial to his AA group. The death of his father and reconciliation with his wife are ascribed to May, both in 1941 or 1942. His father died on November 25, 1941. This makes it easier, although not definitively, to record the events that follow.

9. Manton to McHale, Hazelden II.

10. The impact of the Oxford Group will be investigated in the next essay, "The Evolution of Walker's Spirituality."

11. Second personal witness at AA meeting, September 14, 1943, Hazelden I.

12. Ibid.

13. Ibid.

14. See Richard M. Dubiel, *The Road to Fellowship* (Bloomington, IN: iUniverse, 2004). Of particular interest is chapter 7, "The Jacoby Club and AA," with its pages on Richmond Walker and the corresponding footnotes. Dubiel believes that it was the Jacoby Club that had nurtured Boston AA during its early years.

15. Second personal witness, Hazelden I.

16. Ibid.

17. Walker to Manton, Hazelden II.

18. Manuscript forwarded to me by Gifford Dean, a friend of the Walker family (hereafter referred to as the Dean manuscript). It was composed at Dean's request by an AA member who gathered the memories of other AA members who had known Walker from his attendance at AA meetings around the South Shore. Dean grew up with the Walker children, and his home was adjacent to Walker's in Cohasset.

19. See Hazelden I. Among these materials is an index of sixty-four copies of papers, most of which were handwritten and delivered to AA groups in a variety of locations between 1943 and 1945. The originals of these papers are found at the Daytona Beach Archives.

20. Dean manuscript, Hazelden II.

21. Ibid.

22. Richmond Walker, "Before and After, Taking an Inventory of Myself," October 8, 1943, Hazelden I.

23. Richmond Walker, "Sobriety, A Free Gift of God," May 17, 1944, Hazelden I.

24. Daytona Beach Archives, Vol. I.

25. Agnes Walker to Roberta Manton (no date, but around 1977), Hazelden II. (Mrs. Walker sent the entire manuscript, which is now pictured in full in this book.

26. Hazelden I, Butler Folder.

27. Ibid. (Handwritten chronology of events on Walker and New York.)

28. Ibid.

29. For background on this issue with New York, see Trysh Travis, *The Language of the Heart* (Chapel Hill: University of North Carolina Press, 2009), 148–49, with the accompanying informative footnotes. Her pages on the reasons for the evolution of the Committee for Approved Literature (CAL) are also valuable background material for the Walker episode. She notes that much of the supportive data can be found in the AA Archives, AA World Services Office, New York, in particular Box 73, Folder C. Supplementary handwritten notes regarding the events can be found in the Hazelden Archives I, Butler Folder.

30. Travis, *Language of the Heart,* 148–49.

31. Ibid., 149.

32. Glenn Chesnut, "Richmond Walker and New York, 1953–1954," posted on "AA History Lovers" listserv, Yahoo Groups, August 27, 2004, http://health.groups.yahoo.com/group /AAHistoryLovers /message/1999.

33. Damian McElrath, *Hazelden: A Spiritual Odyssey* (Center City, MN: Hazelden, 1987), 90–91.

34. Patrick Butler to Richmond Walker, May 5, 1954, Hazelden I, Butler Folder.

35. Richmond Walker to Patrick Butler, May 7, 1954, Hazelden I, Butler Folder.

36. Richmond Walker to Patrick Butler, April 28, 1959, Hazelden I, Butler Folder.

37. Manton to McHale, Hazelden II.

38. Carol (Walker) Crane, "Memories of My Father," Hazelden II.

39. Pamela Crane, "My Grandfather, My Favorite Character," ca. 1963, Hazelden II.

40. Richmond Walker, February 14, 1963, Hazelden II.

41. Richmond Walker, May 8, 1947, Hazelden II.

42. Daytona Beach Archives, Vol. II.

43. Pastor Gordon Poteat, "Samaritan Anonymous," *Daytona Beach Journal,* newspaper article on occasion of Walker's death, Hazelden II.

44. Daytona Beach Archives, Vol. III.

45. Richmond Walker, February 25, 1965 (published in *Grapevine,* June 1965), Daytona Beach Archives, Vol. II.

46. Poteat, Hazelden II.

The Evolution of Walker's Spirituality

The seeds of spirituality are implanted in a person at birth. To be truly human is to be truly spiritual, and to be truly spiritual is to be truly human. As human beings develop, so does their spirituality. Yet at times a person's spiritual development can be blocked, as is the case when alcoholism and other addictions are present. This essay will explore how Richmond Walker developed spiritually, delve into the spiritual principles that were critical to his continued recovery and central to his writings, and look at his views on the role of spirituality in Alcoholics Anonymous.[1]

While we know that Richmond Walker attended Union Theological for a brief period after college, it is difficult to know the spiritual ground that Walker walked on before he started drinking and his addictive self began to play the primary role in his life. He clearly recalls the emergence of his self-centeredness as alcohol became the focus of his waking moments. As his relationships with self, with others, and with the Divine Principle in his life continued to deteriorate with his ever-increasing drinking, the spirit associated with his real self was being shut out. The crisis culminated with his wife's lawyer telling him that he was no longer welcome at home.

In the 1958 address he gave to an AA group in Rutland, Vermont, Walker reported having had a connection with the Oxford Group between 1939 and 1941. The extent of that connection we do not know. Perhaps the members of the Oxford Group helped to assuage his intense feelings surrounding the 1935 death of his daughter Hilda. While there are no direct references to the group during that time frame, influences from the Oxford Group can be found in Walker's later writings. In tracing the evolution of Walker's spirituality, his relationship with the Oxford Group does play a role and needs to be examined.

THE OXFORD GROUP

Franklin Nathaniel Daniel Buchman, the founder of the Oxford Group, was born in 1878. Ordained a Lutheran minister, Buchman and a few of his friends formed what they called a First Century Christian Fellowship in 1922. What he conceived to be the essence of the early Christian community became the ideal for his missionary zeal. The message the group promoted was one of "life-changing" by getting right with God. Around 1927, Buchman began working in England and drew several followers from Oxford University, where he eventually located. Although he was never officially connected with Oxford, it was there that he found the base for his movement, and from there that the movement derived its name.[2]

Essential to the group's spirituality were small-group meetings. At their "house parties," the members spent "Quiet Time" in prayer and meditation seeking "guidance" from God on the direction he wished to lead them. Walker adopted a morning quiet time as an integral part of his daily routine in recovery.

It was an Oxford tenet that people had "sick souls," the remedy for which was "soul surgery." The idea was that by cutting out sin, the soul would be cured of its "self-centeredness." Central to the group's beliefs was *surrender* to God, who would then manage the individual's life. Their ideas centered around three themes: (1) the need for people to find God and to change their lives to harmonize with God's will; (2) the surrender of self to God as the required turning point; and (3) "soul surgery"—the cutting out of sin as the way to accomplish this change.

A fundamental Oxford Group principle was that "those who have changed must change others." The ways of going about that were summarized in their slogans: "Win your argument, lose your man," and "Give the news, not your views."[3] If surrendering to God was the cornerstone of the group's spirituality, Quiet Time was the spiritual exercise that sustained this surrender. Bible study was the first part of this practice, followed by prayer—quietly listening for God's voice—and finally journaling one's thoughts. Quiet Time provided the opportunity to communicate with the Holy Spirit and discover the Christ of Faith, the object of faith and worship for the early Christian community.

The four standards against which the "Groupers" could check their spiritual progress (for measuring their walk as Christ defined it) were the absolutes of honesty, unselfishness, purity, and love. Walker referred to these time and again.

Fellowship and sharing were also central to the Oxford Group. Following their aim to be a First Century Christian Fellowship, the group sought first of all fellowship with God, and then with one another as a team, meeting in fellowship, working in groups, and sharing their experiences with others. Buchman often employed the expression "Pass it on."

Author Ernest Kurtz notes that the group's aggressive evangelism, recommended in the book *Soul Surgery,* as well as its members' public allegiance, were replaced in AA by a gentler Twelfth Step approach and the principle of anonymity.[4]

Bill W. acknowledged that AA's debt to the Oxford Group was immense. A library of material on the Oxford Group's influence on AA has been gathered over the years.[5]

Oxford Group Literature

Some of the literature that emanated from the Oxford Group appears to have influenced Walker, though in varying degrees. While he made no direct references to A. J. Russell's *For Sinners Only* (1932), a full-length biographical conversion narrative, at least its title likely influenced Walker's *For Drunks Only* (1945). Both deal with the general idea of conversion or transformation. While Russell's book is clearly biographical in the context of his relationship with the Oxford Group, Walker's book references himself and all drunks. One deals with the Oxford Group, the other with the Fellowship of AA. Both emphasize "Surrender," "Quiet Time," "Sharing," and the "Four Absolutes." Walker adds a fifth tenet: Service. The relationship between the two authors extends also to the meditation book *God Calling,* which Russell edited and wrote a preface for. As noted earlier, Walker used this book for the meditations of *Twenty-Four Hours a Day.*

For Sinners Only

Russell's book was easily one of the most readable and popular books published about the Oxford Group. He spent about a year examining, with a journalist's critical eye, the people and practices associated with the movement. Eventually, he joined the Oxford Group himself. (There is a parallel here between the investigation undertaken by Jack Alexander, who wrote the article on Alcoholics Anonymous in the *Saturday Evening Post,* and Russell's examination of the Oxford Group. Both approached their groups with skeptical and critical eyes.)

In the last chapter of *For Sinners Only,* Russell wrote: "The Oxford Group showed me in practice what I knew in precept: 'that the heart must be at leisure from itself; that to share is better than to preach; to lose is really to find; to 'let go' is to be held secure; to surrender is to possess all things."[6] This strongly resembles the Prayer of St. Francis of Assisi, which was very popular among the early AA members, and it finds a significant place in one of Walker's writings near the end of his life.

The Way

On the inside cover of his personal copy of the Big Book, Walker notes that *The Way* by E. Stanley Jones was the meditation book that he thought of pulling material from for *Twenty-Four Hours a Day;* later, he settled upon *God Calling.* Walker often uses the metaphor of the "Two Ways" and the dichotomy between life before and after recovery. As the format for *Twenty-Four Hours a Day* was evolving, *The Way* may have initially appealed to him as a good model for his meditations. However, *The Way's* meditations are strongly biblical and Christological, with Jesus as the model. Besides the "Way," Walker also used the metaphor of the "beam," which became a popular analogy in Oxford circles. Jones wrote:

> What is it that is wrong in the modern world? Just one thing and only one thing—modern man is not conscious of being on the Way. An airman doesn't mind clouds when he is "on the beam." But when he is "off the beam," he is rightly afraid of clouds—they may hold catastrophe. You can stand anything if you are sure you are on the Way. Can we be sure?[7]

The Upper Room

Another very popular meditation book was *The Upper Room,* which could be found in AA clubs throughout the country. For Dr. Bob—who cofounded AA with Bill W.—it was a favorite. Containing a Reading, Meditation, Thought for the Day, and Prayer for the Day, it could easily have been Walker's model for *Twenty-Four Hours a Day.* Walker himself, in writing and talking about practicing the Eleventh Step, referenced *The Upper Room, Growing Spiritually* by E. Stanley Jones, and *The Eye Opener* as readings that could be used for meditation.

Soul Surgery

The book *Soul Surgery* by Howard A. Walter serves as a link between the Oxford Group and Richmond Walker's participation in AA from 1942 to 1945.[8] It was a staple among the "Groupers," and Walker presented a commentary on it to an AA meeting during those same years. In his presentation, he modified the book's aggressive evangelistic approach with a moderate Twelfth-Stepping presentation to help alcoholics find their way.

Soul Surgery recommends that the surgical procedure for rooting out sin could be found in the Five C's: Confidence, Confession, Conviction, Conversion, and Continuance, the completion of which would allow for full participation in the Oxford Group. Walker employs the same C's not for rooting out sin, but for gently helping the alcoholic to stop drinking and recognize his powerlessness. His commentary is like a little manual for alcoholics seeking recovery. Throughout, he substitutes the phrase *Higher Power* for *God.* At the conclusion of one of his addresses to an AA meeting, Walker indicated that these Five C's would be very helpful in their Twelfth Step work with other alcoholics.[9]

• • •

Despite his relationship with the Oxford Group, very little else suggests that Walker had any particular allegiance to the group's teachings, especially its Christology. There is hardly any mention of Christ in Walker's writings or in archival papers. He was careful to eliminate references when using the meditations from *God Calling.* Like Bill W., he wanted his works to have a universal appeal.

THE BASIC PRINCIPLES OF WALKER'S SPIRITUALITY

The formative years of Walker's spirituality, as outlined in his handwritten talks, were between 1942 and 1945. The essential ingredients of Walker's "Spiritual Protocol" were the Fellowship of AA and the "kit of spiritual tools," the principles of the Twelve Steps to be practiced in all his affairs. The Fellowship and these principles focus on restoring the relationships essential to the full development of every person's life.

Rediscovery: Finding Real Relationships and Real Self [10]

Walker believed that essentially all spirituality is relational—a relationship with our real selves, with others, and with the God of our understanding. Alcoholism blocks the development of those relationships and severs those that already exist, removing us from the land of the living to a barren wasteland. Indeed, one of the most insidious aspects of chemical dependency is that it is *antirelational.* Isolation, self-absorption, and self-centeredness are the largest spiritual blocks. Everything that Walker penned in his early recovery testifies to that. Among his notes is the following: "By following the AA program we recover three things: our personal integrity, our faith in God and our proper relationships with our fellow men."[11]

He wrote that his past life was "absolutely screwy" and he had to re-educate his mind through "quiet time"—prayer several times a day, AA meetings, and Twelfth Step work.

Engaging in these spiritual exercises, said Walker, one is "sure to get a kick out of life."[12]

Walker believed that in AA he had been given the privilege of living two lives in one lifetime.[13] He learned that his alcoholic self was not his real self, but that his "sane, sober self" was. In recovery, individuals come to recognize that their real selves were dying, even dead, when they were drinking and that in recovery they are now alive. The AA program is a way of life and has to become a natural way of living for alcoholics to keep their insane self at bay. Attending AA meetings in Boston, Walker learned to embrace a new way of life. AA is all about finding one's better self.[14]

One of the worst things about drinking is the loneliness associated with it. It cuts one off from others, from the land of the living. One of the best things about AA is the Fellowship and having others walk alongside us.[15] When Walker was drinking, he was choosing his lower self. He wrote that he was hurting himself physically and mentally and causing suffering to others. He was dishonest and selfish. He was forming bad habits to which he became a slave. His whole character was built on a false foundation, and he was helpless to change until he found AA.

When he stopped drinking and began to live the AA program, he began to find his better self. By turning to a Higher Power, he began to overcome his lower self, improve mentally and physically, and become more honest and unselfish. Walker wrote, "I would be a hypocrite if I said that any alcoholic can *suddenly* change from his lower self to his better self. It's a slow process. It took me thirty years to get to my bottom, and I don't ever expect to get to the top. But I'm no longer trying to live two lives at once and I no longer have mental conflict. I know that with the help of God and the AA fellowship, I'm going in the right direction."[16]

When he was drinking, Walker was absolutely selfish, living in the land of objects. When he found AA he discovered a relationship with a group of unselfish people who thought principally about helping others.

In finding recovery, Walker was beginning to comprehend a very important principle, that God works through other people, and that the work done by AA is an example of the grace of God in human lives. It was a demonstration of the power of God available to all of us if we only turn to Him for help. His primary relationship was no longer a pathological relationship with alcohol; instead, he began to discover the intimacy afforded by real relationships.

Rediscovery: Connecting with His Higher Power (Divine Principle)

Walker often reminded his listeners about AA's motto—"But for the grace of God"—which could be found on the walls of clubhouses throughout the country. He believed that the work done by AA was an example of the grace of God in human lives—a demonstration of the power of God available to all if we turn to Him for help.

Alcoholics must honestly want to get well, and they can get well by turning their drinking problem over to that Divine Principle in the Universe that we call God. Early on, Walker used "Divine Principle" when discussing the God of his understanding, but as his thinking evolved, he also employed "Higher Power" and "God." It is interesting to note that in the prayers in *Twenty-Four Hours a Day,* the reference is almost always to "God."

Walker argued that putting one's drinking problem into the hands of God was equivalent to taking out an insurance policy. Paying the premiums required regular attendance at AA meetings, reciting the Lord's Prayer, getting down on our knees before breakfast, and helping other alcoholics. These are the payments that guarantee that the policy will not lapse. At the same time, the person in recovery is building up an endowment that would put him on easy street for the rest of his life.[17]

Let's examine five qualities that stand out as central to Walker's spirituality: surrender, humility, gratitude, honesty, and service.

Surrender

In reflecting upon his relationship with God—his Higher Power—Walker believed that "sobriety is a free gift of God" given to him when God knew that he was ready for it. It is not something that we can obtain through our own efforts. "All we have to do is to stop trying, to relax and take it easy, and to accept the gift with gratitude and humility. . . . The Grace of God does *for* us, what we could never do for ourselves." Walker continued, stating that "we cannot take any credit for having stopped drinking because we did not do it by our own willpower. There's no reason for being proud, or boasting about how long we've been sober. We can only be grateful to God for doing for us, what we could never do for ourselves."[18]

In the Meditation for the Day for September 2 in *Twenty-Four Hours a Day,* Walker wrote, "You should try to stand aside and let God work through you. . . You will have true victory and real success, if you will put yourself in the background and let God work through you."

Walker emphasized this same surrender throughout *For Drunks Only,* but particularly in chapter 4, "The Spiritual Basis of AA," in which he states that it is through the grace of God that an alcoholic gets over his "soul sickness." We surrender our drinking problem to God, having faith in that Divine Principle who is on our side as long as we do the right thing. "The time when a man really gets the programme is when he gets down on his knees and surrenders himself to God as he understands him," Walker wrote.[19]

Likewise, in *The Seven Points of AA,* Walker dedicated chapter 3 to the principle of surrender.

Finally, in his unpublished "Thoughts," he highlights the demands that surrender imposes on the recovering alcoholic:

> Therefore, let the individual who has gone on verbal record as surrendering, investigate the deeper recesses of his mind to ascertain if this is really true and complete. If not, he must make every effort to create this deeper understanding and acknowledgement of the situation, as permanent results can only be gained by men, who as a result of a conviction derived from experience, have completely surrendered to the fact that they cannot indulge in drinking without paying an extortionate price for their pleasure.[20]

For Walker, that was the heart of the matter—the "core" of recovery. The alcoholic had to take it to heart, had to internalize the beliefs that he professed outwardly. What was demanded was a change of heart. What was demanded was not compliance, but unconditional surrender to the program and its principles, and through them to God, or a Higher Power.

Humility

Humility, when properly understood, is the foundation for surrender. It finds a prominent place throughout *Twenty-Four Hours a Day* simply because the expression of surrender is so important for recovering people. Humility is derived from the Latin word *humus,* which means ground, dirt, earth. According to the Torah, when God created man he formed him from the earth and then breathed his spirit into him, thus giving him life. In this sense, *humility* means the acceptance of one's dependence upon the God of one's understanding and the acceptance of a role of equality—neither superiority nor inferiority—with the rest of creation: with the rest of the humus, the earth. In Jewish writings, the holy man is described as one practicing justice and mercy and "walking humbly with God." The Seventh Step is

the "Humility Step": "Humbly asked Him to remove our shortcomings." In its original form, this step included the phrase "Get down on our knees . . ." This was a ritual that Dr. Bob required of those beginning their recovery.

Walker's A.A. Thought for the Day for April 21 stressed the importance of humility:

> After we've been in A.A. for a while, we find that if we're going to stay sober, we have to be humble people. The men we see in A.A. who have really made the grade are all humble people. When I stop to think that but for the grace of God I might be drunk right now, I can't help feeling humble. . . . When I think of the kind of person I was not so long ago, when I think of the man I left behind me, I've got nothing to be proud about. *Am I grateful and humble?*

The August 31 Meditation for the Day conveys the same message:

> You should have a firm foundation of spiritual living which makes you truly humble, if you are going to really help other people. Go easy on them and hard on yourself. That is the way you can be used most to uplift a despairing spirit. And seek no personal recognition for what you are used by God to accomplish.

Humility permeates all of the Little Black Book, including the question in the January 10 A.A. Thought for the Day: "Have I learned that there is power in humility?" Likewise, the Prayer for the Day on January 12 says, "I pray that I may be grateful for the things I have received and do not deserve. I pray that this gratitude will make me truly humble."

Gratitude

Walker united gratitude and humility throughout *Twenty-Four Hours a Day.* He wrote in the Meditation for the Day for July 18:

> We should try to be grateful for all the blessings we have received and which we do not deserve. Gratitude to God for all His blessings will make us humble. Remember that we could do little by ourselves and now we must rely largely on God's grace in helping ourselves and others. People do not care much for those who are smug and self-satisfied or those who gossip and criticize. But people are impressed by true humility. So we should try to walk humbly at all times. Gratitude to God and true humility are what makes us effective.

On that same page, the Prayer for the Day reads: "I pray that I may walk humbly with God. I pray that I may rely on His grace to carry me through."

Humility and gratitude appear again in the Meditation for the Day and the Prayer for the Day for May 30:

> "Praise the Lord." What does praising God mean? It means being grateful for all the wonderful things in the universe and for all the blessings in your life. So praise God by being grateful and humble. Praise of this kind has more power to vanquish evil than has mere resignation. The truly grateful and humble man who is always praising God is not tempted to do wrong. You will have a feeling of security because you know that fundamentally all is well. So look up to God and praise him.
>
> I pray that I may be grateful for all my blessings. I pray that I may be humble because I know that I do not deserve them.

Honesty

Walker believed that the lack of self-honesty could be profoundly damaging and that the ability to look at yourself hard and honestly, admitting both the bad and the good, was the most powerful untapped source of human energy. Self-honesty was not easily achieved, but was something to be worked at slowly and steadily. Recognition of one's weaknesses must be accompanied by a similar recognition of one's strengths. The person who achieves mature self-knowledge is no longer afraid of life's unpredictability. The honest person will develop the self-confidence to handle any situation that life may bring. In truth, being honest is a way of life. The practical implications of this honesty are found in Walker's A.A. Thought for the Day for April 1:

> Since I've been in A.A., have I made a start toward becoming more honest? Do I no longer have to lie to my wife? Am I on time at my work and do I try to earn what I get? Am I making an attempt to be honest with myself? Have I faced myself as I really am and have I admitted to myself that I'm no good by myself, but have to rely on God to help me do the right thing? *Am I beginning to find out what it means to be alive and to face the world honestly and without fear?*

For more on this topic, see A.A. Thoughts for the Day on January 19 and 20; and the essay "Honesty" in "Selected AA Writings by Richmond Walker" on page 288 of this book.

Service

Service, along with the other four absolutes that he borrowed from the Oxford Group, was for Walker an essential benchmark of growth in recovery. Upon his recovery, it was the Twelfth Step that gave meaning and purpose to his life. He believed also that AA groups would be successful and continue to grow if they had a strong sense of and commitment to service. In his talks, especially toward the end of his life, he encouraged all members to practice the Twelfth Step, "having had a spiritual awakening," and never to refuse a Twelfth Step call for help. Walker believed that members of the Fellowship had to be ready at all times to talk to anyone who wanted and needed sobriety. He believed that "carrying the message to others" would keep an AA group both alive and growing. Furthermore, a group would be successful in its service work only if its members had true humility based on gratitude. He wrote, "Each of us should be grateful to God and to A.A. that we have been given another chance to live. This attitude of gratitude should make us humble. If we are humble, if we have a true estimate of our own worth, we will be good A.A. members and the group will run smoothly." (See "A Successful Group," on page 282 of this book, for the full text of the talk quoted here.)

Among Walker's many papers in the Daytona Beach Archives is one entitled "What Spirituality Means to Me." It deserves to be quoted in full here:

> Spirituality means to me a belief in the reality of spiritual things more than the reality of material things. The great astronomers and physicists, in studying the universe, find that its nature is best expressed by a mathematical formula which is thought. This thought is closer to the nature of reality than material things as we know them.
>
> As man goes through the Adam and Eve experience and becomes separated from the world of nature, he feels outcast and lost until he comes to believe in his spiritual nature as apart from the material or animal nature. His soul is restless until it comes to rest in God. *(Another reference to St. Augustine.—D.E.)*
>
> A child sees life as an animal does. The material world around him is the only reality he knows. As he matures, he feels more and more the need for a spiritual world, in which he can feel at home. Gradually, from this strong inner need, he develops his own belief in the reality of his spiritual nature.
>
> Many men are satisfied by a theology and a creed which they are taught to believe in, without any soul searching of their own. This will not do for people

> who form their own conception of God from the facts of their own experience. A free soul develops his own conception of God as the cause behind all the good in the world; the cause of life, of intelligence, love and of everything that we can experience as the good things of life. He thinks of life as God-given, of intelligence as God-given, of Love as God-given.
>
> And so he finds a spiritual home, in which he can feel at ease and have that inner peace which the material world can never give him. This in turn leads him to have that gratitude and humility which cause him to develop a sincere desire to be of service to his fellow man.[21]

These paragraphs were sent to his friend the Reverend E. Trueblood on September 29, 1963, pretty well summing up Walker's thoughts on this subject as he approached the end of his life.

THE SPIRITUAL PROGRAM OF AA

When the AA General Service Office claimed that *Twenty-Four Hours a Day* was too religious, it rankled Walker. He spoke out strongly against those who he thought were losing sight of the spiritual dimension of the AA program and slipping away from its spiritual anchor. Religion was not the issue, he insisted; spirituality was.

Bill W. and Dr. Bob

While the controversy over the "religion" in Walker's book stands as an example of the human element of the AA movement, it also sheds some light on the unfolding of AA spirituality traceable to AA's two founders.

The original meeting between Dr. Bob and Bill W. was mediated not by books but by sharing their own personal stories that confirmed one another's experience. (See "Doctor Bob's Nightmare," page 171 of the Big Book, fourth edition. See page 180 especially.) The one message that developed from their meetings evolved into two ways of communicating it, according to Trysh Travis in *The Language of the Heart:* the *traditional* (deriving from Akron) and the *ecumenical* or "universalist" (evolving from New York).[22]

In Akron, surrender to God by getting down on one's knees was central to the group's spirituality, as was reading the Bible and Quiet Time. The group focused on love and service. The tradition of using Bible readings for Quiet Time remained a staple for Dr. Bob and the Akron and Cleveland groups. When Bill W. stayed at Dr. Bob's home for some length of time in 1935, the Bible held a primary place during their Quiet Times.[23] The New York group, on the other hand, wanted to proselytize to all, and so its spirituality had to appeal to all by relying on the Big Book. Personal stories were critical, as they gave individuals a way to identify with the variety of individual conversion narratives.

The Little Red Book is the closest model we have of how Dr. Bob taught newcomers to work the Twelve Steps to get sober. It focused on the "surrendered life," which stands in opposition to false pride and self-centeredness, and readers are urged to accept the Twelve Steps in their entirety. They were exhorted to root out their "soul-killing habits" and to lead the "AA Way of Life." *Getting down on your knees* while surrendering was the ritual that expressed this surrender, this willingness to embrace the program. Although it was included in earlier versions, the final editing of the Seventh Step deleted the ritual.

After Dr. Bob's death in 1950, Bill W. wrote his own more philosophical/spiritual discussion of the Steps, which became *Twelve Steps and Twelve Traditions,* very different in style and substance from *The Little Red Book.* According to some, Bill W. insisted that the New York office push his book over *The Little Red Book* so the warehouse would not be full of his copies of *Twelve Steps and Twelve Traditions.*[24]

A Program of Surrender

In 1956, Richmond Walker wrote and spoke in support of the spirituality of the AA program in contrast to what he saw as the contemporary emphasis on external organization. At this time, many AA members were worried that the concentration on organization would undermine its spiritual foundation. Walker's challenge was leveled against those in AA who wanted to soft-pedal what they called the spiritual angle. He believed that the AA Way was a spiritual one, and anyone who read the Twelve Steps—especially Steps Two, Three, and Eleven—could have no doubt about its spirituality. "The heart and the power and the strength of AA are its spiritual program," Walker argued, and if the spiritual basis of the program were neglected, AA would eventually die out because it would lose its effectiveness. He believed that "in some places the trend in AA is toward organization at the expense of spirituality—and this could wreck our great spiritual movement. Problems of organization, the trend away from the spiritual basis of the program, those things have a lot of AAs worried."

Moreover, he believed that if its members worked the spiritual principles of the program, the Fellowship could become a great spiritual force for good. Walker declared that he would like to see the AA movement get back to its primary spiritual aim: to help alcoholics recover their sobriety by turning to a Power greater than their own—to God, as the members conceive of Him. In a talk on this subject, he ended with an impassioned plea to the AA members in attendance:

> I am pleading tonight for consecrated AAs who are unashamedly following the spiritual program of Alcoholics Anonymous, who have surrendered their lives to God, as they understand Him, who have put their drink problem in the hands of God. For AAs who are trying to help other alcoholics and know that their success comes from God and nowhere else. For AAs who know they are powerless without God's help. For AAs who are humble for they are grateful to God for saving them from a life of defeat and misery. For AAs who are asking God each morning to direct their thinking during the day, who start each day with prayer and meditation, who pray: Thy will be done in me and thru me today, and mean it. These AAs, both men and women, are the backbone of AA. Without them our fellowship would lose its heart and soul, and eventually would lose its power to help suffering alcoholics.[25]

He had a similar message for an AA group in Rutland, Vermont, urging those present not to "soft-pedal" the spiritual part of the program. He described AA as a spiritual program from start to finish, demanding of its members that they surrender their lives to God. He stated, "This group will be successful if its members have true humility which is based on gratitude. Each of us should be grateful to God and AA that we have been given another chance to live. This attitude of gratitude should make us humble. If we are humble, if we have a true estimate of our own worth we will be good AA members and the group will run smoothly."[26]

At the end of his book *The Seven Points of Alcoholics Anonymous,* Walker summed up his faith in the Fellowship and the importance of active participation:

> We in Alcoholics Anonymous know the joy of giving. We believe that when we come to the end of our lives, it will be only the things that we have given away that we will take with us. We will take no material things with us, but we will take with us the kind deeds we have done, the help we may have given to our fellow alcoholics.
>
> We alcoholics, who have been helped to find AA by someone who was interested in our welfare, believe that we are under a deep obligation to pass the

> own conclusions. To be peaceful inside and to give love outside is the way to live. Many of us want love, but we do not *give,* so we do not *get* love.[30]

In the next two paragraphs, he quotes and comments on the Prayer of St. Francis of Assisi, relating it to this idea. St. Francis's goal was to be an instrument of peace, extending peace and love to all. Inner peace is the goal that we are all seeking, together with love and service to others. AA gave Richmond Walker a chance to discover inner peace through faith in a Power greater than himself.

> I have talked with hundreds of alcoholics during my years in AA. I have never been solely responsible for helping a fellow alcoholic, because if he was ready, I couldn't say the wrong thing, and if he wasn't ready, I couldn't say the right thing. But to endeavor to help my fellow alcoholic has given a purpose to my life and made it worthwhile.
>
> The selfish person can never find happiness, because happiness is a by-product of doing the right thing and trying to help your fellow man. So many people go through life thinking that material things can bring them happiness, and finding out at the end, that only spiritual things like honesty, purity, unselfishness, and love count in the long run.
>
> When we die we will not take anything with us, except perhaps the few kind words we have said, and the few kind deeds we have done during our lifetime. I hope to be remembered as one who, though he misspent many years through drink, at least was able to accomplish some good during the latter part of his life.
>
> The abiding Reality is God, and his order comes thru the moments. [31]

• • •

Notes

1. In addition to the archives at Daytona Beach and Hazelden, another important resource has been the research and publications of Glenn Chesnut of the Hindsfoot Foundation. He has been an important guide as I began my journey into the life, writings, and spirituality of Richmond Walker. Chesnut's book *The Higher Power of the Twelve-Step Program: For Believers & Non-Believers* (New York: Authors Choice Press, 2001), chapter 5, "Two Classical Authors on AA Spirituality," motivated me to examine more thoroughly Walker's Meditations for the Day in *Twenty-Four Hours a Day* as mined from *God Calling*.
2. Ernest Kurtz, *Not God: A History of Alcoholics Anonymous* (Center City, MN: Hazelden, 1979), 39–51. Kurtz offers a compact but excellent summary of the Oxford Group and its early relationship with AA along with the positive and negative influences on Bill W. and AA.
3. Ibid., 50.
4. Ibid., 48.
5. See Dick B., *A Design for Living* (San Rafael, CA: Paradise Research Publications, 1995), and Dick B., *Good Morning!* (Kihei, HI: Paradise Research Publications, 1998).
6. *For Sinners Only,* 292. These words appear to have a clear relationship with the Prayer of St. Francis of Assisi, quoted on page 99 of Bill W.'s *Twelve Steps and Twelve Traditions* (New York: AA World Services, 1952). We shall see that Walker devoted a paragraph to it in a paper written toward the end of his life. I believe it is an excellent expression of the meaning and action required in the practice of the Twelfth Step.
7. E. Stanley Jones, *The Way* (New York: Abington Press, 1946), vii.
8. Howard A. Walter, *Soul Surgery* (published 1919).
9. Richmond Walker, "The Five C's," October 27, 1943, Hazelden I. See also the very abbreviated version in *Twenty-Four Hours a Day,* Thoughts for the Day, May 23–27.
10. Carl Jung, *Modern Man in Search of a Soul* (New York: Harcourt, Brace & Company, 1933), 173. Jung described it best when he commented that "what drives people to war within themselves is the intuition or knowledge that they consist of two people in opposition to one another." It plays itself out in the life of the alcoholic in the strife between the alcoholic self and the person's real self. In one sense, this analogy perfectly illustrates the core of all spirituality. See Damian McElrath, *The Essence of Twelve Step Recovery* (Center City, MN: Hazelden, 2008).
11. Daytona Beach Archives, Vol. IV. (The spirituality of relationships.)
12. Richmond Walker, "First Anniversary of South Shore AA," August 25, 1944, Hazelden I.
13. Daytona Beach Archives, Vol. IV. For a modern version of the "personality problem" and the strife between our two selves, see Craig Nakken, *The Addictive Personality,* 2nd edition (Center City: Hazelden, 1996).
14. Richmond Walker, "Finding My Better Self", September 24, 1943, Hazelden I.
15. Richmond Walker, "Drinking Cuts You Off," June 28, 1944, Hazelden I.

16. Richmond Walker, "Finding My Better Self," September 24, 1943, Hazelden I. A variation on this theme is found in his *Grapevine* article "We Are Two People," October 1953 (vol. 10, no. 5, 19–20), in which he describes the alcoholic as being two different people—the real one and the other in which lurks "our wet subconscious mind."

17. Richmond Walker, "AA Insurance," November 17, 1943, Hazelden I.

18. Richmond Walker, "A Free Gift," May 17, 1944, Hazelden I.

19. Richmond Walker, *For Drunks Only* (1945), 24.

20. Richmond Walker, *Thoughts,* no. 5, Daytona Beach Archives, Vol. I. (Underlining is Walker's.)

21. Daytona Beach Archives, Vol. IV. (The word *religion* is crossed out in the title and the word *spirituality* is inserted.)

22. Trysh Travis, *The Language of the Heart* (Chapel Hill: University of North Carolina Press, 2009), 136–42. (Contains an interesting presentation of New York and Midwest spiritual traditions.)

23. See Bill Pittman, "Dr. Bob's Reading List," *AA: The Way It Began* (Seattle: Glenn Abbey Books, 1988).

24. Glenn Chesnut, "Richmond Walker and New York, 1953–1954," posted on "AA History Lovers" listserv, Yahoo Groups, August 27, 2004, http://health.groups.yahoo.com/group/AAHistoryLovers/message/1999.

25. Richmond Walker, "AA: A Spiritual Program," Hazelden I. Appears to date from 1956, based on internal evidence.

26. Richmond Walker, talk to AA group, Rutland, Vermont (no date), Hazelden I.

27. Richmond Walker, *The Seven Points of Alcoholics Anonymous,* revised edition (Seattle: Glen Abbey Books, 1989; Center City, MN: Hazelden, 1999), page 100.

28. Richmond Walker, "From Our Heads to Our Hearts," Daytona Beach Archives, Vol. IV.

29. Richmond Walker, "A Way to a Reasonable Faith," Hazelden I.

30. Richmond Walker, "Thoughts on Life," Hazelden I.

31. Ibid.

Sources for *Twenty-Four Hours a Day*

As already indicated, the actual roots of *Twenty-Four Hours a Day* lie in Walker's custom of providing thoughts for meditation at AA meetings. These were contained on scraps of paper or index cards that he presented at AA meetings in Boston, the South Shore, and Daytona Beach. Some members of the Daytona Beach Club encouraged him to put them in book form so that other AA members could benefit from the readings. Walker agreed and spent the years between 1946 and 1948 compiling his thoughts for publication.

In beginning this study of the sources for *Twenty-Four Hours a Day,* let's review what Richmond Walker wrote in the foreword to the Little Black Book:

> *Twenty-Four Hours a Day* is intended for members of Alcoholics Anonymous as a help in their program of living one day at a time. It is designed for those who want to start each day with a few minutes of thought, meditation, and prayer.
>
> These daily readings contain most of the material used in the booklet "For Drunks Only" and other A.A. literature; also some passages from "the Big Book," *Alcoholics Anonymous.*
>
> As a basis for the meditations in this book, the author has used many passages from the book *God Calling* by Two Listeners, edited by A. J. Russell. Permission to use the universal spiritual thoughts expressed in this book, without using direct quotations, has been granted. . . .[1]

The sources for *Twenty-Four Hours a Day* can therefore be reduced to four:

- Walker's handwritten talks and presentations between the years 1943 and 1945
- Walker's book *For Drunks Only* published in 1945
- the Big Book, *Alcoholics Anonymous*
- *God Calling* [2]

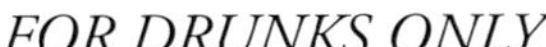

FOR DRUNKS ONLY

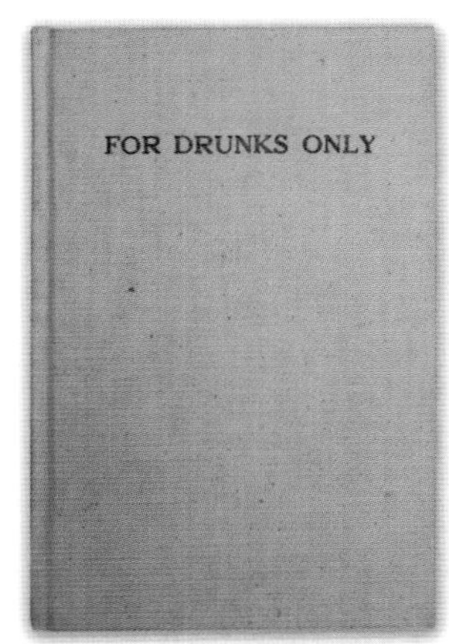

The book *For Drunks Only: One Man's Reaction to Alcoholics Anonymous,* published by Walker in 1945, is very important for two reasons: (1) it pulls together in a logical fashion the thoughts (indeed, his spiritual transformation) contained in the many presentations he made during that period of formation between 1942 and 1945, and (2) as Walker notes in his foreword, the "daily readings contain most of the material used in the booklet 'For Drunks Only' and other A.A. literature." It was published in fall of 1945, about three and a half years after Walker attended his first AA meeting in Boston. In 1980, when Hazelden reissued it, the introduction by Bill Pittman noted that the book had been out of print for thirty-five years. Pittman wrote that the AA South Group in Quincy had published two thousand copies of the book in 1945, and another six thousand in 1946. They sold for twenty-five cents a copy to AA members. Walker sent an autographed copy of the book to "his friend" Bill W. The next year, he offered it for publication by AA. But the offer was declined, as was a similar offer for *Twenty-Four Hours a Day* in 1953.

As mentioned previously, it is possible that the title of Walker's book was influenced by A. J. Russell's book, *For Sinners Only. For Drunks Only* describes in detail the contents of Walker's basic, concrete, action-oriented spirituality, reflecting the ideas that he had internalized over his three and a half years practicing them as a member of AA. As a major source for *Twenty-Four Hours a Day,* at least 90 percent of *For Drunks Only* is repeated in the same sequence and practically word for word in the A.A. Thoughts for the Day from January 1 to May 30 in the Little Black Book. It could be called Walker's manual of ascetical spirituality and contrasts sharply against the more contemplative spirituality found in the Meditations for the Day, which are drawn from *God Calling.*

THE BIG BOOK

The Big Book, *Alcoholics Anonymous,* is the major source for the A.A. Thoughts for the Day from August 8 through September 28.

Richmond Walker's copy of the Big Book is dated May 23, 1942, on the inside cover and was probably purchased at one of the first (if not the first) AA meetings that he attended on Newbury Street in Boston. On the same page, he had also written the passage reproduced in the front of this book: "Make book for morning quiet times—short passages for each day—on different phases of A.A.—Call it Twenty-Four Hours a Day."[3] Below that is this additional phrase in parentheses: (Based on Stanley Jones—"The Way"). *The Way* was a meditation book along Oxford Group lines. It relied heavily on Scripture readings for each day of the year. As noted in the previous essay, *The Way* was not the book that Walker ultimately used. The format was more likely that of *The Upper Room,* also mentioned previously, a booklet of spiritual readings, meditations, and prayers for the day, most widely used by members of the Oxford Group and early members of AA, among whom was Dr. Bob.[4] A little paperback quarterly costing only a nickel, it could easily fit into one's pocket for reference any time of the day. It was first published in 1935.

Walker's copy of the Big Book is the third printing of the first edition. On the inside cover, he lists the addresses for his homes in both Cohasset and Daytona Beach.

Walker has clearly delineated what he has taken from the Big Book with his annotations "Omit" and "End Omit," which indicate the text that he is using in *Twenty-Four Hours a Day.* There are relatively few marginal notes of any significance. One is opposite the text that reads "constitutionally incapable of being honest with themselves." In the margin, Walker wrote that "honesty is the basis of the program." (Again, honesty appears time and again as the core of Walker's recovery.)

Of some interest are the pages that contain the Twelve Steps (pp. 71–72 of first edition, 59–60 of the third edition), where Walker reduces the Twelve Steps to five principles: (1) Admission (Step One); (2) Turn to a Higher Power (Steps Two and Three); (3) Inventory

Walker's Copy of the Big Book

There is a very interesting story related to the discovery of Walker's Big Book.

Gifford Dean, who grew up with the Walker children, sent me a letter (dated April 16, 2009) with an original typewritten manuscript about Walker's involvement in his AA group in Scituate. In the letter, he described how he came into possession of Walker's Big Book after Walker died in 1965. Dean related that Walker's wife, Agnes, knocked on his door one day in Cohasset, where the Walkers and the Deans were neighbors and where she was still residing during the summers. She was carrying a carton of books and pamphlets that she handed to him, saying, "I thought Rich would like you to have these." The box contained some "Golden Books"—a popular series written by Fr. Ralph Pfau, a priest and recovering alcoholic—and miscellaneous AA literature. Most significant in Dean's eyes was Walker's Big Book "with its marginal notes and underlines." Dean kept it for years, and although he considered it important for his own recovery and its relation to Richmond Walker, he "never thought it would have a great value for anyone else."

Dean moved to Florida in 1976. At the dedication ceremony of the Hanley-Hazelden treatment center in West Palm Beach a decade later, he met Dan Anderson, then the president of Hazelden, who showed great interest in the fact that Dean knew Walker and how he had come to have Walker's Big Book. Anderson asked whether Dean would consider making Walker's Big Book a bequest to Hazelden. Dean thought about it, and the next time they met a few years later, he gifted the book to Hazelden. Anderson truly considered it something special and said that he would put it on display at the Richmond Walker Center. This center, on the edge of the large Hazelden campus in Minnesota, was built in 1985 to accommodate the needs of publishing as a result of a surge in demand for Hazelden's educational materials. Fittingly, it was named after Richmond Walker, whose book initiated Hazelden into the publishing field. As is the case with so many other important treasures in other centers, it eventually ended up in a Center City, Minnesota, bank vault, no longer on exhibition, unmissed and forgotten by most everyone.

It was resurrected by Gifford Dean himself, who wrote to me about his relationship with Anderson and the gift of the Big Book, and sent me the manuscript about Walker's life in AA. All this happened but a short time before I was invited to write these essays as an introduction to *The Making of the Little Black Book.*

(Steps Four, Five, Six, and Seven); (4) Restitution (Steps Eight and Nine); (5) Helping Others (Step Twelve). He had written something in the margin regarding Steps Ten and Eleven, but it was erased and is undecipherable.

Most of the other marginal notes are his phrases summarizing the text he is using. It is also significant that in the stories in the second part of the Big Book, the rare underlining is done mostly where reference is made in the story to God or Higher Power.

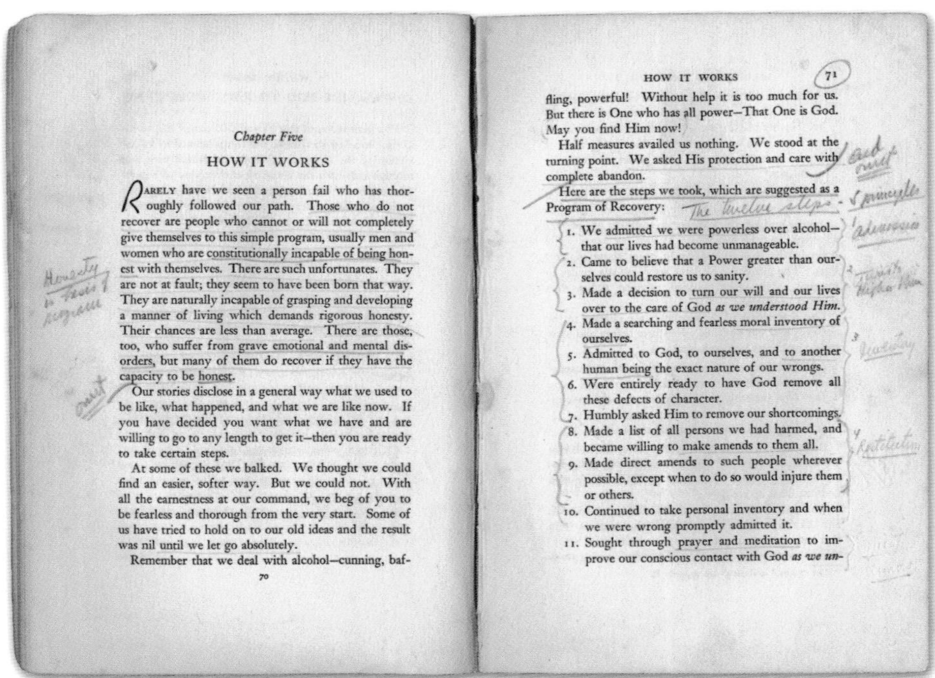

Chapter Five

HOW IT WORKS

RARELY have we seen a person fail who has thoroughly followed our path. Those who do not recover are people who cannot or will not completely give themselves to this simple program, usually men and women who are constitutionally incapable of being honest with themselves. There are such unfortunates. They are not at fault; they seem to have been born that way. They are naturally incapable of grasping and developing a manner of living which demands rigorous honesty. Their chances are less than average. There are those, too, who suffer from grave emotional and mental disorders, but many of them do recover if they have the capacity to be honest.

Our stories disclose in a general way what we used to be like, what happened, and what we are like now. If you have decided you want what we have and are willing to go to any length to get it—then you are ready to take certain steps.

At some of these we balked. We thought we could find an easier, softer way. But we could not. With all the earnestness at our command, we beg of you to be fearless and thorough from the very start. Some of us have tried to hold on to our old ideas and the result was nil until we let go absolutely.

Remember that we deal with alcohol—cunning, baf-

70

HOW IT WORKS 71

fling, powerful! Without help it is too much for us. But there is One who has all power—That One is God. May you find Him now!

Half measures availed us nothing. We stood at the turning point. We asked His protection and care with complete abandon.

Here are the steps we took, which are suggested as a Program of Recovery:

1. We admitted we were powerless over alcohol—that our lives had become unmanageable.
2. Came to believe that a Power greater than ourselves could restore us to sanity.
3. Made a decision to turn our will and our lives over to the care of God *as we understood Him.*
4. Made a searching and fearless moral inventory of ourselves.
5. Admitted to God, to ourselves, and to another human being the exact nature of our wrongs.
6. Were entirely ready to have God remove all these defects of character.
7. Humbly asked Him to remove our shortcomings.
8. Made a list of all persons we had harmed, and became willing to make amends to them all.
9. Made direct amends to such people wherever possible, except when to do so would injure them or others.
10. Continued to take personal inventory and when we were wrong promptly admitted it.
11. Sought through prayer and meditation to improve our conscious contact with God *as we un-*

RICHMOND WALKER'S BIG BOOK

GOD CALLING

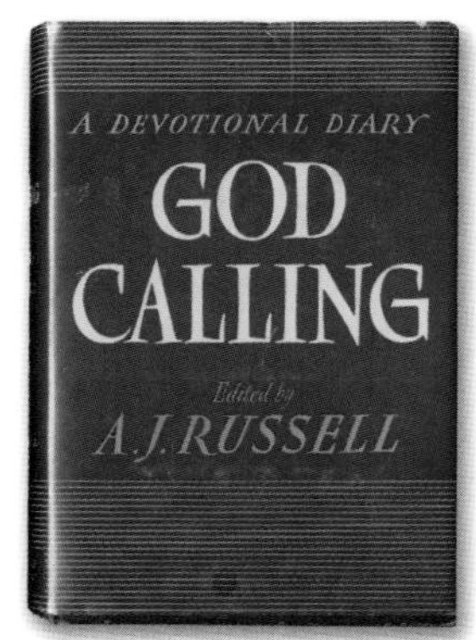

The second major part of *Twenty-Four Hours a Day* is the Meditations for the Day following the A.A. Thoughts for the Day. The source for these daily reflections is the meditation book *God Calling.*[5] Its subtitle reads: *The Power of Love and Joy That Restores Faith and Serenity in Our Troubled World.* It was edited by A. J. Russell and published in 1932.

Russell wrote the preface to *God Calling.* He believed the "astonishing" claim of the "Two Listeners," the authors of the book, that the message they received had been given to them by the "Living Christ Himself," opening their eyes "to many things which they and this generation greatly need to know." As Christ speaks to them, the Two Listeners gain joy and courage to carry on through poverty and ill health, the daily challenges to their faith. Russell urges the reader to inhale the spirit of the book and "live your life in its intimacy with The Master."

The two women who composed the meditations elected to remain anonymous and go by the simple title "Two Listeners." It was Russell's book *For Sinners Only* that had inspired one of the listeners to see if she and her friend, with whom she was living, could get guidance through sharing a quiet time. As the two of them entered into this process, one of them received messages that she claimed came from Christ. These were then written down by her companion every day. Essentially, the messages were "to love and laugh and be joy-bringers to the lives we contacted."

In comparing the readings from *God Calling* with the text in the meditations of *Twenty-Four Hours a Day,* it is clear that Walker had done much editing as well as omitting some of the meditations and substituting his own compositions.[6] *God Calling* was a Christian meditation book, and Walker sought to edit the daily meditations for *Twenty-Four Hours a Day* so they would reach a more ecumenical audience. Because he had done so with much deliberation and forethought, it had been difficult for him to accept the conclusions of AA General Services about the book's "religious overtones." In the foreword to the fortieth anniversary edition of *Twenty-Four Hours a Day,* Mel B. wrote that "Rich W. must have been convinced that the basic principles of *God Calling* supported and reinforced the AA program and thus could benefit recovering alcoholics. So Walker performed what could be called a 'strategic translation' to make the *God Calling* meditations acceptable to recovering alcoholics."[7]

This "strategic translation" actually took a variety of forms. For example, in some cases Walker did his editing simply by changing a word, by changing a phrase, or by rearranging the sentences in the text. He left the major portion of the meditation intact and simply adopted it as his own. In other instances, he surfed through the meditation identifying words, phrases, or passages to omit, change, or rearrange. Or he rearranged sentences within the text to suit his own purposes and free up his own message.

One of the primary reasons for much of the editing is clear: to eliminate the strongly Christological texts in the meditations. Evidence of this emerges early in *Twenty-Four Hours a Day:* In the meditation for January 4, he substitutes *God* for *Christ,* a change maintained throughout the book.

The following are a few examples of Walker's partial editing:

January 1, *Twenty-Four Hours a Day:*

"In the new year, I will live one day at a time. I will make each day one of preparation for better things ahead. I will not dwell on the past or the future; only on the present."] "I will bury every fear of the future, all thoughts of unkindness and bitterness, all my dislikes, my resentments, my sense of failure, my disappointments in others and in myself, my gloom and my despondency. I will leave all these things buried, and go forward, in this new year, into a new life."

January 1, *God Calling:*

["I stand between the years. The Light of My Presence is flung across the years to come —the radiance of the Sun of Righteousness. Backward over the past year is my Shadow thrown, hiding trouble and sorrow and disappointment. Dwell not on the past—only the present."] These sentences precede what follows in *God Calling.*

"Bury every fear of the future, of poverty of those dear to you, of suffering, of loss. Bury all thought of unkindness and bitterness, all your dislikes, your resentments, your sense of failure, your disappointments in others and in yourselves, your gloom, your despondency, and let us leave them all buried, and go forward to a new and risen life."

(This paragraph is then followed by three others in *God Calling,* which Walker did not use.)

January 4, ***Twenty-Four Hours a Day:***

"I will believe that fundamentally all is well. Good things will happen to me. I believe that God cares for me and will provide for me. I will not try to plan ahead. I know that the way will unfold, step by step. I will leave tomorrow's burden to God, because He is the great Burden-Bearer. He only expects me to carry my one-day's share."

January 4, ***God Calling:***

"All is well. Wonderful things are happening. Do not limit God at all. He cares and provides.

Uproot self—the channel-blocker. Do not plan ahead, the way will unfold step by step. Leave tomorrow's burden. Christ is the Great Burden-Bearer. You cannot bear His load and He only expects you to carry a little day-share."

The editing is stronger still when Walker selects a phrase or word from *God Calling* and lets his own thoughts revolve around it. For example, on May 11 of *Twenty-Four Hours a Day,* he selects the phrase "Divine Third," around which he constructs his own Meditation for the Day:

May 11, ***Twenty-Four Hours a Day:***

"Wherever there is true fellowship and love between people, God's spirit is always there as the Divine Third. In all human relationships, the Divine Spirit is what brings them together. When a life is changed through the channel of another person, it is God the Divine Third who always makes the change, using the person as a means. The moving power behind all spiritual things, all personal relationships between people is God, the Divine Third, who is always there. No relationships between persons can be entirely right without the presence of God's Spirit."

May 11, ***God Calling:***

"When I have led you through the storms there will be other words for you, other messages—other guidance.

So deep is your friendship and so great your desire to love and follow and serve Me that soon, when this time of difficulty is over, to be alone together will always mean to be shut in with me.

There are few friendships in the world like that and yet I taught, when in earth, as I have taught you both, the power of the *two together.*

And now tonight I have more to say to you. I say that the time is coming, is even now here, when those who visit you two together, will know that I am the Divine Third in your friendship.

The editing is strongest when Walker strikes out the *God Calling* passage and creates a new one that reveals the practical dimension of his spirituality. For example, August 29:

> Breathe in the inspiration of goodness and truth. It is the spirit of honesty, purity, unselfishness, and love. It is readily available if we are willing to accept it wholeheartedly. God has given us two things: His spirit and the power of choice, to accept or not, as we will. We have the gift of free will. When we choose the path of selfishness and greed and pride, we are refusing to accept God's spirit. When we choose the path of love and service, we accept God's spirit and it flows into us and makes all things new.

The same can be said of the meditation for August 28:

> Happiness cannot be sought directly; it is a by-product of love and service. Service is a law of our being. With love in your heart, there is always some service to your fellow man. A life of power and joy and satisfaction is built on love and service. A man who hates or is too selfish is going against the law of his own being. He cuts himself off from his God and His fellow man. Little acts of love and encouragement, of service and help, erase the rough places of life and help to make the path smooth. If we do these things we cannot help having our share of happiness.

Both passages point to the younger Walker's practical path of spirituality (ascetical, if you will), contrasting with his later, more contemplative writings. Both passages also embrace what Dr. Bob repeated through the years—that love and service are central to the AA way of life:

> And one more thing. None of us would be here today if someone hadn't taken time to explain things to us, to give a little pat on the back, to take us to a meeting or two, to do numerous little kind and thoughtful acts on our behalf. So never let us get a degree of smug complacency that we're not willing to extend, to our less fortunate brothers, that help which has been so beneficial to us.[8]

For Dr. Bob, as well as for Walker, the AA program was measured by love and service.

• • •

A Guide to *Twenty-Four Hours a Day*

This section both summarizes the themes covered in the A.A. Thoughts for the Day of *Twenty-Four Hours a Day* and identifies the specific source of the material, where possible. (All references to *For Drunks Only* refer to the 1980 Hazelden edition.)

PART I: A.A. THOUGHTS FOR THE DAY JANUARY 1 TO MAY 31

The following paragraphs (1) provide a guide to the first five months of *Twenty-Four Hours a Day* in the A.A. Thought for the Day and identify the source of the material, and (2) highlight Walker's early spiritual maturation, as demonstrated in the following digest of the contents of *For Drunks Only.*

For Drunks Only Chapter 1: Personal (pp. 1 and 2)

This very brief chapter contains a condensed version of Walker's life as an alcoholic. There is no mention of the Oxford Group in which he was involved from 1939 to 1941. During that time, Walker intimates that he neither smoked nor drank. (He also writes that his father died in the spring of 1941. Here his memory failed him, for he died in the fall of 1941.) In this abbreviated autobiographical version he states that he was drunk most of the time after the death of his daughter in 1935. He was on a "merry-go-round" and could not stay sober, even after promising his wife that he would after the death of his father. In his introduction, Walker wrote: "I was the type that often becomes an alcoholic. I had an inferiority complex. I was lonely. I didn't know how to make friends. I built a wall between myself and other people. And I took to drink as a duck takes to water" (*For Drunks Only,* p. 1).

For Drunks Only Chapter 2: My Introduction to AA (pp. 3–10)
Twenty-Four Hours a Day January 1 to January 20

Walker employs the phrase "soul sickness" (a phrase common to the Oxford Group) to describe his alcoholic condition. He was desperate and ready for AA. AA works and provides a more natural way of living (without alcohol). It helps us build a new way of life, a long view of what life is all about.

The importance of honesty surfaces throughout the book. This new way of living is "based on honesty, being absolutely honest with ourselves and with other people . . .

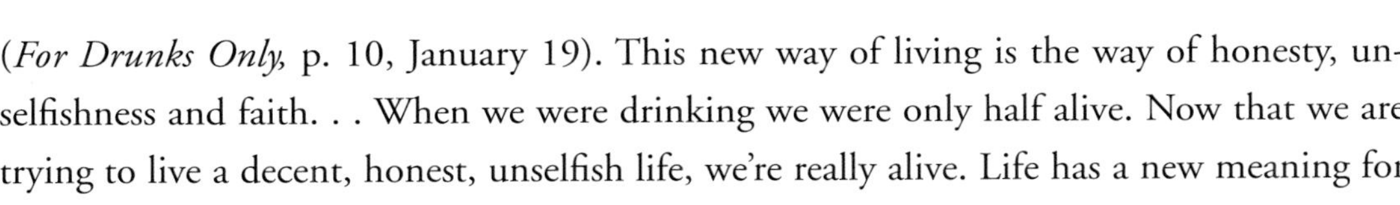

(*For Drunks Only,* p. 10, January 19). This new way of living is the way of honesty, unselfishness and faith. . . When we were drinking we were only half alive. Now that we are trying to live a decent, honest, unselfish life, we're really alive. Life has a new meaning for us so that we can really enjoy it" (*For Drunks Only,* p. 10, January 20).

For Drunks Only Chapter 3: Thinking Things Out (pp. 11–21)
Twenty-Four Hours a Day January 21 to February 23

"When you come into AA and get honest with yourself, and with other people, that terrible load of lying falls off your shoulders" (*For Drunks Only,* p. 13, January 27). Drinking cuts us off from self, others, and God. On the contrary, sobriety restores the spirituality derived from the positive relationships with ourselves, with others, and with God (*For Drunks Only,* p. 14, January 29–31).

For Drunks Only Chapter 4: The Spiritual Basis of AA (pp. 22–26)
Twenty-Four Hours a Day February 24 to March 11

In this chapter, Walker highlights his own understanding of AA's spiritual program: "When I came to my first AA meeting, I looked up at the wall at the end of the room and saw the sign—But for the Grace of God—I knew right then and there that I would have to call on the grace of God to get sober and get over my soul sickness" (*For Drunks Only,* p. 22, February 24). Through AA, Walker began to believe again in that Divine Principle in the universe that he called God. At Quiet Time in the morning, he would ask God for the power to stay sober for twenty-four hours and to thank Him every night for helping to keep him sober (*For Drunks Only,* p. 23, February 26).

Surrender was the spiritual foundation of AA. "Surrender means putting your life into God's hands and making a promise to him that you will try to live the way he wants you to live" (*For Drunks Only,* p. 24, March 2). It's like making a bargain with God not to drink. If we turn our drink problem over to God without reservation, we won't have to worry about it anymore. "We don't leave drink, drink leaves us" (*For Drunks Only,* p. 26, March 11). While sobriety is a free gift, alcoholics must do their part by strengthening their faith through prayer and meditation, listening to and working with other alcoholics, and especially practicing Quiet Time each morning asking God for the strength to stay sober that day (*For Drunks Only,* p. 26, March 9–11).

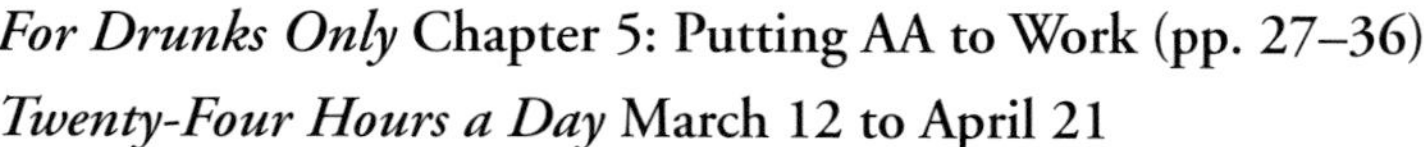

***For Drunks Only* Chapter 5: Putting AA to Work (pp. 27–36)**
***Twenty-Four Hours a Day* March 12 to April 21**

In the beginning of this chapter, Walker makes the case for people's duality (which he also does throughout *Twenty-Four Hours a Day*) by drawing upon the parable of the Prodigal Son. "When he came to himself, he said, 'I will arise and go to my Father.' That's what an alcoholic does in AA. He comes to himself. His alcoholic self is not his real self. His sane, sober, respectable self is his real self. . . . We've got rid of our false, drinking selves and find our real, sober selves" (*For Drunks Only,* p. 27, March 12–13).

It's a twenty-four-hour program, to be bitten off one day at a time. "All we really have is now. We have no past time and no future time. As the saying goes: 'Yesterday is gone, forget it; tomorrow never comes, don't worry; today is here, get busy'" (*For Drunks Only,* p. 29, March 18).

As noted in the previous essay, gratitude and humility are two of the most important qualities that Walker returns to time and again. They are the seeds scattered throughout *For Drunks Only* and the whole of the Little Black Book that are to be harvested by those who practice the program. This passage puts the two together:

> After I had been in AA for a while, I found out that if I was going to stay sober, I'd have to be a humble person. The men I saw in AA who had really made the grade were all humble people. When I stop to think that but for the grace of God I might be drunk right now, I can't help feeling humble. It's not to my credit that I am sober today. Someone said that you can't change a hell into an angel in a few easy lessons. And when I think of the kind of person that I was, not long ago, when I think about the man I left behind me, I've got nothing to be proud about (*For Drunks Only,* p. 36, April 21).

***For Drunks Only* Chapter 6: Enjoying the Benefits of AA (pp. 37–42)**
***Twenty-Four Hours a Day* April 22 to May 15**

Keep grateful, keep loyal, and keep disciplined, and in AA one will find the things one needs to stay sober (*For Drunks Only,* pp. 40–41; May 7–13).

For Drunks Only Chapter 7: Passing AA On to Others (pp. 43–46)
Twenty-Four Hours a Day May 16 to May 30

Walker uses another favorite parable, that of the Good Samaritan, to describe the members of AA who are working to assist others (*For Drunks Only,* p. 43, May 16–17). At the end of the book, he pens: "We in Alcoholics Anonymous can be uniquely useful, just because we have the misfortune or fortune to be alcoholics ourselves. If you are a desperate person, who honestly wants to stop drinking, you can become a sober person by following the AA program. You can become a grateful and humble person. And finally, if you want to, you can become a uniquely useful person by using your own greatest defeat and failure and sickness as a weapon to help others" (*For Drunks Only,* p. 46, May 29–30).

Here ends the material from *For Drunks Only.* If you wish to comprehend the fullness of Walker's spirituality, read either *For Drunks Only* at one sitting or the first five months of A.A. Thoughts for the Day in the Little Black Book. Both serve as his Manual for the Spiritual Life.

Walker then creates a bridge to the months that follow with a ringing tribute to AA, which he calls his AA credo: "I shall not wait to be drafted for service to my fellow men. I shall volunteer. I shall be loyal in my attendance, generous in my giving, kind in my criticism, creative in my suggestions, loving in my attitudes. I shall give to AA my interest, my enthusiasm, my devotion, and most of all, myself. Do I also accept this as my *AA credo*?"[9]

It is interesting that Walker quotes the same credo on December 31, the end of the year, which then serves as a bridge to the rereading of the Little Black Book.

PART II: THOUGHTS FOR THE DAY
JUNE 1 TO AUGUST 7

The tribute to AA serves also as a fitting beginning to the next two and a quarter months of the Thoughts for the Day. While many individual passages find their sources in Walker's papers between 1943 and 1945, there is no one overarching source for these readings. I have assigned them the title "Straight Talk," revolving around topics on the *disease of alcoholism, the AA program,* and *life as a member of Alcoholics Anonymous.*

One of the most important and beautiful of Walker's spiritual themes is to be found in the A.A. Thoughts for the Day from July 29 to July 31:

> There are two days in every week about which we should not worry, two days which should be kept from fear and apprehension. One of those days is yesterday, with its mistakes and cares, its faults and blunders, its aches and pains. Yesterday has passed forever beyond our control. All the money in the world cannot bring back yesterday. We cannot undo a single act we have performed. We cannot erase a single word we said. Yesterday is gone beyond recall. *Do I still worry about what happened yesterday?* (July 29)
>
> The other day we should not worry about is tomorrow, with its possible adversities, its burdens, its large promise and perhaps its poor performance. Tomorrow is also beyond our immediate control. Tomorrow's sun will rise, either in splendor or behind a mask of clouds, but it will rise. Until it does, we have no stake in tomorrow, for it is as yet unborn. *Do I still worry too much about tomorrow?* (July 30)
>
> This leaves only one day—today. Any man can fight the battles of just one day. It is only when you and I add the burdens of these two awful eternities, yesterday and tomorrow, that we break down. It is not the experience of today that drives men mad. It is the remorse of bitterness for something which happened yesterday, or the dread of what tomorrow may bring. Let us therefore do our best to live one day at a time. *Am I living one day at a time?* (July 31)

PART III: THOUGHTS FOR THE DAY
AUGUST 8 TO SEPTEMBER 28

The Big Book, *Alcoholics Anonymous,* is the major source for the A.A. Thoughts for the Day from August 8 through September 28.

A.A. Thoughts for the Day for August 8 and September 28 serve as excellent bookends for the readings from the Big Book.

> For a while, we are going back to the Big Book, *Alcoholics Anonymous,* and pick out passages here and there, so that they may become fixed in our minds, a little at a time, day by day, as we go along. There is no substitute for reading the Big Book. It is our "bible." We should study it thoroughly and make it a part of ourselves. We should not try to change any of it. Within its covers is the full exposition of the A.A. program. There is no substitute for it. We should study it often. *Have I studied the Big Book faithfully?* (August 8)

and

> For the past two months, we have been studying passages and steps from the Big Book, *Alcoholics Anonymous.* Now why not read the book itself again? It is essential that the A.A. program become part of us. We must have its essentials at our fingertips. We cannot study the Big Book too much or too often. The more we read it and study it, the better equipped we are to think A.A., act A.A., and live A.A. We cannot know too much about the program. The chances are that we will never know enough. But we can make as much of it our own as possible. *How much of the Big Book have I thoroughly mastered?* (September 28)

PART IV: THOUGHTS FOR THE DAY
SEPTEMBER 29 TO DECEMBER 31

A.A. Thoughts for the Day, September 29 to October 20

These readings record the obligations of committed and working members of AA. One needs to ask the searching question "just how good an AA am I?" The readings for October 19 and 20 are particularly poignant:

> Do I realize that I do not know how much time I have left? It may be later than I think. Am I going to do the things that I know I should do, before my time runs out? By the way, what is my purpose for the rest of my life? Do I realize all I have to make up for in my past wasted life? Do I know that I am living on borrowed time and that I would not even have this much time left without A.A. and the grace of God? *Am I going to make what time I have left count for A.A.?* (October 19)

> . . . It all boils down to this: I owe a deep debt to A.A. and to the grace of God. Am I going to do all I can to repay that debt? Let us search our souls, make our decisions, and act accordingly. Any real success we have in life will depend on that. Now is the time to put our conclusions into effect. *What am I going to do about it?* (October 20)

A.A. Thoughts for the Day, October 21 to November 26

These pages deal with the rewards that come from being a member of AA. Among these are things that we have lost or that have taken a diminished role in our lives, such as fear, worry, and self-centeredness. This section contains many arresting passages. One that's especially attractive deals with our unfolding journey and the need to keep walking on that path:

> Instead of pretending to be perfectionists, in A.A. we are content if we are making progress. The main thing is to be growing. We realize that perfectionism is only a result of false pride and an excuse to save our faces. In A.A. we are willing to make mistakes and to stumble, provided we are always stumbling forward. We are not so interested in what we are as in what we are becoming. We are on the way, not at the goal. And we will be on the way as long as we live. . . . *Am I making progress?* (November 24)

A.A. Thoughts for the Day, November 27 to December 24

Walker sets out to describe exactly what the Way of AA is—a Way that is not to be abandoned because of "slips." It should be noted that many of the readings from December 9 to the end of the month have the same source as the readings from *The Seven Points of Alcoholics Anonymous.* There are many striking passages throughout this section. We select the following:

> Our faith should control the whole of our life. We alcoholics were living a divided life. We had to find a way to make it whole. When we were drinking, our lives were made up of a lot of scattered and unrelated pieces. We must pick up our lives and put them together again. We do it by a reorganizing faith in a Divine Principle in the universe which holds us together and holds the whole universe together, and gives it meaning and purpose. We surrender our disorganized lives to that Power, we get into harmony with the Divine Spirit, and our lives are made whole again. *Is my life whole again?* (December 20)

This is an important text regarding a person's desire for wholeness, and it builds upon a previous one for November 17, where Walker wrote about being composed of two personalities, good and bad. He continued, "We are all dual personalities to some extent. When we were drinking, the bad personality was in control. We did things when we were drunk that we would never do when we were sober."

Wholeness, integrity, and completeness are what alcoholics are seeking through drinking. With alcohol, they seek to bypass the path that most humans have to take. In his letter to Bill W., Carl Jung anticipated the importance of what has just been written and which plagued Walker for some thirty years. Jung wrote, "Alcoholism is a spiritual disease the basis of which is man's yearning for wholeness."[10]

A.A. Thoughts for the Day, December 25 to December 31

"Many alcoholics will be saying today: 'This is a good Christmas for me,'" reads the A.A. Thought for Christmas Day. Having recovered, this Christmas would be an especially good day for Walker. He wrote a heartwarming description about what that first sober Christmas meant to him, one that had been missing from his life for a long time. But for the grace of God, he might have been spending this Christmas the way he spent so many others in the past. He remembered one Christmas when he was drinking in the Rathskeller in Hingham, which he labeled a "dump." He had bought eight toy reindeer and a toy sleigh from the five and ten to put in the kids' stockings. He put them on the bar and started a contest among the other drunks to see who could name the eight reindeer—Dancer, Prancer, etc. He kept buying drinks for anyone who could remember the right names. He then got too drunk to get home in time to fill any stockings.

He remembered other Christmas mornings coming downstairs in his pajamas and bathrobe and with a terrible hangover, and then sneaking out to get a drink once in a while so that he could at least pretend that he was enjoying watching the kids open their presents.

"By the grace of God" he expected to be sober this Christmas and to hang up the stockings on Christmas Eve with his wife and kids. He would read "The Night Before Christmas" and thank God that through His help, he was sober. He expected to celebrate this Christmas as it should be celebrated, not with rum, but soberly and gratefully for all the blessings that had come to him and his family since he found sobriety through AA.[11]

Walker referred to the A.A. Thoughts for the Day from December 26 to December 31 as his "AA credo." They sum up in lyrical fashion a hymn of praise for what AA means to him:

> . . . I am glad to be able to be useful, to have a reason for living, a purpose in life. I want to lose my life in this great cause and so find it again. (December 26)
>
> I need the A.A. principles for the development of the buried life within me, that good life, which I had misplaced, but which I found again in this fellowship. This life within me is developing slowly but surely . . . As long as I stick close to A.A., my life will go on developing, and I cannot see yet what it will be, but I know that it will be good. . . . (December 27)
>
> A.A. may be human in its organization, but it is divine in its purpose. The purpose is to point me toward God and the good life. . . . Whatever the future holds, it cannot be too much for me to bear. I have the Divine Power with me to carry me through everything that may happen. . . . (December 28)
>
> Participating in the privileges of the movement, I shall share in the responsibilities, taking it upon myself to carry my fair share of the load, not grudgingly but joyfully. . . . (December 29)

To the extent that I fail in my responsibilities, A.A. fails. To the extent I succeed, A.A. succeeds. . . . I shall not wait to be drafted for service to others, but I shall volunteer. . . . (December 30)

I shall be loyal in my attendance, generous in my giving, kind in my criticism, creative in my suggestions, loving in my attitudes. I shall give A.A. my interest, my enthusiasm, my devotion, and most of all, myself. The Lord's Prayer has become part of my A.A. thoughts for each day: "Our Father. . . ." (December 31; as has already been pointed out, this passage is quoted in the A.A. Thought for the Day for May 31, ending the selections from *For Drunks Only.*)

• • •

Notes

1. Richmond Walker, foreword to *Twenty-Four Hours a Day* (Center City, MN: Hazelden, 1954).
2. The other Oxford Group and AA literature that Walker may have had at his disposal and used in A.A. Thoughts for the Day have not been identified. We also know that he was a reader and contributor to the *Grapevine.* A number of his articles appear over the years, especially 1963 to 1965. In Walker's book *The Seven Points of Alcoholics Anonymous* (Center City, MN: Hazelden, 1999), a copy of the original page proofs reveals many references to the *Grapevine* that were omitted in the Hazelden publication.
3. This may have been written in 1946, the same year that *The Way* was published. He had just published *For Drunks Only* in 1945 and was free to take up another writing.
4. See Glenn Chesnut, Hindsfoot Foundation, "The Upper Room and Early AA."
5. Walker wrote in the foreword to *Twenty-Four Hours a Day:* "As a basis for the meditations in this book, the author has used many [but not all] passages from the book *God Calling.*"
6. In the archives at both Daytona Beach and Hazelden are typewritten manuscripts containing passages in parallel columns from both *God Calling* and *Twenty-Four Hours a Day* from January 1 to February 15. The person who compiled the passages sought to show how Walker transcribed the text of *God Calling* and made it compatible with his own thoughts and, in general, with an AA-compatible spirituality. See also Glenn Chesnut, "Twenty-Four Hours a Day" and "God Calling" *(AA Information of Importance)* for a brief explanation of the connection between the two.
7. Mel B., foreword to fortieth anniversary edition of *Twenty-Four Hours a Day* (Center City, MN: Hazelden, 1994).
8. Sunday, July 30, 1950, First International AA Convention, Cleveland, Ohio.
9. See the full credo in Richmond Walker, *The Seven Points of Alcoholics Anonymous,* 98–100.
10. Carl Jung to Bill W. in *Pass It On: The Story of Bill Wilson* (New York: A.A. World Services, Inc., 1984), 384. For the full correspondence, see pages 381–86.
11. Richmond Walker, "A Sober Christmas," 1942, Hazelden I.

The Working Manuscript for *Twenty-Four Hours a Day*

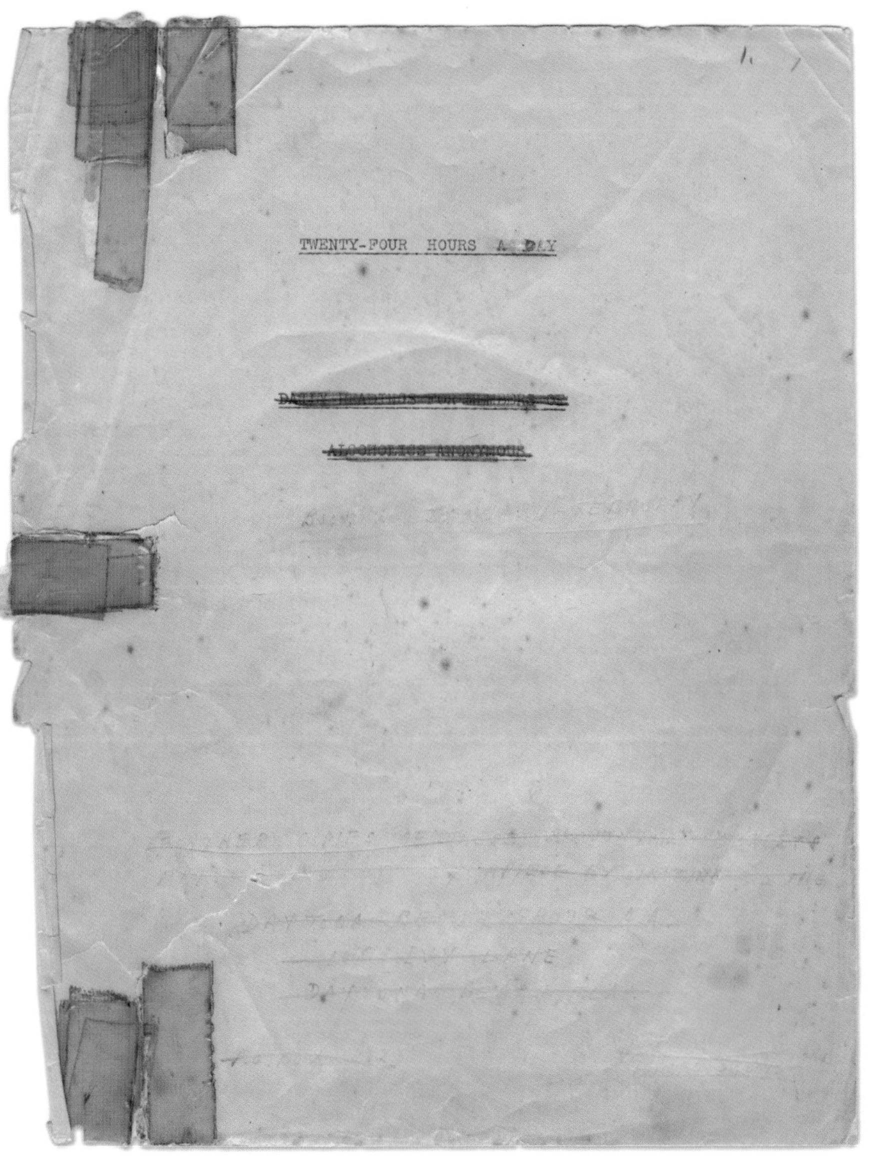

TWENTY-FOUR HOURS A DAY

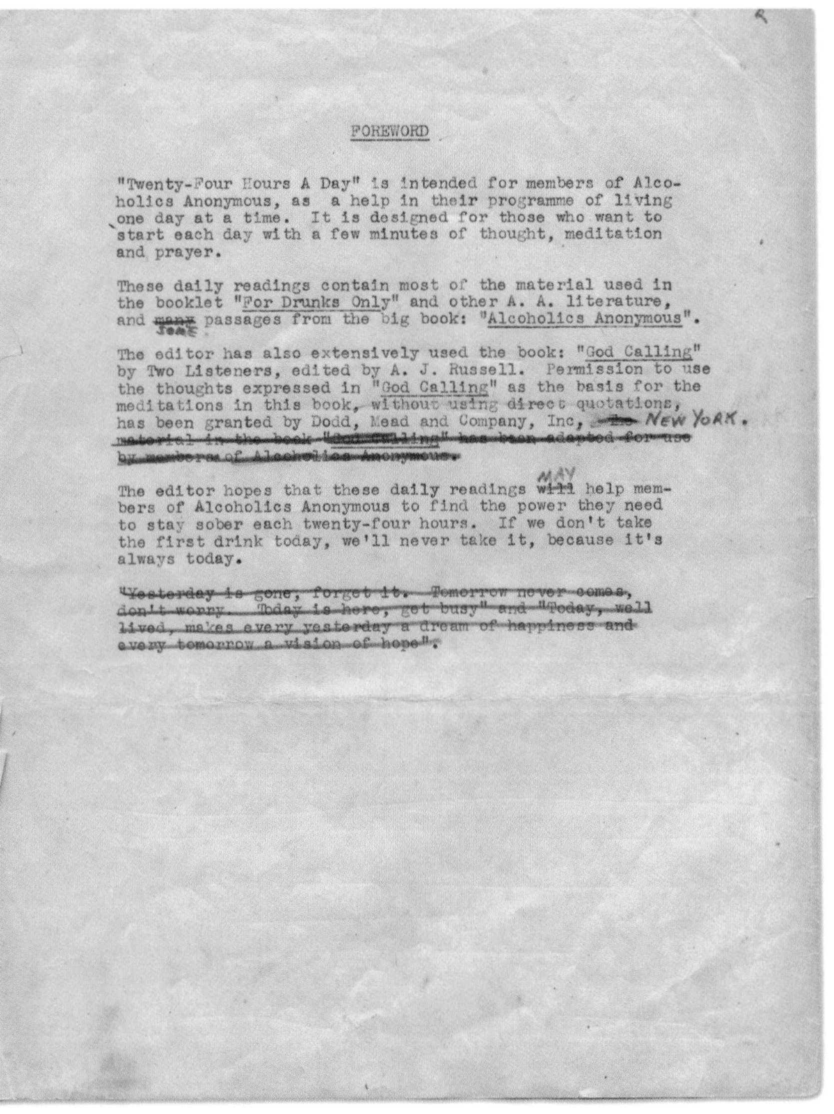

FOREWORD

"Twenty-Four Hours A Day" is intended for members of Alcoholics Anonymous, as a help in their programme of living one day at a time. It is designed for those who want to start each day with a few minutes of thought, meditation and prayer.

These daily readings contain most of the material used in the booklet "For Drunks Only" and other A. A. literature, and ~~many~~ some passages from the big book: "Alcoholics Anonymous".

The editor has also extensively used the book: "God Calling" by Two Listeners, edited by A. J. Russell. Permission to use the thoughts expressed in "God Calling" as the basis for the meditations in this book, ~~without using direct quotations,~~ has been granted by Dodd, Mead and Company, Inc, ~~The~~ NEW YORK. ~~material in the book "God Calling" has been adapted for use by members of Alcoholics Anonymous.~~

The editor hopes that these daily readings ~~will~~ MAY help members of Alcoholics Anonymous to find the power they need to stay sober each twenty-four hours. If we don't take the first drink today, we'll never take it, because it's always today.

~~"Yesterday is gone, forget it. Tomorrow never comes, don't worry. Today is here, get busy" and "Today, well lived, makes every yesterday a dream of happiness and every tomorrow a vision of hope".~~

3.

Look to this day,
For it is life,
The very life of life.
In its brief course lies all
The realities and verities of existence,
The bliss of growth,
The splendor of action,
The glory of power -

For yesterday is but a dream
And tomorrow is only a vision.
But today, well lived,
Makes every yesterday a dream of happiness
And every tomorrow a vision of hope

Look well, therefore, to this day.

Sanskrit Proverb

4

JANUARY 1 -- A. A. Thought for the Day

When I came into A. A., was I a desperate person? Did I have a soul-sickness? Was I so sick of myself and my way of living that I couldn't stand looking at myself in a mirror? Was I ready for A. A.? Was I ready to try anything that would help me to get sober and to get over my soul-sickness? Should I ever forget the condition I was in?

Meditation for the Day

In the new year, I will live one day at a time. I will make each day one of preparation for better things ahead. I will not dwell on the past or future; only on the present. I will bury every fear of the future, all thoughts of unkindness and bitterness, all my dislikes, my resentments, my sense of failure, my disappointments in others and in myself, my gloom and my despondency. I will leave all these things buried and go forward, in ~~the~~ THIS new year, into a new life.

Prayer for the Day

I pray that God will guide me one day at a time in the new year. I pray that for each day, God will supply the wisdom and THE strength that I need.

5

JANUARY 2 -- <u>A. A. Thought for the Day</u>

What makes A. A. work? The first thing is to have a revulsion against myself and against my way of living. Then I must admit I was helpless; that alcohol had me licked, and I couldn't do anything about it. The next thing is to honestly want to quit the old life. Then I must surrender my life to a Higher Power, ~~to~~ put my drinking problem in His hands and leave it there. After these things are done, I should attend meetings regularly for fellowship and sharing. ~~and~~ I SHOULD also try to help other alcoholics. <u>Am I doing these things</u>?

<u>Meditation for the Day</u>

MAN IS SO MADE THAT HE CAN ONLY CARRY THE WEIGHT OF TWENTY-FOUR HOURS NO MORE. DIRECTLY HE WEIGHS HIMSELF DOWN WITH THE YEARS BEHIND AND THE DAYS AHEAD, HIS BACK BREAKS. GOD HAS PROMISED TO HELP YOU WITH THE BURDENS OF THE DAY ONLY. IF YOU ARE FOOLISH ENOUGH TO GATHER AGAIN THAT BURDEN OF THE PAST AND CARRY IT, THEN INDEED YOU CANNOT EXPECT GOD TO HELP YOU BEAR IT. SO FORGET THAT WHICH LIES BEHIND YOU AND BREATHE IN THE BLESSING OF EACH NEW DAY.

<u>Prayer for the Day</u>

I PRAY THAT I MAY REALIZE THAT, FOR GOOD OR BAD, PAST DAYS HAVE ENDED. I PRAY THAT I MAY FACE EACH NEW DAY, THE COMING TWENTY-FOUR HOURS, WITH HOPE AND COURAGE.

6

JANUARY 3 -- <u>A. A. Thought for the Day</u>

When I came into A. A. I learned what an alcoholic was and then I applied this knowledge to myself, to see if I was an alcoholic. When I was convinced that I was an alcoholic, I admitted it openly. Since then, have I been learning to live accordingly? Have I read the book: <u>"Alcoholics Anonymous"</u>? Have I applied the knowledge gained to myself? Have I admitted openly that I am an alcoholic? <u>Am I ready to admit it ~~openly~~ at any time? WHEN I CAN BE OF HELP?</u>

<u>Meditation for the Day</u>

I will be renewed. I will be remade. In this, I need God's help. ~~Everything must rest on God. God's love is a conquering force.~~ His spirit shall flow through me and, in flowing through me, it shall sweep away all the bitter past. I will take heart. The way will open for me. Each day will unfold something good, as long as I am trying to live the way I believe ~~He~~ God wants me to live.

<u>Prayer for the Day</u>

I pray that I may be taught, just as a child would be taught. I pray that I may never question God's plans, but accept them gladly.

7

JANUARY 4 -- A. A. Thought for the Day

Have I admitted I am an Alcoholic? Have I swallowed my pride and admitted I was different from ordinary drinkers? Have I accepted the fact that I must spend the rest of my life without liquor? Have I any more reservations, any idea in the back of my mind that some day I'll be able to drink safely? Am I absolutely honest with myself and with other people? Have I taken an inventory of myself and admitted the wrong I have done? Have I come clean with my friends? HAVE I ~~and~~ tried to make it up to them for the way I have treated them?

Meditation for the Day

I will believe that fundamentally all is well. GOOD ~~Wonderful~~ things will happen to me. I believe that God cares for me and will provide for me. I will not try to plan ahead. I know that the way will unfold, step by step. I will leave tomorrow's burden to God, because He is the great Burden-Bearer. He only expects me to carry my one-day's share.

Prayer for the Day

I pray that I may not try to carry the burden of the universe on my own shoulders. I pray that I may be satisfied to do my share each day.

8

JANUARY 5 -- A. A. Thought for the Day

Have I turned to a Higher Power for help? Do I believe that each man or woman I see in A. A. is a demonstration of the power of God to change a human being from a drunkard into a sober, useful citizen? Do I believe that this Higher Power can keep me from drinking? Am I living one day at a time? Do I ask God to give me the power to stay sober for EACH ~~the next~~ twenty-four hours? Do I attend A. A. meetings regularly? ~~Am I willing to work with other alcoholics?~~

Meditation for the Day

I believe that God's presence brings peace and that peace, like a quiet-flowing river, will cleanse all irritants away. In these quiet times, God will teach me how to rest my nerves. I will not be afraid. I will learn how to relax. When I am relaxed, God's strength will flow into me. ~~And I will let it flow out to others, because I know that God wants me to pass it on, and not to keep it all for myself.~~ I WILL BE AT PEACE.

Prayer for the Day

I PRAY FOR THAT PEACE WHICH PASSES ALL UNDER-STANDING. I PRAY FOR THAT PEACE WHICH THE WORLD CAN NEITHER GIVE NOR TAKE AWAY.

JANUARY 6 -- A. A. Thought for the Day

Keeping sober is the most important thing in my life. The most important decision I ever made was my decision to give up drinking. I am convinced that my whole life depends on not taking that first drink. Nothing in the world is as important to me as my own sobriety. Everything I have, my whole life, depends on that one thing. Can I afford ever to forget this, even for one minute?

Meditation for the Day

I will discipline myself. ~~so that God can use me later in the lives of others~~. I will do this disciplining now. ~~for some day every thought, word and deed of mine can be used by God.~~ I will turn out all useless thoughts. I know that the ~~purity and~~ goodness of my life is a necessary foundation for its usefulness. I will welcome this training, for without it, God cannot give me His power. I believe that this power is a mighty power, when it is used in the right way.

Prayer for the Day

I PRAY THAT I MAY FACE AND ACCEPT WHATEVER DISCIPLINE IS NECESSARY. I PRAY THAT I MAY BE FIT TO RECEIVE GOD'S POWER IN MY LIFE.

JANUARY 7 -- A. A. Thought for the Day

When temptation comes, as it does sometimes to all of us, I will say to myself: No, my whole life depends on not taking that drink and nothing in the world can make me do it. Besides, I have promised that Higher Power that I wouldn't do it. I know that God doesn't want me to drink and I won't break my promise to God. I've given up my right to drink and it's not my decision any longer. Have I made the choice once and for all, so that there's no going back on it?

Meditation for the Day

~~I will cultivate silence, because God speaks in silences.~~ In silence comes God's meaning to the heart. No man can judge when it enters the heart~~, of man~~. He can only judge by results. God's word is spoken to the secret places of my heart and, in some hour of need or temptation, I find that word and realize it's value for the first time. ~~It is all part of the working of the Divine Spirit in the hearts of men.~~ WHEN I NEED IT, I FIND IT THERE.

Prayer for the Day

I pray that I may see ~~wonders unfolding~~ GOD'S MEANING in my life. I pray that I may gladly accept ~~the wonderful gifts of sobriety, peace and serenity.~~ WHAT GOD HAS TO TEACH ME.

11

JANUARY 8 -- A. A. Thought for the Day

Everyone who comes into A. A. knows from bitter experience that he or she can't drink. I know that drinking has been the cause of all my major troubles or has made them worse. Now that I have found a way out, I will hang onto A. A. with both hands. Saint Paul once said that nothing in the world, neither powers nor principalities, life or death, could separate him from the love of God. Once I have given my drink problem to God, should anything in the world separate me from my sobriety?

Meditation for the Day

I know that my new life will not be immune from difficulties, but I will have peace even in difficulties. I know that ~~joy~~ SERENITY is the result of faithful trusting acceptance of God's will, even in the midst of difficulties. Saint Paul said, "Our light afflictions, which ~~is~~ ARE but for a moment, work~~eth~~ for us a far more exceeding and eternal weight of glory".

Prayer for the Day

I pray that I may welcome difficulties. I pray that they may test my strength and build my character.

12

JANUARY 9 -- A. A. Thought for the Day

When we were drinking, most of us had no real faith in anything. We may have said that we believed in God, but we didn't act as though we did. We never honestly asked God to help us and we never really accepted His help. To us, faith looked like helplessness. But when we came into A. A. we began to have faith in God. And we found out that faith gave us the strength we needed to overcome drinking. Have I learned that there is strength in faith?

Meditation for the Day

I will ~~be calm,~~ HAVE FAITH, no matter what may befall me. I will be patient, EVEN IN THE MIDST OF TROUBLES. ~~and let patience have her perfect work.~~ I will not ~~feel~~ FEAR the strain of life, because I believe that God knows just what I can bear. ~~without strain.~~ I know that God will not ask ~~of~~ me TO BEAR anything that could overcome or destroy me.

Prayer for the Day

I pray that I may put ~~today~~ THIS DAY in the hands of God, ~~and be calm.~~ I pray FOR FAITH, SO that nothing will upset me or weaken my determination to stay sober.

13

JANUARY 10 -- A. A. Thought for the Day

When we were drinking, most of us were full of pride and selfishness. We believed we could handle our own affairs, even though we were making a mess of our lives. We were very stubborn and didn't like to take advice. We resented being told what to do. To us, humility looked like weakness. But when we came into A. A., we began to be humble. And we found out that humility gave us the power we needed to overcome drinking. Have I learned that there is power in humility?

Meditation for the Day

I will come to God in faith and He will give me a new WAY OF life. This new way of life will alter my whole existence, the words I speak, the influence I have. They will spring from the life within me. I see how ~~vast, how stupendous,~~ IMPORTANT is work of ~~any soul~~ A PERSON that has this new WAY OF life. The words AND the EXAMPLE OF SUCH A PERSON CAN HAVE A WIDE INFLUENCE ~~influence, go on down the ages forever. I will ponder on these truths that God has given me. They are not surface facts, but the secrets of God's Kingdom.~~ FOR GOOD IN THE WORLD.

Prayer for the Day

I pray that I may ~~find the hidden pearls of great price.~~ LEARN THE PRINCIPLES OF THE GOOD LIFE. I pray that I may meditate upon them and work at them, because they are eternal.

14

JANUARY 11 -- A. A. Thought for the Day

When we were drinking, most of us never thought of helping others. We liked to buy drinks for people, because that made us feel like big shots. But we only used others for our own pleasure. To really go out and try to help somebody who needed help never occurred to us. To us, helping others looked like "a sucker's game." But when we came into A. A., we began to try to help others. And we found out that helping others made us happy and also helped us to stay dry. Have I learned that there is happiness in helping others?

Meditation for the Day

I will pray ~~and God will hear me~~ ONLY FOR STRENGTH AND THAT GOD'S WILL BE DONE. I will use God's unlimited store of strength for my needs. I will seek God's ~~wonderful truths and I will find them~~ WILL FOR ME. I will ~~have~~ STRIVE FOR the consciousness of God's presence, for He is the light of the world. I have become a pilgrim, who needs only my marching orders and strength and guidance for this day.

Prayer for the Day

I pray that I may ~~listen to God's voice eagerly and joyfully~~ SEEK GOD'S GUIDANCE DAY BY DAY. I pray that I may ~~always~~ STRIVE TO abide in God's presence.

15

JANUARY 12 -- A. A. Thought for the Day

The longer we're in A. A., the more natural this way of life seems. Our old drinking lives were a very unnatural way of living. Our present sober lives are the most natural way we could possibly live. During the early years of our drinking, our lives weren't so different from the lives of a lot of other people. But as we gradually became problem drinkers, our lives became more and more unnatural. Do I realize now that the things I thought about and the things I did were far from natural?

Meditation for the Day

I will say thank you to God for everything, even the seeming trials and worries. I will ~~continue~~ STRIVE to be grateful and humble. My whole attitude toward the Higher Power will be one of gratitude. I will be glad for the things I have received. I will pass on what God reveals to me. I believe that more truths will flow in, as I go along in the new way of life.

Prayer for the Day

I pray that I may ~~use all that God gives me and show my gratitude by helping others. I pray that God may come into other hearts through me.~~ BE GRATEFUL FOR THE THINGS I HAVE RECEIVED AND DO NOT DESERVE. I PRAY THAT THIS GRATITUDE WILL MAKE ME TRULY HUMBLE.

16

JANUARY 13 -- A. A. Thought for the Day

When we were drinking, we were living an unnatural life physically and mentally. We were punishing our bodies by loading them with alcohol. We didn't eat enough and we ate the wrong things. We didn't get enough sleep or the right kind of rest. We were ruining ourselves physically. We had an alcoholic obsession and we couldn't imagine life without alcohol. We kept imagining all kinds of crazy things about ourselves and about other people. We were ruining ourselves mentally. Since I came into A. A., am I getting better physically and mentally?

Meditation for the Day

I believe THAT my life is being refined like gold in a crucible. Gold does not stay in the crucible, only until it is refined. I will never despair or be despondent. I now have friends who long for me to conquer. If I should err or fail, it would cause pain and disappointment to them. ~~God's strength is always available.~~ I WILL KEEP TRYING TO LIVE A BETTER LIFE.

Prayer for the Day

I pray that I may always call on God's strength, while the gold of my life is being refined. I pray that I may see it through, with God's help.

17

JANUARY 14 -- A. A. Thought for the Day

When we first came into A. A., a sober life seemed strange. We wondered what life could possibly be like without ever taking a drink. At first, a sober life seemed unnatural. But the longer we're in A. A., the more natural this way of life seems. And now we know that the life we're living in A. A., the sobriety, the fellowship, the faith in God, and the trying to help each other, is the most natural way we could possibly live. Do I believe it's the way God wants me to live?

Meditation for the Day

I will learn to overcome my self, because every blow to selfishness is used to shape the real, eternal, unperishable me. As I overcome my self, I gain that ~~overwhelming~~ power which God releases IN MY SOUL. ~~for the weary world~~. And I too will be victorious. It is not the difficulties of life that I have to conquer, SO MUCH AS ~~only~~ my OWN selfishness.

Prayer for the Day

I pray that I may obey God and walk with Him and listen to Him. I pray that I may ~~see how glorious and marvelous are His revelations~~ STRIVE TO OVERCOME MY OWN SELFISHNESS.

18

JANUARY 15 -- A. A. Thought for the Day

The A. A. programme is a way of life. It's a way of living and we have to learn to live the programme if we're goinG to stay sober. The twelve steps in the book are like guide posts. They point the direction in which we have to go. But each member of the group has to find his own best way of living the programme. We don't all do it exactly alike. Whether by quiet times in the morning, meetings, working with others, or spreading the word, we have to learn to live the programme. Has the A. A. way become my regular, natural way of living?

Meditation for the Day

I will relax and not get tense. I will have no fear, because ~~all is for the best~~ EVERYTHING WILL WORK OUT IN THE END. I will learn soul-balance and poise in a vacillating, changing world. I will claim God's power and use it because if I do not use it, it will be withdrawn. As long as I get back to God and replenish my strength after each task, no work can be too much.

Prayer for the Day

I pray that I may relax and that God's strength will be given to me. I pray that I may ~~bathe my spirit in~~ SUBJECT MY WILL TO God's ~~joy~~ WILL and be free from all tenseness.

19

JANUARY 16 -- <u>A. A. Thought for the Day</u>

The A. A. programme is more a way of building a new life, than just a way of getting over drinking. Because in A. A. we don't just stop drinking. We did that plenty of times in the old days when we went "on the wagon." And of course we always started to drink again, because we were only waiting for the time when we could fall off. Once we've got sober through the A. A. programme, we start going uphill. In our drinking days, we were going downhill, getting worse and worse. We either go down or up. Am I going uphill; getting better and better?

Meditation for the Day

I will try to obey God's will day in and day out, in the wilderness plains as well as on the mountain tops of experience. It is in the daily strivings that perseverance counts. I believe that God is the Lord of little things, the Divine Controller of little happenings. I will persevere in this new way of life. I know that nothing in the day is too small to be part of God's scheme.

Prayer for the Day

I pray that the little stones which I put into the mosaic of my life may make a worthwhile pattern. I pray that I may persevere and so find harmony and beauty.

20

JANUARY 17 -- A. A. Thought for the Day

It doesn't do much good to come to meetings only once in a while and sit around, hoping to get something out of the programme. That's all right at first, but it won't help us for very long. Sooner or later we have to get into action, by coming to meetings regularly, by giving a personal witness of our experience with alcohol, and by trying to help other alcoholics. Building a new life takes all the energy that we used to spend on drinking. Am I spending at least as much time and effort on the new life that I'm trying to build in A. A.?

Meditation for the Day

With God's help, I will build a protective screen around myself which will keep out all evil thoughts. I will fashion it out of my attitude toward God and my attitude toward other people. When one worrying or impatient thought enters my mind, I will put it out at once. I know that love and trust are the solvents for the worry and frets of life. I will use them to form a protective screen around me.

Prayer for the Day

I pray that frets and impatience and worry may not corrode my protective screen against evil thoughts. I pray that I may banish all these from my life.

21

JANUARY 18 -- A. A. Thought for the Day

The new life can't be built in a day. We have to take the programme slowly, a little at a time. Our subconscious minds have to be re-educated. We have to learn to think differently. We have to get used to sober thinking instead of alcoholic thinking. Anyone who tries it, knows that the old alcoholic thinking is apt to come back on us when we least expect it. Building a new life is a slow process, but it can be done if we really follow the A. A. programme. Am I building a new life on the foundation of sobriety?

Meditation for the Day

I will pray daily for faith, for it is God's gift. On faith alone depends the answer to my prayers. God gives it to me in response to my prayers, because it is a necessary weapon for me to possess for ~~the dispersion of evil,~~ the overcoming of all adverse conditions, and the accomplishment of all good in my life. ~~Faith is the envelope in which every request to God should be placed.~~ THEREFORE I WILL WORK AT STRENGTHENING MY FAITH.

Prayer for the Day

I pray that I may so think and live as to feed my faith in God. I pray that my faith may grow because, with faith, God's power becomes available to me.

22

JANUARY 19 -- A. A. Thought for the Day

On the foundation of sobriety, we can build a life of honesty, unselfishness, faith in God and love of our fellow men. We'll never fully reach these goals, but the adventure of building that kind of a life is so much better than the merry-go-round of our old drinking life that there's no comparison. We come into A. A. to get sober, but if we stay long enough we learn a new way of living. We become honest with ourselves and with other people. We learn to think more about others ~~people~~ and less about ourselves. And we learn to rely on the constant help of a Higher Power. Am I living the way of honesty, unselfishness and faith?

Meditation for the Day

I believe that God had already seen my heart's needs before I cried to Him; before I was conscious of those needs myself. I believe that God was already preparing the answer. God does not have to be petitioned with sighs and tears and much speaking, before he reluctantly looses the desired help. He already has anticipated my every want and need. I will try to see this, as His plans unfold in my life.

Prayer for the Day

I pray that I MAY UNDERSTAND my real wants and needs. ~~may be understood.~~ I pray that ~~the~~ MY understanding of THOSE NEEDS AND WANTS ~~God may bring the answer to these needs.~~ MAY HELP TO BRING THE ANSWER TO THEM.

23

JANUARY 20 -- A. A. Thought for the Day

In A. A., we're all through with lying, hangovers, remorse and wasting money. When we were drinking, we were only half alive. Now that we're trying to live decent, honest, unselfish lives, we're really alive. Life has a new meaning for us, so that we can really enjoy it. We feel that we're some use in the world. We're on the right side of the fence, instead of on the wrong side. We can look the world in the face, instead of hiding in alleys. We come into A. A. to get sober and if we stay long enough, we learn a new way of living. Am I convinced that no matter how much fun I got out of drinking, that life never was as good as the life I can build in A. A.?

Meditation for the Day

I want to be at one with the ~~Lord~~ DIVINE SPIRIT of the Universe. I will set my deepest affections on things spiritual, not on things material. As a man thinketh, so is he. So I will think of and desire that which will help, not hinder, my spiritual growth. I will try to be at one with God. No human aspiration can reach higher than this.

Prayer for the Day

I pray that I may think love, and love will surround me. I pray that I may think health, and health will come to me.

24

JANUARY 21 -- A. A. Thought for the Day

To grasp the A. A. programme, we have to think things out. Saint Paul said: "They are transformed by the re-newing of their minds". We have to learn to think straight. We have to change from alcoholic thinking to sober thinking. We must build up a new way of looking at things. Before we came into A. A., we wanted an artificial life of excitement and everything that goes with drinking. That kind of a life looked normal to us then. But as we look back now, that life looks the exact opposite of normal. In fact, it looks ~~absolutely screwy.~~ MOST ABNORMAL. We must re-educate our minds. Am I changing from ~~a screwy~~ AN ABNORMAL thinker to a normal thinker?

Meditation for the Day

I will take the most crowded day ~~with a song.~~ WITHOUT FEAR. I believe that God is with me, and controlling all. I will let ~~love~~ CONFIDENCE be the motif running through all the crowded day. I will not get worried, because I know that God is my helper. Underneath are the Everlasting Arms. I will rest in them, even though the day be full of things crowding in upon me.

Prayer for the Day

I pray that I may be calm and let nothing upset me. I pray that I may not let material things control me and choke out spiritual things.

JANUARY 22 -- <u>A. A. Thought for the Day</u>

In the beginning, you want to get sober, but you're helpless, so you turn to a Power greater than yourself and by trusting in that Power, you get the strength to stop drinking. From then on, you want to keep sober, and that's a matter of re-educating your mind. After a while, you get so that you really enjoy simple, healthy, normal living. You really get a kick out of life without the artificial stimulus of alcohol. All you have to do is to look around at the members of any A. A. group and you will see how their outlook has changed. <u>Is my outlook on life changing</u>?

<u>Meditation for the Day</u>

I will never forget to say thank you to God, even on the greyest days. My attitude will be one of humility and gratitude. Saying thank you to God is a ~~grey day~~ DAILY practice that is absolutely necessary. If a ~~grey~~ day is not one of thankfulness, the ~~lesson~~ PRACTICE has to be repeated until it becomes so. Gratitude is a necessity for those who seek to ~~serve God well.~~ LIVE A BETTER LIFE.

<u>Prayer for the Day</u>

~~I pray that I may carefully train for the work ahead of me. I pray that this training may be spread over many gray days, until God knows I am ready to do His work.~~
I PRAY THAT GRATITUDE WILL BRING HUMILITY.
I PRAY THAT HUMILITY WILL HELP ME TO LIVE A BETTER LIFE.

JANUARY 23 -- <u>A. A. Thought for the Day</u>

An alcoholic is a person whose drinking has got him into a "blind alley". He hasn't been able to learn anything from his drinking experience. He is always making the same mistakes and suffering the same consequences over and over again. He refuses to admit he's an alcoholic. He still thinks he can handle the stuff. He won't swallow his pride and admit that he's different from ordinary drinkers. He won't face the fact that he must spend the rest of his life without liquor. He can't visualize life without ever taking a drink. <u>Am I out of this blind alley</u>?

<u>Meditation for the Day</u>

I believe that God has all power. It is His to give and His to withhold. But He will not withhold it from the ~~soul that~~ PERSON WHO dwells near Him, because then it passes insensibly from God to ~~His disciple.~~ THAT PERSON. It is breathed in by the ~~soul~~ PERSON who lives in God's presence. I will learn to ~~shut myself away~~ LIVE in God's presence and then ~~without speaking~~ I WILL have those things which I desire of Him, strength, power and joy. God's power is available to all who need it and are willing to accept it.

<u>Prayer for the Day</u>

I pray that I may get myself out of the way, so that God's power may flow in. I pray that ~~I will not be selfish, because then I will be weak.~~ I MAY SURRENDER MYSELF TO THAT POWER.

27

JANUARY 24 -- <u>A. A. Thought for the Day</u>

An alcoholic who is living in a "blind alley" refuses to be really honest with himself or with other people. He's running away from life and won't face things as they are. He won't give up his resentments. He's too sensitive and too easily hurt. He refuses to try to be unselfish. He still wants everything for himself. And no matter how many disastrous experiences he ~~'s~~ HAS had with drinking, he still does it over and over again. ~~There's~~ THERE'S only one way to get out of that "blind alley" way of living and that's to change your thinking. <u>Have I changed my thinking</u>?

<u>Meditation for the Day</u>

I know that the vision and power which I receive from God are limitless, as far as spiritual things are concerned. But in temporal ~~affairs~~ AND MATERIAL THINGS, I must submit to limitations. I know that I cannot see the road ahead. I must go just one step at a time, because God does not grant me a longer view. I am in unchartered waters, limited by my temporal and spacial life, but unlimited in my spiritual life.

<u>Prayer for the Day</u>

I pray that, in spite of my ~~bodily~~ MATERIAL limitations, I may follow God's way. I pray that I may learn that ~~serving God~~ TRYING TO DO HIS WILL is perfect freedom.

28

JANUARY 25 -- <u>A. A. Thought for the Day</u>

We used to depend on drinking for a lot of things. We depended on drinking to help us enjoy things. It gave us a "kick". It broke down our shyness and helped us to have a "good time". We depended on drinking to help us when we felt low physically. If we had a toothache or just a hang-over, we felt better after a few drinks. We depended on drinking to help us when we felt low mentally. ~~If~~ IF we'd had a tough day at the office or if we'd had a fight with our wives, or if things just seemed against us, we felt better under the influence of alcohol. For us alcoholics, it got so that we depended on drinking for almost everything. <u>Have I got over that dependence on drinking</u>?

<u>Meditation for the Day</u>

I believe that complete surrender of my life to God is the foundation of ~~happiness. And the superstructure is the joy of communion with Him~~ SERENITY. God has prepared for us many mansions. I do not look upon that promise as referring only to the after-life. I do not look upon this life as something to be struggled through, in order to get the rewards of the next life. I believe that the Kingdon of God is within us and we can enjoy "eternal life" here and now.

<u>Prayer for the Day</u>

I pray that I may ~~carry out God's guidance.~~ TRY TO DO GOD'S WILL. I pray that such understanding, insight AND vision ~~and joy~~ shall be mine, as shall ~~indeed pass all understanding.~~ MAKE MY LIFE ETERNAL HERE AND NOW.

29

JANUARY 26 -- A. A. Thought for the Day

As we become alcoholics, the bad effects of drinking came more and more to outweigh the good effects. But the strange part of it is that, no matter what drinking did to us, loss of our health, our jobs, our money and our homes, we still stuck to it and depended on it. Our dependence on drinking became an obsession. In A. A., we find a new outlook on life. We learn how to change from alcoholic thinking to sober thinking. And we find out that we can no longer depend on drinking for anything. We depend on a Higher Power instead. Have I entirely given up that dependence on drinking?

Meditation for the Day

I will try to keep my life calm and unruffled. ~~I will try to leave everything to God.~~ This is my great task, to ~~get~~ FIND PEACE AND ACQUIRE SERENITY. ~~calm in God's presence.~~ I must not ~~let one ruffled fret stay for one moment.~~ HARBOR DISTURBING THOUGHTS. ~~Years of blessing may be checked in one moment by that.~~ No matter ~~who or what frets me,~~ WHAT FEARS, WORRIES AND RESENTMENTS I MAY HAVE, I MUST TRY TO THINK OF CONSTRUCTIVE THINGS, UNTIL CALMNESS COMES. ~~mine is the task to stop all else, until absolute calm comes. Any block means that God's power is directed to other channels.~~ Only when I am calm can I act as a channel for God's spirit.

Prayer for the Day

I pray that I may ~~pass on every blessing that I have received.~~ BUILD UP INSTEAD OF TEARING DOWN. I pray that I may ~~see how many I can bless each day.~~ BE CONSTUCTIVE AND NOT DESTRUCTIVE.

30

JANUARY 27 -- A. A. Thought for the Day

An alcoholic carries an awful load around with him. What a load lying puts on your shoulders! Drinking makes liars out of all of us alcoholics. In order to get the liquor we want, we have to lie all the time. We have to lie about where we've been and what we've been doing. A man who's lying is only half alive, because of the constant fear of being found out. When you come into A. A. and get honest with yourself and with other people, that terrible load of lying falls off your shoulders. Have I got rid of that load of lying?

Meditation for the Day

I believe that in the spiritual world, as in the material world, there is no empty space. As ~~self and~~ fears and worries AND RESENTMENTS depart out of my life, the things of the spirit ~~rush~~ COME in to take their places. Calm comes after a storm. ~~It is part of God's method to wait until the storm is at its full violence. Jesus' disciples thought that in sleep he had forgotten them. But they were mistaken. He calmed the storm.~~ As soon as I am rid of fears and hates and selfishness, God's love and peace and calm CAN come in.

Prayer for the Day

I pray that I may rid myself of all fears and resentments, so that peace and serenity may take their place. I pray that I may sweep my life clean of evil, so that good may come in.

31

JANUARY 28 -- A. A. Thought for the Day

What a load hangovers put on your shoulders! What terrible physical punishment we've all been through! The pounding headaches and jumpy nerves, the shakes and the jitters, the hot and cold sweats! When you come into A. A. and stop drinking that terrible load of hangovers falls off your shoulders. What a load remorse puts on your shoulders! That terrible mental punishment we've all been through. Ashamed of the things you've said and done. Afraid to face people because of what they might think of you. Afraid of the consequences of what you did when you were drunk. What an awful beating the mind takes! When you come into A. A., that terrible load of remorse falls off your shoulders. Have I got rid of those loads of hangovers and remorse?

Meditation for the Day

When a man seeks to follow ~~God,~~ THE WAY OF THE SPIRIT, it frequently means a complete ~~reversion~~ REVERSAL of the way of the world which he has hitherto followed. But it is a ~~reversion~~ REVERSAL that leads to ~~boundless~~ happiness and peace. Do the aims and ambitions that a man usually strives for bring peace? ~~or~~ DO the world's awards bring heart-rest and happiness? ~~No, I must find a better way of living.~~ OR DO THEY TURN TO ASHES IN THE MOUTH?

Prayer for the Day

I pray that I may not be weary, dis-illusioned and disappointed. I pray that I may ~~change from the warp~~ NOT PUT MY TRUST IN THE WAYS of the world, BUT IN THE WAY OF THE SPIRIT.

32

JANUARY 29 -- A. A. Thought for the Day

What a load wasting money puts on your shoulders! They say the members of the A. A. have paid the highest initiation fee of any club members in the world, BECAUSE we've wasted so much money on liquor. We'll never be able to figure out how much it was. We not only waste our own money, but also the money we should have spent on our families. When you come into A. A., that terrible load of wasted money falls off your shoulders. We alcoholics were getting round-shouldered from carrying all those loads that drinking put on our shoulders. But when we come into A. A., we get a wonderful feeling of release and freedom. Can I throw back my shoulders and look the whole world in the face again?

Meditation for the Day

I believe that ~~God can see the future and can read men's hearts.~~ THE FUTURE IS IN THE HANDS OF GOD. He knows better than I, what ~~I need.~~ THE FUTURE HOLDS FOR ME. I am not at the mercy of fate or buffeted about by life. I am being led in a very definite way, ~~and difficulties are being moved out of my path.~~ AS I TRY TO REBUILD MY LIFE. I am the builder, BUT God is the architect. It is mine to build, ~~knowing that all is well.~~ AS BEST I CAN, UNDER HIS GUIDANCE.

Prayer for the Day

I pray that I may depend on God, since He has planned my life. I pray that I may live ~~each day as best I can.~~ MY LIFE AS I BELIEVE GOD WANTS ME TO LIVE IT.

33

JANUARY 30 -- A. A. Thought for the Day

A drinking life isn't a happy life. Drinking cuts you off from other people and from God. One of the worst things about drinking is the loneliness. And one of the best things about A. A. is the fellowship. Drinking cuts you off from other people & at least from the people who really matter to you, your wife and children, your family and real friends. No matter how much you love them, you build up a wall between you and them by your drinking. ~~And~~ You're cut off from any real companionship with them. As a result, you're terribly lonely. Have I got rid of my loneliness?

Meditation for the Day

I will SOMETIMES go aside into a quiet place of retreat with God. In that place, I will find restoration and healing and power. I will plan ~~retreat~~ QUIET times now and then, times when I will ~~live apart~~ COMMUNE with God and arise rested and refreshed to carry on the work which God has given to me to do. I know that God will never give me a load greater than I can bear. It is in serenity and peace that all true success lies.

Prayer for the Day

I pray that I MAY STRENGTHEN my inner life ~~is all that it should be~~, so that I MAY FIND SERENITY. ~~my work may be accomplished.~~ I pray that ~~I may win these things on the battlefield of the soul.~~ MY SOUL MAY BE RESTORED IN QUIETNESS AND PEACE.

34

JANUARY 31 -- A. A. Thought for the Day

Drinking cuts you off from God. No matter how you were brought up, no matter what your religion is, no matter if you say you believe in God, nevertheless, you build up a wall between you and God by your drinking. You know you're not living the way God wants you to. As a result, you have that terrible remorse. When you come into A. A., you begin to get right with other people and with God. A sober life is a happy life, because by giving up drinking we've got rid of our loneliness and remorse. Do I have real fellowship with other people and with God?

Meditation for the Day

I believe that all sacrifice and all suffering is ~~redemption.~~ OF VALUE TO ME. When I am in pain, I am being tested. Can I trust God, no matter how low I feel? Can I say: Thy will be done, no matter how much I am ~~suffering?~~ DEFEATED? If I can, my faith is real and practical. It works in bad times as well as IN good times. ~~Nothing is by chance.~~ The Divine ~~mind~~ WILL is working in a way that is beyond my finite mind to understand, BUT I CAN STILL TRUST IN IT.

Prayer for the Day

I pray that I may take my suffering in my stride. I pray that I may accept pain AND DEFEAT as part of God's plan for my spiritual growth.

35

FEBRUARY 1 -- <u>A. A. Thought for the Day</u>

When we think about having a drink, we're thinking of the kick we get out of drinking, the pleasure, the escape from boredom, the feeling of self-importance and the companionship of other drinkers. What we don't think of is the let-down, the hangover, the remorse, and waste of money, and the facing of another day. In other words, when we think about that first drink, we're thinking of all the assets of drinking and none of the liabilities. What has drinking really got that we haven't got in A. A.? <u>Do I believe that the liabilities of drinking outweigh the assets</u>?

<u>Meditation for the Day</u>

I will start a new life ~~today and every day.~~ EACH DAY. I will put the old mistakes away and start anew each day. God always offers me a fresh start. I will not be burdened or anxious. If God's forgiveness were only for the righteous and those who had not sinned, where would be its need? I believe that God forgives us all OF our sins, if we are honestly trying to live today the way He wants us to live. God forgives us much and we should ~~love Him much.~~ BE VERY GRATEFUL.

<u>Prayer for the Day</u>

I pray THAT my life may not be ~~soiled~~ SPOILED by worry and fear and selfishness. I pray that I may have a glad, thankful and humble heart.

36

FEBRUARY 2 -- <u>A. A. Thought for the Day</u>

We got a kick out of the first few drinks, before we got stupefied by alcohol. For a while, the world seemed to look brighter. But how about the let-down, the terrible depression that comes the morning after? In A. A., we get a real kick, not a false feeling of exhilaration, but a real feeling of satisfaction with ourselves and self-respect. And a feeling of friendliness toward the world. We got a sort of pleasure from drinking. For a while we thought we were happy. But it's only an illusion. The hangover the next day is the opposite of pleasure. <u>In A. A., am I getting real pleasure and serenity and peace</u>?

<u>Meditation for the Day</u>

I will practice love, because lack of love will block the way. ~~I must~~ I WILL TRY TO SEE GOOD IN ~~love~~ all people, those I like and also those who fret me and go against the grain. They are all children of God. ~~I must~~ I WILL TRY TO GIVE love, otherwise how can I dwell in God's spirit, whence nothing unloving can come? I will TRY TO GET ALONG ~~practice love~~ with all people ~~and God will bless, above all I can ask or imagine. There is no limit to the power of God's love.~~ BECAUSE THE MORE LOVE I GIVE AWAY, THE MORE I WILL HAVE.

<u>Prayer for the Day</u>

I pray that I may do all I can to love ~~people and leave the rest to God. I pray that God will be my advocate and my mediator.~~ MY FELLOW MEN, IN SPITE OF THEIR MANY FAULTS. I PRAY THAT AS I LOVE, SO WILL I BE LOVED.

37

FEBRUARY 3 -- <u>A. A. Thought for the Day</u>

By drinking, we escaped from boredom for a while. We almost forgot our troubles. But, when we sobered up, our troubles were twice as bad. Drinking had only made them worse. In A. A. we really escape from boredom. Nobody's bored at an A. A. meeting. We stick around after it's over and we hate to go home. Drinking gave us a temporary feeling of importance. When we're drinking, we kid ourselves into thinking we are somebody. We tell tall stories to build ourselves up. In A. A., we don't want that kind of self-importance. We have real self-respect and honesty and humility. <u>Have I found something much better and more satisfactory than drinking</u>?

<u>Meditation for the Day</u>

I believe that my faith and God's power can accomplish anything in human relationships. There is no limit to what these two things can do in this field. Only believe, and anything can happen. ~~Saint Paul said: "I can do all things thru ~~Christ~~ HIM who strengtheneth me".~~ All walls that divide you from other human beings can fall by your faith and God's power. These are the two essentials. All men can be moved by these.

<u>Prayer for the Day</u>

I pray that I may ~~rest in the certainty of my faith~~ TRY TO STRENGTHEN MY FAITH DAY BY DAY. I pray that I may rely ~~completely~~ MORE AND MORE on God's power.

38

FEBRUARY 4 -- <u>A. A. Thought for the Day</u>

Treating others to drinks gave us a kind of satisfaction. We liked to say: "Have a drink on me." But we were not really doing the other fellow a favor. We were only helping him to get drunk, especially if he happened to be an alcoholic. In A. A., we really try to help other alcoholics. We build them up instead of tearing them down. Drinking created a sort of fellowship. But it was really a false fellowship, because it was based on selfishness. We used our drinking companions for our own pleasure. In A. A., we have real fellowship, based on unselfishness and a desire to help each other. And we make real friends, not fair weather friends. <u>With sobriety, have I got everything that drinking's got, without the headaches</u>?

<u>Meditation for the Day</u>

I know that God cannot teach a man who is trusting in a crutch. I will throw away the crutch OF ALCOHOL and walk in God's power and spirit. God's power will so invigorate me that I shall indeed walk on to victory. There is never any limit to God's power. I will go step by step, one day at a time. God's will shall be revealed to me as I go ~~on~~ FOREWARD. ~~This is the time of the true learning of trust in God.~~

<u>Prayer for the Day</u>

I pray that I may have ~~absolute~~ MORE AND MORE dependence on God. I pray that I may throw away my ALCOHOLIC crutch and let God's power ~~in~~ TAKE ITS PLACE.

39

FEBRUARY 5 -- <u>A. A. Thought for the Day</u>

One thing we learn in A. A. is to take a long view of drinking instead of a short view. When we were drinking, we thought more about the pleasure or release that a drink would give us, than we did about the consequences which would result from our taking that drink. Liquor looks good from the short view. When we look in a package-store window, we see liquor dressed up in its best wrappings, with fancy labels and decorations. They look swell. <u>But have I learned that what's inside those beautiful bottles is just plain poison to me</u>?

<u>Meditation for the Day</u>

I believe that life is a school, in which I must learn spiritual things. I must ~~walk with~~ TRUST IN God and He will teach me. I must listen to God and He will speak through my mind. I must commune with Him, in spite of all opposition and every obstacle. There will be days when I will hear no voice in my mind and when there will come no intimate heart-to-heart communion. But if I persist, and make a life-habit of schooling myself in spiritual things, God will reveal Himself to me in many ~~marvelous~~ ways.

<u>Prayer for the Day</u>

I pray that I may regularly go to school ~~with God~~ IN THINGS OF THE SPIRIT. I pray that I may grow spiritually, by making a practice of ~~spiritual~~ THESE things.

40

FEBRUARY 6 -- <u>A. A. Thought for the Day</u>

On a dark night, the bright lights of the corner tavern look mighty inviting. Inside, there seems to be warmth and good cheer. But we don't stop to think that if we go in there we'll probably end up drunk, with our money spent, and an awful hangover. A long mahogany bar in the tropical moonlight looks like a very gay place. But you should see the place the next morning. The chairs are piled on the tables and the place stinks of stale beer and cigarette stubs. And often we are there too, trying to cure the shakes by gulping down straight whiskey. <u>Can I look straight through</u> THE NIGHT BEFORE <u>and see the morning after</u>?

<u>Meditation for the Day</u>

God finds, amid the crowd, a few people who follow Him, just to be near Him, just to dwell in His presence. A longing in the Eternal Heart may be satisfied by these few people. I will let God know that I seek just to dwell in His presence, to be near Him, not so much for teaching or a message, as just for Him. It may be that the longing of the human heart to be loved for itself is something caught from the great Divine Heart.

<u>Prayer for the Day</u>

I pray that I may have a listening ear, so that God may speak to me. I pray that I may have a waiting heart, so that God may come to me.

41

FEBRUARY 7 -- <u>A. A. Thought for the Day</u>

A night club crowded with men and women all dressed up in evening clothes looks like a very gay place. But you should see the men's room of that night club the next morning. What a mess! People have been sick all over the place and does it smell! The glamour of the night before is all gone and only the stink of the morning after is left. In A. A., we learn to take a long view of drinking instead of a short view. We learn to think less about the pleasure of the moment and more about the consequences. <u>Has the night before become less important to me, and the morning after more important</u>?

<u>Meditation for the Day</u>

Only a few more steps and then God's power shall be seen and known in my life. I am now walking in darkness, surrounded by the limitations of space and time. But even in this darkness, I can have faith and can be a light to guide feet that are afraid. I believe that God's power will break through the darkness and my prayers will pierce even to the ears of God Himself. But only a cry from the heart, a trusting cry, ever pierces that darkness and reaches to the divine ear of God.

<u>Prayer for the Day</u>

I pray that the divine power of God will help my human weakness. I pray that my prayer may reach through the darkness to the ear of God.

42

FEBRUARY 8 -- <u>A. A. Thought for the Day</u>

When the morning sun comes up on a nice bright day and we jump out of bed, we're thankful to God that we feel WELL AND happy instead of sick and disgusted. Serenity and happiness have become much more important to us than the excitement of drinking, which lifts us up for a short while, but lets us way down in the end. Of course, all of us alcoholics had a lot of fun with drinking. We might as well admit it. We can look back on a lot of good times, before we became alcoholics. But the time comes for all of us alcoholics when drinking ceases to ~~become~~ BE fun and becomes trouble. <u>Have I learned that drinking can never AGAIN be anything but trouble for me</u>?

<u>Meditation for the Day</u>

I must rely on God. I must trust Him to the ~~uttermost~~ limit. I must depend on the Divine Power in all human relationships. I will wait and trust and hope, until God shows me the way. I will wait for guidance on each important decision. I will meet the test of waiting until a thing seems right, before I do it. Every work for God must meet this test of time.

<u>Prayer for the Day</u>

I pray that I may meet the test of waiting for God's guidance. I pray that I will not go off on my own.

43

FEBRUARY 9 -- A. A. Thought for the Day

In the past, we kept right on drinking, in spite of all the trouble we got into. We were foolish enough to believe that drinking could still be fun, in spite of everything that happened to us. When we came into A. A., we found a LOT ~~bunch~~ of people who, like ourselves, had had ~~a lot of~~ fun with drinking, but who now admitted that liquor had become nothing but trouble for them. And when we found that this thing had happened to a lot of other people beside ourselves, we realized that perhaps we weren't such "queer birds" after all. Have I learned to admit that, for me, drinking has ceased to be fun and has become nothing but trouble?

Meditation for the Day

The life-line, the line of rescue, is the line from the soul to God. On one end of the life-line is our faith and on the other end is God's power. It CAN BE ~~is~~ a strong line and no soul can be overwhelmed who is linked to God by it. I will trust in this life-line and never be afraid. God will save me from DOING WRONG ~~sin~~ and from the cares and troubles of life. I will look to God for HELP ~~salvation~~ and trust Him for AID ~~help~~ when I am emotionally ~~or physically~~ upset.

Prayer for the Day

I pray that no lack of trust or fearfulness will make me disloyal to God. I pray that I may keep a strong hold on the life-line of faith.

44

FEBRUARY 10 -- A. A. Thought for the Day

Since I realized that I had become an alcoholic and could never have any more fun with liquor and since I knew that from then on liquor would always get me into trouble, common sense told me that the only thing left for me was a life of sobriety. But I learned another thing in A. A., the most important thing anyone can ever learn, and that was that I could call on a Higher Power to help me keep away from liquor; that I could work with that Divine Principle in the universe and that God would help me to live a sober, useful, happy life. So now I no longer care about the fact that I can never have any more fun with drinking. Have I learned that I am much happier without it?

Meditation for the Day

Like a tree, I must be pruned of a lot of dead branches, before I will be ready to bear good fruit. Think of changed people as trees which have been stripped of their old branches, pruned, cut and bare, but through the dark, seemingly dead branches flows silently, secretly, the new sap, until ~~he~~, with the sun of Spring, comes new life. There are new leaves, buds, blossoms and fruit, MANY ~~a thousand~~ times better because of the pruning. Remember, I am in the hands of a Master Gardener, who makes no mistakes in His pruning.

Prayer for the Day

I pray that I may CUT AWAY THE DEAD BRANCHES OF MY LIFE. ~~be filled by a new life-sap.~~ I pray that I may not mind the pruning, since it helps me to bear GOOD fruit later.

45

FEBRUARY 11 -- A. A. Thought for the Day

If we're going to stay sober, we've got to learn to want something else more than we want to drink. When we first came into A. A., we couldn't imagine wanting anything else so much or more than drinking. So we had to stop drinking on faith, on faith that some day we really would want something else more than drinking. But after we've been in A. A. for a while, we learn that a sober life can really be ~~fun~~ ENJOYED. We learn how nice it is to get along well with our family at home, how nice it is to do our work well at the office, how nice it is to try to help others. Have I found that when I keep sober, everything goes well for me?

Meditation for the Day

There is almost no work in life so hard as waiting. And yet God wants me to wait. All motion is more easy than calm waiting, and yet I must wait until God shows me His will. So many people have marred their work and hindered the growth of their spiritual lives by too much activity. If I wait patiently, preparing myself always, I will be some day at the place where I would be. And much toil and activity could not have accomplished the journey so soon.

Prayer for the Day

I pray that I may wait patiently. I pray that I may trust God and ~~always prepare~~ KEEP PREPARING myself for a better life.

46

FEBRUARY 12 -- A. A. Thought for the Day

As we look back on all those troubles we used to have when we were drinking, the hospitals, the jails, we wonder how we could have wanted that kind of a life. As we look back on it now, we see our drinking life as it really was and we're glad we're out of it. So after a few months in A. A. we find that we can honestly say that we want something else more than drinking. We've learned by experience that a sober life is really ~~a lot of fun~~ ENJOYABLE and we wouldn't go back to the old drunken way of living for anything in the world. Do I want to keep sober a lot more than I want to get drunk?

Meditation for the Day

My spiritual life depends on an inner consciousness of God. I must be led in all things by my consciousness of God and I must trust ~~God~~ HIM in all things. My consciousness of God will always bring ~~joy~~ PEACE to me. ~~I will give God not only trust but also gladness~~. I will have no fear, because a good future lies before me as long as I keep my consciousness of God. If in every single happening, event and plan, I am conscious of God, then no matter what happens, I will be safe in God's hands.

Prayer for the Day

I pray that I may have this ever-consciousness of God. I pray for a new AND BETTER life ~~and a new existence~~ through this God-consciousness.

47

FEBRUARY 13 -- <u>A. A. Thought for the Day</u>

Sometimes we can't help thinking: Why can't we ever drink again? We know that it's because we're alcoholics, but why did we have to get that way? The answer is that at some time in our drinking careers, we passed what is called our "tolerance point". When we passed this point, we passed from a condition in which we could tolerate alcohol to a condition in which we could not tolerate it at all. After that, if we took one drink, we would sooner or later end up drunk. <u>When I think of liquor now, do I think of it as something which I can never tolerate again</u>?

<u>Meditation for the Day</u>

In a race, it is when the goal is in sight that heart and nerves and muscles and courage are strained almost to the breaking point. So with us. The goal of the spiritual life is in sight. All we need is the final effort. The saddest records made by men are those who ran well, with brave, stout hearts, until the sight of the goal and then some weakness or self-indulgence held them back. They never knew how near the goal they were or how near they were to victory.

<u>Prayer for the Day</u>

I pray that I may press on until the goal is reached. I pray that I may not give up in the final stretch.

48

FEBRUARY 14 -- <u>A. A. Thought for the Day</u>

After that first drink, we had a single track mind. It was like a railroad train. The first drink started it off and it kept going on the single track until it got to the end of the line, drunkenness. We knew this would happen when we sat down at a bar to have the first drink, but still we couldn't keep away from liquor. Our will-power was gone. We had become helpless and hopeless before the power of alcohol. It's not the second drink or the tenth drink that does the damage. It's the first drink. <u>Will I ever take that first drink again</u>?

<u>Meditation for the Day</u>

I must keep a time apart with God every day. Gradually I will be transformed mentally and spiritually. It is not the praying so much as just being in God's presence. The strengthening and curative powers of this I cannot understand, because such knowledge is beyond human understanding, but I can experience them. The poor, sick world would be cured, if every day each soul waited before God FOR THE INSPIRATION TO LIVE ARIGHT. My greatest spiritual growth occurs in this time apart with God. ~~And all those who see me or contact with me will be, by this association, brought nearer to God and gradually my influence will spread.~~

<u>Prayer for the Day</u>

I pray that I may faithfully keep a quiet time apart with God. I pray that I may grow spiritually each day.

49

FEBRUARY 15 -- A. A. Thought for the Day

If alcoholism were just a physical allergy, like asthma or hay fever, it would be easy for us, by taking a skin test with alcohol, to find out whether or not we're alcoholics. But alcoholism is not just a physical allergy, It's also a mental allergy or obsession. After we've become alcoholics, we can still tolerate alcohol physically for quite a while, although we suffer a little more after each binge and each time it takes a little longer to get over our hangovers. Do I realize that since I have become an alcoholic, I cannot tolerate alcohol mentally at all?

Meditation for the Day

The world does not need super-men, but super-natural men. Men who will persistently turn the self out of their lives and let Divine Power work through them. Let inspiration take the place of aspiration. Seek to grow spiritually, rather than to acquire fame and riches. ~~My~~ OUR chief ambition should be to be used by God. The Divine Force is sufficient for all the spiritual work in the world. God only needs the instruments for Him to use. His instruments can remake the world.

Prayer for the Day

I pray that I may ~~call on that Divine Power to help me become super-natural.~~ BE AN INSTRUMENT OF THE DIVINE POWER. I pray that ~~I may seek spiritual things first, and all else shall be added unto me.~~ I MAY DO MY SHARE IN REMAKING THE WORLD.

50

FEBRUARY 16 -- A. A. Thought for the Day

One drink started a train of thought, which became an obsession, and from then on we couldn't stop drinking. We developed a mental compulsion to keep drinking until we got good and drunk. People generally make two mistakes about alcoholism. One mistake is that it can be cured by physical treatment only. The other mistake is that it can be cured by will-power only. Most alcoholics have tried both of these ways and have found that they don't work. But we members of A. A. have found a way to arrest our alcoholism. Have I got over my obsession, by following the A. A. programme?

Meditation for the Day

I will try to be unruffled, no matter what happens. I will keep my emotions in check, although others about me are letting theirs go. I will keep calm in the face of disturbance; keep that deep, inner calm through all the experiences of the day. In the rush of work and worry, the deep, inner silence is necessary, to keep me on an even keel. I must learn to take the calm with me into the most hurried days. ~~I will draw hungering breaths for God, as I do for the fresh, pure air of the ocean.~~

Prayer for the Day

I pray that I may ~~get~~ BE still and commune with God. I pray that I may learn patience, humility and peace.

✓1

FEBRUARY 17 -- <u>A. A. Thought for the Day</u>

Alcohol is poison to the alcoholic. Poison is not too strong a word, because alcoholism leads eventually to the death of the alcoholic. It may be a quick death or a slow death. When we go by package stores and see various kinds of liquor all dressed up in fancy packages to make it look attractive, we should always make it a point to say to ourselves, so we'll never forget it: That stuff's all poison to me. And it is. Alcohol poisoned our lives for a long time. <u>Do I know that, since I'm an alcoholic, all liquor is poison to me</u>?

<u>Meditation for the Day</u>

~~I must not expect a perfect church.~~ ~~But I can find in some church~~ I MUST SOMEHOW FIND the means of coming nearer to God. That is what really matters. ~~Then much of the church that is husk falls away and~~ I MUST SOMEHOW SEEK the true bread of life WHICH IS communion with ~~God, is left.~~ HIM. ~~I may hold the husk of no account, but~~ I must grasp at the truth at the center of all worship~~, and try to find God.~~ ~~The~~ THIS central truth is all that matters. ~~The outward church is the husk, but the husk is necessary to carry the grain and to present the life-grain to man.~~ ALL FORMS OF WORSHIP HAVE THIS COMMUNION WITH GOD AS THEIR PURPOSE AND GOAL.

<u>Prayer for the Day</u>

I pray that I may meet God in QUIET communion. I pray that I may partake of the soul-food which God has provided ~~inside of the church and outside of it.~~ FOR ME.

✓2

FEBRUARY 18 -- <u>A. A. Thought for the Day</u>

After I became an alcoholic, alcohol poisoned my love for my family, it poisoned my ambition in business, it poisoned my self-respect. It poisoned my whole life, until I met A. A. My life is happier now than it has been for a long time. I don't want to commit suicide. So with the help of God and the A. A., I'm never going to take any more of that alcoholic's poison into my system. And I'm going to keep training my mind never even to think of liquor again in any way except as a poison. <u>Do I believe that liquor will poison my life, if I ever touch it again</u>?

<u>Meditation for the Day</u>

I will link up my frail nature with the limitless Divine Power. I will link my life ~~onto~~ WITH the Divine Force FOR GOOD IN THE WORLD. It is not the passionate appeal that gains the Divine attention, so much as the quiet placing of the difficulty and worry in the Divine Hands. So I will trust God like a child who places its tangled skein of wool in the hands of a loving mother to unravel. We please God more by our unquestioning confidence than by imploring Him for help. ~~God is always eager to help.~~

<u>Prayer for the Day</u>

I pray that I may put all my difficulties in God's hands and leave them there. I pray that I may fully trust God to take care of them.

53

FEBRUARY 19 -- A. A. Thought for the Day

Many things we do in A. A. are in preparation for that crucial moment when we're walking down the street on a nice sunshiny day and we see a nice cool cocktail lounge and the idea of having a drink pops into our minds. If we've trained our minds so that we're well-prepared for that crucial moment, we won't take that first drink. In other words, if we've done our A. A. homework well, we won't slip when temptation comes. In preparation for that crucial moment when I'll be tempted, will I keep in minD the fact that liquor is my enemy?

Meditation for the Day

How many of the world's prayers have gone unanswered because men who prayed did not endure to the end! They thought it was too late and that they must act for themselves, that God was not going to guide them. "He that endureth to the end, the same shall be saved". Can I endure to the VERY end? If so, I shall be saved. I will try to endure with courage. ~~love and laughter.~~ If I endure, God will unlock those secret spiritual treasures which are hidden from those who do not endure to the end.

Prayer for the Day

I pray that I may follow God's guidance, so that spiritual success shall be mine. I pray that I may never doubt the power of God and so take things into my own hands.

54

FEBRUARY 20 - A. A. Thought for the Day

Liquor used to be my friend. I used to have a lot of fun with drinking. Practically, all the fun I had was connected with drinking. But the time came when liquor became my enemy. I don't know just when liquor turned against me and became my enemy, but I know it happened, because I began to get into trouble. And since I realize that liquor is now my enemy, my main business now is keeping sober. I make a living in business, but that's not my main business. It's secondary to the business of keeping sober. Do I realize that My main business is keeping sober?

Meditation for the Day

I can depend on God to supply me with all the power I need to face any situation, provided that I will sincerely believe in that power and honestly ask for it, at the same time making all my life conform to what I believe God wants me to be. ~~"In everything, by prayer and supplication, let your requests be made known to God".~~ I CAN come to God as a business manager would come to the owner of the business, knowing that to lay the matter before Him means immediate ~~supply,~~ COOPERATION, providing the matter has merit.

Prayer for the Day

I pray that I may ~~find~~ BELIEVE that God is ready and willing to supply me with all that I ~~ask for.~~ NEED. I pray that I may ask ~~with faithful assurance.~~ ONLY FOR FAITH AND STRENGTH TO MEET ANY SITUATION.

FEBRUARY 21 -- A. A. Thought for the Day

I go to the A. A. meetings because it helps me in my business of keeping sober. And I try to help other alcoholics when I can, because that's part of my business of keeping sober. I also have a partner in this business and that's God. I pray to Him every day to help me to keep sober. As long as I keep in mind that liquor can never be my friend again, but now is my deadly enemy, and as long as I remember that my main business is keeping sober and that it's the most important thing in my life, I believe I'll be prepared for that crucial moment when the idea of having a drink pops into my mind. When that idea comes, will I be able to resist it and not take that drink?

Meditation for the Day

I will be more afraid of spirit-unrest, of soul-disturbance, of any ruffling of the ~~spirit,~~ MIND, than of earthquake or fire. When I feel the ~~absolute~~ calm of my spirit has been broken by emotional upset, then I must steal away alone with God, until my heart sings and all is strong and calm again. Un-calm times are the only times when evil can find an entrance. I will beware of unguarded spots of unrest. I will try to keep calm, no matter what turmoil surrounds me.

Prayer for the Day

I pray that no ~~evil force~~ EMOTIONAL UPSETS will hinder God's power in my life. I pray that I may ~~not become upset.~~ KEEP A CALM SPIRIT AND A STEADY HEART.

FEBRUARY 22 -- A. A. Thought for the Day

Now we can take an inventory of the good things that have come to us through A. A. To begin with, we're sober today. That's the biggest asset on any alcoholic's books. Sobriety to us is like good-will in business. Everything else depends on that. Most of us have jobs, which we owe to our sobriety. We know we couldn't hold these jobs if we were drinking, so our jobs depend on our sobriety. Most of us have families, wives and children, which we either had lost or might have lost, if we hadn't stopped drinking. We have friends in A. A., real friends who are always ready to help us. Do I realize that my job, my family, and my real friends are dependent upon my sobriety?

Meditation for the Day

I must trust God ~~wholly.~~ TO THE BEST OF MY ABILITY. This lesson has to be learned. My doubts and fears continually drive me back into the wilderness. Doubts lead me astray, because I am not trusting ~~all to~~ God. I ~~will~~ MUST trust God's ~~tender~~ love. It will never fail me, but I must learn not to fail it, by my doubts and fears. We all have much to learn in turning out fear ~~and being at peace.~~ BY FAITH. All our doubts arrest God's work through us. I must not doubt. I must believe in God ~~absolutely.~~ AND CONTINUALLY WORK AT STRENGTHENING MY FAITH.

Prayer for the Day

I pray that I may live the way God wants me to live. I pray that I may ~~be on the right side of the fence.~~ GET INTO THAT STREAM OF GOODNESS IN THE WORLD.

57

FEBRUARY 23 -- <u>A. A. Thought for the Day</u>

Besides our jobs, our families, our friends and our sobriety, we have something else which many of us found through A. A. That's faith in a Power greater than ourselves, to which we can turn for help. Faith in that Divine Principle in the universe which we call God and which is on our side as long as we do the right thing. There have been many days in the past when, if we had taken an inventory, we'd have found ourselves very much in the red, without sobriety and therefore without jobs, families, friends or faith in God. We now have these things because we're sober. <u>Do I make one resolution every day of my life - to stay sober?</u>

<u>Meditation for the Day</u>

Love the busy life. It is a joy-filled life. Take your fill of joy in the Spring. Live outdoors whenever possible. Sun and air are nature's great healing forces. That inward joy changes poisoned blood into a pure, healthy, life-giving flow. But never forget that the real healing of the spirit comes from within, from the close, loving contact of your spirit with God's spirit. ~~You must keep~~ KEEP in close communion with God's spirit~~, as often as possible.~~ DAY BY DAY.

<u>Prayer for the Day</u>

I pray that I may learn to live the abundant life. I pray that I may ~~try to help others to~~ enjoy ~~the same~~ A close contact with God, THIS DAY AND BE GLAD IN IT.

58

FEBRUARY 24 -- <u>A. A. Thought for the Day</u>

When we came to our first A. A. meeting, we looked up at the wall at the end of the room and saw the sign: "But for the Grace of God". We knew right then and there that we would have to call on the Grace of God in order to get sober and get over our soul-sickness. We heard speakers tell how they had come to depend on a Power greater than themselves. That made sense to us and we made up our minds to try it. <u>Am I depending ~~daily~~ on the Grace of God to help me stay sober?</u>

<u>Meditation for the Day</u>

Share your love, your joy, your happiness, your time, your food, your money gladly with all. Give out all the love you can with a glad, free heart and hand. Do all you can for others and back will come such countless stores of blessings. ~~Silently the work of the spirit is done.~~ Sharing draws others to you. Take all who come as sent by God and give them a royal welcome. You may never see the results of your sharing. Today, they may not need you, but tomorrow may bring ~~good~~ results from the sharing you did today.

<u>Prayer for the Day</u>

I pray that I may make each visitor desire to return. I pray that I may never make anyone feel repulsed or unwanted.

59

FEBRUARY 25 -- A. A. Thought for the Day

Some people find it hard to believe in a Power greater than themselves. But not to believe in such a Power forces us to atheism. It has been said that "atheism is blind faith in the strange proposition that this universe originated in a cipher and aimlessly rushes nowhere". That is practically impossible to believe. I think we can all agree that alcohol is a power greater than ourselves. It certainly was in my case. I was helpless before the power of alcohol. Do I remember the things that happened to me, because of the power of alcohol?

Meditation for the Day

The spiritual and moral will eventually overcome the material and unmoral. That is the purpose and destiny of the human race. Gradually the spiritual is overcoming the material in men's minds. Gradually the moral is overcoming the unmoral. Faith, fellowship and service are cures for most of the ills of the world. ~~They are the spiritual cures for most ailments.~~ There is nothing in the field of personal relationships that they cannot do.

Prayer for the Day

I pray that I may do my share in [MAKING A BETTER WORLD.] ~~conquering the world around me spiritually~~. I pray that I ~~may help ills to vanish, as night vanishes when the sun rises.~~ [MAY BE PART OF THE CURE FOR THE ILLS OF THE WORLD.]

60

FEBRUARY 26 -- A. A. Thought for the Day

When we came into A. A., we came to believe in a Power greater than ourselves. We came to believe in that Divine Principle in the universe which we call God and to which we could turn for help. Each morning, we have a quiet time. We ask God for the power to stay sober for the next twenty-four hours. And each night we thank Him for helping us to keep sober [THAT DAY.] Do I believe that each man or woman I see in A. A. is a demonstration of the power of God to change a human being from a drunkard to a sober person?

Meditation for the Day

I should pray for more faith, as a thirsty man prays for water in a desert. Do I know what it means to feel sure that God will never fail me? Am I as sure of this, as I am that I still breathe? I should pray daily and most diligently that my faith may increase. There is nothing lacking in my life, because really all [I NEED] is mine, only I lack the faith to know it. I am like a king's son who sits in rags and yet all around me are stores of all that I could desire.

Prayer for the Day

I pray for the realization that God has everything I need. I pray that [I MAY KNOW THAT] His power ~~[illegible]~~ [IS] always available~~, to enable me to meet any situation.~~

61

FEBRUARY 27 -- A. A. Thought for the Day

When we came into A. A., the first thing we did was to admit that we couldn't do anything about our drinking. We admitted that alcohol had us licked and that we were helpless against it. We never could decide whether or not to take a drink. We always took the drink. And since we couldn't do anything about it ourselves, we put our whole drink problem into the hands of God. We turned the whole thing over to that Power greater than ourselves. And we have nothing more to do about it, except to trust God to take care of the problem for us. Have I done this honestly and fully?

Meditation for the Day

This is the time for my spirit to touch the spirit of God. I know that the feeling of the spirit-touch is more important than all the sensations of material things. I must seek a silence of spirit-touching with God. Just a moment's contact and all the fever of life leaves me. Then I am well, whole, calm and able to arise and minister to others. God's touch is a potent healer. I must feel that touch and sense God's presence.

Prayer for the Day

I pray that the fever of ~~work, care~~ [RESENTMENT, WORRY] and fear may melt into nothingness. I pray that health, joy, peace [AND SERENITY] ~~and the power to help others~~ may take its place.

62

FEBRUARY 28 -- A. A. Thought for the Day

We should be free from alcohol for good. It's out of our hands and in the hands of God, so we don't need to worry about it or even think about it any more. But if we haven't done this honestly and fully, the chances are that it will become our problem again. Since we don't trust God to take care of the problem for us, we reach out and take the problem back to ourselves. Then it's our problem again and we're in the same old mess we were in before. We're helpless again and we drink. Do I trust God to take care of the problem for me?

Meditation for the Day

No work is of value without preparation. Every spiritual work must have behind it much spiritual preparation. Cut short times of prayer and times of spiritual preparation and many hours of work may be profitless. From the point of view of God, one poor tool working all the time, but doing bad work because of lack of preparation, is of small value compared with the sharp, keen, perfect instrument, working for only a short time, but which turns out perfect work because of long hours of spiritual preparation.

Prayer for the Day

I pray that I may spend more time alone with God. I pray that I may get more strength and joy from such times, so that they will add much to my work.

63

MARCH 1 -- A. A. Thought for the Day

When I find myself thinking about taking a drink, I say to myself: Don't reach out and take that problem back. You've given it to God and there's nothing you can do about it. So I forget about the drink. One of the most important parts of the A. A. programme is to give our drink problem to God honestly and fully and never to reach out and take the problem back to ourselves. If we let God have it and keep it for good and then co-operate with Him, we'll stay sober. Have I determined not to take the drink problem back to myself?

Meditation for the Day

Constant effort is necessary, if I am to grow spiritually and develop my spiritual life. I must keep the spiritual rules persistently, perseveringly, lovingly, patiently and hopefully. By keeping them, every mountain of difficulty shall be laid low, the rough places of poverty of spirit shall be made smooth and all who know me shall know that God is the Lord of all my ways. To get close to the spirit of God is to find life and healing and strength.

Prayer for the Day

I pray that God's spirit may be everything to my soul. I pray that God's spirit may grow within me.

64

MARCH 2 -- A. A. Thought for the Day

Over a period of drinking years, we've proved to ourselves and to everybody else that we can't stop drinking by our own will-power. We have been proved helpless before the power of alcohol. So the only way we could stop drinking was by turning to a Power greater than ourselves. We call that Power God. The time a man really gets this programme is when he gets down on his knees and surrenders himself to God, as he understands Him. Surrender means putting your life into God's hands. Have I made a promise to God that I will try to live the way He wants me to live?

Meditation for the Day

Spirit-power comes from communication with God in prayer and times of quiet meditation. I must constantly seek spirit-communication with God. This is a matter directly between me and God. Those who seek it through the medium of the church do not always get the ~~ecstasy,~~ JOY AND the wonder of spirit-communication direct with God. From this communication come life, joy, peace and healing. Many people do not realize the power that can come to them from direct spirit-communication.

Prayer for the Day

I pray that I may feel that God's power is mine. I pray that I may be able to face anything, through that power.

65

MARCH 3 -- A. A. Thought for the Day

After we've made a surrender, the drink problem is out of our hands and in the hands of God. The thing we have to do is to be sure that we never reach out and take the problem back into our own hands. Leave it in God's hands. Whenever I'm tempted to take a drink, I must say to myself: I can't do that. I've made a bargain with God not to drink. I know God doesn't want me to drink so I won't do it. At the same time I say a little prayer to God for the strength needed to keep the bargain with Him. Am I going to keep my bargain with God?

Meditation for the Day

I will try to grow in this new life. I will think of spiritual things often, and unconsciously I will grow. The nearer I get to the new life, the more I will see my unfitness. My sense of failure is a sure sign that I am growing in the new life. It is only struggle that hurts. In sloth - physical, mental or spiritual - there is no sense of failure or discomfort. But with struggle and effort, I am conscious not of strength but of weakness, until I am really living the new life. BUT in the struggle, I can always rely on the power of God~~,~~ TO HELP ME.

Prayer for the Day

I pray that I may see signs of MY growth in the new life. I pray that I may always keep trying to grow.

66

MARCH 4 -- A. A. Thought for the Day

Having surrendered our lives to God and put our drink problem in His hands doesn't mean that we'll never be tempted to drink. So we must build up strength for the time when temptation will come. In this quiet time, we read and pray and get our minds in the right mood for the day. Starting the day right is a great help in keeping sober. As the days go by and we get used to the sober life, it gets easier and easier. We begin to develop a deep gratitude to God for saving us from that old life. And we begin to enjoy peace and serenity and real quiet happiness. Am I trying to live the way God wants me to live?

Meditation for the Day

The elimination of ~~self~~ SELFISHNESS is the key to happiness and can only be accomplished with God's help. We start out with a spark of the Divine Spirit but a large amount of ~~physical~~ selfishness. As we grow and come in contact with other people, we can take one of two paths. We can become more and more selfish and practically extinguish the Divine Spark within us or we can become more unselfish and develop our spirituality until it becomes the most important thing in our lives.

Prayer for the Day

I pray that I may grow more and more unselfish, honest, pure and loving. I pray that I may ~~help to build a brotherhood among all God's children.~~ TAKE THE RIGHT PATH EACH DAY.

67

MARCH 5 -- A. A. Thought for the Day

Sometimes we try too hard to get this programme. It is better to relax and accept it. It will be given us, with no effort on our part, if we stop trying too hard to get it. Sobriety can be a free gift of God, which He gives us by His Grace when He knows we are ready for it. But we have to be ready. Then we must relax and take it easy, and accept the gift with gratitude and humility. We must put ourselves in God's hands. We must say to God: Here am I and here are all my troubles. I've made a mess of things and can't do anything about it. You take me and all my troubles and do anything you want with me. Do I believe that the Grace of God can do for me what I could never do for myself?

Meditation for the Day

Fear is the curse of the world. Many are men's fears. Fear is everywhere. I must fight fear as I would a plague. I must turn it out of my life. There is no room for fear in the heart in which God dwells. Fear cannot exist where true love is or where faith abides. So I must have no fear. Fear is evil, but "perfect love casteth out all fear". Fear destroys hope and hope is necessary for all of mankind.

Prayer for the Day

I pray that I may have no fear. I pray that I may cast all fear out of my life.

68

MARCH 6 -- A. A. Thought for the Day

In A. A., we must surrender, give up, admit that we're helpless. We surrender our lives to God and ask Him for help. When He knows that we're ready, He gives us by His grace the free gift of sobriety. And we can't take any credit for having stopped drinking, because we didn't do it by our own will-power. There's no place for pride or boasting. We can only be grateful to God for doing for us what we could never do for ourselves. Do I believe that God has made me a free gift of the strength to stay sober?

Meditation for the Day

I must work for God, with God and through God's help. By doing all I can to bring about a true brotherhood of man, I am working for God. I am also working with God, because this is the way God works and He is with me when I am doing such work. I cannot do good work, however, without God's help. In the final analysis, it is through the grace of God that any real change in human personality takes place. I have to rely on God's power and anything I accomplish is through His help.

Prayer for the Day

I pray that I may work for God and with God. I pray that I may be used to change human personalities through God's help.

69

MARCH 7 -- A. A. Thought for the Day

There are two important things we have to do if we want to get sober and stay sober. First,having admitted that we're helpless before alcohol, we have to turn our alcoholic problem over to God and trust Him to take care of it for us. This means asking Him every morning for the strength to stay sober for that day and thanking Him every night. It means really leaving the problem in God's hands and not reaching out and getting the problem back to ourselves. Second, having given our drink problem to God, we must cooperate with Him by doing something about it ourselves. Am I doing these two things?

Meditation for the Day

I must prepare myself by doing each day what I can to develop spiritually and to help others to do so. God tests me and trains me and bends me to His will. If I am not properly trained, I cannot meet the test when it comes. I must want God's will for me above all else. I must not expect to have what I am not prepared for. This preparation consists of quiet communion with God every day and gradually gaining THE strength I NEED.

Prayer for the Day

I pray that I may really try to do God's will in all my affairs. I pray that I may do all I can to help others find God's will for them.

70

MARCH 8 -- A. A. Thought for the Day

We must go to A. A. meetings regularly. We must learn to think differently. We must change from alcoholic thinking to sober thinking. We must reeducate our minds. We must try to help other alcoholics. We must cooperate with God by spending at least as much time and energy on the A. A. programme as we did on drinking. We must follow the A. A. programme to the best of our ability. Have I turned my alcoholic problems over to God and am I cooperating with Him?

Meditation for the Day

The joy of true fellowship shall be mine in full measure. I will revel im the joy of real fellowship. There will come back a wonderful joy, if I share in fellowship now. Fellowship among spiritually-minded people is the ~~embodied spirit~~ EMBODIMENT of God's ~~thoughts of beauty~~ PURPOSE for this world. To realize this will bring me a new life-joy. If I share in mankind's joy and travails, a great blessing will be mine. I can truly live a life not of earth, but a heaven-life here and now.

Prayer for the Day

I pray that I may be helped amd healed ~~not only by knowing things about God, but by knowing God.~~ BY TRUE SPIRITUAL FELLOWSHIP. I pray that I may sense His presence in SPIRITUAL fellowship with His children.

71

MARCH 9 -- A. A. Thought for the Day

If we had absolute faith in the power of God to keep us from drinking and if we turned our drink problem entirely over to God without reservations, we wouldn't have to do anything more about it. We'd be free from drink once and for all. But since our faith in God is apt to be weak, we have to strengthen and build up this faith. We do this in several ways. One way is by going to meetings and listening to others tell how they have found all the strength they need to overcome drink. Is my faith being strengthened by this personal witness of other alcoholics?

Meditation for the Day

It is the quality of my life that determines its value. In order to judge the value of a man's life, we must set up a standard. The most valuable life is one of honesty, purity, unselfishness and love. All men's lives must be judged by this standard in order to determine their value to the world. By this standard, most of the so-called heroes of history were not great men. "What shall it profit a man if he gain the whole world, if he loseth his own soul?"

Prayer for the Day

I pray that I may be honest, pure, unselfish and loving. I pray that I may make the quality of my life good by these standards.

72

MARCH 10 -- A. A. Thought for the Day

We also strengthen our faith by working with other alcoholics and finding that we can do nothing ourselves to help them, except to tell them our own story of how we found the way out. If the other person is helped, it's by the grace of God and not by what we do or say. Our own faith is strengthened when we see another alcoholic find sobriety by turning to God. And finally we strengthen our faith by having quiet times every morning. Do I ask God in this quiet time for the strength to stay sober this day?

Meditation for the Day

My five senses are my means of communication with the material world. They are the links between my physical life and the material manifestations around me. But I must sever all connections with the material world when I wish to hold communion with the Great Spirit of the Universe. I have to hush my ~~heart~~ MIND and bid all my senses be still, before I can become attuned to receive the music of the heavenly spheres.

Prayer for the Day

I pray that I may get my spirit in tune with the Spirit of the Universe. I pray that through faith and communion with Him, I may receive the strength I need.

MARCH 11 -- A. A. Thought for the Day

By having quiet times each morning, we come to depend on God's help during the day, especially if we should be tempted to take a drink. And we can honestly thank Him each night for the strength He has given us. So our faith is strengthened by these quiet times of prayer. By listening to other members, by working with other alcoholics, and by times of quiet meditation, our faith in God gradually becomes strong. Have I turned my drink problem entirely over to God, without reservations?

Meditation for the Day

It seems as though, when God wants to express to men what He is like, he makes a very beautiful character. Think of ~~yourself~~ A PERSONALITY as God's expression of CHARACTER attributes. ~~and you will strive in all ways, in spiritual beauty, in thought-power, in health, to be~~ BE as fit an expression of ~~God~~ GODLIKE CHARACTER as you can. When the beauty of a man's character is impressed upon ~~our souls,~~ US, it leaves an image ~~there~~ which in turn reflects through our own actions. So look for beauty of character in those around you.

Prayer for the Day

I pray that I may look at great souls until their beauty OF CHARACTER becomes a part of my soul. I pray that ~~this beauty may be given back to the world again by me.~~ I MAY REFLECT THIS CHARACTER IN MY OWN LIFE.

MARCH 12 -- A. A. Thought for the Day

The Prodigal Son "took his journey into a far country and wasted his substance with riotous living". That's what we alcoholics do. We waste our substance with riotous living. "When he came to himself, he said I will arise and go to my father". That's what an alcoholic does in A. A. He comes to himself. His alcoholic self is not his real self. His sane, sober, respectable self is his real self. That's why we're so happy in A. A. Have I come to myself?

Meditation for the Day

Simplicity is the Keynote of ~~God's Kingdom.~~ A GOOD LIFE. Choose the simple things always. Life can become complicated if you let it be so. You can be swamped by difficulties if you let them take up too much of your time. Every difficulty can be either solved or ignored and something better substituted for it. Love the humble things of life. Reverence the simple things. Your standard must never be the world's standard of wealth and power.

Prayer for the Day

I pray that ~~my standard may be one of honesty, purity, unselfishness and love.~~ I MAY LOVE THE SIMPLE THINGS OF LIFE. I pray that I may keep my life uncomplicated and free.

75

MARCH 13 -- A. A. Thought for the Day

We've got rid of our false, drinking selves and found our real, sober selves. And we turn to God, our Father, for help, just as the Prodigal Son arose and went to his father. At the end of the story, the father of the Prodigal Son says: "He was dead and is alive again, he was lost and is found". We alcoholics who have found sobriety in A. A. were certainly dead and are alive again. We were lost and are found. Am I alive again?

Meditation for the Day

Gently breathe in God's spirit, that spirit which, if not barred out by selfishness, will enable you to do good works. This means rather that God will be enabled to do good works through you. You can become a channel for God's spirit to flow through you and into the lives of others. The works that you can do will be only limited by your spiritual development. Let your spirit be in harmony with God's spirit and there is no limit to what you can do in the realm of human relationships.

Prayer for the Day

I pray that I may become a channel for God's spirit. I pray that God's spirit may flow through me into the lives of others.

76

MARCH 14 -- A. A. Thought for the Day

Can I get well? If I mean, can I ever drink normally again, the answer is NO. But if I mean, can I stay sober? the answer is definitely yes. I can get well by turning my drink problem over to a Power greater than myself, that Divine Principle in the universe which we call God. And by asking that Power each morning to give me the strength to stay sober for the next twenty-four hours. I know from the experience of thousands of people that if I honestly want to get well, I can get well. Am I faithfully following the A. A. programme?

Meditation for the Day

Persevere in all that God's guidance moves you to do. The persistent carrying out of WHAT SEEMS RIGHT AND GOOD ~~God's commands, as far as you can understand them,~~ will bring you to that place where you would be. If you look back over God's guidance, you will see that His leading has been very gradual and that only as you have carried out His wishes, as far as you can understand them, has God been able to give you more clear and definite leading. Man is led by God's touch on A quickened, responsive ~~spirit nerves.~~ MIND.

Prayer for the Day

I pray that I may persevere in DOING WHAT SEEMS RIGHT. ~~all good things.~~ I pray that I may carry out all of God's leading, as far as I can understand it.

77

MARCH 15 -- <u>A. A. Thought for the Day</u>

We alcoholics were on a merry-go-round, going round and round, and we couldn't get off. That merry-go-round is a kind of hell on earth. In A. A. I got off that merry-go-round by learning to stay sober. I pray to that Higher Power every morning to help me to keep sober. And I get the strength from that Power to do what I could never do with my own strength. I do not doubt the existence of that Power. We're not speaking into a vacuum when we pray. That Power is there, if I will use it. <u>Am I off the merry-go-round of drinking for good</u>?

<u>Meditation for the Day</u>

I must remember that in spiritual matters I am only an instrument. It is not mine to decide how or when I am to act. God plans all spiritual matters. It is up to me to make myself ~~very~~ fit to do God's work. All that hinders my spiritual activity must be eliminated. I can depend on God for all the strength I need to overcome THOSE FAULTS ~~my sins and temptations.~~ WHICH ARE BLOCKS. I must keep myself fit, so that God can use me as a channel for His spirit.

<u>Prayer for the Day</u>

I pray that my SELFISHNESS ~~self~~ may not hinder my progress in spiritual matters. I pray that I may be a GOOD ~~perfect~~ instrument for God to work with.

78

MARCH 16 -- <u>A. A. Thought for the Day</u>

Before we decide to quit drinking, most of us have to come up against a blank wall. We see that we're licked, that we have to quit. But we don't know which way to turn for help. There seems to be no door in that blank wall. A. A. opens the door that leads to sobriety. By encouraging us to honesty admit that we're alcoholics and to realize that we can't take even one drink, and by showing us which way to turn for help, A. A. opens the door in that blank wall. <u>Have I gone through that door to sobriety</u>?

<u>Meditation for the Day</u>

~~I must shut out the distractions of the world.~~ I must have a singleness of purpose, to do my part in God's work. I must not let material distractions interfere with my job of improving personal relationships. It is easy to become distracted by material affairs, so that I lose my singleness of purpose. I do not have time to be concerned about the multifarious concerns of the world. I must concentrate and specialize on what I can do best. ~~helping other alcoholics.~~

<u>Prayer for the Day</u>

I pray that I may not become distracted by material affairs. I pray that I may concentrate on doing what I can do best.

79

MARCH 17 - A. A. Thought for the Day

A. A. also helps us to hang onto sobriety. By having regular meetings so that we can associate with other alcoholics who have come through that same door in the wall, by encouraging us to tell the story of our own sad experiences with alcohol, and by showing us how to help other alcoholics, A. A. keeps us sober. Our attitude toward life changes from one of pride and selfishness to one of humility and gratitude. Am I going to step back through that door in the wall to my old helpless, hopeless, drunken life?

Meditation for the Day

Withdraw into the calm of communion with God. Rest in that calm and peace. When the soul finds its home of rest in God, then it is that real life begins. Only when you are calm and serene can you do good work. Emotional upsets make you useless. The eternal life is calmness and when a man enters into that, then he lives as an eternal being. Calmness is based on complete trust in God. Nothing in this world can separate you from the love of God.

Prayer for the Day

I pray that I may wear the world like a loose garment. I pray that I may keep serene at the center, OF MY BEING.

80

MARCH 18 -- A. A. Thought for the Day

When a man comes into A. A. and faces the fact he must spend the rest of his life without liquor, it often looks like too big an order for him. So A. A. tells him to forget about the future and bite it off one day at a time. All we really have is now. We have no past time and no future time. As the saying goes: "Yesterday is gone, forget it; tomorrow never comes, don't worry; today is here, get busy". All we have is the present. The past is water over the dam and the future never comes. When tomorrow gets here, it will be today. Am I living one day at a time?

Meditation for the Day

Persistence is necessary, if you are to advance in spiritual things. By persistent prayer, persistent firm and simple trust, you achieve the treasures of the spirit. By persistent practice, you can eventually obtain joy, peace, assurance, security, health, happiness and serenity. Nothing is too great, in the spiritual realm, for you to obtain through persistently preparing yourself for it.

Prayer for the Day

I pray that I may persistently carry out my spiritual exercises every day. I pray that I may STRIVE FOR ~~obtain~~ ~~perfect~~ peace, AND SERENITY.

MARCH 19 -- A. A. Thought for the Day

When we were drinking, we used to be ashamed of the past. Remorse is terrible mental punishment. Ashamed of ourselves for the things we've said and done, afraid to face people because of what they might think of us, afraid of the consequences of what we did when we were drunk. In A. A., we forget about the past. Do I believe that God has forgiven me for everything I've done in the past, no matter how black it was, provided I'm honestly trying to do the right thing today?

Meditation for the Day

~~God is here.~~ ~~His~~ GOD'S spirit is all about you all day long. You have no thoughts, no plans, no impulses, no emotions, that He does not know about. You can hide nothing from Him. Do not make your conduct conform only to what the world sees and do not depend on the approval or disapproval of men. God sees in secret, but He rewards openly. If you are in harmony with the Divine Spirit, doing your best to live the way you believe God wants you to live, you will be at peace.

Prayer for the Day

I pray that I may always feel God's presence. I pray that I may realize this PRESENCE constantly all through the day.

MARCH 20 -- A. A. Thought for the Day

When we were drinking, we used to worry about the future. Worry is terrible mental punishment. What's going to become of ~~us~~ ME? Where will ~~we~~ I end up? In the gutter or the ~~bug-house?~~ SANITARIUM? We can see ourselves slipping, getting worse and worse, and we wonder what the finish will be. Sometimes we get so discouraged in thinking about the future that we toy with the idea of suicide. In A. A., have I stopped worrying about the future?

Meditation for the Day

Functioning on a material plane alone takes me away from God. I must also try to function ~~through God.~~ ON A SPIRITUAL PLANE. Functioning ~~through God~~ on a spiritual plane as well as on a material plane will make life what it should be. All material activities are valueless in themselves alone. But all activities, seemingly trivial or of seemingly great moment, are all alike, if directed by God's guidance. I must try to obey God as I would expect a faithful, willing ~~secretary~~ SERVANT to carry out directions. ~~I must have no choice but God's and no will but God's.~~

Prayer for the Day

I pray that the flow of God's spirit may come to me through many channels. I pray that I may function ~~only through God's spirit.~~ ON A SPIRITUAL PLANE AS WELL AS ON A MATERIAL PLANE.

82

MARCH 21 -- A. A. Thought for the Day

In A. A., we forget about the future. We know from experience that as time goes on, the future takes care of itself. Everything works out well, as long as we stay sober. All we need to think about is today. When we get up in the morning and see the sun shining in the window, we thank God that He has given us another day to enjoy because we're sober. A day in which we may have a chance to help somebody. Do I know that this day is all I have and with God's help I can stay sober today?

Meditation for the Day

All is fundamentally well. That does not mean that all is well on the surface of things. But it does mean that God's in His heaven and THAT He has a purpose for the world, which will eventually work out when enough human beings are willing to follow His way. "Wearing the world as a loose garment" means not to be upset by the surface wrongness of things, but to feel deeply secure in the fundamental goodness and purpose in the universe.

Prayer for the Day

I pray that God may be with me in my journey through the world. I pray that I may know that God is planning that journey.

84

MARCH 22 -- A. A. Thought for the Day

We're all looking for the power to overcome drinking. A fellow comes into A. A. and his first question is: How do I get the strength to quit? At first, it seems to him that he will never get the necessary strength. He sees older members who have found the power he is looking for, but he doesn't know the process by which they got it. This necessary strength comes in many ways. Have I found all the strength I need?

Meditation for the Day

You cannot have a spiritual need which God cannot supply. Your FUNDAMENTAL ~~real~~ need is a spiritual need, the need of power to LIVE THE GOOD LIFE. ~~carry on your work.~~ The best spiritual supply is received by you when you WANT ~~wish it~~ to pass on to other people. You get it LARGELY by giving it away. God GIVES YOU STRENGTH AS YOU PASS IT ON TO ANOTHER PERSON. ~~thinks of you, a bud opens, and you convert that bud into cheer for another person.~~ That STRENGTH ~~cheer~~ means increased health; increased health means more GOOD work, and more GOOD work means more PEOPLE ~~souls~~ helped. And so it goes on, a constant supply ~~, but only if the need is a spiritual one.~~ TO MEET ALL SPIRITUAL NEEDS.

Prayer for the Day

I pray that my every spiritual need will be supplied by God. I pray that I may use the power I receive to help others.

85

MARCH 23 -- A. A. Thought for the Day

Strength comes from the fellowship you find when you come into A. A. Just being with men and women who have found the way out gives you a feeling of security. You listen to the speakers, you talk with other members, and you absorb the atmosphere of confidence and hope that you find in the place. Am I receiving strength from the fellowship with other A. A. members?

Meditation for the Day

God is with you, to bless and help you. His spirit is all around you. Waver not in your faith or IN your prayers. All power is the Lord's. Say that to yourself often and steadily. Say it until your heart sings with joy for the safety and personal power that it means to you. Say it until the very force of the utterance drives back and puts to naught all the evils against you. Use it as a battle cry. All power is the Lord's. Then you will pass on to victory over all your sins and temptations and you will begin to live a victorious life.

Prayer for the Day

I pray that with strength from God I may lead an abundant life. I pray that I may lead ~~a life of usefulness and helpfulness to my fellow men.~~ A LIFE OF VICTORY.

86

MARCH 24 -- A. A. Thought for the Day

Strength comes from honestly telling your own experiences with drinking. In religion, they call it confession. We call it witnessing or sharing. You give a personal witness, you share your past experiences, the troubles you got into, the hospitals, the jails, the break-up of your home, the money wasted, the debts, and all the foolish things you did when you were drinking. This personal witness lets out the things you had kept hidden, brings them out into the open, and you find release and strength. Am I receiving strength from my personal witnessing?

Meditation for the Day WE CANNOT FULLY UNDESTAND THE UNIVERSE.

~~Faith is too priceless a possession to be sacrificed on the hypothesis that by doing so we gain knowledge.~~ The simple fact is that we cannot even define space or time. They are both boundless, in spite of all we can do to limit them. We live in a box of space and time, which we have manufactured by our own minds and on that depends all our so-called knowledge of the universe. The simple fact is that we can never know all things, nor are we made to know them. MUCH OF OUR LIVES MUST BE TAKEN ON FAITH.

Prayer for the Day

I pray that my faith may be based on my own experience of the power of God in my life. I pray that I may ~~always keep this priceless possession.~~ KNOW THIS ONE THING ABOVE ALL ELSE IN THE UNIVERSE.

87

MARCH 25 -- <u>A. A. Thought for the Day</u>

Strength comes from coming to believe in a Higher Power that can help you. You can't define this Higher Power, but you can see how it helps other alcoholics. You hear them talk about it and you begin to get the idea yourself. You try praying in a quiet time each morning and you begin to feel stronger, as though your prayers were heard. So you gradually come to believe there must be a Power in the world outside of yourself, which is stronger than you and to which you can turn for help. <u>Am I receiving strength from my faith in a Higher Power</u>?

<u>Meditation for the Day</u>

Spiritual development is achieved by daily persistence in living the way you believe God wants you to live. Like the wearing away of a stone by steady drops of water, so will your daily persistence wear away all the difficulties and gain spiritual success for you. Never falter in this daily, steady persistence. Go forward boldly and unafraid. God will help and strengthen you, as long as you are trying to do His will.

<u>Prayer for the Day</u>

~~I pray that opportunities for service will be given me when God knows that I am ready for them. I pray that I may prepare myself, by daily persistence, for these opportunities.~~ I PRAY THAT I MAY PERSIST DAY BY DAY IN GAINING SPIRITUAL EXPERIENCE. I PRAY THAT I MAY MAKE THIS A LIFETIME WORK.

88

MARCH 26 -- <u>A. A. Thought for the Day</u>

Strength comes ALSO from working with other alcoholics. When you are talking with a prospect and trying to help him, you are building up your own strength at the same time. You see the other fellow in the condition you might be in yourself and it makes your resolve to stay sober stronger than ever. Often you help yourself more than the other fellow, but if you do succeed in helping him to get sober, you are stronger from the experience of having helped another man. <u>Am I receiving strength from working with others</u>?

<u>Meditation for the Day</u>

Faith is the bridge between you and God. It is the bridge ~~that~~ WHICH God has ordained. If all were seen and known, there would be no merit in doing right. Therefore God has ordained that we do not see or know directly. But we can experience the power of His spirit through our faith. It is the bridge between us and Him, which we can take or not, as we will. There could be no morality without free will. We must make the choice ourselves. WE MUST MAKE THE VENTURE OF BELIEF.

<u>Prayer for the Day</u>

I pray that I may choose and decide to cross the bridge of faith. I pray that by crossing this bridge I may receive ~~all~~ the spiritual power I need.

89

MARCH 27 -- A. A. Thought for the Day

You get the power to overcome drinking through the fellowship of other alcoholics who have found the way out. You get power by honestly sharing your past experiences by a personal witness. You get power by coming to believe in a Higher Power, the Divine Principle in the universe which can help you. You get power by working with other alcoholics. In these four ways, thousands of alcoholics have found all the power they needed to overcome drinking. Am I ready and willing to accept this power and work for it?

Meditation for the Day

The power of God's spirit is the greatest power in the universe. Men's conquest of each other, the great kings and conquerors, the conquest of wealth, the leaders of the money society, all amount to very little in the end. But he that conquers himself is greater than he who conquers a city. Material things have no permanence. But God's spirit is eternal. Everything really worth while in the world is the result of the power of God's spirit.

Prayer for the Day

I pray that I may open myself to the power of God's spirit. I pray that ~~all~~ my relationships with my fellow men may be ~~based on this spirit.~~ IMPROVED BY THIS SPIRIT.

90

MARCH 28 -- A. A. Thought for the Day

When you come into an A. A. meeting, you're not just coming into a meeting, you're coming into a new life. I'm always impressed by the change I see in people after they've been in A. A. for a while. I sometimes take an inventory of myself, to see whether I have changed and, if so, in what way. Before I met A. A., I was very selfish. I wanted my own way in everything. I don't believe I ever grew up. When things went wrong, I sulked like a spoiled child and often went out and got drunk. Am I still all get and no give?

Meditation for the Day

There are two things that we must have if we are going to change our way of life. One is faith, the confidence in things unseen, that fundamental goodness and purpose in the universe. The other is obedience, that is living according to our faith, living each day as we believe that God wants us to live, with gratitude, humility, honesty, purity, unselfishness and love. Faith and obedience, these two, will give us all the strength we need to overcome sin and temptation and to live a new and more abundant life.

Prayer for the Day

I pray that I may have more faith and more obedience. I pray that I may live a more abundant life, AS A RESULT OF THESE THINGS.

91

MARCH 29 -- <u>A. A. Thought for the Day</u>

Before I met A. A., I was very dishonest. I lied to my wife constantly about where I had been and what I'd been doing. I took time off from the office and pretended I'd been sick or gave some other dishonest excuse. I was dishonest with myself, as well as with other people. I would never face myself as I really was or admit when I was wrong. I pretended to myself that I was as good as the next fellow, although I suspected I wasn't. <u>Am I now really honest</u>?

<u>Meditation for the Day</u>

~~Am I ready to live a life apart with God? God will reward my seeking with His presence.~~ I must live in the world and yet live apart with God. I can go forth from my secret times of communion WITH GOD TO THE WORK OF THE WORLD. ~~to help others.~~ To get the spiritual strength I need, my INNER ~~real~~ life must be lived apart from the world. I must "wear the world as a loose garment". Nothing in the world should seriously upset me, as long as my INNER ~~real~~ life is lived with God. All successful living arises from this inner life.

<u>Prayer for the Day</u>

I pray that I may live my inner life ~~apart~~ with God. I pray that nothing shall invade OR DESTROY that secret place, OF PEACE.

9√

MARCH 30 -- <u>A. A. Thought for the Day</u>

Before I met A. A., I was very unloving. From the time I went away to school, I paid very little attention to my mother and father. I was on my own and didn't even bother to keep in touch with them. After I got married, I was very unappreciative of my wife. Many a time I left her flat while I went out to have a good time. I paid very little attention to our children and never tried to understand them or make pals of them. My few friends were only drinking companions, not real friends. HAVE I GOTTEN OVER LOVING NOBODY BUT MYSELF? ~~Do I now really love anybody but myself?~~

<u>Meditation for the Day</u>

Be calm, be true, be quiet. Do not get emotionally upset by anything that happens around you. Feel a deep inner security in the goodness and purpose in the universe. Be true to your highest ideals. Do not let yourself slip back into the old ways of reacting. Stick to your spiritual guns. Be CALM ~~quiet~~ always. Do not talk back or defend yourself TOO MUCH against accusation, whether false or true. Accept abuse as well as you accept praise. Only God can judge the real you.

<u>Prayer for the Day</u>

I pray that I may not be upset by THE judgments of others. I pray that I may ~~live the way God wants me to live.~~ LET GOD BE THE JUDGE OF THE REAL ME.

93

MARCH 31 -- A. A. Thought for the Day

Since I've been in A. A., have I made a start towards becoming more unselfish? Do I no longer want my own way in everything? When things go wrong and I can't have what I want, do I no longer sulk? Am I trying not to waste money on myself? And does it make me happy to see my wife have enough money for herself and the children? Am I trying not to be all get and no give?

Meditation for the Day

Each day is a day of progress, steady progress forward, if you make it so. You may not see it, but God does. God does not judge by outward appearance. He judges by the heart. Let Him see in your heart a simple desire always to do His will. Though you may feel that your work has been spoiled or tarnished, God sees it as an offering for Him. When climbing up a steep hill, a man is often more conscious of the weakness of his stumbling feet than of the view, the grandeur, or even of the upward progress.

Prayer for the Day

I pray that I may persevere in all good things. I pray that I may ~~grow~~ ADVANCE each day ~~in every way that I can.~~ IN SPITE OF MY STUMBLING FEET.

94

APRIL 1 -- A. A. Thought for the Day

Since I've been in A. A., have I made a start towards becoming more honest? Do I no longer have to lie to my wife? Am I on time at my work and do I try to earn what I get? Am I making an attempt to be honest with myself? Have I faced myself as I really am and have I admitted to myself that I'm no good by myself, but have to rely on God to help me to do the right thing? Am I beginning to find out what it means to be alive and to face the world honestly and without fear?

Meditation for the Day

~~We shut ourselves off from God by our selfishness and sin.~~ God is all around us. His spirit pervades the universe. And yet we often do not let His spirit in. We try to get along without His help and we make a mess of our lives. We can do nothing of any value without God's help. All our ~~proper~~ human relationships depend on this. ~~and everything worth while depends on human relationships.~~ When we let God's spirit rule our lives, ~~we become more honest, pure, unselfish and loving.~~ WE LEARN HOW TO GET ALONG WITH OUR FELLOW MEN AND HOW TO HELP THEM.

Prayer for the Day

I pray that I MAY LET GOD RUN MY LIFE. ~~cooperate more fully with God. I pray that, with the help of God's spirit, I may improve my relationships with my fellow men.~~ I PRAY THAT I WILL NEVER AGAIN MAKE A MESS OF MY LIFE THROUGH TRYING TO RUN IT MYSELF.

95

APRIL 2 -- A. A. Thought for the Day

Since I've been in A. A., have I made a start towards becoming more loving to my family and friends? Do I visit my parents? Am I more appreciative of my wife than I was before? Am I grateful to her for putting up with me all these years? Have I found a real companionship with my children? Do I feel that the friends I've found in A. A. are real friends? Do I believe that they are always ready to help me and do I want to help them if I can? Do I really care NOW about other people?

Meditation for the Day

Not what you do so much as what you are; that is the miracle-working power. You can be a force for good, with the help of God. ~~[illegible]~~ God is here to help you and TO bless you, here to company with you. You can be ~~a miracle-worker,~~ a worker with God, ~~and for God.~~ Changed by God's grace, you shed one garment of the spirit for a better one. In time, you throw that one aside for a yet finer one. And so, from character to character, you are gradually transformed.

Prayer for the Day

I pray that I may accept every challenge. I pray that each acceptance of a challenge may make me grow into a better man.

96

APRIL 3 -- A. A. Thought for the Day

When I was drinking, I was absolutely selfish. I thought of myself first, last and always. The universe revolved around me at the center. When I woke up in the morning with a hangover, my only thought was how terrible I felt and about what I could do to make myself feel better. And the only thing I could think of was more liquor. To quit was impossible. I couldn't see beyond myself and my own need for another drink. Can I now look out and beyond my own selfishness?

Meditation for the Day

Remember that the ~~finest~~ FIRST quality of greatness is service. In a way, God is the greatest servant of all, because He is always waiting for us to call on Him to help us in all good endeavors. His strength is always available to us, but we must ask it of Him, through our own free will. It is a free gift, but we must sincerely seek for it. A life of service is the finest life we can live. We are here on earth to serve others. That is the beginning and the end of our ~~existence.~~ REAL WORTH.

Prayer for the Day

I pray that I may cooperate with God in all good things. I pray that I may serve God and my fellow men and so lead a useful and happy life.

97

APRIL 4 -- A. A. Thought for the Day

When I came into A. A., I found men and women who had been through the same things I had been through. But now they were thinking more about how they could help others than they were about themselves. They were a lot more unselfish than I ever was. By coming to meetings and associating with them, I began to think a little less about myself and a little more about other people. I also learned that I didn't have to depend on myself alone to get out of the mess I was in. I could get a greater strength than my own. Am I now depending less on myself and more on God?

Meditation for the Day

No man can help, unless he understands the man he is trying to help. To understand the problems and temptations of your fellow man, you must have been through them yourself. You must do all you can to understand your fellow man. You must study his background, his likes and dislikes, his reactions and his prejudices. When you see his weaknesses, do not confront him with them. Share your own weaknesses, sins, AND temptations and let him get his own convictions.

Prayer for the Day

I pray that I may serve as a channel for God's power to come into other men's lives. I pray that I may try to understand my fellow MEN.

98

APRIL 5 -- A. A. Thought for the Day

People often ask what makes the A. A. programme work. One of the answers is that A. A. works because it gets a person away from himself as the center of the universe. And it teaches him to rely more on the fellowship of others and on strength from God. Forgetting ourselves in fellowship, prayer, and working with others, is what makes the A. A. programme work. Are these things keeping me SOBER?

Meditation for the Day

God is the great interpreter of one human personality to another. Even personalities who are the nearest together have much in their natures that remains a sealed book to each other. And only as God enters and controls their lives are the mysteries of each revealed to the other. Each personality is so different. God alone understands perfectly the language of each and can interpret between the two. Here we find the miracles of change and the true interpretation of life.

Prayer for the Day

I pray that I may be in the right relationship to God. I pray that God will interpret to me the personalities of other people, so that I can understand them and help them.

99

APRIL 6 -- A. A. Thought for the Day

Every alcoholic has a personality problem. He drinks to escape from life, to counteract a feeling of loneliness or inferiority, or because of some emotional conflict within himself, so that he cannot adjust himself to life. His alcoholism is a symptom of his personality disorder. An alcoholic cannot stop drinking unless he finds a way to solve his personality problem. That's why going on the wagon doesn't solve anything. That's why taking the pledge usually doesn't work. Was my personality problem ever solved by going on the wagon or taking the pledge?

Meditation for the Day

God irradiates your life with the warmth of His ~~holy~~ spirit. You must open up like a flower to this divine irradiation. Loosen your hold on earth, its cares AND its worries. ~~even its joys.~~ Unclasp your HOLD ON MATERIAL THINGS, ~~personality,~~ relax your grip, and the tide of peace and serenity will flow in. Relinquish every material thing and receive it back again from God. Do not hold on to earth's treasures so firmly that your hands are too occupied to clasp God's hands, as He holds them out to you in love.

Prayer for the Day

I pray that I may be open to receive God's blessing. I pray that I may be willing to ~~sacrifice everything that is necessary, in order to achieve that blessing.~~ RELINQUISH MY HOLD ON MATERIAL THINGS AND RECEIVE THEM BACK FROM GOD.

100

APRIL 7 -- A. A. Thought for the Day

In A. A., an alcoholic finds a way to solve his personality problem. He does this by recovering three things. First, he recovers his personal integrity. He pulls himself together. He gets honest with himself and with other prople. He faces himself and his problems honestly, instead of running away. He takes a personal inventory of himself, to see where he really stands. Then he faces the facts, instead of making excuses for himself. Have I recovered my integrity?

Meditation for the Day

~~Watch out for the "I" in sin. "I" means selfishness and leads to most of the other sins.~~ When trouble comes, do not say: Why should this happen to me? Leave yourself out of the picture. Think of other people and their troubles, and you will forget about your own. Gradually get away from yourself and you will know the ~~joy~~ CONSOLATION of unselfish service of others. After a while, it will not matter so much what happens to you. It is not so important any more, except as your experience can be used to help others who are in the same KIND OF trouble.

Prayer for the Day

I pray that I may become more unselfish. I pray that I may not be thrown off the track by letting the old selfishness creep back into my life.

101

APRIL 8 -- <u>A. A. Thought for the Day</u>

Second, an alcoholic recovers his faith in a Power greater than himself. He admits that he's helpless by himself and he calls on that Higher Power for help. He surrenders his life to God, as he understands Him. He puts his drink problem in God's hands and leaves it there. He recovers his faith in a Higher Power that can help him. <u>Have I recovered my faith</u>?

<u>Meditation for the Day</u>

You must make a stand for God ~~and for the A. A.~~ ~~In life and work and service, you must be outstanding.~~ Believers in God ARE CONSIDERED BY SOME AS PECULIAR PEOPLE. ~~and workers for A. A. may be known as peculiar people.~~ You MUST ~~may~~ even be willing to be deemed a fool for the sake OF YOUR FAITH. ~~of God and the A. A.~~ You must be ready to stand aside and let the fashions and customs of the world go by, when God's PURPOSES ARE THEREBY FORWARDED. ~~glory and the A. A. are thereby serviced.~~ Be known by the marks that distinguish a believer in God. THESE ARE ~~and an A. A.~~ honesty, purity, umselfishness, love, gratitude and humility.

<u>Prayer for the Day</u>

I pray that I may be ready to PROFESS ~~confess~~ my belief in God BEFORE MEN. ~~and my A. A. beliefs before all men.~~ ~~I pray that I may count all other things a loss, so that I may gain these things.~~ I PRAY THAT I MAY NOT BE TURNED ASIDE BY THE SKEPTICISM AND CYNICISM OF UNBELIEVERS.

102

APRIL 9 -- <u>A. A. Thought for the Day</u>

Third, an alcoholic recovers his proper relationships with other people. He thinks less about himself and more about others. He tries to help other alcoholics. He makes ~~him~~ NEW friends, so that he's no longer lonely. He tries to live a life of service instead of selfishness. All his relationships with other people are improved. He solves his personality problem by recovering his personal integrity, his faith in a Higher Power, and HIS ~~a~~ way of fellowship and service to others. <u>Is my drink problem solved,</u> AS LONG AS ~~because~~ <u>my personality problem is solved?</u>

<u>Meditation for the Day</u>

All that depresses you, all that you fear, is really powerless to harm you. These things are but phantoms. So arise from earth's bonds, from depression, distrust, fear and all that hinders your new life. Arise to beauty, joy, peace and work inspired by love. Rise from death to life. You do not even need to fear death. All past sins are forgiven, if you live and love and work with God. Let nothing hinder your new life. Seek to know more and more of that new way of living.

<u>Prayer for the Day</u>

I pray that I may let God live in me AS I WORK FOR HIM. ~~and let my life be a part of His life.~~ I pray that I may go out into the sunlight and WORK ~~walk~~ with God.

103

APRIL 10 -- A. A. Thought for the Day

When I came into A. A., I came into a new world. A sober world. A world of sobriety, peace, serenity and happiness. But I know that if I take just one drink, I'll go right back into that old world. That alcoholic world. That world of drunkenness, conflict and misery. That alcoholic world is not a pleasant place for an alcoholic to live in. Looking at the world through the bottom of a whiskey glass is no fun, after you've become an alcoholic. Do I want to go back to that alcoholic world?

Meditation for the Day

Pride stands sentinel at the door of the heart and shuts out the love of God. God can only dwell with the humble and the obedient. Obedience to God's will is the key unlocking the door to God's Kingdom. No man can obey God to the best of his ability, without in time realizing God's love and responding to that love. The rough stone steps of obedience lead up to WHERE the mosaic floor of love and joy IS LAID. ~~that is laid in God's heaven.~~ Where GOD'S SPIRIT ~~God~~ is, there is your home, There is heaven for you.

Prayer for the Day

I pray that God may make His home in my humble and obedient heart. I pray that I may obey his guidance ~~in all things.~~ TO THE BEST OF MY ABILITY.

104

APRIL 11 -- A. A. Thought for the Day

In that alcoholic world, one drink always leads to another and you can't stop till you're paralyzed. And the next morning it begins all over again. You eventually land in a hospital or jail. You lose your job. Your home is broken up. You're always in a mess. You're on a merry-go-round and you can't get off. You're in a squirrel-cage and you can't get out. Am I convinced that that alcoholic world is not a pleasant place for me to live in?

Meditation for the Day

~~I must deal with myself severely.~~ I must learn to accept self-discipline. I must try never to yield one point that I have already won. I must not let myself go in resentments, hates, fears, pride, ~~lust~~ or gossip. Even if discipline KEEPS ME ~~makes me a peculiar person,~~ separated from SOME people who are without discipline, nevertheless I will carry on. I may have different ways AND a different standard of living THAN SOME OTHERS. ~~different customs.~~ I may be actuated by different motives than SOME ~~many~~ people. But I will try to live the way I believe God wants me to live, NO MATTER WHAT OTHERS SAY.

Prayer for the Day

I pray that I may be an example to others of a better way of living. I pray that I may ~~rely on God's strength always.~~ CARRY ON IN SPITE OF HINDRANCES.

APRIL 12 -- A. A. Thought for the Day

This sober world is a pleasant place for an alcoholic TO LIVE IN. Once you've got out of your alcoholic fog, you find that the world looks good. You find real friends in A. A. You get a job. You feel good in the morning. You eat a good breakfast and you do a good day's work. And at night you come home to a family that welcomes you because you're sober. Am I convinced that this sober world is a pleasant place for an alcoholic to live in?

Meditation for the Day

Man's need is God's ~~chance to help.~~ OPPORTUNITY. First I must recognize my need. Often this means helplessness before some weakness or sickness and an admission of my need FOR HELP. Next comes faith in the ~~strength~~ POWER of God's spirit, available to me to meet that need. ~~Man's need is God's opportunity, But~~ Before ~~the~~ ANY need can be met, man's faith must find expression. That expression of faith is all God needs to manifest His power in my life. Faith is the key that unlocks the storehouse of God's resources.

Prayer for the Day

I pray that I may FIRST admit my needs. I pray that THEN I may have faith that God will meet those needs, IN THE WAY WHICH IS BEST FOR ME.

APRIL 13 -- A. A. Thought for the Day

Having found my way into this new world by the grace of God and the help of A. A., am I going to take that first drink, when I know that just one drink will change my whole world? Am I deliberately going back to the suffering of that alcoholic world? Or am I going to hang onto the happiness of this sober world? Is there any doubt about the answer? With God's help, am I going to hang onto A. A. with both hands?

Meditation for the Day

I ~~must~~ WILL try to make the world better and happier by my presence in it. I ~~must~~ WILL try to help other people find the way God wants them to live. I ~~must~~ WILL try to be on the side of good, in the stream of righteousness, where all things work for good. I ~~must~~ WILL do my duty persistently and faithfully, not sparing myself. I ~~should~~ WILL be gentle with all people. I ~~should~~ WILL try to see the other person's difficulty and help him to correct it. I ~~should~~ WILL always pray to God to act as interpreter between me and the other person.

Prayer for the Day

I pray that I may live in the spirit of prayer. I pray that I may ~~always~~ depend on God for the strength I need to help ~~other people.~~ ME TO DO MY PART IN MAKING THE WORD A BETTER PLACE.

APRIL 14 -- A. A. Thought for the Day

A police captain ONCE told about certain cases he had come across in his police work. The cause of the tragedy in each case was drunkenness. He told his audience about a man who got into an argument with his wife while he was drunk and beat her to death. Then he went out and drank some more. The police captain also told about a man who got too near the edge of an old quarry hole when he was drunk and fell one hundred and fifty feet to his death. When I read or hear these stories, do I think about our motto: "But for the Grace of God?"

Meditation for the Day

I must keep balanced, by keeping ~~God~~ SPIRITUAL THINGS at the center of my life. ~~To be effective in the lives of others, I must learn balance.~~ God will ~~teach~~ GIVE me this poise and balance, if I pray for it. This poise will give me power in dealing with the lives of others. ~~and that poise~~ THIS BALANCE will manifest itself more and more IN MY OWN LIFE. I should keep material things in their proper place and keep spiritual things at the center of my life. ~~The real meaning of my existence will be found in the spiritual concepts of honesty, purity, unselfishness and love.~~ THEN I WILL BE AT PEACE AMID THE DISTRACTIONS OF EVERYDAY LIVING.

Prayer for the Day

I pray that I may dwell with God at the center of my life. I pray that I may ~~fix my whole being with God at its center.~~ KEEP THAT INNER PEACE AT THE CENTER OF MY BEING.

APRIL 15 -- A. A. Thought for the Day

Terrible things could have happened to any one of us. We never WILL know what might have happened to us when we were drunk. We usually thought: "That couldn't happen to ~~me~~ ME." But any one of us could even have killed somebody or have been killed ourselves, if we were drunk enough. But fear of these things never kept us from drinking. Do I believe that in A. A., we have something more effective then fear?

Meditation for the Day

I must keep calm and unmoved in the vicissitudes of life. I must go back into the silence of communion with God to recover this calm, when it is lost even for one moment. I will accomplish more by this calmness than by all the activities of a long day. At all cost, I will keep calm. I can ~~help nobody~~ SOLVE NOTHING when I am agitated. I should keep away from things that are upsetting emotionally. I should run on an even keel and not get tipped over by emotional upsets. I should seek ~~out~~ FOR things that are calm and good and true and stick to those things.

Prayer for the Day

I pray that I may not argue, nor contend, but merely state calmly what I believe to be true. I pray that I may keep myself in ~~the stream of calmness and goodness~~ THAT STATE OF CALMNESS that comes from ~~God.~~ FAITH IN GOD'S PURPOSE FOR THE WORD.

109

APRIL 16 -- A. A. Thought for the Day

In A. A., we have insurance. Our faith in God is a kind of insurance against the terrible things that might happen to us if we ever drank again. By putting our drink problem in the hands of God, we've taken out a sort of insurance policy, which insures us against the ravages of drink, as our homes are insured against destruction by fire. Am I paying my A. A. insurance premiums regularly?

Meditation for the Day I MUST TRY TO LOVE MY FELLOW MEN.

Love comes from THINKING OF ~~believing that~~ every man or woman ~~of whatever race, color or creed is~~ AS your brother or sister, because they are children of God. THIS WAY OF THINKING ~~The fact of their being my brothers or sisters~~ makes me care enough about them to really want to help them. I must put this kind of love into action ~~in my life~~ by serving my fellow men. Love ~~also~~ means no SEVERE judging, no resentments, no MALICIOUS gossip and no DESTRUCTIVE criticism. It means patience, understanding, COMPASSION and helpfulness.

Prayer for the Day

I pray that I may realize that God loves me, since He is THE ~~my~~ Father OF US ALL. ~~in spirit.~~ I pray that I IN TURN may have love for ~~God and for my fellow men.~~ ALL OF HIS CHILDREN.

110

APRIL 17 -- A. A. Thought for the Day

Every time we go to an A. A. meeting, every time we say the Lord's prayer, every time we HAVE A QUIET TIME ~~get down on our knees~~ before breakfast, we're paying a premium on our insurance against taking that first drink. And every time we help another alcoholic, we're making a large payment on our drink insurance. We're making sure that our policy doesn't lapse. Am I building up an endowment in serenity; peace and happiness that will put me on easy street for the rest of my life?

Meditation for the Day

I GAIN ~~find~~ faith by my own experience of God's POWER ~~spiritual strength~~ in my life. The constant, persistent recognition of God's spirit in all my personal relationships, the ever-accumulating weight of evidence in support of God's guidance, the numberless instances in which seeming chance or wonderful coincidence can be traced to God's purpose in my life. All these THINGS gradually engender a feeling of wonder, HUMILITY ~~faith~~ and gratitude to God. These in turn are followed by a more ~~abundant life.~~ SURE AND ABIDING FAITH IN GOD AND HIS PURPOSES.

Prayer for the Day

I pray that my faith may be strengthened every day. I pray that I may find confirmation of my faith in the ~~changed personalities around me.~~ GOOD THINGS THAT HAVE COME INTO MY LIFE.

APRIL 18 -- A. A. Thought for the Day

As I look back over my drinking career, have I learned that "You take out of life what you put into it?" When I put drinking into my life, did I take out a lot of bad things? Hospitals with the D. T.'s? Jails for drunken driving? Loss of job? Loss of home and wife and children? When I put drinking into my life, was almost everything I took out bad?

Meditation for the Day

I should strive for a friendliness and helpfulness that WILL affect all who come near to me. I ~~must~~ SHOULD try to see something to love in them. I SHOULD welcome them, bestow little courtesies and understandings on them, and help them if they ask for help. I must send no one away without a word of cheer, a feeling that I really care about him. God may have put the impulse ~~to come to me~~ in some despairing one's mind, TO COME TO ME. I must not fail God by repulsing that person. He may have deep needs that he will not express to me, unless he is sure of a warm reception.

Prayer for the Day

I pray that I may warmly welcome all who come to me for help. I pray that I may make them feel that I really care.

APRIL 19 -- A. A. Thought for the Day

Since I've been putting sobriety into my life, I've been taking out a lot of good things. I can describe it best as a kind of quiet satisfaction. I feel good. I feel right with the world, on the right side of the fence. As long as I put sobriety into my life, almost everything I take out is good. The satisfaction you get out of living a sober life is made up of a lot of little things. You have the ambition to do things you didn't feel like doing when you were drinking. Am I getting satisfaction out of living a sober life?

Meditation for the Day

It is a glorious way - the upward way. There are wonderful discoveries in the realm of the spirit. There are tender intimacies in the quiet times of communion with God. There is an amazing, almost incomprehensible understanding of your fellow men. On the upward way, you can have all the strength you need from that Higher Power. You cannot make too many demands on Him for ~~strength.~~ POWER. He gives you all the power you need, as long as you are moving along the upward way.

Prayer for the Day

I pray that I may see the beautiful horizons ahead, on the upward way. I pray that I may keep going forward ~~in faith,~~ to the more abundant life.

113

APRIL 20 -- <u>A. A. Thought for the Day</u>

The satisfaction you get out of living a sober life is made up of a lot of little things, but they add up to a satisfactory and happy life. You take out of life what you put into it. So I'd say to people coming into A. A.; Don't worry about what life will be like without liquor. Just stick along and a lot of good things will happen to you. And you'll have that feeling of quiet satisfaction and peace and serenity and gratitude for the grace of God. <u>Is my life becoming really worth living</u>?

<u>Meditation for the Day</u>

There are two paths, one up and one down. We have been given free will to choose either path. We are captains of our souls to this extent only. We can choose the good or the bad. Once we have chosen the wrong path, we go down and down, eventually to death. But if we choose the right path, we go up and up, until we come to the resurrection day. On the wrong path, we have no power for good, because we do not choose to ask for it. But on the right path, we are on the side of good and we have all the power of God's spirit behind us.

<u>Prayer for the Day</u>

I pray that I may be in the stream of goodness. I pray that I may be on the RIGHT side, THE SIDE OF all ~~the~~ good in the universe.

114

APRIL 21 -- <u>A. A. Thought for the Day</u>

After we've been in A. A. for a while, we find out that if we're going to stay sober, we have to be humble people. The men we see in A. A. who have really made the grade are all humble people. When I stop to think that but for the grace of God I might be drunk right now, I can't help feeling humble. Gratitude to God for His grace makes me humble. When I think of the kind of person I was not so long ago, when I think of the man I left behind me, I've got nothing to be proud about. <u>Am I grateful and humble</u>?

<u>Meditation for the Day</u>

I must arise from the death of sin and selfishness and put on a new life of spirituality. All the old sins and temptations must be laid in the grave and a new existence rise from the ashes. Yesterday is gone. All my sins are forgiven if I am honestly trying to do God's will today. Today is here - the time of resurrection and renewal. I must start now - today - to build a new life of complete faith and trust in God and a determination to do His will in all things.

<u>Prayer for the Day</u>

I pray that I may do my share in making the world a better place to live in. I pray that I may do what I can to bring goodness a little nearer to the earth.

115

APRIL 22 -- A. A. Thought for the Day

People believe what they see. They can see A. A. work. An actual demonstration is what convinces them. What they read in books, what they hear people say, doesn't always convince them. But when they see a real honest-to-goodness change take place in a person, a change from a drunkard to a sober, useful citizen, that's something they can believe in because they can see it. There's really only one thing that proves to me that A. A. works. Have I seen the change in people who come into A. A.?

Meditation for the Day

Divine control AND unquestioning obedience to God, ~~these~~ are the only NECESSARY conditions for a spiritual life. Divine control means absolute faith and trust in God, a belief that God is the Divine Principle in the universe and that He is the Intelligence and the Love that controls the universe. Unquestioning obedience to God means living each day the way you believe God wants you to live, constantly seeking the guidance of God in every situation, AND BEING willing to do the right thing at all times.

Prayer for the Day

I pray that I may always be under Divine Control and always practice unquestioning obedience to God. I pray that I may be always ready to serve ~~God.~~ HIM.

116

APRIL 23 -- A. A. Thought for the Day

Men and women keep coming into A. A., licked by alcohol, often given up by doctors as hopeless cases, they themselves admitting they're helpless to stop drinking. When I see these men and women get sober and stay sober over a period of months and years, then I know that A. A. works. The change I see in people who come into A. A. not only convinces me that A. A. works but it also convinces me that there must be a Power greater than ourselves which helps us to make that change. Am I convinced that a Higher Power can help me to change?

Meditation for the Day

Cooperation with God is the great necessity for our lives. All else follows naturally. Cooperation with God is the result of our consciousness of His presence. Guidance is bound to come to us, as we live more and more with God, as our consciousness becomes more and more attuned to the great Consciousness of the universe. We must have many quiet times, when we not so much ask to be shown and led by God, as to feel and realize His presence. New spiritual growth comes naturally from cooperation with God.

Prayer for the Day

I pray that God may supply me with strength and show me the direction in which HE WANTS ME to grow. I pray that these things may come NATURALLY from my cooperation with ~~God.~~ HIM.

117

APRIL 24 -- A. A. Thought for the Day

It's been proved that we alcoholics can't get sober by our will-power. We've failed again and again. Therefore I believe there must be a Higher Power which helps us. I think of that power as the grace of God. And I pray to God every morning for the strength to stay sober today. I know that Power is there because it never fails to help me. Do I believe that A. A. works through the Grace of God?

Meditation for the Day

Once I am "born of the spirit", then that is my life's breath. Within me is the Life of life, so that I can never perish. The Life that down the ages has kept God's children through peril, adversity and sorrow. I must TRY never TO doubt, OR ~~never~~ worry, but follow where the life of the spirit leads. ~~God's spirit supplies wisdom and strength.~~ How often, when I little know it, God goes before me to prepare the way, to soften a heart or to overrule a resentment. As the life of the spirit grows, natural wants BECOME LESS IMPORTANT. ~~drop away.~~

Prayer for the Day

I pray that my life may become centered in God MORE THAN IN SELF. I pray that MY WILL ~~all my activities~~ may be directed towards doing His will.

118

APRIL 25 -- A. A. Thought for the Day

I don't believe that A. A. works because I read it in a book or because I hear people say so. I believe it because I see people getting sober and staying sober. I believe what I see. An actual demonstration is what convinces me. When I see the change in people, I can't help believing that A. A. works. We could listen to talk about A. A. all day and still not believe it, but when we see it work, we have to believe it. Seeing is believing. Do I see A. A. work every day?

Meditation for the Day

TRY SAYING: ~~Say often,~~ "God bless him" of anyone whom you find in disharmony with you~~, or who is in trouble.~~ Also say it of anyone WHO IS IN TROUBLE THROUGH HIS OWN FAULT. ~~whom you desire to help.~~ Say it, willing that showers of blessings may fall upon him. Let God do the blessing. Leave to God the necessary correcting or DISCIPLINING. ~~training.~~ You SHOULD ~~must~~ only desire blessing for him. Leave God's work to GOD. ~~him and~~ Occupy yourself with the task that HE ~~God~~ gives you to do. God's blessing will ALSO break down all your OWN difficulties and build up all your successes. ~~God is the creator of all good.~~

Prayer for the Day

I pray that I may use God's goodness so that it will be a blessing to others. I pray that I may accept God's blessing so that I will have harmony, beauty, joy and happiness.

119

APRIL 26 -- <u>A. A. Thought for the Day</u>

The A. A. programme is one of submission, release and action. When we're drinking, we're submitting to a power greater than ourselves, liquor. Our self-wills are no use against the power of liquor. One drink and we're sunk. In A. A., we stop submitting to the power of liquor. Instead, we submit to a Power, also greater than ourselves, which we call God. <u>Have I submitted myself to that Higher Power?</u>

<u>Meditation for the Day</u>

Ceaseless activity is not God's plan for your life. Times of withdrawal for renewed strength are always necessary. Watch for the faintest tremor of fear and stop all work, everything, and rest before God until you are strong again. Deal in the same way with all tired feelings. Then you need rest of body and renewal of spirit-force. St. Paul said: "I can do all things through Him who strengthens me". This does not mean that you are to do all things and then rely on God to find strength. It means that you are to do ~~as God tells you~~ THE THINGS YOU BELIEVE GOD WANTS YO to do and only then can you rely on His supply of power.

<u>Prayer for the Day</u>

I pray that God's spirit may be my master always. I pray that I may learn how to rest and listen, as well as how to work.

120

APRIL 27 -- <u>A. A. Thought for the Day</u>

By submitting to God, we're released from the power of liquor. It has no more hold on us. We're also released from the things that were holding us down, pride, selfishness and fear. And we're free to grow into a new life, which is so much better than the old life that there's no comparison. This release gives us serenity and peace with the world. <u>Have I been released from the power of alcohol?</u>

<u>Meditation for the Day</u>

We know God by spiritual vision. We feel that He is beside us. We feel His presence. Contact with God is not made by the senses. Spirit-consciousness replaces sight. Since we cannot see God, we have to perceive Him by spiritual perception. God has to span the physical and the spiritual with the gift to us of spiritual vision. Many a man, though he cannot see God, has had a clear spiritual consciousness of Him. We are inside a box of space and time, but we know there must be something outside of that box, limitless space, eternity of time, and God.

<u>Prayer for the Day</u>

I pray that I may have a consciousness of God's presence. I pray that God will give me spiritual vision.

121

APRIL 28 -- A. A. Thought for the Day

We're so glad to be free from liquor that we do something about it. We get into action. We come to meetings regularly. We go out and try to help other alcoholics. We pass on the good news whenever we get a chance. In a spirit of thankfulness to God, we get into action. The A. A. programme is simple. Submit yourself to God, find release from liquor and get into action. ~~That's all there is to it.~~ Do these things and keep doing them and you're all set for the rest of your life. Have I got into action?

Meditation for the Day

God's eternal quest must be the tracking down of souls. You ~~must~~ SHOULD join Him in His quest. Through briars, through waste places, through glades, up mountain heights, down into valleys, God leads you. But ever with His leadership goes your helping hand. Glorious to follow where the Leader goes. You are seeking lost sheep. You are bringing the ~~way~~ GOOD NEWS into places where it has not been known before. You may not know which soul you will help, but you can leave all ~~plans~~ RESULTS to God. Just go with Him in His eternal quest for souls.

Prayer for the Day

I pray that I may follow God in His eternal quest for souls. I pray that I MAY offer God my helping hand.

122

APRIL 29 -- A. A. Thought for the Day

The A. A. programme is one of faith, hope and charity. It's a programme of hope because when a new member comes into A. A., the first thing he gets is hope. He hears the older members tell how they have been through the same kind of hell that he has and how they have found the way out through A. A. And this gives him hope that if they could do it, he can do it. Is hope still strong in me?

Meditation for the Day

The rule of God's kingdom is perfect order, perfect harmony, perfect supply, perfect love, perfect honesty, perfect obedience. There is no discord in God's Kingdon, only some things still unconquered in God's children. The difficulties of life are caused by disharmony in the individual man or woman. People lack power because they lack harmony with God and with each other. They think that God fails because power is not manifested in their lives. God does not fail. People fail because they are out of harmony with Him.

Prayer for the Day

I pray that I may be in harmony with God and with my fellow men. I pray that this harmony will result in strength and success.

123

APRIL 30 -- A. A. Thought for the Day

The A. A. programme is one of faith because we find that we must have faith in a Power greater than ourselves if we are going to get sober. We're helpless before alcohol, but when we turn our drink problem over to God and have faith that He can give us all the strength we need, then we have the drink problem licked. Faith in that Divine Principle in the universe which we call God is the essential part of the A. A. programme. Is faith still strong in me?

Meditation for the Day

Every person is a child of God and as such is full of promise of spiritual growth. When a person is young, he is like the spring-time of the year. The full time of the fruit is not yet, but there is promise of the blossom. There is a spark of the Divine in every one of us. Each has some of God's spirit which can be developed by spiritual exercise. Know that your life is full of glad promise. Such blessings can be yours, such joys, such wonders, as long as you develop in the sunshine of God's love.

Prayer for the Day

I pray that I may develop the Divine spark within me. I pray that by so doing I may fulfill the promise of a more abundant life.

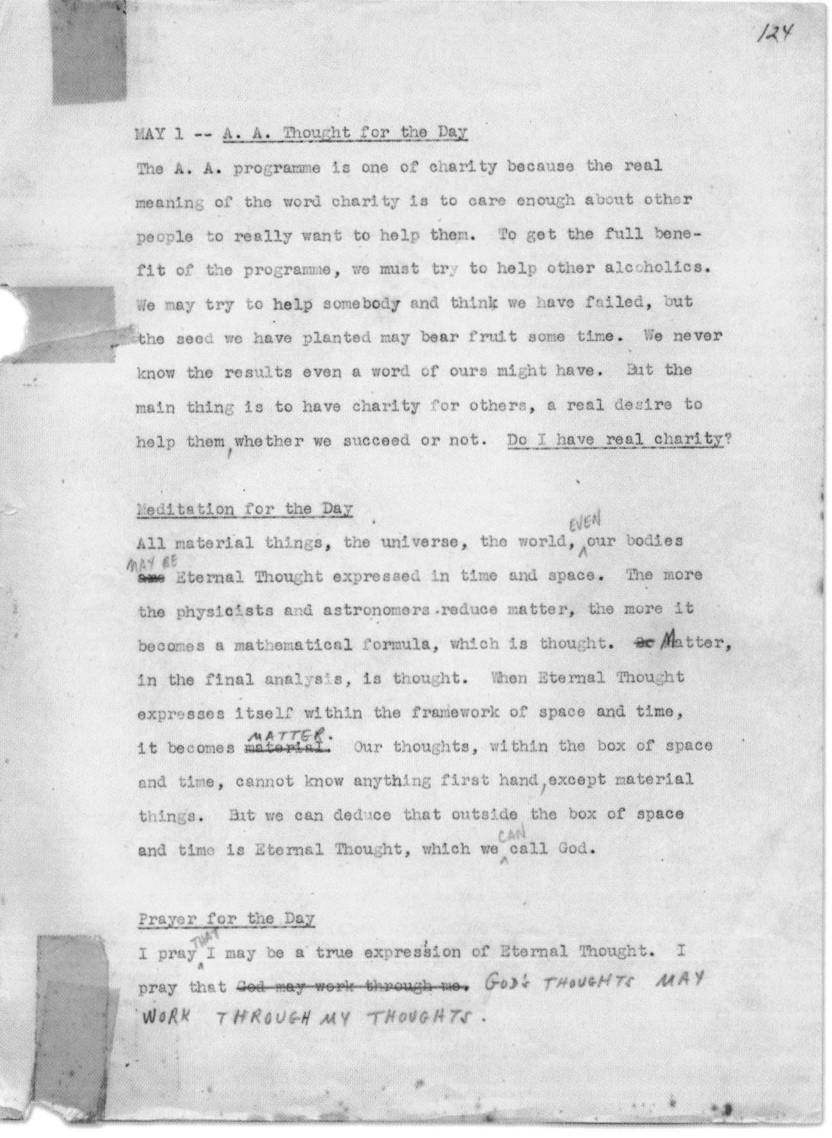

124

MAY 1 -- A. A. Thought for the Day

The A. A. programme is one of charity because the real meaning of the word charity is to care enough about other people to really want to help them. To get the full benefit of the programme, we must try to help other alcoholics. We may try to help somebody and think we have failed, but the seed we have planted may bear fruit some time. We never know the results even a word of ours might have. But the main thing is to have charity for others, a real desire to help them, whether we succeed or not. Do I have real charity?

Meditation for the Day

All material things, the universe, the world, EVEN our bodies ~~are~~ MAY BE Eternal Thought expressed in time and space. The more the physicists and astronomers reduce matter, the more it becomes a mathematical formula, which is thought. ~~So~~ Matter, in the final analysis, is thought. When Eternal Thought expresses itself within the framework of space and time, it becomes ~~material.~~ MATTER. Our thoughts, within the box of space and time, cannot know anything first hand, except material things. But we can deduce that outside the box of space and time is Eternal Thought, which we CAN call God.

Prayer for the Day

I pray THAT I may be a true expression of Eternal Thought. I pray that ~~God may work through me.~~ GOD'S THOUGHTS MAY WORK THROUGH MY THOUGHTS.

125

MAY 2 -- <u>A. A. Thought for the Day</u>

In A. A., we often hear the slogan: Easy does it. Alcoholics always do everything to excess. They drink too much. They worry too much. They have too many resentments. They hurt themselves physically and mentally by too much of everything. So when they come into A. A., they have to learn to take it easy. None of us knows how much longer he has to live. It's probable that we wouldn't have lived very long if we had continued to drink the way we used to. By stopping drinking, we have increased our chances of living for a while longer. <u>Have I learned to take it easy</u>?

<u>Meditation for the Day</u>

You must be, before you can do. To accomplish much, be much. In all cases, the doing must be the expression of the being. It is foolish to think that we can accomplish much in personal relationships, without first preparing ourselves by being honest, pure, unselfish and loving. We must choose the good and keep choosing it, before we are ready to be used by God to accomplish anything worth while. We will not be given the opportunities until we are ready for them. Quiet times of communion with the Higher Power are good preparation for creative action.

<u>Prayer for the Day</u>

I pray that I may constantly prepare myself for better things to come. I pray that I may only have opportunities when I am ready for them.

126

MAY 3 -- <u>A. A. Thought for the Day</u>

A. A. teaches us to take it easy. We learn how to relax, to stop worrying about the past or the future, to give up our resentments and hates and tempers, to stop being critical of people and to try to help them instead. That's what "easy does it" means. So in the time that's left to me to live, I'm going to try to take it easy, to relax and not to worry, to try to be helpful to my fellow men and to trust God. <u>For what's left of my life, is my motto going to be: Easy does it</u>?

<u>Meditation for the Day</u>

I must overcome myself before I can TRULY forgive other people for injuries done to me. The self in me cannot forgive injuries. The very thought of wrongs means that my self is in the foreground. Since the self cannot forgive, I must overcome my selfishness. I must cease trying to forgive those who fretted and wronged me. It is a mistake for me even to think about those ~~things~~ INJURIES. I must aim at overcoming my self in my daily life and then I will find there is nothing in me that remembers injury, because the only thing injured, my selfishness, is gone.

<u>Prayer for the Day</u>

I pray that I may hold no resentments. I pray that my mind may be washed clean of all past hates and fears.

127

MAY 4 -- A. A. Thought for the Day

When I was drinking, I always tried to build myself up. I used to tell tall stories about myself. I told them so often that I half believe some of them now, even though I know they aren't true. I used to hang around low-brow barrooms so I could feel superior to the other customers. The reason I always tried to build myself up was that I knew deep down in my heart that I really didn't amount to anything. It was a kind of defense against my feeling of inferiority. Do I still build myself up?

Meditation for the Day

God thought about the universe and brought it into being. His thought brought me into being. I must think God's thoughts after Him. ~~I cannot live in a vacuum.~~ I must OFTEN keep my mind occupied with ~~the~~ thoughts ABOUT ~~of~~ God and meditate on the way that He wants me to live. I must train my mind constantly in quiet times of communion with God. It is the work of a lifetime to develop to full stature spiritually. ~~and~~ This is what I am here on earth for. It GIVES MEANING TO ~~is the meaning of the universe.~~ MY LIFE.

Prayer for the Day

I pray that I may think God's thoughts after Him. I pray that I may live as He wants me to live.

128

MAY 5 -- A. A. Thought for the Day

I had to show off and boast so that people would think I amounted to something, when of course both they and I knew that I really didn't amount to anything. I didn't fool anybody. Although I've been sober for quite a while, the old habit of building myself up is still with me. I still have a tendency to think too well of myself, and to pretend to be more than I really am. Am I always in danger of getting a swelled head, just because I'm sober?

Meditation for the Day

I cannot ascertain the spiritual by my intellect. I can only do it by my own FAITH AND spiritual faculties~~, and faith.~~ I must think of God MORE with my heart THAN WITH ~~and not~~ my head. I CAN ~~should~~ breathe in God's very spirit in THE LIFE AROUND ME. ~~pure air and fervent desire.~~ I CAN ~~must~~ keep my eyes TURNED TOWARD THE GOOD THINGS IN THE WORLD. ~~upon God.~~ I am shut up in a box of space and time, but I can open a window in that box by faith. I can empty my mind of all THE LIMITATIONS OF ~~that limits me to~~ material things. I CAN SENSE THE ETERNAL.

Prayer for the Day

I pray that whatever is good I may have. I pray that I may leave TO GOD the choice of what good ~~I will get to God.~~ WILL COME TO ME.

MAY 6 -- A. A. Thought for the Day

I've noticed that the ones ~~that~~ WHO do the most for A. A. are not in the habit of boasting about it. The danger of building myself up too much is that, if I do, I'm in danger of having a fall. That pattern of thought goes with drinking. If ONE SIDE OF a boat gets too far up out of the water, it's liable to tip over. Building myself up and drinking go together. One leads to another. So if I'm going to stay sober, I've got to keep small. Have I got the right perspective OF MYSELF?

Meditation for the Day

The way sometimes seems long and weary. So many people today are weary. The weariness of men must be often shared ~~by me~~ BY OTHERS. The weary and the heavy-laden, when they come to me, ~~must~~ SHOULD BE HELPED TO find the rest that I have found. ~~in God.~~ There is only one SURE cure for world-weariness and that is ~~union with God.~~ TURNING TO SPIRITUAL THINGS. In order to help bring about ~~the union~~ THE TURNING of the weary world ~~with~~ TO God, I must dare to suffer, dare to conquer selfishness IN MYSELF AND dare to be filled with ~~sublime~~ SPIRITUAL PEACE, ~~audacity,~~ in the face of all the weariness of the world.

Prayer for the Day

I pray that I may be a help to discouraged people. I pray that I may have the ~~sublime audacity to~~ COURAGE TO HELP TO bring about what the weary world ~~thinks is impossible.~~ NEEDS, BUT DOES NOT KNOW HOW TO GET.

MAY 7 -- A. A. Thought for the Day

It's very important to keep in a grateful frame of mind, if we want to stay sober. We should be grateful that we're living in a day and age when an alcoholic isn't treated as he often used to be treated before Alcoholics Anonymous was started. In the old days, every town had its town drunk who was regarded with scorn and ridicule by the rest of the townspeople. We have come into A. A. and found all the sympathy, understanding and fellowship that we could ask for. There's no other group like A. A. in the world. Am I grateful?

Meditation for the Day

God takes man's efforts for good and blesses them. God needs man's effort. Man needs God's blessing. Together, they mean spiritual success. Man's effort is necessary. He cannot lean on his oars and drift with the tide. He must often direct his efforts against the tide of materialism around him. When difficulties come, man's effort is needed to surmount them. ~~God's blessing is also necessary.~~ BUT God ~~must~~ directs man's efforts into the right channel and God's ~~strength~~ POWER is necessary to help man choose the right.

Prayer for the Day

I pray that I may choose the right. I pray that I may have God's blessing and direction in all ~~that I do.~~ MY EFFORTS FOR GOOD.

131

MAY 8 -- A. A. Thought for the Day

I'm grateful that I found a programme in A. A. that could keep me sober. I'm grateful that A. A. has shown me the way ~~to return~~ to faith in a Higher Power, because the renewing of that faith has changed my way of life. And I've found a happiness and contentment that I had forgotten existed, by simply believing in God and trying to live the kind of a life THAT I know He wants me to live. As long as I stay grateful, I'll stay sober. Am I in a grateful frame of mind?

Meditation for the Day

God can work through you better when you are not hurrying. Go very slowly, very quietly, from one duty to the next, taking time to rest and pray between. Do not be too busy. Take everything in order. Venture often into the rest of God and you will find peace. All work that results from resting with God is good work. Claim the power to work miracles in human lives. Know that you can do ~~all~~ MANY things through the Higher Power. Know that you can do ~~all~~ GOOD things through God who rests you and gives you strength. Partake regularly of ~~the~~ rest ~~of God.~~ AND PRAYER.

Prayer for the Day

I pray that I may not be in too much of a hurry. I pray that I may take time out often to rest with God.

132

MAY 9 -- A. A. Thought for the Day

We alcoholics used so little self-control when we were drinking, we were so absolutely selfish, that it does us good to give up something once in a while. Using self-discipline and denying ourselves a few things is good for us. At first, giving up liquor is a plenty big enough job for all of us, even with God's help. But later on, we can practice self-discipline in other ways and keep a firm grip on ~~ourselves~~ OUR MINDS so that we don't start any wishful thinking. If we day-dream TOO MUCH, we'll be in danger of slipping. Am I practicing ENOUGH self-discipline?

Meditation for the Day

In material things, you must rely on your own wisdom AND THAT OF OTHERS. In spiritual things, you cannot rely SO MUCH on your own wisdom~~, you must rely~~ AS on God's guidance. In dealing with personalities, it is a mistake to step out TOO MUCH on your own. You must TRY TO be guided by God in all human relationships. You cannot accomplish much OF VALUE IN DEALING WITH PEOPLE ~~in the personal realm~~ until God knows you are ready. You ALONE do not have the power or wisdom to put things right between people. You must rely on God to help you ~~to do so.~~ IN THESE VITAL MATTERS.

Prayer for the Day

I pray that I may rely on God ~~to help me to help others.~~ IN DEALING WITH PEOPLE'S PROBLEMS. I pray that I may TRY TO follow His guidance in all personal ~~problems.~~ RELATIONSHIPS.

133

MAY 10 -- A. A. Thought for the Day

One thing that keeps me sober is a feeling of loyalty to the other members of the group. I know I'd be letting them down if I ever took a drink. When I was drinking, I wasn't loyal to anybody. I should have been loyal to my family, but I wasn't. I let them down by my drinking. When I came into A. A., I found a group of people who were not only helping each other to stay sober, but WHO were loyal to each other by staying sober themselves. Am I loyal to my group?

Meditation for the Day

Calmness is constructive of good. Agitation is destructive of good. I should not rush into action. I should first "be still and know that He is God". Then I should act only as ~~He tells~~ GOD DIRECTS me, through my conscience. Only trust, perfect trust in God, can keep me calm when all around me are agitated. Calmness is trust in action. I should seek all things ~~that~~ WHICH can help me to cultivate calmness. To attain material things, the world learns to attain speed. To attain spiritual things, I have to learn to attain a state of calm.

Prayer for the Day

I pray that I may learn how to have inner peace. I pray that I may be calm, so that God can work through me.

134

MAY 11 -- A. A. Thought for the Day

We can depend on those members of any group who have gone all-out for the programme. They come to meetings. They work with other alcoholics. We don't have to worry about their slipping. They're loyal members of the group. I'm trying to be a loyal member of the group. When I'm tempted to take a drink, I'll tell myself that if I did I'd be letting down the other members, who are the best friends I have. Am I going to let them down, if I can help it?

Meditation for the Day

Wherever there is true friendship and love between people, ~~God~~ GOD'S SPIRIT is always there as the Divine Third. In all human relationships, the Divine Spirit is what brings them together. When a life is changed through the channel of another person, it is God the Divine Third who always makes the change, using the ~~other~~ person as a means. The moving power behind ALL spiritual things, all ~~personality~~ PERSONAL relationships between people is God, the Divine Third, who is always there. No relationships between persons can be ENTIRELY right without ~~God's~~ THE PRESENCE OF GOD'S SPIRIT.

Prayer for the Day

I pray that I may be used as a channel by God's spirit. I pray that I may feel that the Divine Third is always there, TO HELP ME.

135

MAY 12 -- A. A. Thought for the Day

When we come into A. A., looking for a way out of drinking, we really need a lot more than that. We need fellowship. We need to get the things that are troubling us out into the open. We need a new outlet for our energies and we need a new strength beyond ourselves that will help us to face life instead of running away from it. In A. A., we find these things that we need. Have I found the things that I need?

Meditation for the Day

Turn out all thoughts of doubt and fear and resentment. Never tolerate them [IF YOU CAN HELP IT.] ~~for one minute.~~ Bar the windows and doors of your mind against them, as you would bar your home against a thief who would steal in to take away your treasures. What greater treasures can you have then faith and courage and love? All these are stolen from you by doubt and fear and resentment. Face each day with peace and [HOPE.] ~~joy.~~ They are the results of true faith in God. Faith ~~also~~ gives you a feeling of protection and safety that you can get in no other way.

Prayer for the Day

I pray that I may ~~not~~ feel protected and safe [BUT NOT] only when I am in the harbor. I pray that I may [HAVE] ~~sense~~ protection and safety even in the midst of [THE] storms~~.~~ [OF LIFE.]

136

MAY 13 -- A. A. Thought for the Day

In A. A., we find fellowship and release and strength. And having found these things, the real reasons for our drinking are taken away. Then drinking, which was a symptom of underlying troubles, has no more justification in our minds. We no longer need to fight against drink. Drink just naturally leaves us. At first, we are sorry that we can't drink, but we get so that we are glad that we don't have to drink. Am I glad that I don't have to drink?

Meditation for the Day

[TRY] Never [TO] judge. The [MIND] ~~heart~~ of mankind is so delicate, so complex, that only its Maker can know it [WHOLLY.] Each [MIND] ~~heart~~ is so different, actuated by such different motives, controlled by such different circumstances, influenced by such different sufferings. You cannot know all the influences that have gone to make up a personality. Therefore it is impossible for you to [WHOLLY] judge that personality. But God knows that person wholly and He can change it. Leave to God ~~alone~~ the unravelling of the puzzles of personality. And leave [IT] to God [TO TEACH YOU] ~~the teaching of~~ the proper understanding.

Prayer for the Day

I pray that I may [NOT JUDGE MY FELLOW MEN.] ~~bring each personality to God, its Maker, and leave it with Him.~~ I pray that I may be [CERTAIN] ~~secure in the certainty~~ that God can set right what is wrong in ~~each~~ [EVERY] ~~person.~~ [PERSONALITY.]

137

MAY 14 -- <u>A. A. Thought for the Day</u>

Having got over drinking, we have only just begun to enjoy the benefits of A. A. We find new friends, so that we are no longer lonely. We find new relationships with our families, so that we are happy at home. We find release from our troubles and worries through a new way of looking at things. We find an outlet for our energies in helping other people. <u>Am I enjoying these benefits of A. A.</u>?

<u>Meditation for the Day</u>

~~In you, there is God.~~ The kingdom of heaven is ~~also~~ within YOU. God sees, as no man can see, what is within you. He sees you growing more and more like Himself. That is your reason for existence, to grow more and more like God, to develop more and more the spirit of God ~~in~~ WITHIN you. You can often see in your fellow man those qualities and aspirations ~~that~~ WHICH you yourself possess. So also can God recognize His own spirit in you. Your motives and aspirations can only be understood by those who have attained the same spiritual level AS YOU HAVE.

<u>Prayer for the Day</u>

I pray that I may not expect complete understanding from others. I pray that I may only expect ~~it~~ THIS from God, as I TRY TO grow more like Him.

138

MAY 15 -- <u>A. A. Thought for the Day</u>

In A. A., we find a new strength and peace from the realization that there must be a Power greater than ourselves which is running the universe and which is on our side when we live ~~the~~ A good life. So the A. A. programme really never ends. You begin by overcoming drink and you go on from there to many new opportunities for happiness and usefulness. <u>Am I really enjoying the FULL benefits of A. A.?</u>

<u>Meditation for the Day</u>

"Seek ye first the Kingdom of God and His righteousness and all these things shall be added unto you". WE SHOULD NOT ~~Jesus said not to~~ seek material things first, but ~~to~~ seek spiritual things first and material things will come to ~~you, as a result of your being right spiritually.~~ US, AS WE HONESTLY WORK FOR THEM. Many people seek material things first and think they can then grow into knowledge of spiritual things. YOU CANNOT SERVE GOD AND MAMMON AT THE SAME TIME. ~~But~~ The first requisites of an abundant life are the spiritual things; honesty, purity, unselfishness and love. Until you have these QUALITIES, QUANTITIES OF material things are of little REAL use to you.

<u>Prayer for the Day</u>

I pray that I may put much effort into acquiring spiritual things. I pray that I may ~~trust God in everything.~~ NOT EXPECT GOOD THINGS UNTIL I AM RIGHT SPIRITUALLY.

MAY 16 -- <u>A. A. Thought for the Day</u>

In the story of the Good Samaritan, the wayfarer fell among robbers and was left lying in the gutter, half dead. And a priest and a Levite both passed by on the other side of the road. But the Good Samaritan was moved with compassion and came to him and bound up his wounds and brought him to an inn and took care of him. ~~Would~~ DO I treat a fellow alcoholic like the PRIEST AND THE LEVITE OR LIKE THE Good Samaritan?

<u>Meditation for the Day</u>

Never weary in prayer. When one day you see how ~~marvelously~~ UNEXPECTEDLY your prayer has been answered, then you will deeply regret that you have prayed so little. Prayer changes ~~all~~ things, FOR YOU. ~~It re-creates.~~ ~~It is irresistible.~~ ~~Pray without ceasing~~ PRACTICE PRAYING until your trust in God has become ~~rock-like.~~ STRONG. And then pray on, because it has become so much a habit that you NEED IT DAILY. ~~cannot resist it.~~ ~~Always~~ Keep praying until prayer seems to become ~~praise.~~ COMMUNION WITH GOD. That is the note on which true TIMES OF prayer should end.

<u>Prayer for the Day</u>

I pray that ~~my attitude toward men will be determined by my attitude toward God.~~ I MAY FORM THE HABIT OF DAILY PRAYER. I pray that ~~my attitude toward God may be one of prayer and praise.~~ I MAY FIND THE STRENGTH I NEED, AS A RESULT OF THIS COMMUNION.

MAY 17 -- <u>A. A. Thought for the Day</u>

A lot of well-meaning people treat an alcoholic like the priest and the Levite. They pass by on the other side by scorning him and telling him what a low person he is, with no will-power. Whereas, he really has fallen for alcohol, in the same way as the man in the story fell among robbers. And the member of A. A. who is working with others is like the Good Samaritan. <u>Am I moved with compassion and do I go to another alcoholic and take care of him?</u>

<u>Meditation for the Day</u>

I must constantly live in preparation for something better to come. All of life is a preparation for something better. I must anticipate the morning to come. ~~and~~ I MUST feel, in the night of sorrow, that understanding joy that tells of confident expectation of better things to come. "Sorrow may endure for a night, but joy cometh in the morning". Know that God has something better in store for you, as long as you are making yourself ready for it. ~~Even~~ ALL your existence in this world is a training for a better life to come.

<u>Prayer for the Day</u>

I pray that, when this life is over, I will return to an eternal, spaceless life with God. I pray that I may make this life a preparation for ~~something~~ A better LIFE to come.

141

MAY 18 -- A. A. Thought for the Day

We're in A. A. for two main reasons, to keep sober ourselves and to help others to keep sober. It's a well known fact that helping others is a big part of keeping sober yourself. It's also been proved that it's very hard to keep sober all by yourself. A lot of people have tried it and failed. They come to a few A. A. meetings and then stay sober alone for a few months, but USUALLY ~~then~~ they EVENTUALLY ~~usually~~ get drunk. Do I know that I can't ~~do it alone?~~ STAY SOBER SUCCESSFULLY ALONE?

Meditation for the Day

~~With faith,~~ Look BY FAITH into that place beyond space or time where God dwells and whence you came and to which you shall EVENTUALLY return. "Look unto ~~me~~ HIM and be ~~ye~~ saved". To look beyond material things is within the power of everyone's imagination. Faith's look saves you from despair. Faith's look saves you from worry and care. Faith's look brings a peace beyond all understanding. Faith's look brings YOU all the strength you need. ~~to overcome sin and temptation.~~ Faith's look gives you a new and vital power and a wonderful peace and serenity.

Prayer for the Day

I pray that ~~I may wear the world as a loose garment.~~ I MAY HAVE FAITH'S LOOK. I pray that by faith I may look BEYOND THE NOW to eternal life.

142

MAY 19 -- A. A. Thought for the Day

Fellowship is a BIG part of staying sober. The doctors call it group therapy. We never go to an A. A. meeting without taking something out of it. Sometimes we don't feel like going to a meeting and we think of excuses for not going. But we usually end up by going anyway. And we always get ~~a~~ SOME lift out of every meeting. Meetings are part of keeping sober. AND ~~We~~ we get more out of a meeting if we TRY TO contribute something to it. Am I contributing my share AT MEETINGS?

Meditation for the Day

"He brought me up out of a horrible pit, out of the miry clay, and set my feet upon a rock and established my goings". The first part: "He brought me up out of a horrible pit" means that by turning to God and putting my problems in His hands, I am able to overcome my sins and temptations. "He set my feet upon a rock" means that when I trust God in all things, I have TRUE security. "He established my goings" means that if I honestly try to live the way God wants me to live, I will have God's guidance, IN MY DAILY LIVING.

Prayer for the Day

I pray that ~~I may be secure from sin and temptation.~~ MY FEET MAY BE SET UPON A ROCK. I pray that I may rely on ~~God's guidance always.~~ GOD TO GUIDE MY COMINGS AND GOINGS.

MAY 20 -- A. A. Thought for the Day

If we get up in a meeting and tell something about ourselves in order to help the other fellow, we feel a whole lot better. It's the old law of the more you give, the more you get. Witnessing and confession are part of keeping sober. You never know when you may help somebody. Helping others is ONE OF the best ways to stay sober yourself. And the satisfaction you get out of helping a fellow human being is one of the finest experiences you can have. Am I helping others?

Meditation for the Day

Without God, no real victory is ever won. All the military victories of great conquerors have passed into history. The world might be better off without military conquerors. The real victories are won in the spiritual realm. "HE THAT CONQUERS HIMSELF IS GREATER THAN HE WHO CONQUERS A CITY." The real victories are victories over sin and temptation, leading to ~~the~~ A victorious ~~life, the~~ AND abundant life. ~~of human brotherhood under the fathership of God.~~ THEREFORE Keep a brave and trusting heart. Face all your difficulties in the spirit of conquest. Remember that where God is, there is the true victory.

Prayer for the Day

I pray that the forces of evil IN MY LIFE will flee ~~at~~ BEFORE God's presence. I pray that with God I ~~may~~ WILL win the ~~only~~ real victory OVER MYSELF.

MAY 21 -- A. A. Thought for the Day

One of the finest things about A. A. is the sharing. Sharing is a wonderful thing because the more you share the more you have. In our old drinking days, we didn't do much sharing. We used to keep things to ourselves, partly because we were ashamed, but mostly because we were selfish. And we were very lonely, because we did't share. When we came into A. A., the first thing we found was sharing. We heard other alcoholics frankly sharing their experiences with hospitals, jails, and all the usual mess that goes with drinking. Am I sharing?

Meditation for the Day

Character is developed by the daily discipline of ~~daily~~ duties done. Be obedient to the heavenly vision AND Take the straight ~~and narrow~~ way. Do not fall into the error of calling Lord, Lord, and doing not the things that should be done. ~~The~~ A man NEEDS A ~~who wants the~~ life of prayer and meditation BUT HE must still do his work in the busy ways of life. ~~And~~ The busy man is ~~bidden~~ WISE to rest and wait patiently for God's guidance. If you are obedient to the heavenly vision, you can be at peace. ~~in the busy ways of life.~~

Prayer for the Day

I pray that I may be obedient to the heavenly vision. I pray that if I fall, I ~~may~~ WILL pick myself up ~~again~~ and go on.

145

MAY 22 -- A. A. Thought for the Day

What impresses us most at an A. A. meeting is the willingness to share, without holding anything back. And pretty soon we find ourselves sharing also. We start telling our own experiences and by so doing we help the other fellow. And when we've got these things off our chest, we feel a lot better. It does us a lot of good to share with some other poor unfortunate PERSON who's in the same box that we were in. And the more we share with him, the more we have left for ourselves. Do I know that the more I share, the better chance I'll have to stay sober?

Meditation for the Day

Constantly claim God's strength. Once convinced of the right of a course of action, once REASONABLY sure of God's guidance, claim that strength now. You can claim all the strength you need to meet any situation. You can claim a new supply, when your own supply is exhausted. You have a right to claim it, and you should use your right. A beggar supplicates, a son appropriates. When you supplicate, you are often kept waiting, but when you appropriate God's strength in a good cause, you have it at once.

Prayer for the Day

I pray that I may claim God's strength whenever I need it. I pray that I may try to live as a ~~son~~ CHILD of God.

146

MAY 23 -- A. A. Thought for the Day

The twelfth step of A. A., working with others, can be subdivided into five steps, five words beginning with the letter C, confidence, confession, conviction, conversion and continuance. The first thing in trying to help another alcoholic is to get his confidence. We do this by telling HIM our own experiences with drinking, so that he sees that we know what we're talking about. If we share our experiences frankly, he will know that we are sincerely trying to help him. He will realize that he's not alone and that others have had experiences as bad or worse than his. This gives him confidence that he can be helped. Do I care enough about another alcoholic to get his confidence?

Meditation for the Day

I fail not so much when tragedy happens as I did before the happening, by all the little things I might have done, but did not do. I must PREPARE FOR THE FUTURE BY DOING ~~learn to do~~ the right thing at the right time NOW. If a thing should be done, I should deal with that thing today and get it righted with God, before I allow myself to undertake any new duty. I should look upon myself as performing God's errands and then coming back to Him, to tell Him in quiet COMMUNION that the message has been delivered or the task done.

Prayer for the Day

I pray that I may SEEK ~~take~~ no credit for the result of ~~the good that I may do.~~ WHAT I DO. I pray that I may leave the outcome OF MY ACTIONS to God.

147

MAY 24 -- <u>A. A. Thought for the Day</u>

In twelfth step work, the second thing is confession. By frankly sharing with the prospect, we get him talking about his own experiences. He will open up and confess things to us that he hasn't been able to tell to other people. And he feels better when this confession has got these things off his chest. It's a great load off his mind to get these things out into the open. It's the things that are kept hidden that weigh on the mind. He feels a sense of release and freedom when he has opened up his heart to us. <u>Do I care enough about another alcoholic to help him to make a a confession?</u>

<u>Meditation for the Day</u>

~~I do not help enough.~~ I SHOULD ~~must~~ help OTHERS all I can. Every troubled soul that God puts in my path is THE one for me to help. As I SINCERELY TRY TO help, a supply of strength will flow into me from God, ~~and~~ My circle of helpfulness will widen more and more. God hands out the spiritual food to me and I pass it on TO OTHERS. I must NEVER ~~not~~ say: THAT "I have only enough STRENGTH for my own need". The more I give away, the more I will keep. That which I keep TO MYSELF I WILL lose, IN THE END.

<u>Prayer for the Day</u>

I pray that I may HAVE A SINCERE WILLINGNESS TO GIVE. ~~get a feeling of bounteous giving into my being.~~ I pray that I may ~~accept the strength which God gives without limit.~~ NOT HOLD BACK THE STRENGTH I HAVE RECEIVED FOR MYSELF ALONE.

198

MAY 25 -- <u>A. A. Thought for the Day</u>

In twelfth step work, the third thing is conviction. The prospect must be convinced that he honestly wants to stop drinking. He must see and admit that HIS LIFE IS UNMANAGEABLE. ~~he's definitely an alcoholic~~. He must face the fact that he must ~~spend the rest of his life without liquor~~ DO SOMETHING ABOUT HIS DRINKING. He must be absolutely honest with himself and face himself as he really is. He must be convinced that he must give up drinking ~~for good~~ and he must see that his whole life depends on this conviction. <u>Do I care enough about another alcoholic to help him reach this conviction?</u>

<u>Meditation for the Day</u>

There is no limit to what you can accomplish in HELPING OTHERS. ~~human relationships.~~ Keep that thought always. Never relinquish any ~~spiritual~~ work or give up the thought of any ~~spiritual~~ accomplishment because it seems beyond your power. GOD WILL HELP YOU IN ALL GOOD WORK. Only give it up if you FEEL ~~see~~ that it's not God's will for you. IN HELPING OTHERS, Think of the tiny seed under the ~~snow and~~ the dark, hard ground. THERE IS No certainty ~~even~~ that when it has forced its way up to the surface that sunlight and warmth will greet it. Often a ~~spiritual~~ task seems beyond your power, but there is no limit to what you can accomplish, WITH GOD'S HELP.

<u>Prayer for the Day</u>

I pray that I may never BECOME ~~be~~ discouraged IN HELPING OTHERS. I pray that I may always RELY ~~call~~ on the power of God to help me.

149

MAY 26 -- <u>A. A. Thought for the Day</u>

In twelfth step work, the fourth thing is conversion. Conversion means change. The prospect must learn to change his way of thinking. Up till now, everything he's done has been connected with drinking. Now he must face a new kind of life, without liquor. He must see and admit that he cannot overcome drinking by his own will power, so he must turn to a Higher Power for help. He must start each day by asking this Higher Power for the strength to stay sober. This conversion to belief in a Higher Power comes gradually, as he tries it and finds that it works. <u>Do I care enough about another alcoholic to help him to make this conversion?</u>

<u>Meditation for the Day</u>

Discipline OF YOURSELF is absolutely necessary, before the power of God is given to you. When you see others manifesting the power of God, you PROBABLY have not seen the discipline that went before. THEY MADE THEMSELVES READY. All your life is a preparation for ~~something~~ MORE good to be accomplished when God knows that you are ready for it. So keep discipling yourself in the spiritual life every day. ~~You may feel that you have learned~~ LEARN so much of the spiritual LAWS that your life cannot again be a failure. ~~That is right, but~~ Others ~~have to~~ WILL see the outward manifestation OF THE INWARD DISCIPLINE in your daily living. ~~before they can see God's power at work in you.~~

<u>Prayer for the Day</u>

I pray that I may manifest God's power in my daily living. I pray that I may ~~be disciplined.~~ DISCIPLINE MYSELF SO AS TO BE READY TO MEET EVERY OPPORTUNITY.

150

MAY 27 -- <u>A. A. Thought for the Day</u>

In twelfth step work, the fifth thing is continuance. Continuance means our staying with the prospect after he has started on the new way of living. We must stick with him and not let him down. We must encourage him to go to meetings regularly for fellowship and help. He will learn that keeping sober is a lot easier in the fellowship of others who are trying to do the same thing. We must continue to help him, by going to see him regularly or telephoning him or writing him, so that he doesn't get out of touch with A. A. CONTINUANCE MEANS GOOD SPONSORSHIP. <u>Do I care enough about another alcoholic to continue with him as long as necessary?</u>

<u>Meditation for the Day</u>

Every strong and beautiful flower must have a strong root in the ground. It must send a root down, so that it may be rooted and grounded, while at the same time it sends a shoot up to be the flower that shall gladden the world. Both growths are necessary. Without the strong root, it would soon wither. The higher the growth upward, the deeper must be the rooting. My life cannot flower into ~~spiritual beauty and~~ success and helpfulness, unless it is rooted in a strong faith ~~in God~~, or unless it feels deeply secure in the goodness and purpose of the universe.

<u>Prayer for the Day</u>

I pray that my life may be deeply rooted in faith. I pray that I may feel deeply secure.

151

MAY 28 -- A. A. Thought for the Day

In A. A., we learn that since we are alcoholics we can be uniquely useful people. That is, we can help another alcoholic when perhaps somebody who ~~had~~ HAS not had our experience with drinking could not help him. That makes us uniquely useful. The A. A.'s are a ~~great bunch~~ FINE GROUP of people because they have taken their own greatest defeat and failure and sickness and used it as a means of helping others. We who have been through the mill are the ones who can best help other alcoholics. Do I believe that I can be uniquely useful?

Meditation for the Day

I ~~must~~ SHOULD TRY TO practice the presence of God. I ~~must~~ CAN feel that He is with me and near me, protecting and strengthening me always. In spite of every difficulty, every trial, every failure, the presence of God suffices. Just ~~to be with God,~~ to believe that He is ~~beside~~ NEAR me, brings strength and peace. ~~I must keep praying for more love for God and for my fellow man.~~ ~~I must~~ I SHOULD TRY TO live ~~constantly~~ as though God were beside me. I cannot see Him because I was not made with the ability to see Him, ELSE THERE WERE NO ROOM FOR FAITH. But I can feel His spirit ~~within~~ WITH me. ~~when I practice His presence.~~

Prayer for the Day

I pray that I may TRY TO practice the presence of God. I pray that by doing so, I may ~~find strength and peace.~~ NEVER FEEL ALONE OR HELPLESS AGAIN.

152

MAY 29 -- A. A. Thought for the Day

We who have learned to put our drink problem in God's hands, can help others to do so. We can be used as a connection between an alcoholic's need and God's supply of strength. We in Alcoholics Anonymous can be uniquely useful, just because we have the misfortune or fortune to be alcoholics ourselves. Do I want to be a uniquely useful person? ~~by~~ WILL I ~~using~~ USE my own greatest defeat and failure and sickness as a weapon to help others?

Meditation for the Day

I WILL TRY TO HELP OTHERS. I WILL TRY NOT TO LET A DAY PASS WITHOUT REACHING OUT AN ARM OF LOVE TO SOMEONE. EACH DAY I WILL TRY TO DO SOMETHING TO LIFT ANOTHER HUMAN BEING OUT OF THE SEA OF DISCOURAGEMENT INTO WHICH HE OR SHE HAS FALLEN. MY HELPING HAND IS NEEDED TO RAISE THE HELPLESS TO COURAGE, TO STRENGTH, TO FAITH, TO HEALTH. IN MY OWN GRATITUDE, I WILL TURN AND HELP ANOTHER ALCOHOLIC WITH THE BURDEN THAT IS PRESSING TO HEAVILY UPON HIM.

Prayer for the Day

I PRAY THAT I MAY BE USED BY GOD TO LIGHTEN MANY BURDENS. I PRAY THAT MANY SOULS MAY BE HELPED THROUGH MY EFFORTS.

152

MAY 30 -- <u>A. A. Thought for the Day</u>

"I am part of A. A., one among many, but I am one. I need the A. A. principles for the development of the buried life within me. A. A. may be human in its organization, but it is Divine in its purpose. The purpose is to point me toward God AND A BETTER LIFE. Participating in the privileges of the movement, I shall share in the responsibilities, taking it upon myself to carry my fair share of the load, not grudgingly, but joyfully. To the extent that I fail in my responsibilities, A. A. fails. To the extent that I succeed, A. A. succeeds." Do I accept this as my A. A. credo?

<u>Meditation for the Day</u> "PRAISE THE LORD".

~~"Our Lord, we praise thee".~~ What does praising God mean? It means being grateful for all the wonderful things in the universe and FOR all the blessings in your life. So praise God by being grateful and humble. Praise OF THIS KIND has more power to vanquish evil than has resignation or obedience. The truly humble and grateful man, who is always praising God, is not tempted to do wrong. ~~So look up to God and praise Him.~~ You will have ~~a thrill of joy and~~ a feeling of security, because you know that fundamentally all is well. ~~It's a wonderful world when you praise God.~~ SO LOOK UP TO GOD AND PRAISE HIM.

<u>Prayer for the Day</u>

I pray that I may be grateful for all my blessings. I pray that I may be humble because I KNOW THAT I do not deserve them.

154

MAY 31 -- <u>A. A. Thought for the Day</u>

"I shall not wait to be drafted for service to my fellow men; I shall volunteer. I shall be loyal in my attendance, generous in my giving, kind in my criticism, creative in my suggestions, loving in my attitudes. I shall give to A. A. my interest, my enthusiasm, my devotion, most of all, myself." Do I also accept this as my A. A. credo?

<u>Meditation for the Day</u>

Prayer is of many kinds, but of whatever kind, prayer is the linking up of the soul and mind ~~and heart~~ to God. So that if prayer is only a glance of faith, a look or a word of love, or JUST a feeling of confidence in the goodness and purpose in the universe, still the result of that prayer is added strength to meet all temptations and to overcome them. Even if no supplication is expressed, all the supply of strength that is necessary is secured. Because the soul, being linked and united to God, receives ~~in and through~~ FROM Him all spiritual ~~things.~~ HELP NEEDED. ~~And~~ The soul, when in ~~a~~ ITS human body, still needs the things belonging to its heavenly habitation.

<u>Prayer for the Day</u>

I pray that I may ~~learn~~ BE TAUGHT how to pray. I pray that I may be linked through prayer to the mind AND WILL of God.

155

JUNE 1 -- A. A. Thought for the Day

Some things I do not miss since becoming dry: That over all, awful feeling physically, including the shakes, a splitting headache, pains in my arms and legs, bleary eyes, fluttering stomach, droopy shoulders, weak knees, a three-day beard and a flushed complexion. Also facing my wife at breakfast and looking at my breakfast. Also composing the alibi and sticking to it. Also trying to shave with a hand that won't behave. Also opening up my wallet to find it empty. I don't miss these things, do I?

Meditation for the Day

By thinking of God, praying to Him, AND having communion with Him, ~~living with Him,~~ you gradually grow more like Him. The way of your transformation from the material to the spiritual is the way of Divine Companionship. You were born with a spark of the Divine within you. IT HAD BEEN ALL BUT SMOTHERED BY THE LIFE YOU WERE LIVING. That celestial fire has to be tended and fed so that it will grow eventually into a REAL ~~consuming flame of~~ desire to LIVE THE RIGHT WAY. BY TRYING TO DO ~~do~~ the will of God, ~~and~~ YOU GROW ~~to be~~ more and more ~~like Him in every way.~~ IN THE NEW WAY OF LIFE.

Prayer for the Day

I pray that I may tend the spark of the Divine within me so that it will grow. I pray that I may be gradually transformed from the OLD LIFE TO THE NEW LIFE. ~~material to the spiritual.~~

156

JUNE 2 -- A. A. Thought for the Day

Some more things I do not miss since becoming dry: Wondering if the car is in the garage and how I got home. Struggling to remember where I was and what I did since my last conscious moment. Trying to delay getting off to work. Wondering how I will look when I arrive at the office. Dreading the day ahead of me. I'm quite sure I don't miss these things, am I not?

Meditation for the Day

~~You belong to God and you will gradually grow more and more like Him, as you live the good life.~~ No man can believe in God and keep his selfish ways. The self shrivels up and dies and upon the soul becomes stamped God's image. The gradual elimination of selfishness in the growth of love for God and your fellow men is the goal of life. At first, you have only a faint liknesss to the Divine, but the picture grows and takes on more and more of the likeness of God, until ~~all~~ THOSE who see you can see in you SOME OF the power of God's grace at work, IN A HUMAN LIFE.

Prayer for the Day

I pray that I may develop ~~the~~ THAT faint likeness I have to the Divine. I pray that others may see in me SOME OF the power of God's grace at work.

157

JUNE 3 -- A. A. Thought for the Day

Some more things I do not miss since becoming dry: Running all over town to find a bar open to get that "pick-up". Meeting my friends and trying to cover up that I feel "lousy". Looking at myself in the mirror and calling myself a damn fool. Struggling with myself to snap out of it for two or three days, Wondering what it is all about. I'm positive I don't miss these things, am I not?

Meditation for the Day

Love is the power that transforms YOUR LIFE. ~~the world.~~ TRY TO ~~love God,~~ love your family, AND ~~love~~ your friends and then TRY TO love everybody that you possibly can, even "the sinners, the publicans and the harlots" - everybody. ~~Drive out sin with love.~~ LOVE ~~Praise~~ of God is AN EVEN GREATER ~~the~~ power. ~~that transforms your life.~~ It is the result of gratitude to God and IT is the acknowledgment of ~~all~~ the blessings that God has sent you. LOVE ~~Praise~~ of God acknowledges His gifts ~~and blesses you~~ and leaves the way open for God to shower yet more blessings on your thankful heart. ~~Learn to keep saying~~ SAY: thank you ~~to~~ God~~-~~until it becomes a habit.

Prayer for the Day

I pray that I may TRY TO love God and all men. I pray that I may CONTINUALLY THANK ~~praise~~ God for all His blessings.

158

JUNE 4 -- A. A. Thought for the Day

Some things I like since becoming dry: Feeling good in the morning. Happy home surroundings. Full use of my intelligence. Joy in my work. Money in my pocket. A complete lack of remorse. The confidence of my friends. The prospect of a happy future. The appreciation of the beauties of nature. Knowing what it is all about. I'm sure THAT I like these things, am I not?.

Meditation for the Day

~~"Mould us into thy likeness".~~ MOLDING YOUR LIFE ~~Moulding~~ means cutting ~~and chiselling~~ and shaping YOUR ~~the~~ material into something GOOD, ~~beautiful~~, something which can express the spiritual. All material things are the clay out of which WE MOLD SOMETHING SPIRITUAL. ~~you mould a spiritual likeness to God.~~ You must FIRST recognize the selfishness in your desires and motives, actions and words, ~~and thoughts~~ and THEN MOLD ~~shape~~ that selfishness until is is sublimated into a spiritual weapon FOR GOOD. ~~the glory of God.~~ As the work of MOLDING ~~moulding~~ proceeds, you see more and more clearly ~~all that~~ WHAT MUST ~~yet remains to~~ be done, TO MOLD YOUR LIFE INTO SOMETHING BETTER.

Prayer for the Day

I pray that I may MOLD MY LIFE ~~mould my selfishness~~ into something USEFUL AND GOOD. ~~useful for God.~~ I pray that I may not be discouraged by the slow progress that I make.

159

JUNE 5 -- A. A. Thought for the Day

WE ARE ALCOHOLICS FORTUNATE TO BE LIVING IN A DAY AND AGE ~~TIME~~ WHEN THERE IS SUCH A THING AS ALCOHOLICS ANONYMOUS. BEFORE A.A. CAME INTO BEING, THERE WAS VERY LITTLE HOPE FOR THE ALCOHOLIC. A.A. IS A GREAT REBUILDER OF HUMAN WRECKAGE. IT TAKES A MAN OR A WOMAN WHOSE PERSONALITY PROBLEM EXPRESSES ITSELF IN ALCOHOLISM AND OFFERS THEM A PROGRAMME WHICH, IF THEY ARE WILLING TO ACCEPT IT, ALLOWS THEM NOT ONLY TO GET SOBER BUT TO FIND A MUCH BETTER WAY OF LIVING. HAVE I LEARNED A ~~MUCH~~ BETTER WAY OF LIVING?

Meditation for the Day

~~Listen for God's voice.~~ Very quietly ~~He~~ GOD speaks through your thoughts and feelings. Heed the Divine voice of your conscience. Listen for ~~God~~ THIS and you will never be disappointed in the results in your life. Listen for ~~God~~ THIS SMALL, STILL VOICE and your tired nerves will become rested. The Divine voice comes to you as strength as well as tenderness, as power as well as restfulness. ~~This tenderness and restfulness will make you strong. Then it must be your task to let all your power be God's power.~~ Man's ~~power~~ MORAL STRENGTH derives its effectiveness from the ~~power~~ STRENGTH that comes when we listen PATIENTLY for the still, small Voice.

Prayer for the Day

I pray that I may listen for the still, small Voice of God.
I pray that I may obey the leading of ~~that voice.~~ MY CONSCIENCE.

160

JUNE 6 -- A. A. Thought for the Day

ALCOHOLISM IS USUALLY A SYMPTOM OF SOME UNDERLYING PERSONALITY PROBLEM. IT'S THE WAY WE ALCOHOLICS EXPRESS OUR MALADJUSTMENTS TO LIFE. I BELIEVE THAT I WAS A POTENTIAL ALCOHOLIC FROM THE START. I HAD AN INFERIORITY COMPLEX. I DIDN'T MAKE FRIENDS EASILY. THERE WAS A WALL BETWEEN ME AND OTHER PEOPLE. AND I WAS LONELY. I WAS NOT WELL ADJUSTED TO LIFE. DID I DRINK TO ESCAPE FROM MYSELF?

Meditation for the Day

According to the varying needs of each person, so does each person think of God. It is not necessary that you think of God as others think of Him, but it is necessary that you think of Him as supplying ~~all that~~ WHAT you personally need. The weak need God's strength. The strong need God's tenderness. The tempted and fallen need God's saving grace. The righteous need God's pity for sinners. The lonely need God as a friend. The fighters for righteousness need a leader in God. You may think of God in any ~~of these relationships to man.~~ WAY YOU WISH. WE USUALLY DO NOT TURN TO GOD UNTIL WE NEED HIM.

Prayer for the Day

I pray that I may think of God as supplying my needs. I pray that ~~my need will be supplied by Him, when I turn to Him and put my need before Him.~~ I WILL BRING ALL MY PROBLEMS TO HIM FOR HELP IN MEETING THEM.

161

JUNE 7 -- A. A. Thought for the Day

ALCOHOLISM IS A PROGRESSIVE ILLNESS. WE GO THROUGH THE THREE STAGES OF SOCIAL DRINKING, TROUBLE DRINKING AND MERRY-GO-ROUND DRINKING. WE LAND IN HOSPITALS AND JAILS. WE EVENTUALLY LOSE OUR HOMES, OUR FAMILIES AND OUR SELF-RESPECT. YES, ALCOHOLISM IS A PROGRESSIVE ILLNESS ~~DO I BELIEVE THAT~~ AND THERE ARE ONLY THREE ENDS TO IT ~~WILL I~~ — THE INSANE ASYLUM, THE MORGUE OR TOTAL ABSTINENCE.

Meditation for the Day WILL I CHOOSE NOT TO TAKE THE FIRST DRINK?

~~"Your soul shall live"~~, YOU CAN not only live ~~but~~ A NEW LIFE BUT YOU CAN grow in grace and power and beauty. Reach ever forward and upward after the things of the spirit. In the animal world, the very form of ~~an animal~~ A GIRAFFE changes to enable it to reach that upon which it delights to feed. Your whole character changes as you reach upward for the things of the spirit, for beauty, for love, for honesty, for purity and for unselfishness. ~~By~~ Reaching after these things of the spirit, your whole nature becomes changed, so that you can best receive and delight in the wonders of the abundant life.

Prayer for the Day

I pray that I may reach forward and upward. I pray that my character may be changed by this reaching ~~up~~ UPWARD for the things of the spirit.

16[illegible]

JUNE 8 -- A. A. Thought for the Day

ONCE AN ALCOHOLIC, ALWAYS AN ALCOHOLIC. WE ALWAYS GET WORSE, NEVER BETTER. WE ARE NEVER CURED. OUR ALCOHOLISM CAN ONLY BE ARRESTED. NO MATTER HOW LONG A MAN HAS BEEN SOBER, IF HE TRIES LIQUOR AGAIN, HE'S AS BAD OR WORSE THAN HE EVER WAS. THERE IS NO EXCEPTION TO THIS RULE IN THE WHOLE HISTORY OF A.A. ~~DO I KNOW THAT~~ WE CAN NEVER RECAPTURE THE GOOD TIMES OF THE PAST BY DRINKING? THEY ARE GONE FOREVER. WILL I TRY TO RECAPTURE THEM?

Meditation for the Day

Your life has been given to you MAINLY for the purpose of training your soul. This life WE LIVE is not SO MUCH for the body, ~~it is~~ AS for the soul. ~~But~~ ~~man~~ MEN often choose the way of life that best suits the body, not the way that best suits the soul. God wants you to choose what best suits the soul AS WELL AS THE BODY. Accept this BELIEF and a wonderful ~~moulding~~ MOLDING of the character is the result. Reject it and God's purpose for your life is frustrated and your spiritual progress is delayed. ~~Picture~~ Your soul ~~as being~~ IS BEING trained ~~by God's spirit and~~ by ~~what~~ THE good you choose, ~~and then you will share in the feeling that~~ THUS the purpose of your life is being accomplished.

Prayer for the Day

I pray that I may choose what is good for my soul. I pray that I may realize God's purpose for my life.

163

JUNE 9 -- A. A. Thought for the Day

WE FINALLY CAME TO THE BOTTOM. WE DID NOT HAVE TO BE FINANCIALLY BROKE, ALTHOUGH MANY OF US WERE. BUT WE WERE SPIRITUALLY BANKRUPT. WE HAD A SOUL-SICKNESS, A REVULSION AGAINST OURSELVES AND AGAINST OUR WAY OF LIVING. LIFE HAD BECOME IMPOSSIBLE FOR US. WE HAD TO END IT ALL OR DO SOMETHING ABOUT IT. AM I GLAD I DID SOMETHING ABOUT IT?

Meditation for the Day

Faith is not seeing, but believing. I am in a ~~[illegible]~~ box of space and time and cannot see [SPACELESSNESS OR] eternity. But God ~~breaks~~ [IS NOT WITHIN] the shell of time and space. He is timeless and spaceless. [HE CANNOT BE FULLY COMPREHENDED BY OUR FINITE MINDS.] ~~So when I look at God I see eternity and then faith becomes both seeing and believing.~~ [BUT] ~~We~~ [WE] must [TRY TO] make a union between ~~my~~ [OUR] purposes and the purposes of God. By [TRYING TO MERGE OUR] ~~merging my~~ hearts and minds with the ~~heart and~~ mind of God, a oneness of purpose results. This oneness of purpose puts ~~me~~ [US] in harmony with God and ~~my~~ [OUR] fellow ~~man~~ [MEN]. ~~and with nature.~~ ~~All~~ Evil comes from being in disharmony with God and ~~all~~ good comes from being in harmony with Him.

Prayer for the Day

~~I pray that God's kingdom may come in me today. I pray that God's kingdom may come through me today.~~ I PRAY THAT I MAY BE IN HARMONY WITH GOD. I PRAY THAT I MAY GET INTO THE STREAM OF GOODNESS IN THE UNIVERSE.

164.

JUNE 10 -- A. A. Thought for the Day

IF A MAN HAS HAD SOME MORAL, RELIGIOUS OR SPIRITUAL TRAINING, HE'S A BETTER PROSPECT FOR A.A. WHEN HE REACHES THE BOTTOM, AT THIS CRUCIAL MOMENT WHEN HE'S THOROUGHLY LICKED, HE TURNS INSTINCTIVELY TO WHATEVER DECENCY IS LEFT IN HIM. HE CALLS UPON WHATEVER RESERVES OF MORALITY AND FAITH ARE LEFT DOWN DEEP IN HIS HEART. HAVE I HAD THIS SPIRITUAL EXPERIENCE?

Meditation for the Day

The world wonders when it sees the man who can so unexpectedly draw large and unsuspected sums of money from his bank for some emergency. ~~in charity.~~ But what the world has not seen are the countless small sums paid into that bank, earned by faithful work [OVER A LONG TIME.] ~~in many fields.~~ And so is ~~God's~~ [THE] bank [OF THE SPIRIT]. The world sees the man of faith make a sudden demand ~~upon God,~~ upon God's stores of power, and the demand is met. The world does not see ~~that~~ [WHAT] the man has been ~~praying~~ [PUTTING] in, in thanks and praise, in prayer and communion, in small good deeds done, faithfully, steadily over the years.

Prayer for the Day

I pray that I may keep making deposits in God's bank. I pray that in my hour of need, I may call upon these.

165

JUNE 11 -- A. A. Thought for the Day

WE ALCOHOLICS HAVE TO BELIEVE IN SOME POWER GREATER THAN OURSELVES. YES, WE HAVE TO BELIEVE IN GOD. NOT TO BELIEVE IN A HIGHER POWER DRIVES US TO ATHEISM. ATHEISM, IT HAS BEEN SAID, IS BLIND FAITH IN THE STRANGE PROPOSITION THAT THIS UNIVERSE ORIGINATED IN A CYPHER AND AIMLESSLY RUSHES NOWHERE. THAT'S PRACTICALLY IMPOSSIBLE TO BELIEVE. SO WE TURN TO THAT DIVINE PRINCIPLE IN THE UNIVERSE WHICH WE CALL GOD. HAVE I STOPPED TRYING TO RUN MY OWN LIFE?

Meditation for the Day

"Lord, we thank Thee for the great gift of peace, that peace which passeth all understanding, that peace which the world can neither give nor take away". That is the peace ~~that~~ WHICH only God can give in the midst of a restless world and surrounded by trouble and difficulty. To know that peace is to have received the stamp of the kingdom of God. When you have earned that peace, you are fit to judge between true and false values, between the values of the Kingdom of God and the values of all that the world has to offer. ~~That peace is faith at rest.~~

Prayer for the Day

I pray that today I may have an inner peace. I pray that TODAY I may ~~wear the world~~ ~~[illegible]~~ BE AT PEACE WITH MYSELF.

166

JUNE 12 -- A. A. Thought for the Day

WHEN WE CAME INTO A.A., WE MADE A TREMENDOUS DISCOVERY. WE FOUND THAT WE WERE SICK PERSONS RATHER THAN MORAL LEPERS. WE WERE NOT SUCH QUEER BIRDS AS WE THOUGHT WE WERE. WE FOUND OTHER PEOPLE WHO HAD THE SAME ILLNESS THAT WE HAD, WHO HAD BEEN THROUGH THE SAME EXPERIENCES THAT WE HAD BEEN THROUGH. THEY HAD RECOVERED. IF THEY COULD DO IT, WE COULD DO IT. WAS HOPE BORN IN ME THE DAY I WALKED INTO A.A.?

Meditation for the Day

"He that heareth these sayings and doeth them is like unto a man who built his house upon a rock and the rain descended and the floods came and the wind blew and beat upon that house and it fell not for it was founded upon a rock". When your life is built upon ~~complete~~ obedience to God and upon doing His will as you understand it, you will be steadfast and unmovable even in the midst of storms. The serene, steadfast, unmovable life, the rock home, is laid stone by stone, foundations, walls and roof, by acts of obedience TO THE HEAVENLY VISION, The daily following ~~out~~ of God's guidance, AND the daily doing of His will, ~~AS YOU UNDERSTAND IT,~~ BUILDS YOUR HOUSE UPON A ROCK.

Prayer for the Day

I pray that my life may be founded upon the rock of faith. I pray that I may be obedient to the heavenly vision.

167

JUNE 13 -- A. A. Thought for the Day

IN A.A. WE HAVE TO REEDUCATE OUR MINDS. WE HAVE TO LEARN TO THINK DIFFERENTLY. WE HAVE TO TAKE A LONG VIEW OF DRINKING INSTEAD OF A SHORT VIEW. WE HAVE TO LOOK THROUGH THE GLASS TO WHAT LIES BEYOND IT. WE HAVE TO LOOK THROUGH THE NIGHT BEFORE TO THE MORNING AFTER. (NO MATTER HOW GOOD LIQUOR LOOKS FROM THE SHORT VIEW, WE MUST REALIZE THAT IN THE LONG RUN IT IS POISON TO US.) HAVE I LEARNED TO LOOK THROUGH THE BOTTLE TO THE BETTER LIFE THAT LIES AHEAD?

Meditation for the Day

~~Your thoughts can be God-inspired, if you look to Him for guidance.~~ If you are honestly trying to live the way you believe God wants you to live, ~~with honesty, purity, unselfishness and love,~~ you can get guidance from God in TIMES OF quiet communion with Him, provided your thoughts are directed towards God's will and all good things. The attitude of "Thy will, not mine, be done" leads to clear guidance. Act on this guidance and you will be led on to better things. Your impulses seem to become less your own and more the leading of God's spirit, acting through your thoughts. Obeyed, they will bring you the answers to your prayers.

Prayer for the Day

I pray that I may try to think God's thoughts after Him.

I pray that my thoughts may be guided by His thoughts.

168

JUNE 14 -- A. A. Thought for the Day

IN A.A. WE HAVE TO LEARN THAT DRINK IS OUR GREATEST ENEMY. ALTHOUGH WE USED TO THINK THAT LIQUOR WAS OUR FRIEND, THE TIME CAME WHEN IT TURNED AGAINST US AND BECAME OUR ENEMY. WE DON'T KNOW JUST WHEN THIS HAPPENED, BUT WE KNOW THAT IT DID, BECAUSE WE BEGAN TO GET INTO TROUBLE. JAILS AND HOSPITALS. WE REALIZE THAT LIQUOR IS NOW OUR ENEMY. IS MY MAIN BUSINESS KEEPING SOBER?

Meditation for the Day

It is not your circumstances that need altering so much as yourself. After you have changed, conditions will naturally change. Spare no effort to become all God would have you become. Follow every good leading OF YOUR CONSCIENCE. Take each day with no backward look. Face the day's problems with God and seek God's help and guidance as to what you should do in every situation that may arise. ~~Never look back, and~~ Never leave until tomorrow ~~that~~ THE thing ~~about which you can get God's guidance today~~ THAT YOU ARE GUIDED TO DO TODAY.

Prayer for the Day

I pray that God will ~~make me~~ HELP ME TO BECOME all that He would have me be.

I pray that I may face today's problems with good grace.

169

JUNE 15 -- A. A. Thought for the Day

IN A.A., WE HAVE THREE THINGS, FELLOWSHIP, FAITH AND SERVICE. FELLOWSHIP IS WONDERFUL, BUT IT LASTS JUST SO LONG. THEN SOME GOSSIP, DISILLUSIONMENT AND BOREDOM COME IN. WORRY AND FEAR COME BACK AT TIMES, AND WE FIND THAT FELLOWSHIP IS NOT THE WHOLE STORY. THEN WE NEED FAITH. WHEN WE'RE ALONE, WITH NOBODY TO PAT US ON THE BACK, WE MUST TURN TO GOD FOR HELP. CAN I SAY "THY WILL BE DONE" AND MEAN IT?

Meditation for the Day

There is beauty in a God-guided life. There is wonder in the feeling of being led by God. TRY TO realize God's bounty and goodness more and more. God is planning for you. Wonderful are His ways; they are beyond your knowledge. But God's ~~guidance~~ LEADING will enter your consciousness more and more and bring you ever more peace and joy. Your life is being planned and blessed by God. You ~~should~~ MAY count all material things as loss if they prevent your winning your way to the consciousness of God's guidance.

Prayer for the Day

I pray that I may earn the rewards of God's power and peace. I pray that I may ~~have~~ DEVELOP the feeling of being led by God.

170

JUNE 16 -- A. A. Thought for the Day

BUT EVEN FAITH IS NOT THE WHOLE STORY. THERE MUST BE SERVICE. WE MUST GIVE THIS THING AWAY IF WE WANT TO KEEP IT. THE DEAD SEA HAS NO OUTLET AND IT IS STAGNANT AND FULL OF SALT. THE SEA OF GALLILEE IS CLEAR AND CLEAN AND BLUE, AS THE JORDAN RIVER CARRIES IT OUT INTO THE LIVES OF OTHERS. TO BE OF SERVICE TO OUR FELLOW MEN MAKES OUR LIVES WORTH LIVING. DOES SERVICE TO OTHERS GIVE ME A REAL PURPOSE IN LIFE?

Meditation for the Day

Seek God early in the day, before He gets crowded out by life's ~~troubles~~ PROBLEMS, difficulties ~~and~~ OR pleasures. In that early quiet time, gain a calm, strong confidence in the goodness and purpose ~~of~~ IN the universe. Do not ~~only~~ seek God ONLY when the world's struggles prove too much and too many for you to bear or face alone. Seek God early, when you ~~need the~~ CAN HAVE A consciousness of God's spirit in the world. People ~~usually~~ OFTEN only seek God when their difficulties are too great to be surmounted IN any other way, forgetting that if they sought God's companionship before they need it, ~~most~~ MANY of their difficulties would never arise.

Prayer for the Day

I pray that I may not let God be crowded out by the hurly-burly of life. I pray that I may seek God early and often.

171

JUNE 17 - A.A. THOUGHT FOR THE DAY

WE IN A.A. HAVE THE PRIVILEGE OF LIVING TWO LIVES IN ONE LIFETIME. ONE LIFE OF DRUNKENNESS, FAILURE AND DEFEAT. THEN, THROUGH A.A., ANOTHER LIFE OF SOBRIETY, PEACE OF MIND AND USEFULNESS. WE WHO HAVE RECOVERED OUR SOBRIETY ARE MODERN MIRACLES. AND WE'RE LIVING ON BORROWED TIME. SOME OF US MIGHT HAVE BEEN DEAD LONG AGO. BUT WE HAVE BEEN GIVEN ANOTHER CHANCE TO LIVE. DO I OWE A DEBT OF GRATITUDE TO A.A. THAT I CAN NEVER REPAY AS LONG AS I LIVE?

Meditation for the Day

~~Think of God often.~~ ~~The very~~ Thinking about God in love and worship drives away ~~all~~ evil. It is the thought before which ~~all~~ the hosts of evil flee. The thought of ~~God~~ A POWER GREATER THAN YOURSELF is the call for a life-line to rescue you from temptation. The thought of God banishes loneliness and dispels gloom. It summons help to conquer your faults. ~~It will set you on high, because you are a child of God.~~ Think of God ~~more~~ AS often AS POSSIBLE. Use the thought prayerfully and purposefully. It will carry your thoughts away from material things and toward the SPIRITUAL things that make life worth while.

Prayer for the Day

I pray that I may think of God often. I pray that I MAY rest in peace at the thought of His ~~goodness.~~ LOVE AND CARE.

172

JUNE 18 -- A. A. Thought for the Day

THE A.A. WAY OF LIVING IS NOT AN EASY ONE. BUT IT'S AN ADVENTURE IN LIVING THAT IS REALLY WORTH WHILE. AND IT'S SO MUCH BETTER THAN OUR OLD DRUNKEN WAY OF LIVING THAT THERE'S NO COMPARISON. OUR LIVES WITHOUT A.A. WOULD BE WORTH NOTHING. WITH A.A., WE HAVE A CHANCE TO LIVE REASONABLY GOOD LIVES. ~~Do I BELIEVE THAT~~ IT'S WORTH THE BATTLE, NO MATTER HOW TOUGH THE GOING IS FROM DAY TO DAY. ISN'T IT WORTH THE BATTLE?

Meditation for the Day

The spiritual life has two parts. One is the life apart, the life of prayer and quiet ~~and~~ communion with God. You spend this part of your life apart with God. Every day your mind can be set in the right direction so that your thoughts will be of the right kind. The other is the life impart; imparting to others what you have learned from your own meditative experience. The victories you have won over ~~sin and temptation~~ YOURSELF through the help of God can be shared with your fellow men. You can ~~impart~~ HELP THEM BY IMPARTING to them some of the victory and security which you have gained in your life apart.

Prayer for the Day

I pray that I may grow strong from my times apart with God. I pray that I may pass on some of this strength to others.

173

JUNE 19 -- A. A. Thought for the Day

WE HAVE THIS CHOICE EVERY DAY OF OUR LIVES. WE CAN TAKE THE PATH THAT LEADS TO INSANITY OR DEATH. AND REMEMBER, OUR NEXT DRUNK COULD BE OUR LAST ONE. OR WE CAN TAKE THE PATH THAT LEADS TO A REASONABLY HAPPY AND USEFUL LIFE. THE CHOICE IS OURS EACH DAY OF OUR LIVES. GOD GRANT THAT WE TAKE THE RIGHT PATH. HAVE I MADE MY CHOICE TODAY?

Meditation for the Day

~~Your~~ ONE real work in life is to grow spiritually, ~~and to help others to grow spiritually~~. To do this, you must follow the path of ~~obedience which leads to the throne of God.~~ DILIGENTLY SEEKING THE GOOD. The hidden spiritual wonders are revealed ~~by God~~ to those who diligently seek this treasure. From one point to the next, you have to follow the way of obedience to God's will until finally you reach greater and greater spiritual heights. Work on the material plane ~~is only~~ SHOULD BE secondary to your real life's work. The material things which you need MOST are those which help you to attain the spiritual.

Prayer for the Day

I pray that I may keep growing spiritually. I pray that I may make this my real life's work.

174

JUNE 20 -- A. A. Thought for the Day

You ~~must~~ SHOULD be ready and willing to help carry the A. A. message when called upon to do so. Live for some purpose greater than yourself. Each day you will have something to work for. You have received so much from this programme that you should have a vision that gives your life direction and a purpose that gives meaning to each new day. Let us not slide along through life. Let us have a purpose for each day and let us make that purpose for something greater than just ourselves. What is my purpose for today?

Meditation for the Day

To see God with the eyes of faith is to cause God's power to manifest itself in the material world. God cannot do ~~mighty works~~ HIS WORK because of unbelief. In response to your belief, God can work a miracle in your personality. All miracles happen in the realm of personality and all are caused by and based on belief in God's never-failing power. But God's power cannot manifest itself in personalities, ~~in the material world,~~ unless those personalities make His power available by their faith. We can only see God with the eyes of faith, but this kind of seeing produces great changes in ~~personalities.~~ OUR WAY OF LIVING.

Prayer for the Day

I pray that I may see God with the eyes of faith. I pray that this seeing will produce a change in my personality.

176

JUNE 21 -- A. A. Thought for the Day

Intelligent faith in that Power greater than ourselves can be counted on to stabilize our emotions. It has an incomparable capacity to help us look at life in balanced perspective. We look up, around and away from ourselves and we see that nine out of ten things which at the moment upset us will shortly disappear. Problems solve themselves, criticism and unkindness vanish as though they had never been. Have I got the proper perspective toward life?

Meditation for the Day

A truly spiritual man would like to have ~~"the mind which was in Jesus" as Saint Paul said.~~ A SERENE MIND. The only way to keep calm and sane in this troubled world is to have ~~the~~ A SERENE mind. ~~which was in Jesus.~~ ~~That~~ THE calm and sane mind ~~which saw~~ SEES spiritual things as the true realities and material things as only temporary and fleeting. That sort of mind you can never obtain by reasoning, because your reasoning powers are limited by space and time. That kind of mind you can never obtain by reading, because other minds are also limited in the same way. You can only have that mind by an act of faith~~, by accepting it as a free gift of God.~~

Prayer for the Day

I pray that I may have a calm and sane mind. I pray that I may look up, around and away from myself.

176

JUNE 22 -- A. A. Thought for the Day

If you have any doubt, just ask any of the older members of the A. A. group and they will readily tell you that since they turned their lives over to the care of God as they understand Him, MANY OF their problems ~~vanish~~ HAVE VANISHED into the forgotten yesterdays. When you allow yourself to be upset over one thing, you succeed only in opening the door for the coming of hundreds of other upsetting things. Am I allowing myself to be upset over little things?

Meditation for the Day

~~I must go forward fearlessly.~~ I ~~must~~ WOULD DO WELL not TO think of the Red Sea of difficulties that lie ahead. I am sure that when I come to that Red Sea, the waters will part and I will be given all the power I need to face and overcome ~~every difficulty~~ MANY DIFFICULTIES and meet what is in store for me with courage. ~~and faith.~~ I believe that I will pass through that Red Sea to the promised land, the land of the spirit where ~~all~~ MANY souls meet in perfect comradeship. I believe that when that time comes, I will be freed of all the dross of material things ~~by the light of the Father's presence.~~ AND FIND PEACE.

Prayer for the Day

I pray that I may face the future with courage. I pray that I may be given the strength to face both life and death fearlessly.

177

JUNE 23 -- A. A. Thought for the Day

No chain is stronger than its weakest link. Likewise, if you fail in the ~~day-by-day~~ programme, in all probability it will be at your weakest point. Great faith and constant contact with God's power can help you discover, guard and under-gird your weakest point with a strength not your own. Intelligent faith in God's power can be counted on to help you master your emotions, help you to think kindly of OTHERS, ~~everyone,~~ AND help you with any task THAT you undertake, no matter how difficult. Am I master of my emotions?

Meditation for the Day

You ~~must~~ NEED TO BE constantly ~~become~~ recharged by the power of the spirit of God. Commune with God in quiet times until the life from God, the Divine life, by that very contact, flows into your being and revives your fainting spirit. When weary, sit by the well and rest. Rest and gain power and strength from God and then you will be ready to meet whatever opportunities come your way, ~~and to do effective work.~~ Rest, until every care and worry and fear have gone and then the tide of ~~power and strength and~~ peace and serenity, ~~and~~ love and joy, will flow into your ~~being.~~ CONSCIOUSNESS.

Prayer for the Day

I pray that I may rest and become recharged. I pray that I may pause and wait for the renewing of my strength.

178

JUNE 24 -- A. A. Thought for the Day.

Alcohol is our weakness, ~~and it's~~ THE origin OF OUR ALCOHOLISM can be ~~greatly~~ LARGELY attributed to our unstable emotions. We suffer from mental conflicts from which we look for escape by drowning our problems in drink. We try through drink to push away from us the realities of life. But alcohol does not feed, alcohol does not build, it only borrows from the future and it ultimately destroys. We try to drown our feelings in order to escape life's realities, little realizing or caring that in continued drinking we are only multiplying our problems. Have I got control over my unstable emotions?

Meditation for the Day

When I let personal piques and resentments interfere with what I know to be my proper conduct, I am on the wrong track and ~~then~~ I am undoing all I have built up by doing the right thing. I must never let personal piques interfere with living the way I know God wants me to live. ~~My greatest danger is going against God's guidance.~~ When I have no clear guidance from God, I must go forward quietly along the path of duty. This attitude of quiet faith will receive its reward as surely as acting upon God's direct guidance. I must not weaken my spiritual power by letting personal piques upset me.

Prayer for the Day

I pray that I may not let myself BECOME TOO ~~be~~ upset. I pray that I may go quietly along the path I have chosen.

179

JUNE 25 -- A. A. Thought for the Day

One of the most encouraging facts of life is that your weakness can become your greatest asset. Kites and airplanes rise against the wind. In climbing up a high mountain, we need the stony crags and rough places to aid us in our climb. So your weakness can become an asset if you will face it, examine it and trace it to its origin. Set it in the very center of your mind. No weakness, such as drinking, ever turned into an asset until it was first fairly faced. Am I making my weakness my greatest asset?

Meditation for the Day

When men seek to worship God, they think of the great universe that God rules over, of creation, of mighty law and order throughout the universe. Then men feel the awe that precedes worship. I too must feel awe, feel the desire to worship God in wondering amazement. My mind is in a box of space and time and it is so made that I cannot conceive of what is beyond space or time, the limitless and the eternal. But I know that there must be something beyond space and time, and that something must be the limitless and eternal Power behind the universe. I also know that I can experience that Power in my life.

Prayer for the Day

I pray that I may accept the limitless and ~~the~~ eternal SPIRIT. I pray that It may express Itself in my life.

180

JUNE 26 -- A. A. Thought for the Day

We must know the nature of our weakness before we can determine how to deal with it. When we are honest about it's presence, we may discover that it is imaginary and can be overcome by a change of thinking. We admit that we are alcoholics and we would ~~only~~ be foolish if we refused to accept our handicap and do something about it. So by honesty facing our weakness and keeping ever present the knowledge that for us alcoholism is a disease with which we are afflicted, we can take the necessary steps to arrest it. Have I fully accepted my handicap~~s~~?

Meditation for the Day

There is a proper time for everything. I must learn not to do things at the wrong time, that is, before I am ready or before conditions are right. It is always a temptation to do something at once, instead of waiting until the proper time. TIMING IS IMPORTANT. I must learn, in the little daily ~~things~~ SITUATIONS of life, to delay action until I am sure that I am doing the right thing at the right time. So many lives lack balance AND TIMING. ~~Now~~ In the momentous decisions and ~~the~~ crises of life, they MAY ask God's guidance, but into the small ~~things~~ SITUATIONS of life they rush alone. ~~By whether or not I do the right thing at the right time, those around me are helped or hindered.~~

Prayer for the Day

I pray that I may delay action until I feel that I am doing the right thing. I pray that I may not rush in alone.

181

JUNE 27 -- A. A. Thought for the Day

If you can take your troubles as they come; if you can maintain your calm and composure amid pressing duties and unending engagements; if you can rise above the distressing and disturbing circumstances in which you are set down, you have discovered a priceless secret of daily living. Even if you are forced to go through life weighed down by some unescapable misfortune or handicap and yet live each day as it comes with poise and peace of mind, you have succeeded where most people have failed. You have wrought a greater achievement than ~~many~~ a person who rules a nation. Have I achieved poise and peace of mind?

Meditation for the Day

Take a blessing with you wherever you go. You have been blessed, so bless others. Such stores of blessings are awaiting you in the months and years that lie ahead. Pass on your blessings. Blessing can and does go around the world, passed on the currents from man to man. Shed a little blessing in the heart of one person. That person is cheered to pass it on and so God's vitalizing, joy-giving message travels on. Be a transmuter of God's blessings.

Prayer for the Day

I pray that I may pass on my blessings. I pray that they may flow ~~as they grow.~~ INTO THE LIVES OF OTHERS.

182

JUNE 28 -- A. A. Thought for the Day

You can prove to yourself that life is basically and fundamentally an inner attitude. Just try to remember what troubled you most a week ago. You probably will find it difficult to remember. Why then should you unduly worry or fret over the problems that arise today? Your attitude toward them can be changed by putting yourself and your problems in God's hands, and trusting Him to see that everything will turn out all right, provided you are trying to do the right thing. Your changed mental attitude toward your problems relieves you of their burden and you can face them without fear. Has my mental attitude changed?

Meditation for the Day

You cannot see the future. It's a blessing that you cannot. You could not bear to know all the future. That is why God only reveals it to you day by day. The first step each day is to lay your will before God as an offering, ready for God to do what is best for you. Be sure that, if you trust God, what He does for you will be FOR the best. The second step is to be confident that God is powerful enough to do anything He wills and that no miracle IN HUMAN LIVES is impossible with Him. Then leave the future to God.

Prayer for the Day

I pray that I may gladly leave ~~all my affairs~~ MY FUTURE in God's hands. I pray that I may be confident that good things will happen, AS LONG AS I AM ON THE RIGHT PATH.

183

JUNE 29 -- A. A. Thought for the Day

The programme of Alcoholics Anonymous involves a continuous striving for improvement. There can be no ^[LONG] resting period. We must ^[TRY TO] work at it all the time. We must continually keep in mind that it is a programme not to be measured in years, because am alcoholic never fully reaches his goals nor is he ever cured. His alcoholism is only kept in abeyance by daily living of the programme. It is a timeless programme in every sense. We live it day by day, or more precisely moment by moment - now. Am I always striving for improvement?

Meditation for the Day

Life is all a preparation for something better to come. God has a plan for your life and it will work out, if you try to do His will. God has things planned for you, far beyond what you can imagine now. But you must prepare yourself so that you will be ready for the better things to come. Now is the time for discipline and prayer. The time of expression will come ^[LATER]. Life can be flooded through and through with joy and gladness. So prepare[, YOURSELF FOR ^THESE BETTER THINGS TO COME.]

Prayer for the Day

I pray that I may prepare myself for better things ^[WHICH GOD HAS IN STORE FOR ME] ~~to come~~.
I pray that I may trust God for the future.

184

JUNE 30 -- A. A. Thought for the Day

An alcoholic is unable or unwilling, during his addiction to alcohol, to live in the present. The result is that he lives in a constant state of ~~loneliness~~ [REMORSE] and fear[,] because of his ~~morbid~~ [UNHOLY] past and it's ~~unholy~~ [MORBID] attraction or the uncertain future and it's vague forbodings. So the only real hope for the alcoholic is to face the present. Now is the time. Now is ours. The past is beyond recall. The future is as uncertain as life itself. Only the now belongs to us. Am I living in the now?

Meditation for the Day

I must forget the past ^[AS MUCH AS POSSIBLE.] The past is water over the dam. Nothing can be done about the past[,] except to make what restitution I can. I must not carry the burden of my past failures. I must go on in faith. The clouds will clear and the way will lighten. The path will become less stony with every forward step I take. God has no reproach for anything that He has healed. I can be made whole and free[,] even though I have wrecked my life in the past. ^[REMEMBER THE SAYING:] "Neither do I condemn thee, go and sin no more".

Prayer for the Day

I pray that I may not carry the burden of the past. I pray that I may ^[CAST IT OFF AND] press on in faith.

185

JULY 1 -- A. A. Thought for the Day

In following the A. A. programme with its twelve steps, we have ~~all~~ the advantages of a better understanding of our problems. Day after day our sobriety results in the formation of new habits, normal habits. As each twenty-four hour period ends, we find that the business of staying sober is a much less trying and fearsome ordeal than it ~~was~~ SEEMED in the beginning. Do I find it easier as I go along?

Meditation for the Day

Learn daily the ~~sublime~~ lesson of trust and calm in the midst of THE storms OF LIFE. Whatever of sorrow or difficulty the day may bring, God's command to you is the same. Be grateful, humble, calm and loving to all people. Leave each soul the better for having met you or heard you. For all kinds of people, this should be your attitude, a loving desire to help and an infectious spirit of calmness and trust in God. You have the one answer to loneliness and fear, which is a calm faith in the goodness and purpose in the universe.

Prayer for the Day

I pray that I may be calm in the midst of storms. I pray that I may pass on this calmness to others who are lonely and full of fear.

186

JULY 2 -- A. A. Thought for the Day

In the association with members of the A. A. group to which we belong, we have the advantage of the sincere friendship and understanding of the other members who, through social and personal contact, take us away from our old haunts and environments and ~~tend~~ HELP to remove in a large measure the occasions of alcoholic suggestion. We find in this association A sympathy and a willingness on the part of ~~all~~ MOST members to do everything in their power to help ~~each other.~~ US. Do I appreciate the wonderful fellowship of A. A.?

Meditation for the Day

"Except ye become as little children, ye cannot enter the kingdom of heaven". IN THIS SAYING It is urged that all who ~~sought~~ SEEK heaven on earth or in the hereafter should become ~~as~~ LIKE little children. In SEEKING things of the spirit and in OUR faith, we should ~~seek~~ TRY to become child-like. Even as we grow older, the years OF SEEKING can ~~add to~~ GIVE us the attitude of the trusting child. Not only for its simple trust, should we have the childlike spirit, but also for its joy in life, its ready laughter, its lack of criticism, and its desire to share. In CHARLES Dicken's STORY A "Christmas Carol", even old Scrooge changed, when he got the child-spirit.

Prayer for the Day

I pray that I may become like a child in faith and hope. I pray that I may, like a child, be friendly and ~~loving towards all.~~ TRUSTING.

187

JULY 3 -- A. A. Thought for the Day

In the beginning of Alcoholics Anonymous, there were only two persons. Now there are many groups and thousands of members. True, the surface has only been scratched. There are probably two million persons in America who need our help. More and more people are making a start in A. A. each day. In the case of each individual member, the beginning has been accomplished when he turns to a Power greater than himself, admitting that his life has become unmanageable. That Higher Power works for good in all things, and helps us to accomplish much in individual growth and in the growth of the A. A. groups. Am I doing my part in helping A. A. to grow?

Meditation for the Day

"Blessed are they that hunger and thirst after righteousness, for they shall be filled". Only in the fullness of faith can the heart-sick and faint and weary be satisfied, healed and rested. Think of the wonderful spiritual revelations still to be found by those who are trying to live the spiritual life. Much of life is spiritually unexplored country. Only to the consecrated and loving people who walk with God in spirit, can these great spiritual discoveries be revealed. Keep going forward and keep growing in righteousness.

Prayer for the Day

I pray that I may not be held back by the material things of the world. I pray that I may let God lead me forward.

188

JULY 4 -- A. A. Thought for the Day

In Alcoholics Anonymous, there is no thought of individual profit. No greed or gain. No membership fees, no dues. All that we hope for is sobriety and regeneration, so that we can live normal, respectable lives and be recognized by others as men and women willing to do unto others as we would be done by. These things we can accomplish by the help of each other, by following the twelve steps and by the grace of God. Am I fully willing to work without material gain to myself?

Meditation for the Day

What is sometimes called conversion is often only the discovery of God as a friend in need. What is sometimes called religion is often only the experiencing of the help and strength of God's power in the world. What is sometimes called holiness is often only the invitation of the Great Friend. As God becomes your friend, you become a friend to other men. We experience human friendship and from this we can imagine what kind of a Great Friend God can be. the tireless, selfless, all conquering, miracle-working Friend. Reach out to this Great Friend and figuratively take His hand in yours.

Prayer for the Day

I pray that I may think of God as a friend in need. I pray that I may go along with Him.

189

JULY 5 -- A. A. Thought for the Day

Until we came into A. A., most of us had tried desperately to stop drinking. We were filled with the delusion that we could drink like our friends. We tried time and again to take it or leave it, but could do neither. We always lapsed into ceaseless, unhappy drinking. Wives, mothers, families, friends and employers threw up their hands in hurt bewilderment, in despair, and finally in disgust. We wanted to stop. We realized that every reason for drinking was only a crazy excuse. Have I given up every excuse for drinking?

Meditation for the Day

Many things can upset you and you can easily get off the track. But remember that God is ~~with~~ NEAR you all the time, ~~blessing and helping you.~~ READY TO HELP YOU, IF YOU CALL ON HIM. No man can FOREVER stand ~~alone~~ against God's will for him, nor can he FOREVER upset God's plan for his life, even though ~~it~~ GOD'S PLAN may be postponed by ~~his~~ A MAN'S willfulness and deliberate choice of evil. A whole world of men and women cannot PERMANENTLY change God's laws nor His purpose for the universe. ~~To the passenger on a rough sea, it may seem as if each wave would overwhelm the ship or turn it from its course. But the Captain knows that, in spite of wind and wave, He steers a straight course to the Haven where He would be.~~ THE SEA OF LIFE MAY LOOK VERY ROUGH TO US, BUT WE CAN BELIEVE THAT OUR CAPTAIN STEERS THE BOAT ON A STRAIGHT COURSE.

Prayer for the Day

I pray that I may TRY TO steer a straight course. I pray that I may accept God's ~~will for~~ DIRECTION IN my life's JOURNEY.

190

JULY 6 -- A. A. Thought for the Day

We tried to study our alcoholic problem, wondering what was the cause of our strange obsession. Many of us took special treatments, hospitalization, even confinement in institutions. In every case, the relief was only temporary. We tried through crazy excuses to convince ourselves that we knew why we drank, but we went on regardless. Finally, drinking had gone far beyond even a habit. We had become alcoholics, men and women who had been destroying themselves against their own will. Am I completely free from my alcoholic obsession?

Meditation for the Day

"Ask and ye shall receive". Never let yourself think that you cannot do something USEFUL or that you never will be able to accomplish a ~~certain~~ USEFUL task. The fact is that you can do practically anything in the field of human relationships, if you are willing to call on God's supply of strength. The supply may not be immediately available, ~~for you~~ because you may not be ENTIRELY ready to receive it. But it will surely come when you ~~are~~ PROPERLY prepared for it. As you grow spiritually, a feeling of being plentifully supplied by God's strength will possess you and you will be able to accomplish ~~greater~~ MANY USEFUL things.

Prayer for the Day

I pray that I may claim God's supply OF STRENGTH by my faith in Him. I pray that it shall be given me, according to my faith.

191

JULY 7 -- A. A. Thought for the Day

We had become hopelessly sick people, spiritually, emotionally and physically. The power that controlled us was greater than ourselves; it was John Barleycorn. Many drinkers have said: I hadn't gone that far, I hadn't lost my job on account of drink, I still had my family, I managed to keep out of jail. True, I took too much sometimes and I guess I managed to make quite an ass of myself when I did, but I still thought ~~that~~ I could control my drinking. I didn't really believe that I was an alcoholic. ~~Am I one~~ IF I WAS of these, ~~and~~ have I fully changed my mind?

Meditation for the Day

~~Each death is~~ only change. ~~It is merely the doorway to immortality, beyond space and time.~~ Painful as the present time may be, you will one day see the reason for it. You will see that it was not ~~cruel~~ ONLY testing, but ALSO A ~~tender~~ preparation for the ~~wonderful~~ life-work which you are to do. ~~Try to realize~~ HAVE FAITH that your prayers and aspirations will SOME DAY be answered. Answered ~~perhaps~~ in a way that PERHAPS seems painful to you, but ~~is just now~~ the only RIGHT way. Selfishness and pride OFTEN MAKE US WANT THINGS THAT ARE NOT GOOD FOR US. THEY need to be burned out of ~~your~~ OUR nature. ~~You~~ WE must be rid of the blocks which are holding ~~you~~ US back, BEFORE WE CAN EXPECT OUR PRAYERS TO BE ANSWERED.

Prayer for the Day

I pray that I may be willing to go through a time of testing. I pray that I may trust God for the outcome.

192

JULY 8 -- A. A. Thought for the Day

~~Every~~ A. A. members will tell you that they can look back and clearly see that they were out of control long before they finally admitted it. Every one of us has gone through that stage ~~where~~ WHEN we wouldn't admit that we were alcoholics. It takes a lot of punishment to convince us, but one thing is certain, we all know from actual experience that when it comes to dishing out punishment, John Barleycorn has no ~~master~~ EQUAL. Have I any reservations as to my status as an alcoholic?

Meditation for the Day

There is a force for good in the world and when you are co-operating with that force for good, good things happen to you. You have free-will, the choice to be on the side of the right or on the side of the wrong. This force for good we call God's will. God has a purpose for the world and He has a purpose for your life. He wants you to bring all your desires into oneness with His desires. He can only work through people. ~~You must~~ IF YOU try to make God's will your ~~only~~ will, ~~Then~~ you will be guided by ~~His will~~ HIM. You will be in the stream of goodness, carried along by everything that is right. You will be on God's side.

Prayer for the Day

I pray that I may TRY TO make God's will my will. I pray that I may keep in the stream of goodness in the world.

193

JULY 9 -- A. A. Thought for the Day

Disillusionment and spiritual confusion mark our age. Many of us ~~had~~ HAVE cast aside old ideals without acquiring new ones. Many men and women are creeping through life on their hands and knees, merely because they refuse to rely upon any power but themselves. Many of them feel that they are being brave and independent, but actually they are only courting disaster. Anxiety and the inferiority complex have become the greatest of all modern plagues. IN A.A. WE HAVE THE ANSWER TO THESE ILLS. Have I ~~gotten over relying~~ CEASED TO RELY on myself only?

Meditation for the Day

Disillusionment and doubt spoil life. The doubting ones are the disillusioned ones. When you are in doubt, you are on the fence. You are not going anywhere. Doubt poisons all action. It is saying to life: "Well, I don't know, so ~~I~~ YOU ~~won't~~ DON'T do anything. You should meet life with a Yes, an affirmative attitude. There is good in the world and ~~I will~~ WE CAN follow ~~the~~ THAT good. There is power available for ~~me~~ US, to HELP US TO do ~~good,~~ THE RIGHT THING, therefore ~~I~~ WE will accept that power. There are miracles of change in people's lives, therefore ~~I~~ WE will accept those miracles as evidence of God's power.

Prayer for the Day

I pray that I will not be paralyzed by doubt. I pray that I may go along on the ~~assumptions~~ VENTURE of faith.

194

JULY 10 -- A. A. Thought for the Day

We in Alcoholics Anonymous do not enter into theological discussions, but in carrying our message we attempt to explain the simple How of ~~religion~~ THE SPIRITUAL LIFE. How faith in a Higher Power can help you to overcome loneliness, fear and anxiety. How it can help you get along with other people. How it can make it possible for you to rise above pain, sorrow, AND despondency. How it can help you overcome YOUR desires for the things that destroy. Have I reached a simple, effective faith?

Meditation for the Day

Expect ~~many~~ miracles OF CHANGE IN PEOPLE'S LIVES. Do not be held back by unbelief. People can be changed AND they are often ready and waiting to be changed. NEVER BELIEVE THAT HUMAN NATURE CANNOT BE CHANGED. WE SEE CHANGED PEOPLE EVERY DAY. Do you have the faith to make those changes possible? ~~An unlimited supply of God's strength is available to you, if you are willing to put it to use.~~ Modern miracles happen every day in the lives of people. All miracles are in the realm of ~~personal relationships.~~ PERSONALITIES. Human nature can be changed and is always being changed. But ~~you~~ WE must have enough faith so that ~~you~~ WE can be ~~a~~ channels for God's strength into ~~another man's life.~~ THE LIVES OF OTHERS.

Prayer for the Day

I pray that I may HAVE THE FAITH TO expect miracles. I pray that I may be ~~used as a channel for God's supply of strength.~~ USED BY GOD TO HELP CHANGE THE LIVES OF OTHERS.

195

JULY 11 -- A. A. Thought for the Day

We in Alcoholics Anonymous do not try to chart the path for the human soul or to lay out a blueprint of the workings of faith, as one might plan a charity drive. We do tell the newcomer that we have renewed our faith ~~anew~~ IN A HIGHER POWER. In telling him, our faith is further renewed. We believe that faith is always close at hand, waiting for those who will listen to the heartbeat of the spirit. We believe there is a force for good in the universe and that if we will link up with this force, we are carried ~~on~~ ONWARD to a ~~good~~ NEW life. Am I in this stream of goodness?

Meditation for the Day

God will protect you ~~against~~ FROM the forces of evil, if you WILL rely on him. You can face all things through the power of God which strengthens you. Once God has set on you His stamp and seal of ownership, all His strength will serve and protect you. Remember that you are a child of the Father. Realize that the Father's help is always ready and available to all His children, so that they can face anything. God will do all that is necessary for your spiritual well-being, IF YOU WILL LET HIM HAVE HIS WAY. ~~Trust Him. Rely on him.~~

Prayer for the Day

I pray that I may rely on God as I go through this day. I pray that I may feel deeply SECURE, NO MATTER WHAT HAPPENS TO ME. ~~that all will be well.~~

196

JULY 12 -- A. A. Thought for the Day

Today is ours. Let us live today as we believe God wants us to live. Each day will have a new pattern, which we cannot foresee. But we can open each day with a quiet period in which we say a little prayer, asking God to help us through the day. Personal contact with God, as we understand Him, will from day to day bring us nearer to an understanding of His will for us. At the close of the day, we offer Him thanks for another day of sobriety. A full, constructive day has been lived and we are grateful. Am I asking God each day for strength and thanking Him each night?

Meditation for the Day

If you believe that God's ~~strength~~ GRACE has saved you, then you must believe that He is meaning to save you yet more and to keep you in the way that you should go. Even a human rescuer does not save a man from drowning, only to place him in other deep and dangerous waters. But rather to place him on dry land and there to restore him~~, to his home.~~ God, WHO IS your rescuer, would certainly do this and even more. God will complete the task He sets out to do. He will not throw you overboard, IF YOU ARE DEPENDING ON HIM.

Prayer for the Day

I pray that I may trust God to keep me in the way. I pray that I may rely on Him not to let me go.

197

JULY 13 -- A. A. Thought for the Day

An alcoholic before he comes into A. A., is "flying blind". But A. A. gives him a directed beam in the A. A. programme. As long as he keeps on this beam, the signal of sobriety keeps coming through. If he has a slip, the signal is broken. If he swings [illegible] into drunkenness, the signal stops. Unless he regains the A. A. directed beam, he is in danger of crashing against the mountain peak of despair. Am I on the beam?

Meditation for the Day

Be expectant. Constantly expect better things. Believe that what God has in store for you is better than anything you ever had before. The way to grow old happily is to expect better things right up to the end of your life and even beyond that. A good life is a growing, expanding life, with ever widening horizons, an ever greater circle of friends and acquaintances and an ever greater opportunity for usefulness.

Prayer for the Day

I pray that I may await with complete faith for the next good thing in store for me. I pray that I may keep the expectant attitude of faith.

198

JULY 14 -- A. A. Thought for the Day

One of the best things about the A. A. programme is the peace of mind and the serenity that it brings us. In our drinking days, we had no peace of mind or serenity. We had the exact opposite, a kind of turmoil or that "quiet desperation" we knew so well. The turmoil of our drinking days was caused partly by physical suffering, the terrible hangovers, the cold sweats, the shakes and the jitters. But it was caused even more by mental suffering, the loneliness, the feelings of inferiority, the lying, the remorse that every alcoholic understands. Have I achieved peace of mind?

Meditation for the Day

Look for God's hand in all personal relationships, in all happenings of the day. God will take care of all our relationships with people, if we are willing to let Him. Rejoice that God protects you and keeps you from temptation and sin. God protects you in all things. Rely on His strength and go forward. You are entering upon the stage of success. You must not doubt that better things are ahead for you. Go forward unafraid because you are under God's protection.

Prayer for the Day

I pray that God may protect and keep me as long as I try to serve Him. I pray that I may go forward unafraid.

199

JULY 15 -- A. A. Thought for the Day

After we had sobered up through the A. A. programme, we gradually began to get a peace of mind and a serenity which we never thought were possible. This peace of mind is based on a feeling that fundamentally all is well. That does not mean that all is well on the surface of things. Little things can keep going wrong and big things can keep on upsetting us. But deep down [IN OUR HEARTS] we know that everything is [EVENTUALLY] going to be all right [NOW THAT WE ARE LIVING SOBER LIVES]. Have I [ACHIEVED] a deep down, inner calm?

Meditation for the Day

You are climbing up the ladder of life, which reaches into eternity. Would God plant your feet upon an insecure ladder? It's supports may be out of sight, hidden in ~~the~~ secret places, ~~of the Most High,~~ but if God has asked you to step on and up firmly, then surely He has secured your ladder. ~~Have~~ Faith [GIVES YOU THE STRENGTH TO] ~~as you~~ climb [STEADILY] this ladder of life. [YOU SHOULD] Leave [YOUR SECURITY] ~~everything~~ to God and trust Him not to let you fall, ~~but~~ [HE IS THERE] to give you all the [POWER] ~~strength~~ you need to keep on climbing. ~~to the top.~~

Prayer for the Day

I pray that I may climb [THE LADDER OF LIFE] without fear. I pray that I may ~~leave the result to God.~~ [PROGRESS STEADILY THROUGH THE REST OF MY LIFE WITH FAITH AND CONFIDENCE.]

200

JULY 16 -- A. A. Thought for the Day

[WE CAN BELIEVE THAT] God is in His heaven and [THAT] He has a purpose for our lives, which will eventually work out, as long as we try to live the way we believe He wants us to live. A colored mammy once said [THAT] she "wore the world like a loose garment". That meant that nothing could seriously upset her, because she had a deep, abiding faith that God would always take care of her. To us, that means not to be too upset by the surface wrongness of things, but to feel deeply secure in the fundamental goodness and purpose in the universe. Do I feel deeply secure?

Meditation for the Day

"Like the shadow of a great rock in a desert land", God is your refuge [FROM THE ILLS OF LIFE. THE OLD HYMN SAYS:] "Rock of ages, cleft for me, let me hide myself in Thee". God [CAN BE] ~~is~~ your shelter from the storm. God's power can protect you from every ~~sin and~~ temptation [AND DEFEAT. TRY TO FEEL] ~~Know~~ His divine power, call on it, accept it and use it. [ARMED] With that power, you can face anything. [EACH DAY,] Seek safety in God's secret place, in communion with Him. You cannot be [WHOLLY] touched or [SERIOUSLY] harmed there. God [CAN BE] ~~is~~ your refuge.

Prayer for the Day

I pray that I may find [A] haven in the thought of God. I pray that I may [ABIDE] ~~be~~ in that Strong Tower, strongly guarded.

201

JULY 17 -- <u>A. A. Thought for the Day</u>

The new life of sobriety we are learning to live in A. A. is slowly growing on us and we are beginning to get SOME OF that deep peace of mind and serenity that we never thought were possible. At first, we may have doubted that this could happen TO US, but after ~~a~~ ANY considerable length of time in A. A., looking at the happy faces around us, we know that SOMEHOW it is happening to us. In fact, it cannot help happening to ~~anybody~~ ANYONE who takes the A. A. programme seriously DAY BY DAY. <u>Can I see my own happiness reflected in the faces of others?</u>

<u>Meditation for the Day</u>

God does not withhold His presence from you. He does not refuse to reveal more of His truth to you. He does not hold back His ~~holy~~ spirit from you. He does not withhold the strength that you need. His presence, His truth, His spirit, His strength are always immediately available to you, whenever you are FULLY willing to receive them. But they ~~are~~ MAY BE blocked off by selfishness, intellectual pride, fear, greed and materialism. WE MUST TRY TO Get rid of these blocks, and let ~~God~~ GOD'S SPIRIT come in.

<u>Prayer for the Day</u>

I pray that I may remove all blocks THAT ARE KEEPING ME FROM GOD. I pray that I may let God come into my life with power.

202

JULY 18 -- <u>A. A. Thought for the Day</u>

Two things can spoil group unity, gossip and criticism. To avoid these divisive things, we must realize that we're all in the same boat. We're like a bunch of people in a life-boat after the steamer has sunk. If we're going to be saved, we've got to pull together. It's a matter of life ~~and~~ OR death with us. Gossip and criticism are sure ways of disrupting any A. A. group. We're all in A. A. to keep sober ourselves and to help each other to keep sober. And neither gossip nor criticism help anyone to stay sober. <u>Am I EVER guilty of gossip or criticism?</u>

<u>Meditation for the Day</u>

~~Walk very humbly with your God.~~ WE SHOULD TRY TO Be grateful for all the blessings ~~you~~ WE have received and which ~~you~~ WE do not deserve. Gratitude to God for all His blessings will make ~~you~~ US humble. Remember that ~~you can~~ WE COULD do little by ~~yourself but you~~ OURSELVES AND NOW WE must rely largely on God's ~~strength~~ GRACE in helping ~~yourself~~ OURSELVES and others. People do not care MUCH for those who are smug and self-satisfied OR THOSE WHO GOSSIP AND CRITICIZE. But people are impressed by true humility. So WE SHOULD TRY TO walk humbly at all times. ~~Never rely wholly on your own strength, but rely a great deal on God.~~ Gratitude to God and true humility are what make ~~you~~ US effective.

<u>Prayer for the Day</u>

I pray that I may walk humbly with God. I pray that I may rely on His ~~strength~~ GRACE to carry me ~~[illegible]~~ THROUGH.

203

JULY 19 -- A. A. Thought for the Day

Personalities have no place in an A. A. clubroom. Every man in A. A. is a brother and every woman is a sister, as long as he or she is a member of A. A. We ought not to gossip about the relationships of any man or women in the group. And if we say about a fellow member: "I think he's taking a few drinks on the side", it's the worst thing we could ~~to~~ DO to that person. If a man or a woman is not living up to A. A. principles, or IF HE has a slip, it's up to him or her to stand up in a meeting and say so. If he doesn't do that, he's only hurting himself. Do I talk about other members behind their backs?

Meditation for the Day

To God, a miracle OF CHANGE IN A PERSON'S LIFE is only a natural happening. But it is a natural happening ~~operating~~ OPERATED by spiritual forces. There is no miracle in ~~human relationships~~ PERSONALITIES too marvelous to be an everyday happening. But miracles happen only to those who are fully guided and strengthened by God. Marvelous changes in people's natures happen so simply, ~~so~~ AND YET THEY ARE free from all other agency than the grace of God. But these miracles have been ~~achieved~~ PREPARED FOR by days, AND MONTHS OF LONGING FOR SOMETHING BETTER. ~~of prepa-ration.~~ They are ALWAYS accompanied by a real desire to con-quer self and to surrender ONE'S LIFE to God.

Prayer for the Day

I pray that I may expect miracles in the lives of people. I pray that I may be used to help people change.

204

JULY 20 -- A. A. Thought for the Day

We must be loyal to the group and to each member of it. We must never accuse a member behind his back or even to his face. It's up to him to tell us himself if any-thing's wrong. More than that, we must try not to think bad things about any member, because if we do, we're consciously or unconsciously hurting that person. We must be loyal to each other, if A. A. is going to be successful. While we're in this life-boat, trying to save ourselves and each other from alcoholism, we must be truly and sincerely helpful to each other. Am I a loyal member of ~~the~~ MY group?

Meditation for the Day

Carry out God's guidance AS BEST YOU CAN. ~~and~~ Leave the results to Him. Do this obediently and faithfully with no question that, if the working out of the guidance is left in God's hands, the results will be all right. Believe that the guidance God gives you has already been worked out by God to produce the required results ~~in~~ ACCORDING TO your case and in your circumstances. So follow God's guidance ~~as well as you can.~~ ACCORDING TO YOUR CONSCIENCE. God has knowledge of your individual life and character, your capabilities and your weaknesses. ~~So God's guidance for you must have been given with full knowledge of the required result.~~

Prayer for the Day

I pray that I may live ~~the way I believe God wants me to live.~~ ACCORDING TO THE DICTATES OF MY CONSCIENCE. I pray that I may be content to leave the results to ~~Him.~~ GOD.

205

JULY 21 -- A. A. Thought for the Day

If we feel the need of saying something to put another member on the right track, we should say it to him with understanding and sympathy and not with a critical attitude. We should keep everything out in the open and above board. The A. A. programme is wonderful, but we must really follow it. We must all pull together or we'll all be sunk. We enjoy the privilege of being associated with A. A. and we are entitled to all its benefits. But gossip and criticism are not tolerance and tolerance is an A. A. principle that is absolutely necessary ~~for~~ TO group unity. Am I truly tolerant of my fellow members?

Meditation for the Day

"Faith can move mountains". That expression means that faith can change any situation in the field of personal relationships. IF YOU TRUST HIM, God shows you the way to "move mountains". If you are humble enough to know that you can do little by yourself TO CHANGE A SITUATION, if you have enough faith to ask God to give you the ~~strength~~ POWER you need and if you are grateful enough to God for the ~~strength~~ GRACE He gives you, you can "move mountains". ~~That is, there is no limit to the changes you can be used to bring about in human lives.~~ SITUATIONS WILL BE CHANGED FOR THE BETTER BY YOUR PRESENCE.

Prayer for the Day

I pray that I may have enough faith to make me really effective. I pray that I may LEARN TO depend less on myself and more on God.

206

JULY 22 -- A. A. Thought for the Day

One of the finest things about A. A. is the diversity of its membership. We come from all walks and stations of life. All types and classes of people are represented in an A. A. group. Being different from each other in certain ways, we can each make a different contribution to the whole. Some OF US are weak in one respect, but strong in another. A. A. can use the strong points of all its members and can disregard their weaknesses. A. A. is strong NOT ONLY BECAUSE WE ALL HAVE THE SAME PROBLEM, BUT ALSO because of the diversified talents of its members. Each CAN contribute~~s~~ his ~~best~~ PART. Do I recognize the good points of my fellow members?

Meditation for the Day

"And greater works than these shall ye do". Each ~~person~~ INDIVIDUAL has the ability to do good works through the power of God's spirit. This is the wonder of the world, the miracle of the ~~universe~~ EARTH, that God's power goes out to bless THE HUMAN RACE through the agency of ~~any person~~ SO MANY PEOPLE WHO ARE actuated by His ~~spirit~~ GRACE. ~~So arise from~~ WE NEED NOT BE HELD BACK BY doubt, despondency and ~~all other limitations~~ FEAR. A wonderful future ~~lies~~ CAN LIE before any person who depends on God's power, ~~A~~ a future of unlimited power to do good works~~, in the world~~.

Prayer for the Day

I pray that I may not limit myself by doubting. I pray that I may have confidence that I can be effective, FOR GOD.

207

JULY 23 -- A. A. Thought for the Day

We ~~must~~ SHOULD remember that all A. A.'s have "clay feet." We should not set any member of A. A. upon a pedestal and mark him out as a perfect A. A. It's not fair to the person to be singled out in this fashion and if he is wise, he will not wish it. If we single out any member as our ideal ~~in~~ A. A. and if he has a fall, we are ~~apt~~ IN DANGER OF ~~to~~ fall~~ing~~ with him. WITHOUT EXCEPTION, We are all only one drink away from a drunk, no matter how long we have been in A. A. NOBODY IS ENTIRELY SAFE. A. A. ITSELF should be our ideal, not any PARTICULAR member of it. Am I putting my trust in A. A. principles, AND NOT IN ANY ONE ~~or in some particular~~ member of the group?

Meditation for the Day

The inward peace that comes from trust in God truly passes all understanding. That peace no man can take from you. No ~~man~~ PERSON has the power to disturb that INNER peace. But you must be careful not to let in the world'S ~~and it's~~ worries and distractions. You must TRY not TO give entrance to fears and despondency. You must ~~not~~ REFUSE TO open the door to the distractions that disturb your ~~inner~~ INWARD peace. ~~Set yourself to this task,~~ MAKE IT A POINT to allow nothing TODAY to disturb your ~~inward~~ INNER peace, your heart-calm.

Prayer for the Day

I pray that I ~~will not let~~ MAY NOT ALLOW those about me TO spoil my peace of mind. I pray that I may keep a deep inner calm, THROUGHOUT THE DAY.

208

JULY 24 -- A. A. Thought for the Day

A. A. is like a dike, holding back the ocean of liquor. If we take one glass of liquor, it is like making a small hole in the dike, and once a hole has been made, the whole ocean of alcohol will ~~come~~ RUSH in upon us. By practicing the A. A. principles we keep the dike strong and in repair. We spot any weakness OR CRACK in that dike and make the necessary repairs before any damage is done. Outside the dike is the whole ocean of alcohol, waiting to engulf us again in despair. Am I keeping the dike strong?

Meditation for the Day

Keep as close as you can to the Higher Power. TRY TO Think, act and live as though you were always in God's presence. Keeping close to a Power greater than yourself is the solution to ~~all~~ MOST OF earth's problems. TRY TO Practice the presence of God in ~~everything~~ THE THINGS you think, ~~say~~ and do. That is the secret of ~~all~~ PERSONAL power, ~~and all peace and all~~ IT IS THE THING WHICH influenceS ~~in~~ the lives of others FOR GOOD. ~~Keep near to God.~~ Abide in the Lord, AND rejoice in His love. ~~Great things are ahead for you if you~~ Keep close to ~~God~~ THE DIVINE SPIRIT IN THE UNIVERSE. ~~Live in His presence and~~ Keep ~~Him~~ GOD CLOSE ~~at the bottom of all~~ BEHIND your thoughts.

Prayer for the Day

I pray that I may keep close to THE MIND OF God. I pray that I may live with Him in my heart, AND MIND.

209

JULY 25 -- A. A. Thought for the Day

We are living on borrowed time. We are living today because of A. A. and the grace of God. And what there is left of our lives we owe to A. A. and to God. We should make the best use we can of our borrowed time and in some small measure pay back for that part of our lives WHICH we wasted before we came into A. A. Our lives from now on are not our own. We hold them in trust for God and A. A. And we must do all we can to forward the great movement that has given us a new lease on life.

Am I holding my life in trust for A. A.?

Meditation for the Day

You ~~must~~ SHOULD hold your life in trust for God. Think DEEPLY ON what that means. Is anything too ~~wonderful for~~ MUCH TO EXPECT FROM such a life? Do you begin to see how ~~wonderful~~ DEDICATED a life in trust for God can be? IN SUCH A LIFE ~~Always expect~~ miracles ~~to~~ CAN happen. IF YOU ARE FAITHFUL, ~~Always~~ YOU CAN believe that God has many good things in store for you. God ~~is~~ CAN BE Lord of your life, controller of your days, OF your present and your future. ~~Only~~ TRY TO act as God guides, AND leave all results to Him. Do not hold back, ~~so~~ BUT GO all out ~~for God~~ AND THE BETTER LIFE. MAKE GOOD YOUR TRUST.

Prayer for the Day

I pray I may hold my life in trust for God. I pray that ~~I give it all to Him.~~ I MAY NO LONGER CONSIDER MY LIFE AS ALL MY OWN.

210

July 26 -- A. A. Thoughts for the Day

When we come to the end of our lives on earth, we will take no material thing with us. We will take not one cent in our cold, dead hands. The only things that we ~~will~~ MAY take are the things we have given away. If we have helped our fellow men, we ~~will~~ MAY take that with us; if we have given of our time and money for the good of A. A., we ~~will~~ MAY take that with us. Looking back over our lives, what are we proud of? Not what we have gained for ourselves, but what few good deeds we have done. Those are the things that really matter IN THE LONG RUN. What will I take with me when I go?

Meditation for the Day

"~~Our Lord, we thank Thee for so much. We bless Thee and praise Thy glorious name."~~ ~~Here "name" is used in the sense of "spirit".~~ "Hallowed ~~be~~ BE Thy name". WHAT DOES THAT MEAN TO US? ~~means thanks for God's spirit.~~ HERE 'NAME' IS USED IN THE SENSE OF 'SPIRIT'. ~~"Bless Thy name" means bless God's spirit in you.~~ THE WORDS MEAN PRAISE TO GOD FOR HIS SPIRIT IN THE WORLD, MAKING MEN BETTER. ~~You~~ WE should be especially grateful for God's spirit, which gives ~~you~~ US THE strength to overcome ~~all sin and temptation.~~ ALL THAT IS BASE IN OUR LIVES. HIS SPIRIT IS POWERFUL. ~~His spirit~~ It can help us to face anything and to live a conquering, abundant life. SO WE PRAISE AND THANK HIM FOR HIS SPIRIT IN OUR LIVES AND IN THE LIVES OF OTHERS.

Prayer for the Day

I pray that I may be grateful for God's spirit in me. I pray that I may TRY TO live in accordance with it.

211

JULY 27 -- A. A. Thought for the Day

"TO PARAPHRASE THE PSALM: We alcoholics declare the power of liquor and drunkenness sheweth its handiwork. Day unto day uttereth hangovers and night unto night sheweth suffering. The law of A. A. is perfect, converting the drunk. The testimony of A. A. is sure, making wise the simple. The statutes of A. A. are right, rejoicing the heart. The programme of A. A. is pure, enlightening the eyes. The fear of the first drink is clean, enduring forever." Have I any doubt about the power of liquor?

Meditation for the Day

"Walk humbly with Thy Lord". Walking with God means practicing the presence of God in ~~all~~ your DAILY affairs. It means asking God for strength to face each new day. It means turning to Him often during the day in prayer for yourself and for other people. It means thanking Him at night for the blessings you have received during the day. ~~Walk with God. Wear the world as a loose garment.~~ Nothing can seriously upset you if you are "walking with God." YOU CAN BELIEVE THAT HE ~~He~~ is beside you in spirit, to help YOU and to guide you, ON YOUR WAY.

Prayer for the Day

I pray that I may TRY TO walk humbly with God. I pray that I may turn to Him often, as to a close friend.

212

JULY 28 -- A. A. Thought for the Day

"TO CONTINUE THE PARAPHRASE OF THE PSALM: The judgments of the twelve steps are true and righteous altogether. More to be desired are they than whiskey, yea, than much fine whiskey, sweeter also than wine, ~~or beer.~~ Moreover, by them are alcoholics warned and in the keeping of them there is great reward. Who can understand his alcoholism? Cleanse us from secret faults. Keep us from presumptuous resentments. Let them not have dominion over us. Then shall we be upright, and free of the great transgression." Am I resolved that liquor will never again have dominion over me?

Meditation for the Day

~~Faith in God brings inward peace.~~ God ~~is~~ CAN BE your shield. THEN No buffets of the world can harm you. Between you and all scorn and indignity FROM OTHERS is your trust in God, like a ~~strong~~ SAINING shield. Nothing ~~should~~ CAN THEN have the power to spoil your inward peace. WITH THIS SHIELD, YOU CAN Attain this inward peace quickly, in your surroundings as well as in your heart. With this inward peace, you do not need to ~~overcome~~ RESENT the person who troubles you. Instead, you CAN overcome the ~~weakness~~ RESENTMENT in your own ~~nature~~ MIND which ~~has~~ MAY HAVE been aroused by ~~this~~ THAT person.

Prayer for the Day

I pray that I may ~~have the~~ STRIVE FOR inward peace. I pray that I may not be seriously upset, no matter what happens around me.

213

JULY 29 -- A. A. Thought for the Day

There are two days in every week about which we should not worry, two days which should be kept from fear and apprehension. One of these days is yesterday, with its mistakes and cares, its faults and blunders, its aches and pains. Yesterday has passed forever beyond our control. All the money in the world cannot bring back yesterday. We cannot undo a single act we performed. We cannot erase a single word we said. Yesterday is gone [BEYOND RECALL.] Do I still worry about [WHAT HAPPENED] yesterday?

Meditation for the Day

"God will not suffer you to be tempted above ~~that~~ [WHAT] ye are able, but with the temptation He will also find a way of escape, that ye may be able to bear it." If you have [ENOUGH] faith and trust in God, He will give you all the strength you need to face every temptation and to overcome it. Nothing will prove too hard for you to bear. You can face any situation. "Be of good cheer, I have overcome the world." You can overcome any temptation with God's help. So fear nothing.

Prayer for the Day

I pray that I may face every ~~temptation~~ [SITUATION] without fear. I pray that nothing will prove too hard for me to bear.

214

JULY 30 -- A. A. Thought for the Day

The other day we should not worry about is tomorrow, with its possible adversities, its burdens, its large promise and perhaps its poor performance. Tomorrow is also beyond our immediate control. Tomorrow's sun will rise, either in splendor or behind a mask of clouds, but it will rise. Until it does, we have no stake in tomorrow, for it is as [AS] yet unborn. Do I still worry [TOO MUCH] about tomorrow?

Meditation for the Day

"Faith is the substance of things hoped for, the evidence of things not seen." Faith is not seeing, but believing. Down through the ages, there have always been those who obeyed [THE HEAVENLY VISION,] not seeing but believing in God. And their faith was rewarded. So shall it be to you. [GOOD THINGS WILL HAPPEN TO YOU.] You cannot see God, but you can see the results of ~~His power~~ [FAITH] in human lives, ~~lives changed~~ [CHANGING THEM] from defeat to victory. ~~That strength~~ [GOD'S GRACE] is available to all who have faith, not seeing, but believing. ~~Keep firm in that faith, because life is not worth living without it.~~ With ~~it~~ [FAITH], life can be victorious and happy.

Prayer for the Day

I pray that I may have faith enough to believe without seeing. I pray that I may be content with the results of [MY] faith~~, which I see in changed human beings.~~

215

JULY 31 -- A. A. Thought for the Day

This leaves only one day, today. Any man can fight the battles of just one day. It is only when you and I add the burdens of those two awful eternities, yesterday and tomorrow, that we break down. It is not the experience of today that drives men mad. It is the remorse or bitterness for something which happened yesterday or the dread of what tomorrow may bring. Let us, therefore, DO OUR BEST TO live but one day at a time. Am I living one day at a time?

Meditation for the Day

Give God the gift of a thankful heart. TRY TO see causes of thankfulness in your everyday life. When life seems hard and troubles crowd, then look for SOME REASONS ~~causes~~ for thankfulness. There is NEARLY always something you can be thankful for. The offering of thanksgiving is indeed a sweet incense going up to God throughout the busy day. Seek diligently for something to be glad and thankful about. ~~Soon no search will be required.~~ You will AQUIRE IN TIME THE HABIT OF REMG ~~be~~ constantly grateful to God for all His blessings~~, most of which you do not deserve.~~ EACH ~~Every~~ day SOME new cause~~s~~ for joy and gratitude will spring to TO YOUR MIND ~~greet you~~ and you will thank God sincerely.

Prayer for the Day

I pray for a TRULY thankful heart. I pray that I may be constantly reminded of CAUSES FOR SINCERE GRATITUDE. ~~my own unworthiness.~~

216

AUGUST 1 -- A. A. Thought for the Day

The Alcoholics Anonymous programme has borrowed from medicine, psychiatry, and religion. It has taken from these what it wanted, and combined them into the programme which they consider best suited to the alcoholic mind, and which would best help alcoholics to recover. The results HAVE ~~has~~ been very satisfactory. We do not try to improve on the A. A. programme. Its value has been proved by the success it has had in helping THOUSANDS OF alcoholics to recover. It has everything we alcoholics need TO ARREST OUR ILLNESS. Do I TRY TO follow the A.A. programme just as it is?

Meditation for the Day

You SHOULD STRIVE FOR ~~must make~~ a union between your purposes IN LIFE and the purposes of the Divine Principle DIRECTING ~~in~~ the universe. There is no bond of union on earth to compare with the union between a HUMAN soul ~~that loves God~~ and God. Priceless beyond all earth's REWARDS ~~imaginings~~ is that UNION. ~~friendship.~~ In merging your heart and mind with the heart and mind of the HIGHER POWER, ~~universe,~~ a oneness of purpose results, which only those who experience it can even dimly realize. That oneness of purpose puts you in harmony with God and with ALL OTHERS WHO ARE TRYING TO DO HIS WILL. ~~your fellow men.~~

Prayer for the Day

I pray that I may become attuned to THE WILL OF God. I pray that I may be in harmony with the music of the spheres.

217

AUGUST 2 -- A. A. Thought for the Day

Alcoholics Anonymous has no quarrel with medicine, psychiatry or religion. We have great respect for the methods of each. And we are glad for ~~the~~ ANY success they MAY have had with alcoholics. We are desirous always of cooperating with them in every way. The more doctors, the more psychiatrists, the more ministers ~~, the more~~ OR priests we can get to work with us, the better we like it. We have many WHO TAKE A REAL INTEREST IN OUR PROGRAMME and would like many more. ~~Do I always~~ AM I READY cooperate with those ~~that~~ WHO take ~~an~~ A SINCERE interest in A. A.?

Meditation for the Day

God ~~loves~~ IS ALWAYS READY to pour His blessings INTO OUR HEARTS IN GENEROUS ~~down in rich and choicest~~ measure. But like the seed-sowing, the ground must be prepared before the seed is dropped in. ~~It~~ IT is ~~yours~~ OUR TASK to prepare the soil, God's to drop the seed. This preparation of the soil means MANY days ~~and years~~ of right living, EACH DAY choosing the right and avoiding the wrong. As you go along, each day ~~is~~ YOU ARE better prepared for God's ~~seasoning~~ PLANTING until you reach the TIME OF harvest. Then you ~~and~~ ~~God~~ share in the harvest WITH GOD - ~~[illegible]~~ the harvest of A USEFUL AND a more abundant life.

Prayer for the Day

I pray that my ~~life~~ WAY OF LIVING may be ~~a preparation for something better to come~~ PROPERLY PREPARED DAY BY DAY. I pray that I may STRIVE TO make MYSELF ready for the harvest, WHICH GOD HAS PLANTED IN MY HEART.

218

AUGUST 3 -- A. A. Thought for the Day

We in A. A. must remember that we are offering something intangible. We are offering a psychological and spiritual programme. We are not offering a medical programme. If a man needs medical treatment, we call in a doctor. If a man needs ~~sedatives or B-vitamins~~ A MEDICAL PRESCRIPTION, we let the doctor ~~give them to~~ PRESCRIBE FOR him. If a man needs hospital treatment, we let the hospital take care of him. Our vital A. A. work begins when a man is physically able to receive it. ~~Do I realize that I am not offering a medical programme?~~ AM I WILLING TO LEAVE MEDICAL CARE TO DOCTORS?

Meditation for the Day

~~God must prize the gift of every~~ EACH moment of your DAY WHICH YOU DEVOTE TO ~~life for Him~~ THIS NEW WAY OF LIFE IS A GIFT TO GOD. The gift of the moments. Even when your ~~longing~~ DESIRE to serve ~~Him has offered Him all of your life, every hour, every day, even then it is a long and~~ GOD IS SINCERE, IT IS not an easy THING ~~lesson~~ to learn ~~what it means~~ to give HIM MANY OF THESE ~~God all the~~ moments. The ~~little~~ DAILY things you had planned to do given up gladly so that you can ~~joyfully serve your fellow man~~ PERFORM A GOOD SERVICE OR SAY A KIND WORD. If you can see ~~God in everything~~ GOD'S PURPOSE IN MANY SITUATIONS, it will be easier to give Him ~~all the~~ MANY moments of your day. Every situation has two interpretations, your own and God's. ~~Try to give up your own for His.~~ TRY TO HANDLE EACH SITUATION IN THE WAY YOU BELIEVE GOD WOULD HAVE IT HANDLED.

Prayer for the Day

I pray that I may make my day count SOMEWHAT for God. I pray that I may not ~~waste them~~ SPEND IT ALL selfishly.

219

AUGUST 4 -- A. A. Thought for the Day

We in A. A. are offering a [KIND OF] psychological programme[, AS WELL AS A SPIRITUAL ONE]. ~~A~~ [FIRST, A] man must be mentally able to receive it. He must have made up his mind that he wants to quit drinking and he must be willing to do something about it. ~~Then we must get his confidence,~~ [HIS CONFIDENCE MUST BE OBTAINED. WE MUST] show him that we are his friends and really desire to help him. When we have his confidence, he will listen to us. ~~After that, it's a matter of group therapy, the~~ [THEN THE AA FELLOWSHIP IS A KIND OF GROUP THERAPY. A NEWCOMER NEEDS THE] fellowship of other alcoholics who understand his probems, because they have ~~been through~~ [HAD] it themselves. [THE INDIVIDUAL MUST LEARN TO REEDUCATE HIS MIND. HE MUST LEARN TO THINK DIFFERENTLY.] ~~Do I realize that I am offering a psychological programme?~~ [DO I DO MY BEST TO GIVE MENTAL HELP?]

Meditation for the Day

~~Draw into your being more and more of the wonderful Eternal Life.~~ It is the flow of the life eternal through spirit, mind and body that cleanses, heals, restores and renews, ~~youth. It passes on from you to others, with the same miracle-working power.~~ "And this is life eternal, that they may know Thee". Seek conscious contact with God more and more [EACH DAY]. Make God ~~the one~~ [AN] abiding presence ~~of your~~ [DURING THE] day. Be conscious of His spirit helping you. All that is done without ~~being done in the power of~~ God's spirit is passing. All that is done ~~in~~ [WITH] ~~that spirit~~ [GOD'S SPIRIT] is ~~life~~ eternal.

Prayer for the Day

I pray that I may be in the stream of eternal life. I pray that I may be cleansed and healed[, BY THE ETERNAL SPIRIT].

220

AUGUST 5 -- A. A. Thought for the Day

We in A. A. are ~~also~~ offering a spiritual programme. The fundamental basis of A. A. is belief in some Power greater than ourselves. This [BELIEF] takes a man off the center of the universe and allows him to transfer his problems to some Power outside of himself. He turns to this Power for the strength he needs to get sober and to stay sober. [HE PUTS HIS DRINK PROBLEM IN GOD'S HANDS AND LEAVES IT THERE. HE STOPS TRYING TO RUN HIS OWN LIFE AND SEEKS TO LET GOD RUN IT FOR HIM.] ~~Do I realize that I am offering a spiritual programme?~~ [DO I DO MY BEST TO GIVE SPIRITUAL HELP?]

Meditation for the Day

God is your healer and your strength, ~~forever.~~ You do not have to ask Him to come [TO YOU]. He is always with you [IN SPIRIT]. At your moment of need, He is there to help you. Could you know God's love, ~~could you know~~ [AND HIS] His desire to help you, you would know that He needs no pleading for help. Your need is God's opportunity. You must learn to rely on God's strength whenever you need it. Whenever you feel inadequate ~~for~~ [TO] any situation, you ~~must~~ [SHOULD] realize that the feeling of inadequacy is disloyalty to God. ~~Simply~~ [JUST] say to yourself: I know that God is with me and will help me to think and say and do the right thing.

Prayer for the Day

I pray that I may never feel inadequate [TO ANY SITUATION]. I pray that I may be buoyed up by the feeling that God is with me.

221

AUGUST 6 -- A. A. Thought for the Day

Psychologists are turning to religion, because just knowing about ourselves is not enough. A man needs the added dynamic of faith in a Power outside of himself, on which he can rely. Books on psychology and psychiatric treatments are not enough, without the strength that comes from faith in God. And ministers and priests are turning to psychology, because faith is an act of the mind ~~and~~ [AND WILL.] Religion must be presented in psychological terms [TO SOME EXTENT, IN ORDER] to satisfy the modern man. Faith must be built [LARGELY] on our own psychological experience. Have I taken ~~the best~~ [WHAT I NEED] from both phychology and religion? [WHEN I LIVE THE A.A. WAY?]

Meditation for the Day

Refilling with the spirit is something you need every day. For this refilling with the spirit, ~~you must turn more often to God.~~ You need these times of quiet communion, away, alone, without noise, without activity. [YOU NEED] ~~That~~ [THIS] dwelling apart, ~~that~~ [THIS] shutting yourself away in the very secret place of your being, away alone with ~~God.~~ [YOUR MAKER.] From these times of communion you come forth ~~into~~ [WITH] new power. ~~to bless and heal.~~ This refilling is the [BEST] preparation for effective work. When you are [SPIRITUALLY] filled, there is no work too hard for you. ~~Your God and you together go forth to bless and heal.~~

Prayer for the Day

I pray that I may be [DAILY] refilled with the [RIGHT] spirit. ~~of God.~~ I pray that I may be full of the joy of [TRUE] living.

222

AUGUST 7 -- A. A. Thought for the Day

We in A. A. are offering an intangible thing, a psychological and apiritual programme. [IT'S A WONDERFUL PROGRAMME. WHEN WE LEARN TO] ~~The newcomer must turn~~ [TURN TO] to a Higher Power, with faith that that Power can give ~~him~~ [US] the strength ~~he~~ [WE] need, [WE FIND PEACE OF MIND.] When ~~We must~~ [WE] re-educate ~~his~~ [OUR] mind by learning to think differently, [WE FIND NEW INTERESTS THAT MAKE LIFE WORTH WHILE.] ~~The man~~ [WE] who [HAVE] achieved sobriety through faith [IN GOD] and mental re-education ~~is a~~ [ARE] modern miracles. [IT IS] The function of [OUR] A. A. [PROGRAMME] ~~is~~ to produce modern miracles. ~~Is~~ [DO I CONSIDER] the change in my life a modern miracle?

Meditation for the Day

You ~~must~~ [SHOULD] never doubt that ~~God~~ [GOD'S SPIRIT] is always with you, wherever you are, to keep you ~~from harm~~ [ON THE RIGHT PATH]. God's keeping power is never at fault, ~~but~~ only your realization of it. You must [TRY TO] believe in God's nearness and the availability of His ~~power~~ [GRACE]. It is not a question of whether God can provide a shelter from the storm, but of whether [OR NOT] you ~~fail to~~ seek the security of that shelter. Every fear, ~~and every~~ [WORRY OR] doubt is disloyalty to God. You must [ENDEAVER TO] trust God wholly. Practice saying: All is [GOING TO BE] well. Say it [TO YOURSELF] until you feel it [DEEPLY.] ~~and know it.~~

Prayer for the Day

I pray that I may feel deeply that all is well. I pray that nothing will [IS ABLE TO] move me from that deep conviction.

223

AUGUST 8 -- A. A. Thought for the Day

For a while, we are going back to the big book: "Alcoholics Anonymous", and pick out passages here and there, so that they may become fixed in our minds, a little at a time, DAY BY DAY, as we go along. There is no substitute for reading the big book. It is our "bible". We should study it THOROUGHLY and make it a part of ourselves. We should not TRY TO change any of it. ~~It~~ WITHIN ITS COVERS is the full exposition of the A. A. programme. There is no substitute for it. WE SHOULD STUDY IT OFTEN. Have I studied the big book faithfully?

Meditation for the Day

ALL OF LIFE IS A FLUCTUATION BETWEEN EFFORT AND REST. ~~You need effort and rest, a union of the two.~~ YOU NEED BOTH EVERY DAY. But effort is not TRULY effective until first you have had the proper preparation FOR IT, BY RESTING IN A TIME OF QUIET MEDITATION. ~~, which is a quiet time and communion with God.~~ ~~Then you have~~ THIS DAILY TIME OF REST AND MEDITATION GIVES YOU the power necessary to make your BEST effort. ~~The law of supply for yourself is to give away something. All of life is a fluctuation between effort and rest.~~ There are days when you are called ~~to~~ ON FOR much effort and then comes a time when you need ~~to~~ MUCH rest. ~~But~~ IT IS NOT GOOD TO ~~do not~~ rest too long ~~, or you will get lazy, and do not~~ AND IT IS NOT GOOD TO carry on ~~one~~ GREAT effort too long ~~or you will get stale~~ WITHOUT REST. ~~There has to be a~~ THE SUCCESSFUL LIFE IS A PROPER balance between the two.

Prayer for the Day

I pray that I may ~~never refuse any opportunity.~~ BE READY TO MAKE THE PROPER EFFORT. I pray that I may also recognize the need for relaxation.

224

AUGUST 9 -- A. A. Thought for the Day

"We have an allergy to alcohol. The action of alcohol on chronic alcoholics is a manifestation of an allergy. We allergic types can never safely use alcohol in any form at all. We cannot be reconciled to a life without alcohol, unless we can experience an entire psychic change. Once this psychic change has occurred, we who seemed doomed, we who had so many problems that we despaired of ever solving them, find ourselves able to control our desire for alcohol." Have I had a ~~complete~~ psychic change?

Meditation for the Day

~~Rely on~~ ASK God IN DAILY PRAYER to give you the strength to change. ~~As much as is retained by you, that much less will be gained from God.~~ When you ask God to change you, you must AT THE SAME TIME FULLY trust ~~wholly to~~ Him. If you do not FULLY TRUST HIM, God ~~will~~ MAY answer your prayer ~~for help~~ as a rescuer does that of a drowning man who is putting up too much of a struggle. The rescuer must first render ~~him~~ THE DROWNING MAN still more helpless, until he is wholly at the rescuer's mercy. Just so MUST WE BE WHOLLY AT GOD'S MERCY ~~must an alcoholic reach his bottom~~, before ~~he~~ WE can be ~~saved.~~ RESCUED.

Prayer for the Day

~~I pray that I may empty myself quickly, to ensure Divine supply. I pray that I may pay out all, in perfect trust that more will come to meet my need.~~ I PRAY THAT I MAY BE DAILY WILLING TO BE CHANGED. I PRAY THAT I MAY PUT MYSELF WHOLLY AT THE MERCY OF GOD.

AUGUST 10 -- A. A. Thought for the Day

"The tremendous fact for every one of us is that we have discovered a common solution. We who have found this solution to our alcoholic problem, who are properly armed with THE facts about ourselves, can generally win the entire confidence of another alcoholic. We who are making the approach to a new prospect have had the same difficulty as he has had, we obviously know what we are talking about, our whole deportment shouts at the new prospect that we are men with a real answer." Am I a person with the real answer ~~?~~ TO THE ALCOHOLIC PROBLEMS OF OTHERS?

Meditation for the Day

For straying ~~or slipping~~ FROM THE RIGHT WAY there is no cure except to keep so close to THE THOUGHT OF God that nothing, no OTHER interest, ~~no temptation,~~ can SERIOUSLY come between you and God. Sure of that, you can ~~but~~ stay on God's side. Knowing ~~that as God is~~ the way, ~~itself~~ nothing can prevent your staying in the way and nothing can cause you to SERIOUSLY stray from it. God has promised peace if you stay close to Him, but not leisure. YOU STILL HAVE TO CARRY ON IN THE WORLD. He has promised heart-rest and comfort, but not pleasure in the ordinary sense. ~~"In the world ye shall have tribulation, but be of good cheer, I have overcome the world".~~ PEACE AND COMFORT BRING REAL INWARD HAPPINESS.

Prayer for the Day

I pray that I may keep my feet on the way. I pray that I may stay ~~close to God.~~ ON GOD'S SIDE.

AUGUST 11 -- A. A. Thought for the Day

"While an alcoholic keeps strictly away from drink, he reacts to life much like other men. But the first drink sets the terrible cycle in motion. An alcoholic usually has no idea why he takes the first drink. Some drinkers have excuses with which they are satisfied, but in their hearts they really do not know why they do it. The truth is that at some point in their drinking they have passed into a state where the most powerful desire to stop drinking is of no avail." Am I satisfied that I have passed my tolerance POINT for alcohol?

Meditation for the Day

He who made the ordered world out of chaos and set the stars in their courses and made each plant to know its season, He can bring peace and order out of your private chaos, if you will let Him. God is watching over you too, to bless you and care for you. Out of the darkness He is leading you to light, out of unrest to rest, out of disorder to order, out of faults and failure to ~~perfection.~~ SUCCESS. You belong to God and your affairs are His affairs and can be ordered by Him, IF YOU ARE WILLING.

Prayer for the Day

I pray that I may be led out of disorder into order. I pray that I may be led out of ~~darkness into light.~~ FAILURE INTO SUCCESS.

AUGUST 12 -- A. A. Thought for the Day

"There was nothing left for us but to pick up the simple kit of spiritual tools laid at our feet by Alcoholics Anonymous. By doing so, we have a spiritual experience which revolutionizes our whole attitude toward life, toward our fellows and toward God's universe. The central fact of our lives today is the absolute certainty that our Creator has entered into our hearts and lives there in a way which is indeed miraculous. He has commenced to accomplish those things for us which we could never do by ourselves." Have I let God come into my life?

Meditation for the Day

The moment a thing seems wrong to you, or a person's actions to be not what you think they should be, at that moment begins your obligation and responsibility to pray ~~and work~~ for those wrongs to be righted or that person to be ~~different.~~ CHANGED. What is wrong in your surroundings, OR in the people you know? Think ~~out~~ ABOUT these things and make these matters your responsibility. Not to interfere or be a busybody, but to pray that a change may come THROUGH YOUR INFLUENCE. You ~~will~~ MAY see lives altered and evils banished IN TIME. You can become a force for good ~~in your community.~~ WHEREVER YOU ARE.

Prayer for the Day

I pray that I may be a fellow-worker with God. I pray that I may help people by my example.

AUGUST 13 -- A. A. Thought for the Day

"We had but two alternatives, one was to go on to the bitter end, blotting out the consciousness of our intolerable situation as best we could, and the other was to accept spiritual help. We became willing to maintain a certain simple attitude toward life. What seemed at first a flimsy reed, has proved to be the loving and powerful hand of God. A new life has been given us, a design for living that really works. Each individual establishes in his own way his personal relationship with God." Have I established my own relationship with God?

Meditation for the Day

Make it a DAILY practice to review your character. Take your character in relation to YOUR DAILY life, to your dear ones, your friends, your acquaintances and your work. EACH DAY, TRY TO See where God wants you to change. Plan how best each fault can be eradicated or each mistake ~~or omission be avoided.~~ BE CORRECTED. Never be satisfied with a comparison with those around you. Strive toward ~~perfection~~ A BETTER LIFE as your ultimate goal. God is your helper ~~through darkness to light,~~ through weakness to power, through danger to security, through ~~indifference~~ FEAR AND WORRY to ~~love, through resentment to forgiveness.~~ TO PEACE AND SERENITY.

Prayer for the Day

I pray that I may make REAL progress toward a better life. I pray that I may never be satisfied with my present state.

229

AUGUST 14 -- A. A. Thought for the Day

"No person likes to think he is bodily and mentally different from his fellows. Our drinking careers have been characterized, by countless vain attempts to prove that we could drink like other people. This delusion that we are like other people has to be smashed. It has been definitely proved that no real alcoholic has ever recovered control. Over any considerable period we get worse, never better. There is no such thing as making a normal drinker out of an alcoholic." Am I convinced that I can never again drink normally?

Meditation for the Day

We should have life and have it more abundantly, spiritual, mental, physical, abundant life, joyous life, powerful life. These we can have if we follow the RIGHT way. Not all people will accept from God the gift of an abundant life, ~~the best~~ A gift held out free to all. ~~And~~ Not all people care to stretch out a hand to take it. God's gift, the richest ~~heaven~~ HE has to offer, IS the precious gift of abundant life, People often turn away from IT, reject IT, and will have none of IT. ~~Let~~ DO not LET this be true of you.

Prayer for the Day

I pray that I may hasten to accept the gift of abundant SPIRITUAL life. I pray that I may ~~accept the gift gratefully.~~ LIVE THE GOOD LIFE TO THE BEST OF MY ABILITY.

230

AUGUST 15 -- A. A. Thought for the Day

"Once an alcoholic, always an alcoholic. Commencing to drink after a period of sobriety, we are in a short time as bad as ever. If we have admitted we are alcoholics, we must have no reservations of any kind, nor any lurking notion that some day we will be immune to alcohol. What sort of thinking dominates an alcoholic who repeats time after time the desperate experiment of the first drink? Parallel with sound reasoning, there inevitably runs some insanely trivial excuse for taking the first drink. There is little thought of what the terrific consequences may be." Have I given up all excuses FOR TAKING A DRINK?

Meditation for the Day

"Where two or three are gathered together, I will be there in the midst of them." When God finds two or three people in union, who only want His will to be done, WHO WANT ONLY to serve ~~only~~ Him, He has a plan that can be revealed to them. The ~~spirit~~ GRACE of God can come to people who are together in one place with one accord. A union like this is miracle-working. God is ~~ready~~ ABLE to use such people. Only good can come through such consecrated people, brought together in unified groups, ~~Such groups can change the world.~~ FOR A SINGLE PURPOSE AND OF A SINGLE MIND.

Prayer for the Day

I pray that I may be part of a unified group. I pray that I may contribute my share, TO ITS CONSECRATED PURPOSE.

231

AUGUST 16 -- A. A. Thought for the Day

"The alcoholic is absolutely unable to stop drinking on the basis of self-knowledge. We must admit we can do nothing about it ourselves. Will power and self-knowledge will never help in the strange mental blank spots when we are tempted to drink. An alcoholic mentality is a hopeless condition. The last flicker of conviction that we can do the job ourselves must be snuffed out. The spiritual answer and the programme of action are the only Hope. Only spiritual principles will solve our problems. We are completely helpless apart from Divine help. Our defense against drinking must come from a Higher Power." Have I accepted the spiritual answer and the programme of action?

Meditation for the Day

Rest NOW ~~until~~ life, eternal life, flowing through your veins and heart and mind, bids you TO bestir yourself. Then glad work will follow. Tired work is never effective. The strength of God's spirit is always available to the tired mind and body. He is your physician and healer. Look to THESE quiet times of communion with God ~~for cure,~~ for rest, for peace, FOR CURE. Then rise refreshed IN SPIRIT and go out to work, knowing that your strength is able to meet any ~~difficulties~~ PROBLEMS because it is reinforced by God's ~~strength.~~ POWER.

Prayer for the Day

I pray that THE PEACE I HAVE FOUND WILL MAKE ME EFFECTIVE. ~~rest and work may follow each other naturally.~~

I pray that I may be relieved of all strain, DURING THIS DAY.

232

AUGUST 17 -- A. A. Thought for the Day

"To one who feels he is an atheist or agnostic, a spiritual experience seems impossible, but to continue as he is means disaster. To be doomed to an alcoholic death or to live on a spiritual basis are not always easy alternatives to face. But we have to face the fact that we must find a spiritual basis of life - or else. Lack of power is our dilemma. We have to find a power by which we can live, and it has to be a Power greater than ourselves." Have I found that Power BY WHICH I CAN LIVE?

Meditation for the Day

~~Sunshine helps to make glad the heart of man.~~ ~~It~~ SUNSHINE is the laughter of nature. Live ~~much~~ out in the sunshine. The sun and air are good medicine. Nature is a good nurse for tired bodies. Let her have her way with you. ~~And there is sunshine in God's spirit.~~ GOD'S GRACE IS LIKE THE SUNSHINE. ~~Your~~ LET whole being ~~can~~ be enwrapped in the Divine spirit. Faith is the soul's breathing in of the Divine spirit. It makes glad the heart of man. The Divine Spirit heals and cures THE MIND. Let it have its way with you and ~~you~~ ALL will be well.

Prayer for the Day

I pray that I may live in the sunshine of God's spirit.

I pray that ~~I~~ MY MIND AND SOUL may be energized by it.

AUGUST 18 -- A. A. Thought for the Day

"We of agnostic temperament have found that as soon as we were able to lay aside prejudice and express a willingness to believe in a Power greater than ourselves, we commenced to get results, even though it was impossible for any of us to fully define or comprehend that Power, which we call God. As soon as a man can say that he does believe, or is willing to believe, he is on his way. Upon this simple cornerstone a wonderfully effective spiritual structure can be built." Am I willing to depend on a Power that I cannot fully define or comprehend?

Meditation for the Day

~~You~~ [WE] seek God's presence and "they who seek shall find." It is not a question of searching so much as [AN INNER] consciousness, ~~a consciousness~~ of the presence of ~~God near you at all times.~~ [THE DIVINE SPIRIT IN YOUR HEART.] To realize God's presence, you must surrender to His will in the small, as [WELL AS] in the big things of life. This makes God's guidance possible. Some things separate you from God, a false word, a fear-inspired failure, a harsh criticism, [A STUBBORN RESENTMENT.] These are the things that put a distance between your ~~soul~~ [MIND] and God. A word of love, [A SELFLESS RECONCILIATION,] a kind act of helpfulness, these bring God closer.

Prayer for the Day

I pray that I may think and say and do the things that bring God closer [TO ME]. I pray that I [MAY] find Him in [A SINCERE PRAYER,] a kind word, ~~or~~ [OR AN UNSELFISH] deed.

AUGUST 19 -- A. A. Thought for the Day

"People of faith have a logical idea of what life is all about. There is a wide variation in the way each one of us approaches and conceives of the Power greater than himself. Whether we agree with a particular approach or conception seems to make little difference. These are questions for each individual to settle for himself. But in each case the belief in a Higher Power has accomplished the miraculous, the humanly impossible. There has come a revolutionary change in their way of living and thinking." Has there been a revolutionary change in me?

Meditation for the Day

Worship is consciousness of God's divine majesty. As you ~~kneel in~~ [PAUSE TO] worship, God will ~~make known to you His desire to~~ [HELP YOU TO] raise your humanity to His divinity. The earth is a material temple to enclose God's divinity. God brings to those who worship ~~Him~~ [A] divine power, [A] divine love and [A] divine healing. You only have to open your ~~heart~~ [MIND] to Him and try to ~~live the way you believe He wants you to live.~~ [ABSORB SOME OF HIS DIVINE SPIRIT.] ~~Kneeling~~ [PAUSING QUIETLY] in the spirit of worship, turn your inward ~~eyes heavenward~~ [THOUGHTS UPWARD] and realize ~~the~~ [THAT HIS] divine power that may be yours, ~~for the asking.~~ [THAT YOU CAN EXPERIENCE HIS LOVE AND HEALING.]

Prayer for the Day

I pray that I may ~~truly~~ worship God by sensing the eternal [SPIRIT]. I pray that I may ~~see life whole.~~ [EXPERIENCE A NEW POWER IN MY LIFE.]

235

AUGUST 20 -- A. A. Thought for the Day

"When many hundreds of people are able to say that the consciousness of the presence of God is today the most important fact of their lives, they present a powerful rea~~s~~on [s] why one should have faith. When we see others solve their problems by simple reliance upon the ~~s~~pirit [S] of the universe, we have to stop doubting the power of God. Our ideas did not work, but the God-idea does. Deep down in every man, woman and child is the fundamental idea of God. Faith in a Power greater than ourselves and miraculous demonstrations of that power in human lives, are facts as old as man Himself." Am I willing to rely on the ~~s~~pirit [S] of the universe?

Meditation for the Day

You ~~should~~ SHOULD not dwell TOO MUCH on the mistakes, faults and ~~bad habits~~ FAILURES of the past. Be done with shame and remorse and contempt for yourself. With God's help, develop a new self-respect. Unless you respect yourself, others will not respect you. You ~~run~~ RAN a race, you ~~have~~ stumbled and ~~fallen~~ FELL, you have risen again, and now you press on toward the goal of a ~~good~~ BETTER life. Do not stay to examine the spot where you fell, only feel sorry for the delay, the shortsightedness that prevented ~~your anticipating and avoiding the obstacles.~~ YOU FROM SEEING THE REAL GOAL SOONER.

Prayer for the Day

I pray that I may not look back. I pray that I may KEEP PICKING MYSELF UP AND mak~~e~~ING a fresh start ~~today.~~ EACH DAY.

236

AUGUST 21 -- A. A. Thought for the Day

"Who are you to say there is no God? This challenge comes to all of us. Are we capable of denying that there is a design and purpose in all of life as we know it? Or are we willing to admit that faith in some kind of Divine Principle is a part of our make-up, just as much as the feeling we have for a friend? We find a great Reality deep down within us, if we face ourselves as we really are. In the last analysis, it is only there that God may be found. When we find this Reality within us, we are restored to our right minds." Have I found the great Reality?

Meditation for the Day

"Behold, I make all things new." When you change to a new way of life, you leave ~~earthly~~ MANY things behind you. It is only the earth-bound spirit that cannot soar. ~~You should~~ Loosen SOMEWHAT the strands that tie you to the earth. It is only the earthly ~~strands~~ DESIRES that bind you. Your new freedom will depend on your ABILITY TO RISE ~~rising~~ above earthly things. Clipped wings can grow again. Broken ~~voices~~ WINGS can regain a strength and beauty unknown before. IF YOU WILL, You can be released and free.

Prayer for the Day

I pray that I may be freed from ~~the~~ things that ~~drag~~ HOLD me down. I pray that my spirit may soar in freedom.

237

AUGUST 22 -- A. A. Thought for the Day

"Those who do not recover are people who are constitutionally incapable of being honest with themselves. There are such unfortunates. They are not at fault. They seem to be born that way. They are naturally incapable of grasping and developing a manner of living which demands rigorous honesty. Their chances are less than average. There are those too who suffer from grave emotional and mental disorders, but many of them do recover, if they have the capacity to be honest." Am I completely honest with myself and with other people?

Meditation for the Day

You can make use of your mistakes, failures, losses and sufferings. It is not what happens to you, SO MUCH AS ~~but~~ what use you make of it. Take your sufferings, difficulties and hardships and MAKE use OF them to help some UNFORTUNATE ~~troubled~~ soul, WHO ~~so~~ IS FACED WITH THE SAME TROUBLES. ~~meet some need that must be met.~~ Then something good will come out of your suffering and the world will be A better PLACE because of it. The good YOU DO ~~of~~ each day will live on, after the troubles and distress have gone, after the difficulty and the pain have passed away.

Prayer for the Day

I pray that I may make good use of my mistakes and failures.
I pray that some good may result from my painful experienceS.

258

AUGUST 23 -- A. A. Thought for the Day

"We who have accepted the A. A. principles have all been faced with the necessity for a thorough personal house-cleaning. We must face and be rid of the things in our-selves which have been blocking us. We therefore take a personal inventory. We take stock honestly. We search out the flaws in our make-up which caused our failure. Resentment is the number one offender. Life which includes deep resentment leads only to futility and unhappiness. If we are to live, we must be free of anger." Am I free of resentment and anger?

Meditation for the Day

Keep in mind the goal you are striving for, the good life you are trying to attain. Do not let little things divert you from the path. Do not be overcome by the small trials and vexations of each day. TRY TO See the ~~one~~ purpose and plan to which all is leading. If WHEN ~~in~~ climbing a mountain you keep your eyes on each stony or difficult place, how weary IS ~~and profitless~~ your climb. But if you think of each step as leading to the summit of achievement from which a glorious landscape will open out before you, then your climb will be ENDURABLE ~~profitable~~ and you will achieve your goal.

Prayer for the Day

I pray that I may REALIZE ~~see,~~ that life without a goal is FUTILE. ~~wasted.~~
I pray that I may find the good life worth ~~building.~~ STRIVING FOR.

239

AUGUST 24 -- A. A. Thought for the Day

"When we saw our faults, we listed them. We placed them before is in black and white. We admitted our wrongs honestly and we were willing to set these matters straight. We reviewed our fears thoroughly. We asked God to remove our fears and we commenced to outgrow fear. Many of us needed an overhauling in regard to sex. We came to believe that sex powers were God-given and therefore good if used properly. Sex is never to be used lightly or selfishly, nor is it to be despised or loathed. If sex is troublesome, we threw ourselves the harder into helping others, and so took our minds off ourselves." Am I facing ~~my fears and~~ my sex problems ~~honestly?~~ IN THE PROPER WAY?

Meditation for the Day

~~"I can do all things through Him who strengthens me."~~

Cling to the ~~truth~~ BELIEF that all things are possible with God. IF ~~This~~ ~~truth accepted and firmly believed in~~ BELIEF IS TRULY ACCEPTED, IT is the ladder ~~up~~ UPON which a HUMAN soul can climb from the lowest pit of despair to the sublimest heights of ~~abundant living.~~ PEACE OF MIND. IT IS POSSIBLE FOR GOD TO CHANGE YOUR WAY OF LIVING. When you see the ~~complete~~ change in ~~a~~ ANOTHER person through ~~the power of the~~ grace of God, you cannot doubt that ~~in the realm of personality~~ all things are possible IN THE LIVES OF PEOPLE through the strength that comes from faith in Him, WHO RULES US ALL.

Prayer for the Day

I pray that I may live expectantly. I pray that I may ~~expect miracles to happen in human lives.~~ BELIEVE DEEPLY THAT ALL THINGS ARE POSSIBLE WITH GOD.

240

AUGUST 25 -- A. A. Thought for the Day

"Unless we discuss our defects with another person, we do not acquire enough humility, fearlessness, and honesty to really get the programme. We must be entirely honest with somebody, if we expect to live happily in this world. We must be hard on ourselves, but always considerate of others. We pocket our pride and go to it, illuminating every twist of character and every dark cranny of the past. Once we have taken this step, withholding nothing, we can look the world in the eye." Have I discussed ALL my defects with another person?

Meditation for the Day

Never yield to weariness of the spirit. At times, the world's cares and distractions will intrude and the spirit will become weak. At times like this, carry on and soon the spirit will become strong again. God's spirit is always with you, to replenish and renew. None ever SINCERELY sought God's help in vain. Physical weariness and exhaustion make a time of rest and communion with God MORE necessary. When you are overcome by temporary conditions which you cannot control, keep quiet and wait for the power of the spirit to flow back.

Prayer for the Day

I pray that I may not speak or act in the midst of emotional upheaval. I pray that I may wait until the tempest is past.

241

AUGUST 26 -- A. A. Thought for the Day

"If we are still clinging to something that we will not let go, we must sincerely ask God to help us to be willing to let even that go too. We cannot divide our lives into compartments and keep some for ourselves. We must give all the compartments to God. We must say: My Creator, I am now willing that you should have all of me, good and bad. I pray that you now remove from me every single defect of character which stands in the way of my usefulness to you and my fellows." Am I still clinging to something that I will not let go?

Meditation for the Day

The laws of nature cannot be changed and must be obeyed, IF YOU ARE TO STAY HEALTHY. No exceptions will be made in your case. Submit to the laws of nature or they will FINALLY break you. ~~But~~ AND in the realm of the spirit, in all human relationships, submit to THE MORAL LAWS AND TO the will of God. If you CONTINUE TO break the laws of honesty, purity, unselfishness or love, you will be TO SOME EXTENT broken yourself. The MORAL AND SPIRITUAL laws of God, like the laws of nature, are unbreakable without SOME disaster. If you are dishonest, impure, selfish or unloving, you will be NOT BE ~~unhappy.~~ LIVING ACCORDING TO THE LAWS OF THE SPIRIT AND YOU WILL SUFFER THE CONSEQUENCES.

Prayer for the Day

I pray that I may submit to the laws of nature and TO the laws of God. I pray that I may live in harmony with ALL THE LAWS OF LIFE. ~~the universe.~~

242

AUGUST 27 -- A. A. Thought for the Day

"We must be willing to make amends to all the people we have harmed. We must do the best WE CAN to repair the damage done in the past. When we make amends, when we say: I'm sorry, the person is sure to at least TO be impressed by our sincere desire to set right the wrong. Sometimes a person we are making amends to admits his own fault, so feuds of long standing melt away. Our most ruthless creditors will sometimes surprise us. In general, we must be willing to do the right thing, no matter what the consequences may be for us." Have I made a sincere effort to make amends to the people I have harmed?

Meditation for the Day

~~God~~ THE GRACE OF GOD cures disharmony and disorder in human relationships. Directly you put your affairs, with their confusion and their difficulties, into God's hands, He begins to effect a cure of all the disharmony and disorder. You ~~must know~~ CAN BELIEVE that He ~~shall~~ WILL cause you no more pain in the doing of it than a physician, who plans and knows that he can effect a cure, would cause his patient. ~~He~~ YOU CAN HAVE FAITH THAT GOD will do all THAT IS NECESSARY as painlessly as possible. But you must be willing to submit to His treatment, EVEN IF YOU CANNOT NOW SEE THE MEANING OR PURPOSE OF IT.

Prayer for the Day

~~I pray that I may be calm in all disrupting situations. I pray that I may face the consequences of my actions calmly.~~ I PRAY THAT I MAY WILLINGLY SUBMIT TO WHATEVER SPIRITUAL DISCIPLINE IS NECESSARY. I PRAY THAT I MAY ACCEPT WHATEVER IT TAKES TO LIVE A BETTER LIFE.

243

AUGUST 28 -- A. A. Thought for the Day

"We must continue to take personal inventory and continue to set right any new mistakes as we go along. We should grow in understanding and effectiveness. This is not an overnight matter; it should continue for our life time. Continue to watch for selfishness, dishonesty, resentment and fear. When these crop up, we ask God at once to remove them. We must not rest on our laurels. We are headed for trouble if we do. We are not cured of alcoholism. What we really have is a daily reprieve, contingent on the maintenance of our spiritual condition." Am I checking my [SPIRITUAL] condition daily?

Meditation for the Day

Happiness [CANNOT BE SOUGHT DIRECTLY; IT] is a by-product of love and service. Service is a law of ~~God~~ [OUR BEING]. With love in your heart, there is always [SOME] service ~~of~~ [TO] your fellow man. A life of power and joy [AND SATISFACTION] is built on love and service. A man who hates or is [TOO] selfish is going against the law of ~~God~~ [HIS OWN BEING]. He cuts himself off from God and His fellow man. Little acts of love and encouragement, of service and help, ~~smooth out~~ [ERASE] the rough places of life and [HELP TO] make the path ~~easy.~~ [SMOOTH. IF WE DO THESE THINGS, WE CANNOT HELP HAVING OUR SHARE OF HAPPINESS.]

Prayer for the Day

I pray that ~~my life may be built on~~ [I MAY GIVE MY SHARE OF] love and service. I pray that I may not grow weary in my attempts to do the right thing.

244

AUGUST 29 -- A. A. Thought for the Day

"We cannot get along without prayer and meditation. On awakening, let us think about the twenty-four hours ahead. We consider our plans for the day. Before we begin, we ask God to direct our thinking. Our thought lives will be placed on a much higher plane, when we start the day with prayer and meditation. We conclude this period of meditation with a prayer that we will be shown through the day what our next step is to be. The basis of all our prayers is: Thy will be done in me and through me today." Am I sincere in my desire to do God's will [TODAY]?

Meditation for the Day

Breathe in ~~God's spirit. It is the spirit of right human relationships.~~ [THE INSPIRATION OF GOODNESS AND TRUTH.] It is the spirit of honesty, purity, unselfishness and love. It is readily available if we are willing to accept it [WHOLEHEARTEDLY]. God has given us two things: His spirit and the power of choice, to accept it or not, as we will. We have [THE GIFT OF] free will. When we choose the path of selfishness and greed and pride, we are refusing to accept God's spirit. When we choose the path of love and service, we accept God's spirit and it flows into us and makes all things new.

Prayer for the Day

I pray that I may choose the right ~~path.~~ [WAY.] I pray that I may [TRY TO] follow it to the end.

248

AUGUST 30 -- A. A. Thought for the Day

"Practical experience shows that nothing will so much insure immunity from drinking as intensive work with other alcoholics. Carry the message to other alcoholics. You can help when no one else can. You can secure their confidence when others fail. Life will take on a new meaning for you. To watch people recover, to see them help others in turn, to watch loneliness vanish, to see a fellowship grow about you, to have a host of friends, this is an experience you must not miss." Am I ~~trying~~ ALWAYS READY AND WILLING to help other alcoholics?

Meditation for the Day

~~The~~ ONE secret of abundant living is THE ART OF giving. THE PARADOX OF LIFE IS THAT The more you give, the more you have. If you lose your life in THE service OF OTHERS, you will save it. YOU CAN Give abundantly AND SO LIVE ABUNDANTLY. You are rich in one respect. You have a spirit that is inexhaustible. ~~Have~~ LET no mean or selfish thought ~~in your heart.~~ KEEP YOU FROM SHARING THIS SPIRIT. Of love, of help, of ~~all you have,~~ UNDERSTANDING AND OF SYMPATHY, give and keep giving. Give your ~~time, your~~ personal ease and comfort, ~~your healing, your strength, your sympathy; of all these and many more.~~ YOUR TIME, YOUR MONEY AND MOST OF ALL, YOURSELF. AND YOU WILL BE LIVING ABUNDANTLY.

Prayer for the Day

~~I pray that I may learn the lesson of giving.~~ I pray that I may live to give. I PRAY THAT I MAY LEARN THE SECRET OF ABUNDANT LIVING.

246

AUGUST 31 -- A. A. Thought for the Day

"Call on a prospect while he is still jittery. He may be more receptive when depressed. See him alone if possible. Tell him enough about your drinking habits, symptoms, and experiences to encourage him to speak of himself. If he wishes to talk, let him do so. If he is not communicative, talk about the troubles liquor has caused you, being careful not to moralize or lecture. When he sees you know all about the drinking game, commence to describe yourself as an alcoholic, and tell him how you learned you were sick." ~~Do I mind talking~~ AM I READY TO TALK about myself to a prospect?

Meditation for the Day

~~Do~~ TRY not TO give way to criticism, BLAME, scorn or judgment of others, ~~or to uncontrolled emotion.~~ WHEN YOU ARE TRYING TO HELP THEM. Effectiveness in helping others depends on controlling yourself. You may be swept away by A temporary natural urge, TO CRITICIZE OR BLAME, unless you keep a tight rein on your emotions. You ~~must~~ SHOULD have a firm foundation of spiritual living, WHICH MAKES YOU TRULY HUMBLE, if you are going to really help other people. ~~Pray for others and deny~~ GO EASY ON THEM AND BE HARD ON yourself. That is the MOST way you can be used ~~by God to help other people.~~ TO UPLIFT A DESPAIRING SPIRIT. AND SEEK NO PERSONAL RECOGNITION FOR WHAT YOU ARE USED BY GOD TO ACCOMPLISH.

Prayer for the Day

I pray that I may ~~avoid emotional upsets.~~ TRY TO AVOID JUDGMENT AND CRITICISM. I pray that I may ~~keep a tight rein upon myself.~~ ALWAYS TRY TO BUILD UP A PERSON INSTEAD OF TEARING HIM DOWN.

247

September 1 -- A. A. Thought for the Day

"Be careful not to brand the prospect as an alcoholic. Let him draw his own conclusion. But talk to him about the hopelessness of alcoholism. Tell him exactly what happened to you and how you recovered. Stress the spiritual feature freely. If the man be AN agnostic or atheist, make it emphatic that he does not ave to agree with your conception of God. He can choose any nception he likes, provided it makes sense to him. The main thing is that he be willing to believe in a Power greater than himself and that he live by spiritual principles." ~~Can I get over the spiritual basis to a prospect?~~ DO I HOLD BACK TOO MUCH IN SPEAKING OF THE SPIRITUAL PRINCIPLES OF THE PROGRAM?

Meditation for the Day

"I will never leave nor forsake thee". Down through the centuries, thousands have BELIEVED IN ~~proved~~ God's constancy, untiringness, AND unfailing love. ~~God's love will never leave you. His understanding will~~ never leave you. His strength ~~will~~ never leave ~~you~~. God HAS ~~is~~ love. Then forever you are sure of HIS love. God HAS ~~is~~ POWER. ~~strength~~. Then forever, YOU ARE SURE, in every difficulty and temptation, ~~you are sure~~, of HIS strength. God HAS ~~is~~ patience. Then always there is One who can never tire. God HAS ~~is~~ understanding. Then always you will understand and be understood. UNLESS YOU WANT HIM TO GO, God will never leave you. ~~He is in the universe.~~ HE IS ALWAYS READY WITH POWER.

Prayer for the Day

I pray that I may ~~set my affection on God.~~ FEEL THAT GOD'S LOVE WILL NEVER FAIL. I pray that ~~I may never lose the sense of His presence.~~ I MAY HAVE CONFIDENCE IN HIS UNFAILING POWER.

248

September 2 -- A. A. Thought for the Day

"Outline the programme of action to a new prospect, explaining how you made a self-appraisal, how you straightened out your past, and why you are now endeavoring to be helpful to him. It is important for him to realize that your attempt to pass this on to him plays a vital part in your own recovery. The more hopeless he feels, the better. He will be more likely to follow your suggestions. Tell him about the fellowship of A. A. and if he shows interest, lend him your copy of the book." Can I get over THE A.A. ~~my~~ story to another alcoholic?

Meditation for the Day

You SHOULD TRY TO STAND ASIDE AND ~~must~~ let the Lord work through you. You SHOULD TRY ~~must~~ not TO block Him off BY YOUR OWN EFFORTS, or prevent His spirit working through you. ~~as a channel.~~ God desires your obedient service and your loyalty to the ideals of TH NEW LIFE YOU ARE SEEKING ~~honesty, purity, unselfishness and love~~. If you are loyal to God, He will give you protection against MISTAKES ~~temptation~~. His spirit will ~~fight for you,~~ plan for you, AND secure FOR you a sufficiency TRUE VICTORY AND REAL SUCCESS, of all spiritual HELP ~~things~~. You will have ~~all the power you need,~~ if you WILL PUT YOURSELF IN THE BACKGROUND AND let God work through you.

Prayer for the Day

I pray that I may not interfere with the working of God's spirit in me and through me. I pray that I may give it full rein.

249

September 3 -- <u>A. A. Thought for the Day</u>

"Offer a new prospect friendship and fellowship. Tell him that if he wants to get well you will do anything to help. Burn the idea into the consciousness of the prospect that he can get well, regardless of anyone else. Job or no job, wife or no wife, he cannot stop drinking as long as he places dependence on other people ahead of dependence on God. Let no alcoholic say he cannot recover unless he has his family back. This just isn't so. His recovery is not dependent on other people. It is dependent upon his own relationship to God." <u>Can I recognize all excuses made by a prospect</u>?

<u>Meditation for the Day</u>

~~The real life is in the Unseen.~~ [THE] ~~It is~~ a spiritual life [DEPENDS UPON THE UNSEEN]. To ~~really~~ [THE SPIRITUAL LIFE] live, you must ~~abide in the life of~~ [BELIEVE IN] the Unseen~~; with God.~~ ~~Do~~ [TRY TO] not ~~ever~~ lose [THE] consciousness of God's spirit in you [AND IN OTHERS]. As a child in its mother's arms, stay sheltered in the ~~spirit~~ [UNDERSTANDING] and ~~strength~~ [LOVE] of God. God will relieve you of the weight of ~~sin~~ [WORRY] and care, misery and depression, want and woe, faintness and heartache [IF YOU WILL LET HIM]. Lift up your ~~head~~ [EYES] from earth's troubles and view the glory ~~of God.~~ [OF THE UNSEEN GOD.] Each day ~~see more of heaven on earth.~~ [TRY TO SEE MORE GOOD IN PEOPLE, MORE OF THE UNSEEN IN THE SEEN.]

<u>Prayer for the Day</u>

I pray that I may rest and abide in ~~God's spirit,~~ [PRESENCE OF THE UNSEEN GOD.] I pray that I may leave my burdens ~~with God.~~ [IN HIS CARE.]

250

September 4 -- <u>A. A. Thought for the Day</u>

"We must be careful never to show intolerance or hatred of drinking as an institution. Experience shows that such an attitude is not helpful to anyone. We are not fanatics or intolerant of people who can drink normally. Every prospect ~~is~~ [IS] relieved when he finds we are not witch-burners. Temperate drinking is O.K., but we alcoholics can't get away with it. And no alcoholic likes to be told about alcohol by anyone who hates it. We shall be of little use if our attitude is one of bitterness or hostility." <u>Do I have tolerance for those who can drink normally</u>?

<u>Meditation for the Day</u>

Do not become encumbered by petty annoyances. Never respond to emotional upsets by emotional upset. [TRY TO] Keep calm in all circumstances. ~~Do~~ [TRY] not [TO] fight back. Call on the ~~spirit~~ [GRACE] of God to calm you [WHEN YOU FEEL LIKE RETALIATING]. ~~You need peace constantly, that perfect peace that the world can neither give not take away.~~ Look to God for ~~that peace.~~ [THE INNER STRENGTH]. ~~Rely on God to keep you calm.~~ [TO] Drop ~~the burdens~~ [THOSE RESENTMENTS] that ~~seem to~~ drag you down. If you are burdened by annoyances, you will lose your [INWARD] peace and the spirit of God will be shut out. [TRY TO] Keep ~~perfect peace~~ [PEACEFUL] within.

<u>Prayer for the Day</u>

I pray that I may do the things that make for peace. I pray that I may have a mission of conciliation.

251

September 5 -- A. A. Thought for the Day

One of the mottoes of A. A. is "First Things First". This means that we should always keep in mind that alcohol is our number one problem. We must never let any other problem, whether of family, business, friends or anything else take precedence in our minds over our alcoholic problem. As we go along in A. A., we learn to recognize the things that may upset us emotionally. When we find ourselves getting upset over something we must realize that it's a luxury we alcoholics cannot afford. Anything that may make us forget our number one problem is dangerous to us. Am I keeping ~~avoidance of alcohol~~ SOBRIETY in first place in my mind?

Meditation for the Day

Spiritual progress is the law of ~~the universe~~ YOUR BEING. ~~Higher, ever higher, rise to life and~~ TRY TO SEE AROUND YOU MORE AND MORE OF beauty, AND TRUTH, knowledge and power. Today TRY TO be stronger, braver, more loving, as a result of what you did yesterday. This law of SPIRITUAL progress gives ~~a~~ meaning and ~~a~~ purpose to YOUR life. Always expect better things AHEAD. ~~Always expect miracles.~~ You can ~~do anything~~ ACCOMPLISH MUCH GOOD through the strength of God's spirit, IN YOU. Never be TOO discouraged. The world is ~~getting~~ SURE TO GET better, in spite of set-backs of war, ~~and~~ hate and greed. Be a part of ~~God's kingdom on earth.~~ THE CURE OF THE WORLD'S ILLS RATHER THAN PART OF THE DISEASE.

Prayer for the Day

I pray that I may ~~keep in the stream of progress.~~ KEEP PROGRESSING IN THE BETTER LIFE. I pray that I may be A part of ~~it.~~ THE FORCES FOR GOOD IN THE WORLD.

252

September 6 -- A. A. Thought for the Day

Another of the mottoes of A. A. is "Live and Let Live". This of course means tolerance of people who think differently than we do, whether they are in A. A. ~~of~~ OR outside of A. A. We cannot afford the luxury of being intolerant or critical of other people. We do not try to impose our wills on those who differ from us. We are not "holier than thou". We do not have all the answers. We are not better than other good people. We live the best WAY we can and we allow others to do likewise. Am I willing to live and let live?

Meditation for the Day

~~Look not so much at the things that are seen, as at the real, eternal things.~~ "And this is life eternal, that we may know thee, the only true God". Learning to know God AS BEST WE CAN draws the ~~life~~ eternal LIFE NEARER TO YOU. ~~very near.~~ Freed from SOME OF the limitations of humanity, you can ~~serve your fellow men's real spiritual needs, understand them and their difficulties and temptations.~~ GROW IN THE THINGS THAT ARE ETERNAL. YOU CAN STRIVE FOR WHAT IS REAL AND OF ETERNAL VALUE. The more you try to live in THE CONSCIOUSNESS OF the unseen world, the gentler will be your passing into it when the time comes FOR YOU TO GO. This life on earth ~~is all~~ SHOULD BE LARGELY a preparation for the eternal life to come.

Prayer for the Day

~~I pray I may make my life a preparation by putting eternal things first. I pray that my life may be one of faith, fellowship and service.~~ I PRAY THAT I MAY LIVE EACH DAY AS THOUGH IT WERE MY LAST. I PRAY THAT I MAY LIVE MY LIFE AS THOUGH IT WERE EVERLASTING.

253

September 7 -- A. A. Thought for the Day

Another of the mottoes of A. A. is "Easy Does It". This means that we just go along in A. A., doing the best we can and not getting ~~stewed~~ STEAMED up over problems that arise in A. A. or outside of ~~A. A.~~ IT. We alcoholics are emotional people and we have gone to excess in almost everything we have done. We have not been moderate in many things. We have not ~~learned~~ KNOWN HOW to relax. Faith in a Higher Power ~~helps~~ CAN HELP us to LEARN TO take it easy. We are not running the world. I AM ONLY ONE AMONG MANY. We are resolved to live normal, REGULAR lives. FROM OUR A.A. EXPERIENCE WE LEARN THAT EASY DOES IT. Have I learned to take it easy?

Meditation for the Day

"The Eternal God is thy refuge, AND Underneath are the everlasting arms." Sheltering arms express the loving ~~tenderness~~ PROTECTION of God's spirit. Man, in his troubles and difficulties, needs nothing so much as a refuge, a place to ~~hide in~~ RELAX, a place ~~where nobody and nothing can touch him.~~ WHERE WE CAN LAY DOWN HIS BURDENS AND GET RELIEF FROM HIS CARES. Say to yourself: God is my refuge. Say it until its truth sinks into your very soul. Say it until you know it and are sure of it. Nothing can SERIOUSLY UPSET YOU OR make you afraid, if God is TRULY your refuge.

Prayer for the Day

I pray that I may ~~keep going~~ GO EACH DAY to God as a refuge, until fear goes and peace AND SECURITY come~~s~~. I pray that I may feel DEEPLY secure in ~~God's everlasting arms.~~ THE HAVEN OF HIS SPIRIT.

254

September 8 -- A. A. Thought for the Day

Another of the mottoes of A. A. is "But for the Grace of God". Once we have fully accepted the programme, we become humble about our achievement. We do not take too much credit for our sobriety. When we see another suffering alcoholic in the throes of alcoholism, we say to ourselves: But for the grace of God, there go I. We do not forget the kind of people we were. We remember the men we left behind us. And we are very grateful to the grace of God which has given us another chance. Am I truly grateful for the Grace of God?

Meditation for the Day

~~Walk in God's love.~~ A consciousness of God's presence as ~~love~~ ONE WHO LOVES YOU makes all life different. The consciousness of God's love ~~means~~ PROMOTES the opening of your whole being to God. ~~That~~ IT brings WONDERFUL relief from ~~all sin and temptation.~~ THE CARES AND WORRIES OF OUR DAILY LIVES. Relief brings peace AND Peace brings ~~joy~~ CONTENTMENT. TRY TO Walk in God's love. You will have that peace ~~that~~ WHICH passes all understanding and A CONTENTMENT ~~joy~~ that no man can take from you. ~~Be~~ FEEL sure of God's UNFAILING love and care for you and for all His children. There is ~~gladness and helpfulness~~ FREEDOM AND SERENITY in those who walk in God's love, HELD SAFE IN HIS LOVING CARE.

Prayer for the Day

I pray that ~~my walk with God will become a glad, conquering and useful march.~~ I MAY WALK IN GOD'S LOVE. I pray that, as I go, I may feel ~~a~~ THE spring of God's power in my steps, AND THE JOY OF HIS LOVE IN MY HEART.

255

September 9 -- A. A. Thought for the Day

"When an alcoholic is offered a life of sobriety by following the A. A. programme, he will look at the prospect of living without alcohol and he will ask: Am I to be consigned to a life where I shall be stupid, boring and glum, like some OF THE righteous people I see? I know I must get along without liquor, but how can I? Have you a sufficient substitute?" ~~In talking with a prospect, have I got the answers to these questions?~~ HAVE I FOUND A MORE THAN SUFFICIENT SUBSTITUTE FOR DRINKING?

Meditation for the Day

In God's strength you conquer LIFE. Your conquering power is the grace of God. There can be no COMPLETE failure with God. Do you want to make the best of life? Then live AS ~~very~~ near AS POSSIBLE to God, the Master and Giver of all life. Your reward for depending on God's strength will be sure. Sometimes the reward will be ~~people changed,~~ RENEWED POWER TO FACE LIFE, sometimes ~~the diseases of the mind~~ WRONG THINKING overcome, sometimes people brought to a new way of living. Whatever success comes, ~~it~~ will not be ALL your OWN doing, but LARGELY THE WORKING OUT OF the grace of God.

Prayer for the Day

I pray that I may ~~be content with God's judgment.~~ TRY TO RELY MORE FULLY ON THE GRACE OF GOD. I pray that I ~~may not mind the judgment of the world.~~ MAY LIVE A VICTORIOUS LIFE.

256

September 10 -- A. A. Thought for the Day

"Here are the answers to the question of how ~~can~~ a man CAN live without liquor and be happy. The things we put in place of drinking are more than substitutes for it. One is the fellowship of Alcoholics Anonymous. In this company, you find release from care, boredom and worry. Your imagination will be fired. Life will mean something at last. The most satisfactory years of your existence lie ahead. Among fellow A. A.'s you will make lifelong friends. You will be bound to them with new and wonderful ties." Does life mean something to me now?

Meditation for the Day

~~"You cannot serve both God and mammon".~~ Do you want the full and complete satisfaction that you find in SERVING God and ALL the satisfactions of the world also? It is not easy to serve both God and the world. ~~You cannot~~ IT IS DIFFICULT TO claim the ~~wages~~ REWARDS of both. If you work for God, you will STILL have great rewards ~~in the world~~. But you must be ~~ready~~ PREPARED TO sometimes ~~to~~ stand apart from the world. You ~~must not~~ CANNOT always turn to the world and expect ALL the rewards WHICH LIFE HAS TO OFFER. ~~of the world.~~ If you are trying ~~honestly~~ SINCERELY to serve God, ~~then do not expect all the satisfactions of the world.~~ YOU WILL HAVE OTHER AND GREATER REWARDS THAN THE WORLD HAS TO OFFER.

Prayer for the Day

I pray that I may ALSO ~~be content with~~ the rewards that come from serving God. I pray that I may not expect too much from the world.

September 11 -- A. A. Thought for the Day

"Continuing the answers to the question of how ~~can~~ a man CAN live without liquor and be happy." ~~We~~ "We tell him he will be bound to the other A. A.'s with new and wonderful ties, for he and they will escape disaster together and all will commence shoulder to shoulder the common journey to a better and more satisfactory life. He will know what it means to give of himself that others may survive and rediscover life. He will become happy, respected and useful once more. Since these things have happened to us, they can happen to him." Have these things happened to me?

Meditation for the Day

God manifests ~~Himself~~ in human ~~beings~~ LIVES as strength to overcome ~~sin~~ EVIL and power to resist temptation. ~~The grace of God is that strength that~~ POWER WHICH enables a human being to change from a ~~useless~~, HOPELESS ~~individual to a useful, normal person~~. God also manifests Himself as love~~, love to~~ FOR our fellow men, compassion for their problems, and a ~~true charity toward them~~ REAL WILLINGNESS TO HELP THEM. ~~God also manifests Himself as love, love to our fellow men, compassion for their problems, and a true charity toward them.~~ THE GRACE OF God also manifests ~~Himself~~ ITSELF as peace ~~and serenity after the change in a person has taken place~~ OF MIND AND SERENITY OF CHARACTER. ~~God brings strength,~~ love and peace. WE CAN HAVE PLENTY OF POWER, LOVE AND SERENITY IN OUR LIVES IF WE ARE WILLING TO ASK GOD FOR THESE THINGS EACH DAY.

Prayer for the Day

I pray that I may see ~~God~~ GOD'S GRACE in the strength I receive, the love I know and the peace I have. I pray that I may be ~~very~~ grateful for ~~these blessings~~ THE THINGS I HAVE RECEIVED THROUGH THE GRACE OF GOD.

September 12 -- A. A. Thought for the Day

"What draws the newcomer to A. A. and gives him hope? He hears the stories of men whose experience ~~tallies~~ TALLY with his own. The expressions on the faces of the women, that undefinable something in the eyes of the men, the stimulating and electric atmosphere of the A. A. clubroom, conspire to let him know that here is haven at last. The very practical approach to his problems, the absence of intolerance of any kind, the informality, the genuine democracy, the uncanny understanding which these people in A. A. have is irresistable." Have I found a real haven in A. A.?

Meditation for the Day

"If thine eye be single, thy whole body shall be full of light." The eye of the soul is the will. If your ~~one~~ will is to do the will of God, to ~~find God in~~ SERVE HIM WITH your ~~own~~ life, ~~to serve God~~ HIM by ~~helping others~~, then truly shall your whole body be full of light. The ~~first~~ IMPORTANT thing is to ~~be sure~~ STRIVE that your will ~~is for~~ BE ATTUNED TO the will of God, a single eye to God's ~~Kingdom~~ PURPOSE, desiring nothing less than that His ~~Kingdom, come on earth~~ PURPOSES BE FULFILLED. TRY TO Seek in all things the advance of His Kingdom, ~~know no values but~~ SEEK THE spiritual values, AND EARNESTLY DESIRE SPIRITUAL GROWTH. ~~no real profit but spiritual gain.~~ THEN YOUR LIFE WILL EMERGE FROM THE DARKNESS OF FUTILITY INTO THE LIGHT OF VICTORY.

Prayer for the Day

I pray that my eye may be single. I pray that my life may be ~~full of light.~~ LIVED IN THE LIGHT OF THE BEST THAT I KNOW.

259

September 13 -- A. A. Thought for the Day

"No one is too discredited, nor has sunk too low, to be welcomed cordially into A. A., if he means business. Social distinctions, petty rivalries and jealousies, these are laughed out of countenance. Being wrecked in the same vessel, being restored and united under one God, with hearts and minds attuned to the welfare of others, the things which matter so much to some people no longer signify much to us. In A. A. we have true democracy and true brotherhood." Has A. A. taught me to be truly democratic?

Meditation for the Day

When you call on God in prayer to help you overcome weakness, sorrow, pain, ~~sin and temptation,~~ DISCORD AND CONFLICT, God never fails IN SOME WAY to answer the appeal. When you are in need of strength for yourself or ~~in trying to help~~ FOR THE HELP OF some other person, call on God ~~for strength.~~ IN PRAYER. ~~It~~ THE POWER YOU NEED will come simply, naturally and forcefully. ~~Call on~~ PRAY TO God not only when you need help, but ~~also to express love.~~ ALSO JUST TO COMMUNE WITH HIM. ~~God's grace~~ THE SPIRIT OF PRAYER can alter an atmosphere from one of discord to one of ~~love.~~ RECONCILIATION. It will raise the quality of ~~talk and~~ thought, AND WORD AND ~~It will~~ bring order out of chaos.

Prayer for the Day

~~I pray that I may be part of the answer, not part of the problem. I pray that I may be an apostle of conciliation.~~

I PRAY THAT I MAY BRING PEACE WHERE THERE IS DISCORD. I PRAY THAT I MAY BRING CONCILIATION WHERE THERE IS CONFLICT.

260

September 14 -- A. A. Thought for the Day

"How does A. A. grow? ~~[obliterated]~~

Some of us are salesmen who go about. Little clusters of twos and threes and fives keep springing up in different communities, through contact with the larger centers. Those of us who travel drop in at other groups as often as we can. This practice enables us to lend a hand to new groups which are springing up all over the land. New groups are being started each month. A. A. is even spreading outside the United States and is slowly becoming world-wide. Thus we grow." Am I doing all I can to spread A. A. wherever I go?

Meditation for the Day

"Lord, we believe. Help thou our unbelief." This cry of the human heart is an expression of human ~~need.~~ FRAILTY. It signifies the SINCERE DESIRE FOR soul's progress. As a person ~~realizes~~ FEELS THE EXISTENCE God and his power, ~~to save,~~ that person believes in ~~God~~ HIM more and more. At the same time, a person is more conscious of his falling short of absolute trust in God. The soul's progress is an increasing belief, then a cry for more faith, a plea to conquer all unbelief, all lack of trust. WE CAN BELIEVE THAT That cry is heard by God and that prayer is answered IN DUE TIME. AND SO OUR FAITH GROWS LITTLE BY LITTLE, DAY BY DAY.

Prayer for the Day

I pray that with more power in my life will come more faith. I pray that I may come to trust God ~~absolutely.~~ MORE EACH DAY.

September 15 -- A. A. Thought for the Day

"We all realize that we know only a little. God will constantly disclose more to all of us. Ask Him in your morning meditation what you can do each day for the man who is still sick. The answers will come, if your own house is in order. See to it that your relationship with God is right and great events will come to pass for you and countless others. Give freely of what you find in A. A. But obviously you cannot transmit something which you haven't got. So make a life-study of A. A." Am I always looking for new ways of presenting the A. A. programme?

Meditation for the Day

"In quietness and confidence shall be your strength". Confidence means to have faith in something. When you have confidence in God's grace, you can face anything. When you have confidence you are serene and at peace. You rest in the faith that God will take care of you. Rest in God until His life-power flows through you. Have no fear for the future. Be still, and in that stillness God's strength and peace will come. It lies in quietness, that peace of strength and that strength of peace.

Prayer for the Day

I pray that I may find my strength in quietness. I pray that I may rest content.

September 16 -- A. A. Thought for the Day

Today, let us begin the study of the twelve suggested steps of A. A. These twelve suggested steps seem to embody five principles. The first step is the membership requirement step. The second, third and eleventh steps are the spiritual steps of the programme. The fourth, fifth, sixth, seventh and tenth steps are the personal inventory steps. The eighth and ninth steps are the restitution steps. The twelfth step is the passing on of the programme or helping others step. So the five principles are membership requirement, spiritual basis, personal inventory, restitution and helping others. Have I made these steps a part of me?

Meditation for the Day

You live not only in time but in eternity. In the unseen, your future is being planned. Abide in God, and He in you, and so shall you bring forth fruit for eternity. Let your life flow as some calm river through the dry land of earth. It will cause the trees and flowers of life to spring forth and yield abundantly. Successful work is done for eternity, not just for now. Such work can yield a real spiritual increase, which goes on forever.

Prayer for the Day

I pray that my life may be like a cool river in a thirsty land. I pray that I may give freely to all who come.

263

September 17 -- A. A. Thought for the Day

Step One is: "We admitted we were powerless over alcohol, that our lives had become unmanageable." This step states the membership requirement of A. A. We must admit that ~~we are definitely alcoholics~~ OUR LIVES ARE DISTORTED. We must accept the fact that we are helpless before the power of alcohol. We must admit that we are licked AS FAR AS DRINKING IS CONCERNED AND THAT WE NEED HELP. We must be willing to accept this bitter fact THAT WE CANNOT DRINK. We must make ~~a graceful~~ AS GRACEFULLY AS POSSIBLE, A surrender to the inevitable AND FACT THAT WE MUST STOP DRINKING. ~~Is it difficult for me to admit that I was an alcoholic?~~ AM DIFFERENT FROM NORMAL DRINKERS? ARE NORMAL PEOPLE.

Meditation for the Day

"Show us the way, O Lord, and let us walk in Thy paths". There ~~is~~ SEEMS TO BE a right way to live and a wrong way. YOU CAN MAKE A PRACTICAL TEST. When you live the right way, ~~everything works~~ THINGS SEEM TO out well for you. When you live the wrong way, ~~everything works~~ THINGS SEEM TO out badly for you. You SEEM TO take out of life ABOUT what you put into it. If you disobey the laws of nature, THE CHANCES ARE THAT you will be unhealthy. If you disobey the spiritual AND MORAL laws, THE CHANCES ARE THAT you will be unhappy. By following the laws of nature and the spiritual laws of honesty, purity, unselfishness and love, you ~~will be~~ CAN EXPECT TO BE REASONABLY healthy and happy.

Prayer for the Day

I pray that I may ~~take~~ TRY TO LIVE the right way. I pray that I may follow the ~~upward~~ path, THAT LEADS TO A BETTER LIFE.

264

September 18 -- A. A. Thought for the Day

Step Two is: "Came to believe that a Power greater than ourselves could restore us to sanity." Step Three is: "Made a decision to turn our will and our lives over to the care of God as we understood Him." Step Eleven is: "Sought through prayer and meditation to improve our conscious contact with God as we understood Him, praying only for knowledge of His will for us and the power to carry that out." The fundamental basis of A. A. is a belief in some Power greater than ourselves. Let us not water this down. We cannot fully get the programme without this venture of belief. ~~Have I surrendered myself to a Higher Power?~~ HAVE I MADE THE VENTURE OF BELIEF IN A POWER GREATER THAN MY OWN?

Meditation for the Day

"He that dwelleth in the secret place of the Most High, shall abide under the shadow of the Almighty". Dwell FOR A MOMENT EACH DAY in a secret place, the place of communion with God, apart from the world, and thence receive strength to face the world. Material things cannot intrude upon this secret place, they cannot ever find it, because it is outside the realm of material things. When you abide in this secret place, you are under the shadow of the Almighty. God is close to you in ~~the~~ THIS quiet place of communion. ~~Make~~ EACH DAY DWELL FOR A WHILE IN this secret place. ~~your dwelling place.~~

Prayer for the Day

I pray that I may ~~be where God's shadow falls over me.~~ RENEW MY STRENGTH IN QUIETNESS. I pray that I may ~~abide there in peace.~~ FIND REST IN QUIET COMMUNION WITH GOD.

265

September 19 -- A. A. Thought for the Day

Let us continue with Steps Two, Three and Eleven. We must turn to a Higher Power for help, because we are helpless ourselves. When we put our drink problem in God's hands and leave it there, we have made the most important decision of our lives. From then on, we trust God for the strength to keep sober. This takes us off the center of the universe and allows us to transfer our problems to a Power outside of ourselves. By prayer and meditation, we seek to improve our conscious contact with God. We try to live each day the way we believe God wants us to live. Am I trusting God for the strength to stay sober?

Meditation for the Day

"These things have I spoken unto you, that your joy may be full". ~~The full~~ EVEN A PARTIAL relization of the spiritual life brings, ~~among other things,~~ ~~great~~ MUCH joy. You feel at home in the world when you are in touch with ~~God.~~ THE DIVINE SPIRIT OF THE UNIVERSE. Spiritual ~~truths~~ EXPERIENCE brings ~~an~~ A DEFINITE ~~overwhelming joy.~~ SATISFACTION. Search for the ~~joy in~~ REAL MEANING OF life by following spiritual laws. ~~Love and laugh. Delight yourself in the Lord.~~ God wants you to have ~~full joy~~ SPIRITUAL SUCCESS and He intends that you have it. If you live your life AS MUCH AS POSSIBLE according to the spiritual laws, you ~~will~~ CAN have ~~the fullness of joy.~~ EXPECT YOUR SHARE OF JOY AND PEACE, SATISFACTION AND SUCCESS.

Prayer for the Day

I pray that I ~~may~~ WILL find ~~the~~ happiness ~~of~~ IN doing the right thing. ~~There is no other real happiness.~~ I PRAY THAT I WILL FIND SATISFACTION IN OBEYING SPIRITUAL LAWS.

266

September 20 -- A. A. Thought for the Day

Step Four is: "Made a searching and fearless moral inventory of oirselves." Step Five is: "Admitted to God, to ourselves, and to another human being the exact nature of our wrongs." Step Six is: "Were entirely ready to have God remove all these defects of character." Step Seven is: "Humbly asked Him to remove our shortcomings." Step Ten is: "Continued to take personal inventory and when we were wrong, promptly admitted it." In taking a personal inventory, we have to be absolutely honest with ourselves and with other people. Have I taken an honest inventory of myself?

Meditation for the Day GOD IS GOOD.

You can OFTEN tell whether or not a thing is of God. If it is of God, it ~~is~~ MUST BE good. Honesty, purity, unselfishness and love are all good, ~~Selfish pleasure is bad and leads often to death.~~ ~~Unselfish helpfulness is good,~~ and THESE THINGS ALL ~~leads~~ lead to THE abundant life. ~~God is good.~~ Leave in ~~His~~ GOD'S hands the present and the future, knowing only that He ~~is good.~~ THE HAND THAT VEILS THE FUTURE IS THE HAND OF GOD. He can bring order out of chaos, good out of evil, AND peace out of turmoil. WE CAN BELIEVE THAT everything really good comes from God, AND THAT HE ~~God~~ shares His goodness with ~~His children,~~ US. ~~and you are His child.~~

Prayer for the Day

I pray that I may reach out for the good. I pray that I may TRY TO choose the best in life.

267

September 21 -- A. A. Thought for the Day

Let us continue with Steps Four, Five, Six, Seven and Ten. In taking a personal inventory of ourselves, we have to face facts as they really are. We have to stop running away. We must face reality. We must see ourselves as we really are. We must admit our faults openly and try to correct them. We must TRY TO see where we have been dishonest, impure, selfish and unloving. We do not do this once and forget it. We do it every day OFTEN of ~~our lives,~~ as long as we live. WE ARE NEVER DONE WITH CHECKING UP ON OURSELVES. ~~Am I constantly taking inventory of myself and trying to improve?~~ AM I TAKING A DAILY INVENTORY OF MYSELF?

Meditation for the Day

IN IMPROVING OUR PERSONAL LIVES, WE HAVE UNSEEN HELP. ~~"Lord, show us the Father, and it sufficeth us".~~ ~~You are~~ WE WERE not MADE SO THAT WE COULD ~~meant to~~ see God. That would be too easy for ~~everybody.~~ US AND THERE WOULD BE NO MERIT IN OBEYING HIM. It takes an act of faith, a venture of belief, to ~~believe in God.~~ REALIZE THE UNSEEN POWER. ~~But you~~ YET WE have MUCH evidence of God's existence in the strength that ~~you~~ MANY PEOPLE HAVE receive~~d~~ from that act of faith, THAT VENTURE OF BELIEF. ~~You~~ WE are in a box of space and time and ~~you cannot see spiritual things.~~ WE CAN SEE NEITHER OUR SOULS NOR GOD. God and the human spirit are both outside the limitations of space and time. Yet ~~they are~~ OUR UNSEEN HELP IS effective here and now. THAT HAS BEEN PROVED IN THOUSANDS OF CHANGED LIVES.

Prayer for the Day

I pray that I may make the great venture of belief. I pray that ~~I~~ MY VISION may not be blocked by intellectual pride.

268

September 22 -- A. A. Thought for the Day

Step Eight is: "Made a list of all persons we had harmed, and became willing to make amends to them all." Step Nine is: "Made direct amends to such people wherever possible, except when to do so would injure them or others." Making restitution for the wrongs we have done is often very difficult. It hurts our pride. But the rewards are great. When we go to a person and say we are sorry, the reaction we get is almost invariably good. It takes courage to make the plunge, but the results more than justify it. A load is off our chest and often an enemy has been turned into a friend. Have I done my best to make ALL THE restitution~~s~~ POSSIBLE?

Meditation for the Day

There should be joy in living the spiritual life. A faith without joy is not ENTIRELY genuine. If you are not HAPPIER ~~having a good time~~ as a result of your faith, there is PROBABLY something wrong with it. Faith in God should bring you a deep feeling of HAPPINESS AND security, no matter what happens on the surface OF YOUR LIFE. Each new day is ~~a new~~ ANOTHER opportunity to SERVE GOD AND improve your relationships with your fellow men. THIS SHOULD BRING JOY. Life should be abundant and out-reaching. It should be glowing and outgoing, in ever widening circles.

Prayer for the Day

I pray that my horizons may grow ever wider. I pray that I MAY ~~they~~ keep reaching out, FOR MORE SERVICE AND COMPANIONSHIP.

269

September 23 -- A. A. Thought for the Day

Step Twelve is: "Having had a spiritual awakening as the result of those steps, we tried to carry this message to alcoholics, and to practice these principles in all our affairs." Note that the basis of our effectiveness in carrying the message to others is the reality of our own spiritual awakening. If we are not changed, we cannot be used to change others. To keep this programme, we must pass it on to others. We cannot hoard it ~~to~~ [FOR] ourselves. We [MAY] lose it unless we give it away. It cannot flow into us and stop; it must continue to flow into us, as it flows out to others. Am I always ~~giving?~~ [READY TO GIVE AWAY WHAT I HAVE LEARNED IN A.A.?]

Meditation for the Day

"Draw nigh unto God and He will draw nigh unto you". [WHEN YOU ARE FACED WITH A PROBLEM BEYOND YOUR STRENGTH,] You must turn to God by an act of faith. It is that turning to God [IN EACH TRYING SITUATION] that you must cultivate. ~~in every circumstance.~~ The turning may be one of glad thankfulness [FOR GOD'S GRACE IN YOUR LIFE.] ~~or mute appeal for strength.~~ [OR] Your appeal to God may be a ~~simple~~ [PRAYERFUL] claiming of [HIS] strength to face a situation and a finding that you have it [WHEN THE TIME COMES]. Not only ~~strength~~ [THE POWER TO FACE TRIALS,] but [ALSO] the comfort and joy of God's nearness and companionship [ARE YOURS FOR THE ASKING].

Prayer for the Day

I pray that I may [TRY TO] draw near ~~unto~~ [TO] God [EACH DAY IN PRAYER]. I pray that I may feel ~~his~~ [His] nearness and his strength [IN MY LIFE].

270

September 24 -- A. A. Thought for the Day

Let us continue with Step Twelve. We must practice these principles in all our affairs. This part of the twelfth step must not be overlooked. It is the carrying on of the whole programme. We do not just practice these principles in regard to our drinking problems. We practice them in all our affairs. We do not give one compartment of our lives to God and keep the other compartments to ourselves. We give our whole lives to God and we try to do His will in every respect. Herein lies our growth; herein lies all the promise of the future, an ever widening horizon. Do I carry the A. A. principles with me, wherever I go?

Meditation for the Day

"Lord, to whom shall we go but to Thee? Thou hast the words of eternal life." The words of eternal life are ~~all~~ the words [FROM GOD] controlling your [TRUE] being, ~~even~~ controlling ~~your temporal life~~ [THE REAL SPIRITUAL YOU]. They are the words from God which are heard by men in their hearts and minds [WHEN THEY ARE WIDE OPEN TO HIS SPIRIT]. These are the words of eternal life which express the [TRUE] way you are to live. They say to you [IN THE STILLNESS OF YOUR HEART AND MIND AND SOUL]: Do this and live."

Prayer for the Day

I pray that I may follow the dictates of my conscience. I pray that I may follow the inner urging [OF MY SOUL].

271

September 25 -- A. A. Thought for the Day

Let us consider the term "spiritual experience" as given in Appendix II of the big book, "Alcoholics Anonymous": "A spiritual experience is something that brings about a personality change. By surrendering our lives to God as we understand Him, we are changed. The nature of this change is evident in recovered alcoholics. This personality change is not necessarily in the nature of a sudden and spectacular upheaval. We do not need to acquire an immediate and overwhelming God-consciousness, followed at once by a vast change in feeling and outlook. In most cases, the change is gradual." Do I see ~~the~~ A GRADUAL AND CONTINUING change in myself?

Meditation for the Day

"Come unto me all ye that labor and are heavy laden and I will give you rest." ~~For rest from the cares of life,~~ you ~~must~~ CAN turn to God EACH DAY IN PRAYERFUL CONTEMPLATION. ~~Complete rest~~ REAL RELAXATION AND SERENITY comes ~~only~~ from a deep sense of the fundamental goodness of the universe. God's everlasting arms ARE UNDERNEATH ALL, AND WILL ~~will~~ support you. ~~Go to~~ COMMUNE WITH God, not SO MUCH ~~just~~ for petitions to be granted, ~~but~~ AS for the rest that comes from relying ~~on His strength~~ HIS WILL AND HIS PURPOSE FOR YOUR LIFE. Be sure of God's strength available to you, be conscious of His support, and wait QUIETLY until ~~God's rest~~ THAT TRUE REST FROM GOD fills your ~~soul.~~ BEING.

Prayer for the Day

I pray that I may be conscious of God's support TODAY. I pray that I may rest safe and sure therein.

272

September 26 -- A. A. Thought for the Day

Continuing the consideration of the term "spiritual experience": "The acquiring of an immediate and overwhelming God-consciousness, resulting in a dramatic transformation, though frequent, is by no means the rule. Most of our spiritual experiences are of the educational variety, and they develop slowly over a period of time. Quite often friends of the newcomer are aware of the difference long before he is himself. He finally realizes that he has undergone a profound alteration in his reaction to life and that such a change could hardly have been brought about by himself alone." ~~Has my change been gradual?~~ IS MY OUTLOOK ON LIFE CHANGING FOR THE BETTER?

Meditation for the Day

Look at the world as your Father's house. ~~Look on~~ THINK OF all people you meet as guests in your Father's house, to be treated with love and consideration. Look at yourself as a servant in your Father's house, as a servant of all. Think of no work as beneath you. Be ever ready to do all you can for others WHO NEED YOUR HELP. THERE IS MUCH SATISFACTION IN SERVING THE HIGHEST THAT YOU KNOW. There is gladness in God's service. Express your love for God in service to ~~others.~~ ALL WHO ARE LIVING WITH YOU IN YOUR FATHER'S HOUSE.

Prayer for the Day

I pray that I may serve others out of gratitude to God. I pray that my work may be ~~an expression of His love.~~ A SMALL REPAYMENT FOR HIS GRACE SO FREELY GIVEN ME.

273

September 27 -- A. A. Thought for the Day

Continuing the consideration of the term "spiritual experience": "What often takes place in a few months could seldom have been accomplished by years of self-discipline. With few exceptions, our members find that they have tapped an unsuspected inner resource which they presently identify with their own conception of a Power greater than themselves. Most of us think this awareness of a Power greater than ourselves the essence of spiritual experience. Some of us call it God-Consciousness. In any case, willingness, honesty and open-mindedness are the essentials of recovery." Have I tapped ~~the~~ THAT inner resource ~~and do I identify it with a Power greater than myself?~~ WHICH CAN CHANGE MY LIFE?

Meditation for the Day

God's power ~~to save~~ IN YOUR LIFE increases as your ability to understand His ~~salvation~~ GRACE increases. The power of God's grace is only limited by the understanding and will of each individual, ~~soul.~~ God's miracle-working power is only limited in each individual soul by the lack of SPIRITUAL vision of that soul. God respects free will, the right of each person to accept or reject His miracle-working power. Only the ~~call~~ SINCERE DESIRE of the soul gives Him the opportunity to bestow it.

Prayer for the Day

I pray that I may not limit God's power by my lack of vision. I pray that I may keep my mind open TODAY to His influence.

274

September 28 -- A. A. Thought for the Day

For the past two months, we have been studying passages AND STEPS from the big book: "Alcoholics Anonymous." Now why not read the book itself again? It is essential that the A. A. programme become part of us. We must have its essentials at our finger tips. We cannot study the big book TOO MUCH OR too often. The more we read it and study it, the better equipped we are to think A. A., act A. A., and live A. A. We cannot know too much about the programme. The chances are that we will never know enough. But we can make as much of it our own as possible. How much of the big book have I thoroughly mastered?

Meditation for the Day

~~You must fully~~ WE NEED TO accept the difficulties and disciplines of life, so as to fully share the ~~human life with all your~~ COMMON LIFE OF OUR fellow men. ~~Much~~ MANY THINGS that ~~you~~ WE must accept in life ~~is~~ ARE not to be ~~accepted~~ TAKEN SO MUCH as being necessary for ~~you~~ US personally, ~~but to be accepted~~ AS TO BE EXPERIENCED in order ~~to set an example to your fellow men and to prove that you are sharing~~ THAT WE MAY SHARE in the sufferings and ~~difficulties~~ PROBLEMS of mankind. WE NEED SYMPATHY AND UNDERSTANDING. ~~You~~ WE must share ~~all~~ MANY OF the experiences of life, in order to understand and ~~appreciate other people's point of view~~ SYMPATHIZE WITH OTHERS. Unless ~~you~~ WE have been through the same experience, ~~you~~ WE cannot understand another person OR HIS MAKEUP well enough to be able to help him.

Prayer for the Day

I pray that I may accept everything that comes my way as a part of life. I pray that I may MAKE ~~use~~ USE OF it, IN HELPING MY FELLOW MEN.

275

September 29 -- A. A. Thought for the Day

Having got this far, shall we pause and ask ourselves some searching questions? [WE NEED TO CHECK UP ON OURSELVES PERIODICALLY.] Just how good an A. A. am I? Am I attending meetings regularly? Am I doing my share to carry the load? When there is something to be done, do I volunteer? Do I speak at the meetings when asked, no matter how nervous I am? Do I accept ~~every~~ [EACH] opportunity to do twelfth step work [AS A CHALLENGE?] ~~giving~~ [DO I GIVE] freely of my time and money? Am I [TRYING TO] ~~spreading~~ [spread] A. A. wherever I go? Is my daily life a demonstration of A. A. [PRINCIPLES?] Am I a good A. A.?

Meditation for the Day

~~"As thy days, so shall thy strength be."~~ How do I get the strength to be effective and to accept responsibility? By asking ~~God~~ [THE HIGHER POWER] for the strength ~~you~~ [I] need each day. It has been proved in countless lives that for every day ~~you~~ [I] live, the necessary ~~strength~~ [POWER] shall be given ~~you~~ [ME]. [I MUST] Face each challenge that comes to ~~you~~ [ME] during the day, sure that God will give ~~you~~ [ME] the strength to face it. ~~In the realm of personal relationships, which is the true world,~~ For every task that is given ~~you~~ [ME], there is also given [ME] all the power necessary for the performance of that task. [I DO NOT NEED TO HOLD BACK.]

Prayer for the Day

I pray that I may accept every task as a challenge. I know I cannot [WHOLLY] fail if God is with me.

276

September 30 -- A. A. Thought for the Day

There are no leaders in A. A., except as they volunteer to accept responsibility. The work of carrying on A. A., leading group meetings, serving on committees, speaking before ~~the~~ [OTHER] ~~public~~ [GROUPS], doing twelfth step work, spreading A. A. among the ~~people~~ [ALCOHOLICS] of the community; all these things are done on a volunteer basis. If I don't volunteer to do something concrete for A. A., ~~A. A.~~ [THE MOVEMENT] is that much less effective. I must do my [FAIR] share to carry the load. A. A. depends on all its members to keep alive and [TO] keep growing. Am I doing my share [FOR A.A.?]

Meditation for the Day

When you look to God for strength to face responsibility and are quiet before Him, His healing touch causes the Divine Quiet to flow into your very being. When in weakness you cry to God, His touch brings healing, the renewal of your courage, and the power to meet every situation and be victorious. When you faint by the way or are distracted by ~~the world's hubbub~~ [FEELINGS OF INFERIORITY], then [RELY ON] the touch of God's spirit ~~supports~~ [TO SUPPORT] you on your way. [THEN ARISE AND GO FORTH WITH CONFIDENCE.]

Prayer for the Day

I pray that I may lay myself open [TODAY] to the healing ~~power~~ [TOUCH] of God. I pray that I may not falter or faint by the wayside, [BUT RENEW MY COURAGE THROUGH PRAYER.]

277

October 1 -- <u>A. A. Thought for the Day</u>

A. A. will lose some of its effectiveness if I do not do my share. Where am I failing? Are there some things I do not feel like doing? Am I held back by self-consciousness or fear? Self-consciousness is a form of pride. It is a fear that something may happen to you. What happens to you is not very important. The impression you make on others does not depend SO MUCH on the KIND OF ~~fine~~ job you do, ~~but only~~ AS on your sincerity and honesty of purpose. Am I holding back because of I AM ~~being~~ afraid of not making a good impression?

Meditation for the Day

Look to God ~~and to no other source~~ for the TRUE power that will MAKE YOU EFFECTIVE. ~~save you.~~ ~~Only look to God.~~ See no other WHOLLY DEPENDABLE supply of strength, ~~that you can depend on.~~ ~~Regard God as your only real supply~~ HELPER. ~~of power.~~ That is the secret of A TRULY EFFECTIVE ~~the abundant~~ life. ~~for you.~~ And you, in your turn, will be used to help many others find EFFECTIVENESS. ~~the right road.~~ ~~Whenever temptation comes, look to God.~~ Whatever SPIRITUAL HELP you need, whatever SPIRITUAL HELP you desire for others, look unto God. ~~Only~~ Seek THAT God's will to be done IN YOUR LIFE and seek that your will conforms to His. FAILURES COME FROM DEPENDING TOO MUCH ON YOUR OWN STRENGTH.

Prayer for the Day

I pray that I may FEEL ~~know~~ that nothing GOOD IS TOO MUCH FOR ME ~~can seriously harm me~~, if I look to God FOR HELP. I pray that I may ~~feel this with my whole being.~~ BE EFFECTIVE THROUGH HIS GUIDANCE AND HELP.

278

October 2 -- <u>A. A. Thought for the Day</u>

What makes an effective talk in an A. A. meeting? It is not a fine speech with fine choice of words and an impressive delivery. Often a few simple words direct from the heart are more effective than the most polished speech. There is always a temptation to speak beyond your own experience, in order to make a good impression. This is never effective. What does not come from the heart does not reach the heart. What comes from personal experience and a sincere desire to help the other person, reaches the heart. Do I speak for effect or with a deep desire to help?

Meditation for the Day

"Thy will be done" must be your oft-repeated prayer. And in the willing of God's will there should be gladness. You should delight to do that will, because when you do, all your life goes right and everything TENDS TO WORK ~~works~~ well for you IN THE LONG RUN. When you are honestly trying to do God's will and humbly accepting the results, nothing can seriously HURT ~~upset~~ you. He who accepts the will of God IN HIS LIFE MAY NOT ~~shall~~ inherit the earth, BUT HE WILL INHERIT REAL PEACE OF MIND.

Prayer for the Day

I pray that I may have a yielded will. I pray that my will MAY BE be attuned to the will of God.

October 3 -- A. A. Thought for the Day

How do I talk with a new prospect? Am I always trying to dominate the conversation? Do I lay down the law and tell the prospect what he will have to do? Do I judge him and privately feel that he has small chance of making the programme? Do I belittle him to myself? Or am I willing to bare my soul, so as to get him talking about himself? And then am I willing to be a good listener, not interrupting, but hearing him out to the end? Do I feel deeply that he is my brother, and that I will do all I can to help him along the path to sobriety?

Meditation for the Day

"The work of righteousness shall be peace and the effect of righteousness shall be quietness and assurance forever". "Be still and know that I am God". Only when the soul attains this calm, can there be true spiritual work done, and mind and soul and body be strong to conquer and to bear all things. Peace is the result of righteousness, living the way God wants you to live, quietness and assurance follow. Assurance is that calmness born of a deep certainly of God's strength available to you and in His power to love and guard you from all harm.

Prayer for the Day

I pray that I may attain true calm. I pray that I may live in quietness and peace.

October 4 -- A. A. Thought for the Day

Am I critical of other members of A. A. or of new prospects? Do I ever say about a fellow member: I don't think he's sincere, I think he's bluffing, or I think he's taking a few drinks on the quiet? Do I realize that my doubtful and skeptical attitude is hurting that man, if only in my attitude toward him, which he cannot help sensing? Do I say about a new prospect: He'll never make the programme, or He'll only last a few months? If I take this attitude, I am unconsciously hurting that man's chances. Is my attitude always constructive and never destructive?

Meditation for the Day

To be attracted to God, you must be spirit-guided. There is wonderful illumination of thought given to those who are spirit-guided. To those who are material-guided, there is nothing in God to appeal to them or attract them. But to those who are spirit-guided there is strength and peace and calm to be found in communion with an Unseen Lord. To those who believe in this God they cannot see, life has a real meaning and purpose. They are children of the Unseen God and all human beings are their brothers.

Prayer for the Day

I pray that I may be spirit-guided. I pray that I may feel God's presence and power in my life.

281

October 5 -- A. A. Thought for the Day

Do I have any hard feelings about my fellow members or for any other A. A. group? Am I critical of the way a fellow member thinks or acts? Do I feel that another group is operating in the wrong way, and do I broadcast it? Or do I realize that every A. A. member, no matter what his limitations, has something to offer, some good, however little, that he can do for A. A., in spite of his handicaps? Do I believe that there is a place for all kinds of groups in A. A., PROVIDED THEY ARE FOLLOWING A.A. TRADITIONS, and that they can be effective, even if I do not agree with their procedure? Am I tolerant of people and groups?

Meditation for the Day

"The Lord shall preserve thy going out and thy coming in, from this time forth and even forever more". All your movements, your goings and THY comings, ~~controlled by God.~~ CAN BE GUIDED BY THE UNSEEN SPIRIT. Every visit to help another man, every VALELPFUL effort to assist, CAN BE blessed by ~~God.~~ THAT UNSEEN SPIRIT. THERE CAN BE ~~A~~ blessing on all you do, on every interview with a suffering fellow man. Every meeting of a need, MAY NOT BE not a chance meeting, but IT MAY HAVE BEEN planned by ~~God.~~ THE UNSEEN SPIRIT. Led by the spirit of the Lord, you can ~~accomplish much.~~ BE TOLERANT, SYMPATHETIC AND UNDERSTANDING OF OTHERS AND SO ACCOMPLISH MUCH.

Prayer for the Day

I pray that I may be led by the spirit of God. I pray that the Lord will preserve my goings and MY comings.

282

October 6 -- A. A. Thought for the Day

Is it my desire to be a big shot in A. A.? Do I always want to be up front in the limelight? Do I feel that nobody else can do as good a job as I can? Or am I willing to take a seat in the back row once in a while and let somebody else carry THE BALL? ~~one~~ Part of the effectiveness of any A. A. group is the development of new men to carry on, to take over the load FROM THE OLDER MEMBERS. Am I reluctant to give up authority? Do I try to carry the load for the whole group? If so, I am not being fair to the ~~other~~ NEWER members. Do I realize that no one man is essential? ~~and~~ DO I KNOW that A. A. could carry on without me, if it had to?

Meditation for the Day

THE UNSEEN GOD CAN HELP TO MAKE US TRULY GRATEFUL AND HUMBLE. Since we cannot see God, we must believe in Him without seeing. What we can see CLEARLY is the change in a human being, when he sincerely asks God for the strength to change. WE SHOULD Cling to faith in God and in His power to ~~help you.~~ CHANGE OUR WAYS. ~~Your~~ OUR faith IN AN UNSEEN GOD WILL ~~shall~~ be rewarded by ~~an~~ ~~abundant life, a conquering~~ USEFUL AND SERVICEABLE life. God will not fail ~~you,~~ TO SHOW US THE WAY WE SHOULD LIVE, when in ~~your helplessness you~~ REAL GRATITUDE AND TRUE HUMILITY WE turn to Him.

Prayer for the Day

I pray that I may believe that ~~there is no miracle of change that God cannot perform.~~ GOD CAN CHANGE ME. I pray that I may ~~expect miracles,~~ BE ALWAYS WILLING TO BE CHANGED FOR THE BETTER.

283

October 7 -- <u>A. A. Thought for the Day</u>

Do I put too much reliance on any one member of the group? Do I make a tin God out of some one person? Do I set him on a pedestal and worship him? If I do, I am building my house on sand. All A. A. members have clay feet. They are all only one drink away from a drunk, no matter how long they have been in A. A. THIS HAS BEEN PROVED TO BE TRUE MORE THAN ONCE. It's not fair to any man to be singled out as an outstanding leader of A. A. and TO quote him on every phase of the programme. If he should fail, where would I be? <u>Can I afford to be tipped over by the failure of my ideal?</u>

<u>Meditation for the Day</u>

You must always remember that you are weak but that God is strong. God knows all about your weakness. He hears every cry for mercy, every sigh of weariness, every plea for help, every sorrow over failure, every weakness FELT AND expressed. ~~His sympathy is for you.~~ WE ONLY FAIL WHEN WE TRUST TOO MUCH TO OUR OWN STRENGTH. Do not feel bad about your weakness. When you are weak, that is when God is strong to help you. Trust God ENOUGH, and your weakness will not matter. God is ALWAYS strong to save.

<u>Prayer for the Day</u>

I pray that I may LEARN TO lean on God's strength. I pray that I may know that ~~all is well.~~ MY WEAKNESS IS GOD'S OPPORTUNITY.

284

October 8 -- <u>A. A. Thought for the Day</u>

~~Do I have too much loyalty to my own A. A. group?~~ There is such a thing as being too loyal to any <u>one</u> group. Do I feel put out when another group starts, and some members of my group leave IT and branch out into new territory? Or do I send them out with my blessing? ~~So I go to~~ DO I VISIT that new offshoot group and help it along? Or do I sulk in my own tent? A. A. grows by the starting of new groups all the time. I must realize that it's a good thing for a large group to split up into smaller ones EVEN IF IT MEANS THAT THE LARGE GROUP - MY OWN GROUP - BECOMES SMALLER. <u>Am I a member of A. A. or just a member of my own particular group?</u>

<u>Meditation for the Day</u>

Pray~~,~~ and keep praying until it brings peace and serenity, and a feeling of communion with One who is near and ready to help. The thought of God is balm for our ~~sorrows.~~ HATES AND FEARS. In praying to God, ~~you~~ WE find healing for ~~all spiritual ills.~~ HURT FEELINGS AND RESENTMENTS. In thinking of God, doubts and fears leave ~~you~~ US. Instead of those doubts and fears, there will flow into ~~your~~ OUR heart such ~~strength~~ FAITH AND LOVE as is beyond the ~~strength~~ POWER of material things TO GIVE and such peace as the world can neither give nor take away. ~~With~~ AND With God, ~~you~~ WE can ~~feel secure even in the darkest places.~~ HAVE THE TOLERANCE TO LIVE AND LET LIVE.

<u>Prayer for the Day</u>

I pray that I may ~~keep my conscious contact with the Higher Power.~~ HAVE TRUE TOLERANCE AND UNDERSTANDING. I pray that I may ~~keep on praying.~~ KEEP STRIVING FOR THESE DIFFICULT THINGS.

285

October 9 -- A. A. Thought for the Day

Am I willing to be bored sometimes at meetings? Am I willing to listen to much repetition of A. A. principles? Am I willing to hear the same thing over and over again, AM I WILLING TO LISTEN TO A LONG, ALIN AY-ALON PERSONAL STORY, because it might help some new member? Am I willing to sit quietly and listen to a long-winded member go into every detail of his past? Am I willing to "take it," because it is doing him good to get it off his chest? My feelings are not THE important. The good of A. A. comes first, even if it is not always comfortable for me. Have I learned to take it?

Meditation for the Day

God would draw ~~you~~ US ALL closer to Him in the bonds of the spirit. He would have all people drawn closer to each other in the bonds of the spirit. God, the Great Spirit of the universe, of which each of our own spirits is a SMALL part, MUST WANT ~~wants~~ unity between HIMSELF ~~Him~~ and all His children. "Unity of the spirit in the bonds of peace." Each experience of A MAN'S ~~your~~ life, of joy, of sorrow, of danger, of safety, of difficulty, of success, of hardship, of ease; each should be LISTENED TO AND ACCEPTED IN THE ~~met and taken with the spirit and unity of God.~~ SPIRIT AND THE BONDS OF TRUE FELLOWSHIP.

Prayer for the Day

I pray that I may WELCOME THE BONDS OF TRUE BROTHERHOOD. ~~rely on God's spirit in every situation.~~ I pray that ~~in all things~~ I may be brought closer to unity with God, AND MY FELLOW MEN.

286

October 10 -- A. A. Thought for the Day

When a new member comes into my A. A. group, do I make a special effort to make him feel at home? Do I put myself out to listen to him, even if his ideas of A. A. are very vague? Do I make it a habit to talk to each new member myself, or do I OFTEN leave that to someone else? I may not be able to help him, but then again it may be something that I might say that would put him on the right track. When I see any member sitting alone, do I put myself out to be nice to him, ~~even if I am bored?~~ OR DO I STAY AMONG MY OWN SPECIAL GROUP OF FRIENDS AND LEAVE HIM OUT IN THE COLD? ~~Are all~~ new A. A.'s my responsibility?

Meditation for the Day

You are God's servant. Serve Him cheerfully and readily. Nobody likes a servant who avoids extra work, who complains about being called from one task to do one less enjoyable. A master would feel that he was being ill-served by such a servant. But is that not how you so often serve God? ~~Think of this and lay it to heart.~~ View your day's work in this light. Try to do your day's work the way you believe God wants you to do it, never shirking any responsibility, AND OFTEN ~~always~~ going out of your way to be of service.

Prayer for the Day

I pray that I may be a good servant. I pray that I may ~~do my day's work faithfully.~~ BE WILLING TO GO OUT OF MY WAY TO BE OF SERVICE.

287

October 11 -- A. A. Thought for the Day

How good a sponsor am I? When I have brought a new man to a meeting, do I feel that my responsibility has ended? Or do I make it my job to stay with him through thick and thin, until he has become a good member of A. A.? If he doesn't show up at a meeting, do I say to myself: Well, he's had it put up to him, if he doesn't want it, there's nothing more I can do? Or do I look him up and find out whether there is ~~any~~ reason for his absence? Do I go out of my way to check up on him, to see if there is anything further I can do to help? Am I a good sponsor?

Meditation for the Day

"First be reconciled to your brother and then come and offer your gift to God". First, get right with ~~your~~ fellow man and then get right with God. ~~Always see something good in your fellow man.~~ Always look for the best in him and encourage ~~that. And in every situation always look for a reason to be~~ thankful to God. ~~Gratitude to God makes you humble. Thank~~ God always for what His power has done for you. Establish a line of communication between yourself and God by the prayer in the morning and the prayer of thanks at night.

Prayer for the Day

I pray that I may see something good in every person. I pray that I may ~~encourage the best in that person.~~

288

October 12 -- A. A. Thought for the Day

Am I still on a "free ride" in A. A.? Am I all get and no give? Do I go to meetings and sit in the back row and let the others do all the work? Do I think it's enough, just because I'm sober, and can I rest on my laurels? If so, I haven't gone very far in the programme, not am I getting nearly enough of what it has to offer. I will be a "weak sister" until I get in there and help to carry the load. I must get off the ~~sidelines~~ and get into the game. I'm not a spectator, I'm one of the team. ~~Why don't~~ I go in there and carry the ball?

Meditation for the Day

Be thankful ~~to the heavenly~~ vision ~~that~~ you have. Perform, in the little things, faithful service to God. Do your small ~~tasks~~ every day ~~for God. You can bring joy by faithful ser-vice.~~ Be a doer of God's word, not a hearer only. In your daily ~~tasks,~~ keep faith with God. Every day brings a new opportunity to ~~live again.~~ ~~Live for God and your fellow man.~~ Even when you are tempted to rest or let things go or evade the issue, make a habit ~~of meeting~~ the issue squarely.

Prayer for the Day

I pray that I may perform each task faithfully. I pray that I may meet each issue of life squarely.

289

October 13 -- A. A. Thought for the Day

A. A. work is one hundred percent voluntary. It depends on each and every one of ~~its~~ [OUR] members to volunteer to do ~~their~~ [HIS OR HER] share. A newcomer can sit on the sidelines until he has got over his nervousness and his confusion. He has a right to be helped by all, until he can stand on his own feet. But the time inevitably comes when he has to step up and volunteer to do his share in meetings and in twelfth step work. Until that time comes, he is not a ~~real~~ [VITAL] part of A. A. He is only in the process of becoming assimilated. Has my time come to volunteer?

Meditation for the Day

God's Kingdom on earth is growing slowly, like [A SEED] ~~seeds~~ in the ground. In the growth of His Kingdon there is always progress among the few, ~~a going on from strength to strength.~~ [WHO ARE OUT AHEAD OF THE CROWD.] ~~Be in God's Kingdom and of God's Kingdom~~ [KEEP STRIVING FOR SOMETHING BETTER] and there can be no stagnation in your life. Eternal life, abundant life is yours for the ~~asking.~~ [SEEKING.] Do not misspend time over past failures. Count the lessons learned from failures as rungs upon the ladder of progress. [PRESS ONWARD TOWARD THE GOAL.]

Prayer for the Day

I pray that I may be willing to grow. I pray that I may keep stepping up on the rungs of the ladder of ~~progress.~~ [LIFE.]

290

October 14 -- A. A. Thought for the Day

How big a part of my life is A. A.? Is it just one of my activities and a small one at that? Do I only go to A. A. meetings once a week, and sometimes even miss that meeting? Do I think of A. A. only occasionally? Am I reticent about mentioning the subject [OF A.A.] to ~~my friends~~ [PEOPLE] who might need help? Or does A. A. fill a large part of my life? Is it the foundation of my whole life? [WHERE WOULD I BE WITHOUT A.A.?] Does everything I have and do depend on my A. A. foundation? ~~Do I realize that I would be utterly useless without A. A. to keep me on the ball?~~ [SOBER?] [IS A.A. THE FOUNDATION ON WHICH I BUILD MY LIFE?]

Meditation for the Day

Lay upon God your failures and mistakes and shortcomings. Do not dwell upon your failures, upon the fact that in the past you have been nearer a beast than an angel. You have a mediator between you and God, ~~the spirit,~~ [YOUR GROWING FAITH] which can lift you up from the mire and [POINT YOU] toward the heavens. You can [STILL] be reconciled with ~~Him and in tune~~ [THE SPIRIT OF GOD.] ~~with the spirit of the universe.~~ [YOU CAN STILL REGAIN YOUR HARMONY WITH THE DIVINE PRINCIPLE OF THE UNIVERSE.]

Prayer for the Day

I pray that I may not let the beast in me hold me back from my spiritual destiny. I pray that I may rise and walk upright ~~again.~~ [LIKE A MAN.]

291

October 15 -- A. A. Thought for the Day

Am I deeply grateful to A. A. for what it has done for me in regaining my sobriety and opening up an entirely new life for me? ~~Of course,~~ A. A. has made it possible for me to carry on other interests, in business and in various other associations with people. It has made a full life possible for me. It would [PERHAPS] be wrong if all my activities were limited to A. A. [WORK.] It has made a well-rounded life possible for me, in work, in play and in hobbies of various kinds. [BUT WILL I DESERT A.A. BECAUSE OF THIS? WILL I ACCEPT A DIPLOMA AND BECOME A GRADUATE OF A.A.?] ~~But do I constantly realize~~ [DO I REALIZE] that I could have nothing worth while without A. A.?

Meditation for the Day

There is only one way to get full satisfaction from life and that is to live the way you believe God wants you to live. Live with God, in that secret place of the spirit, and you will have a feeling of [BEING ON THE RIGHT ROAD.] ~~full satisfaction.~~ You will have a [DEEP] sense of [SATISFACTION.] ~~plenty.~~ The world will have meaning and you will have a place in the world, work to do that counts in the eternal order of things. ~~Everything~~ [MANY THINGS] will work for you and with you as long as you [FEEL YOU] are on God's side. ~~The abundant life is yours when you sincerely try to do God's will.~~

Prayer for the Day

I pray that I may have a sense of the [ETERNAL] value of the work I do. I pray that I may not only work for now, but [ALSO] for eternity.

292

October 16 -- A. A. Thought for the Day

How seriously do I take my obligations to A.A.? Have I taken all the good I can get out of it, and then let my obligations slide? Or do I constantly feel a deep debt of gratitude and a deep sense of loyalty to the whole A. A. movement? Am I not only grateful but proud to be a part of such a wonderful fellowship, ~~that~~ [WHICH] is doing such marvelous work among alcoholics? Am I glad to be a part of the great work that A. A. is doing and do I feel a deep obligation to carry on that work at every opportunity? Do I ~~realize~~ [FEEL] that I owe A. A. my loyalty and devotion?

Meditation for the Day [IF YOUR HEART IS RIGHT, YOUR WORLD WILL BE RIGHT.]

The beginning of all reform must be in yourself. [ITS NOT WHAT HAPPENS TO YOU, ITS HOW YOU TAKE IT.] However restricted your circumstances, however little you may be able to remedy financial affairs, you can always turn to [YOUR INWARD SELF] ~~yourself~~ and, seeing something not in order there, seek to right it. And as all reform is from within outward, you will always find that the outward is improved, as the inward is improved. As you improve yourself, your outward circumstances will change [FOR THE BETTER] ~~from disorder to order, from chaos to calm.~~ The power released from within yourself will ~~work miracles in the world.~~ [WILL CHANGE YOUR OUTWARD LIFE.]

Prayer for the Day

I pray that the hidden power within me may be released. I pray that I may not imprison the spirit [THAT IS] within me.

293

October 17 -- A. A. Thought for the Day

What am I going to do today for A.A.? Is there someone I should call up on the telephone or someone I should go ~~and~~ TO see? Is there a letter I should write? Is there an opportunity somewhere to advance the work of A. A. which I have been putting off or neglecting? If so, will I do it today? Will I be done with procrastination and do what I have to do today? Tomorrow may be too late. How do I know there will be a tomorrow for me? How about getting out of that easy chair and getting going? Do I feel that A. A. depends PARTLY on me today?

Meditation for the Day

TODAY Look upward toward God, not downward toward yourself. Look away from ~~sordid~~ UNPLEASANT surroundings, from lack of beauty, from the imperfections in yourself and in those around you. In your unrest, behold God's calmNESS, in your impatience, God's patience, in your ~~lack and~~ limitations, God's perfection. Looking upward toward God, ~~you~~ YOUR SPIRIT will begin to grow ~~more like Him~~. Then others will see ~~that you have~~ something IN YOU that they also want. As you grow in the spiritual life, you will be enabled to do ~~the~~ MANY things ~~you were never able to do before.~~ THAT SEEMED TOO HARD FOR YOU BEFORE.

Prayer for the Day

I pray that I may keep my eyes trained ~~on a level~~ above the horizon OF MYSELF. I pray that I may ~~realize the~~ SEE infinite possibilities ~~ahead~~. FOR SPIRITUAL GROWTH.

294

October 18 -- A. A. Thought for the Day

Have I ~~entirely~~ got~~ten~~ over MOST OF my sensitiveness, my feelings which are too easily hurt, and my just plain laziness and self-satisfaction? Am I willing to go all out for A. A., at no matter what cost to my precious self? Is my own comfort more important to me than doing the things that need to be done? Have I got to the point where what happens to me is not so important? Can I face up to things that are embarrassing or uncomfortable, if they are the right things to do for the good of A.A.? Have I given A. A. just a small piece of myself? ~~or~~ AM I WILLING TO GIVE all of myself whenever necessary?

Meditation for the Day

Not until a man has failed can he learn true humility. Humility arises from a deep sense of gratitude to God for giving him the strength to rise above past failures. Humility is not inconsistent with self-respect. The true man has self-respect and the respect of others and yet he is humble. The humble man is tolerant of others' failings, he does not have a critical attitude toward the foibles of his fellow men. ~~He has their welfare at heart and wishes them well.~~ HE IS HARD IN HIMSELF AND EASY ON OTHERS.

Prayer for the Day

I pray that I may be ~~truly humble~~ AND YET HAVE SELF RESPECT. ~~I pray that, with all humility, I may see the possibilities within myself.~~ I PRAY THAT I MAY SEE THE GOOD IN MYSELF AS WELL AS THE BAD.

295

October 19 -- A. A. Thought for the Day

Do I realize that I do not know how much time I have left? It may be later than I think. Am I going to do the things that I know I should do, before my time runs out? By the way, what is my plan for the rest of my life? Do I realize all I have to make up for in my past wasted life? Do I know that I am living on borrowed time, and that I would not have even this much time left, without A. A. and the grace of God? Am I going to make what time I have left count ~~for God and~~ for A. A.?

Meditation for the Day

We can believe that somehow the cry of the human soul is never unheard by God. It may be that God hears the cry, even if man fails to notice God's response to it. The human cry for help ~~and strength~~ must always evoke a response of some sort from God. It may be that ~~a~~ man's failure to discern properly keeps him unaware of the response. ~~and so not helped by it.~~ But ONE THING we can believe IS that the grace of God is always available for every ~~suffering~~ human being, WHO SINCERELY CALLS FOR HELP. MANY CHANGED LIVES ARE LIVING PROOFS OF THIS FACT.

Prayer for the Day

I pray that I may trust God to answer my prayer as He sees fit. I pray that I may be content with whatever form ~~the~~ THAT answer MAY TAKE. ~~takes.~~

296

October 20 -- A. A. Thought for the Day

For the past few ~~days~~ WEEKS we have been asking ourselves some searching questions. WE HAVE NOT BEEN ABLE TO ANSWER THEM ALL AS WE WOULD LIKE. BUT On the right answers to those questions will depend the usefulness and effectiveness of ~~my life~~ OUR LIVES and to some extent the usefulness and effectiveness of the whole A. A. movement. It all boils down to this: I owe a deep debt to A. A. and to the grace of God. Am I going to do all I can to repay that debt? Let us search our souls, make our decisions, and ~~get into action~~ ACT ACCORDINGLY. Any real success we have in life will depend on that. Now is the time to ~~get going~~ PUT OUR CONCLUSIONS INTO EFFECT. What am I going to do about it?

Meditation for the Day

"Our Lord and our God, be it done unto us according to Thy will." Simple acceptance of God's will IN WHATEVER HAPPENS is the key to abundant living. We must continue to pray: Not my will, but Thy will be done. It may not turn out the way you want it to, but it will be the best way in the long run, ~~if~~ BECAUSE it is God's way. If you decide to accept WHATEVER HAPPENS AS God's will for yourself, whatever it may be, your burdens will be lighter. Try to see in all things ~~the same~~ SOME fulfillment of THE Divine Intent.

Prayer for the Day

I pray that I may see the working out of God's will in ~~all~~ MY LIFE. ~~things.~~ I pray that I may be content with ~~that.~~ WHATEVER HE WILLS FOR ME.

297

October 21 -- A. A. Thought for the Day

~~Let us now examine what our life is like~~, [HAVE CONSIDERED THE OBLIGATIONS OF] ~~N~~now that we [ARE] ~~are~~ real working members of A. A., [LET US EXAMINE] What ~~are~~ [ARE] the rewards that have come to ~~me~~ [us] as a result of ~~my~~ [our] new way of living? First, I understand myself more than I ever did before. I have learned what was the matter with me and I know now [A LOT OF] what makes me tick. I will never be alone again. I am just one of many who have the ~~disease~~ [illness] of alcoholism and one of many who have learned what to do about it. I am not an odd fish or a square peg in a round hole. I [seem to] have found my right place in the world. ~~Do~~ [Am I beginning] ~~I~~ [to] understand myself?

Meditation for the Day

"Behold, I stand at the door and knock. If any man hear my voice and open the door, I will come in to him, and will remain with him, and him with me". The knocking of God's spirit, asking to come into your life, is due to no merit of yours, though it is in response to the longing of your heart. Keep a listening ear, an ear bent to catch the sound of the gentle knocking at the door of your heart by the spirit of God. Then open the door of your heart and let God's spirit come in.

Prayer for the Day

I pray that I may let God's spirit ~~take charge of~~ [COME INTO] my heart. I pray that it may fill me ~~to overflowing.~~ [WITH AN ABIDING PEACE.]

298

October 22 -- A. A. Thought for the Day

Second, I am content to face the rest of my life without alcohol. I have made the great decision once and for all. I have surrendered [as] gracefully [as possible] to the inevitable. I [hope I] have no more reservations. [I hope that] Nothing can happen to me now that would justify my taking a drink. No death of a dear one. No great calamity in any area of my life ~~would~~ [should] justify me in drinking. Even if I were on some desert isle, far from the rest of the world, but not far from God, ~~would~~ [should] I ever feel it right to drink? [For me,] Alcohol is out - period. [I will always be safe unless I take that first drink.] Am I fully resigned to this fact?

Meditation for the Day

Day by day ~~you must~~ [we should] slowly build up an unshakable faith in a Higher Power and in that Power's ability to give ~~you~~ [us] all the ~~strength you~~ [help we] need. By having ~~a~~ [these] quiet time each morning, ~~you~~ [we] start each day with a renewing of ~~your~~ [our] faith, until ~~at last~~ it becomes [almost] a part of ~~you~~ [us] and is ~~unshakable.~~ [a strong habit.] ~~You~~ [We] should keep furnishing the quiet places of ~~your~~ [our] soul with all the furniture of faith. ~~Fill your thoughts~~ [We should try to fill our thoughts each day] with all that is harmonious and good, beautiful and enduring.

Prayer for the Day

I pray that I may build a house in ~~myself~~ [my soul] for the spirit of God to dwell in. I pray that I may come at last to an unshakable faith, [in a Power greater than myself.]

299

October 23 -- A. A. Thought for the Day

Third, I have learned how to be honest. What a relief! No more ducking or dodging: No more tall tales. No more pretending to be what I am not. My cards are on the table, for all the world to see. I am what I am, as Popeye says, and that's all I am. I have had an unsavory past. I am sorry, yes. But it cannot be changed now. All that is yesterday and is done. But now my life is an open book. Come and look at it, if you want to. I'm trying to do the best I can. I will fail often. But I won't make excuses. I will face things as they are. Am I honest?

Meditation for the Day

Though it may seem a paradox, you must believe in spiritual forces which you cannot see, rather than in material things which you can see, especially when you are dealing with personal relationships. Between man and man, only spiritual forces will suffice to keep them in harmony. These spiritual forces we know, because one can see their results, although we cannot see them. A changed life results from the power of unseen spiritual forces.

Prayer for the Day

I pray that I may believe in the Unseen. I pray that I may be satisfied by the results of the Unseen, which I do see.

300

October 24 -- A. A. Thought for the Day

Fourth, I have turned to a Power greater than myself, thank God. I am no longer the center of the universe. All the world does not revolve around me any longer. I have a Father in heaven, and I am only one of his children and a small one at that. But I can depend on Him to show me what to do and to give me the strength to do it. I am on the Way, and the whole power of the universe is behind me when I do the right thing. I do not have to depend on myself any longer. With God, I can face anything. Is my life in the hands of God?

Meditation for the Day

The grace of God is an assurance against evil. It holds security for the believing soul. The grace of God means safety in the midst of evil. You can be kept unspotted by the world, through the grace of God. You can have a new life. But only in close contact with the grace of God, is its keeping power realized. In order to realize it and benefit from it, you must have daily quiet communion with God, so that the keeping power of His grace will come unhindered unto your soul.

Prayer for the Day

I pray that I may be kept from evil by the grace of God. I pray that henceforth I will be unspotted by the world.

301

October 25 -- <u>A. A. Thought for the Day</u>

Fifth, I have learned to live one day at a time. I have finally realized the great fact that all I have is <u>now</u>. This sweeps away all vain regret and it ~~wipes the~~ MAKES MY THOUGHT OF future free of fear~~s~~. Now is mine. I can do what I want with it. I own it, for better or worse. What I do now, in this present moment, is what makes up my life. My whole life is only a succession of nows. I will take this moment, ~~that~~ WHICH has been given TO me by the grace of God, and I will do something with it. What I do with each now, will make me or break me. <u>Am I living IN THE now?</u>

<u>Meditation for the Day</u>

~~You~~ WE should work at overcoming ~~your self,~~ OURSELVES, ~~your~~ OUR selfish desires and ~~your~~ OUR self-centeredness. This can never be fully accomplished. WE CAN NEVER BECOME ENTIRELY UNSELFISH. But ~~you~~ WE can come to realize that ~~you~~ WE are not AT the center of the universe, and THAT everything does not revolve around ~~you~~ US at the center. ~~You are~~ I AM only one cell in a vast network of human cells. ~~So you should~~ I CAN AT LEAST make the effort to conquer the self-life, and seek daily to obtain more and more OF this self-conquest. "He that overcomes himself is greater than he who conquers a city".

<u>Prayer for the Day</u>

I pray that I may STRIVE TO overcome ~~myself~~ MY SELFISHNESS. I pray that I may ~~get~~ ACHIEVE the right perspective of my position in the world.

302

October 26 -- <u>A. A. Thought for the Day</u>

Sixth, I have A. A. meetings to go to, thank God. Where would I go without them? Where would I be without them? Where would I find the sympathy, the understanding, the fellowship, the companionship? Nowhere else in the world. I have come home. I have found the place where I belong. I no longer wander alone over the face of the earth. I am at peace and at rest. What a great gift has been given me by A. A.! I do not deserve it. But it is nevertheless mine. I have a home at last. I am content. <u>Do I thank God every day for the A. A. fellowship?</u>

<u>Meditation for the Day</u>

Walk all the way with your fellow man and with God. Do not go part of the way and then stop. Do not push God so far into the background that He has no effect on your life. Walk all the way with Him. Make a good companion of God, by praying to Him often during the day. Do not let your contact with Him be broken for too long a period. Walk all the way with God and with your fellow man, along the path of life, ~~that leads to eternity.~~ WHEREVER IT MAY LEAD YOU.

<u>Prayer for the Day</u>

I pray that I may keep my feet upon the path that leads ~~to~~ UPWARD. ~~endless life.~~ I pray that I may walk ~~with my fellow man~~ IN COMPANIONSHIP WITH GOD along the way.

303

October 27 -- A. A. Thought for the Day

Seventh, I can help other alcoholics. I am of some use in the world. I have a purpose in life. I am worth something at last. My life has a direction and a meaning. All that feeling of futility is gone. I can do something worth while. God has given me a new lease on life, so that I can help my fellow alcoholic. He has let me live through all the hazards of my alcoholic life, to bring me at last to a place of real usefulness in the world. He has let me live for this. This is my destiny and my opportunity. I am worth something! Will I give ~~all~~ AS MUCH OF MY LIFE AS I CAN TO ~~I have for~~ A.A.?

Meditation for the Day

Each of us has his own battle to win, the battle between the material VIEW OF LIFE and the spiritual VIEW. Something must guide ~~your life.~~ OUR LIVES. Will it be ~~money~~ WEALTH, pride, selfishness, greed, or will it be faith, honesty, purity, unselfishness, love, AND SERVICE? ~~helping others?~~ Each man has the choice. We can choose good or evil. ~~You~~ WE cannot choose both. Are ~~you~~ WE going to keep striving until ~~you~~ WE win the battle? If ~~you~~ WE win the victory, WE CAN BELIEVE THAT even God in His heaven will rejoice.

Prayer for the Day

I pray that I may choose the good and resist the evil. I pray that I will not be a loser in the battle for righteousness.

304

October 28 -- A. A. Thought for the Day

What other rewards have come to me as a result of my new way of living? Each one of us can answer this question in many ways. My relationships with my wife and children are on an entirely new plane. The TOTAL selfishness is gone and MORE cooperation has taken its place. My home is a home again. Understanding has taken the place of misunderstanding, recriminations, bickering and ~~despair~~ RESENTMENT. A new companionship has developed which bodes well for the future. "There ~~is a home~~ ARE HOMES where fires burn and there is bread, lamps are lit and prayers are said. Though people falter through the dark and nations grope, with God Himself back of ~~this~~ THESE little homes, we still can hope". Have I ~~my~~ COME home?

Meditation for the Day

We ~~must~~ CAN bow to God's will in anticipation of the thing happening which will, in the long run, be the best for all concerned. It may not ALWAYS seem the best thing at the present time, but we cannot see as far ahead as God can. We do not know how His ~~plan is~~ PLANS ARE laid, we only NEED TO BELIEVE ~~know~~ that if we ~~bow to His will~~ TRUST HIM and accept whatever happens AS HIS WILL AND in a spirit of faith, everything will work out for the best in the end.

Prayer for the Day

I pray that I may not ask to see the distant scene. I pray that one step MAY be enough for me.

305

October 29 -- A. A. Thought for the Day

My relationships with my children have greatly improved. Those children who saw me drunk and were ashamed, those children who turned away in fear and even loathing, have seen me sober and liked me, have turned to me in confidence and trust and have forgotten the past as best they could. They have given me a chance for companionship that I had completely missed. I am their father now. Not just that man that mother married and God knows why. I am part of my home and a stranger in the house no more. ~~Have I my children?~~ HAVE I FOUND SOMETHING THAT I HAD LOST?

Meditation for the Day

~~Your~~ OUR true measure of success in life is the measure SPIRITUAL PROGRESS ~~of God's will~~ that ~~you~~ WE have revealed in ~~your life~~ OUR LIVES. ~~to those around you.~~ Others ~~must~~ SHOULD BE ABLE TO see a demonstration of God's will in ~~your life.~~ OUR LIVES. The measure of His will that those around ~~you~~ US have seen worked out in ~~your~~ OUR daily living, is the measure of ~~your~~ OUR TRUE success. ~~Try~~ WE CAN DO OUR BEST to be a demonstration ~~every~~ EACH day of the power of God in ~~a~~ human ~~life~~ LIVES, an example of the working OUT of the grace of God, IN THE HEARTS OF MEN.

Prayer for the Day

I pray that I may so live that others will see in me something of the working out of the ~~grace~~ WILL of God. I pray that ~~they may want something of what they see in me.~~ MY LIFE MAY BE A DEMONSTRATION ~~TO OTHERS~~ OF WHAT THE GRACE OF GOD CAN DO.

306

October 30 -- A. A. Thought for the Day

I have REAL friends, where I had none before. My drinking companions could hardly be called my REAL friends, though when drunk we ~~were bosom companions~~ SEEMED TO BE BOSOM PALS and hail fellows well met. My idea of friendship has changed. Friends are no longer people whom I can use for my own pleasure OR PROFIT. Friends are now people who understand me, and I them, whom I ~~can~~ CAN help and who can help me TO LIVE A BETTER LIFE. I have learned not to hold back and wait for friends to come to me, but to go half way and to be met half way, ~~gladly~~ OPENLY and freely. ~~Have I friends?~~ DOES FRIENDSHIP HAVE A NEW MEANING FOR ME?

Meditation for the Day

There is a time for everything. ~~You~~ WE should learn to wait patiently until the right time comes. EASY DOES IT. We waste our energies in trying to get things before we are ready to ~~receive~~ HAVE them, before we have earned the right to receive them. ~~The~~ A GREAT lesson we have to learn is how to wait WITH PATIENCE. WE CAN BELIEVE THAT ALL OUR LIFE IS ~~All your life is~~ a preparation for something better to come WHEN WE HAVE EARNED THE RIGHT TO IT. ~~in this life and in the next.~~ ~~You must~~ WE CAN believe that God has a plan for ~~your life~~ OUR LIVES and that ~~that~~ THIS plan will work out in the fullness of time.

Prayer for the Day

I pray that I may learn the lesson of waiting patiently. I pray that I may not expect things until I have earned the right to have them.

307

October 31 -- A. A. Thought for the Day

I have MORE peace and contentment. Life has fallen into place. The pieces of the jig saw puzzle have found their correct position. Life is whole, all of one piece. I am not cast hither and yon on every wind of circumstance ~~and~~ OR fancy. I am no longer a dry leaf cast up and away by the breeze. I have found my place of rest, my place where I belong. I am content. I do not vainly wish for things I cannot have. I have "the serenity to accept the things I CANNOT CHANGE ~~must~~, courage to change the things I can, and wisdom to know the difference". ~~Am I content?~~ HAVE I FOUND CONTENTMENT IN A.A.?

Meditation for the Day

In all of us there is an inner consciousness that tells of God, ~~a~~ AN INNER voice that speaks to our hearts. It is a voice that speaks to us intimately, personally, in a time of quiet meditation. It is LIKE a lamp unto our feet and a light unto our path". WE CAN REACH OUT INTO THE DARKNESS AND FIGURATIVELY TOUCH THE HAND OF GOD. AS THE BIG BOOK PUTS IT: "Deep down in every man, woman and child is the fundamental idea of God. We can find the Great Reality deep down within us. And when we find it, it changes our whole attitude toward life."

Prayer for the Day

I pray that I may follow the leading of the inner voice. I pray that I may not turn a deaf ear to the urging of my CONSCIENCE. ~~heart.~~

308

November 1 -- A. A. Thought for the Day

I have hope. That magic thing that I had lost or misplaced. The future looks dark no more. I do not even look at it, except when necessary to make plans. I TRY TO let the future take care of itself. The future ~~is~~ WILL BE made up of todays and todays, stretching out as SHORT ~~long~~ as now, and as long as eternity. Hope is ~~made up of~~ JUSTIFIED BY many right nows, ~~Hope is justified~~ by the rightness of the present. Nothing can happen to me that God does not WILL FOR ME, ~~want to have happen~~. I can hope for the best, as long as I have what I have, and it is good. Have I hope?

Meditation for the Day

Faith is the messenger that bears your prayers to God. Prayer can be like incense, rising ever higher and higher. The prayer of faith is the prayer of TRUST, ~~joy,~~ that feels the PRESENCE ~~love~~ of God which it RISES ~~uses~~ to meet. It CAN BE ~~is~~ sure of SOME ~~a~~ response from God. WE ~~You~~ can say a prayer of thanks to God every day for His grace, which has kept US ~~you~~ on the right way and allowed US ~~you~~ to start living the good life. So WE SHOULD pray to God with faith and TRUST ~~joy~~ and gratitude.

Prayer for the Day

I pray that I may feel sure of SOME ~~a~~ response to my prayerS ~~from God.~~ I pray that I may be content with whatever form that response takes.

November 2 -- A. A. Thought for the Day

I have faith. That thing that makes the world seem right. That thing that makes sense at last. That awareness of the Divine Principle in the universe which holds it all together and gives it unity and purpose and goodness and meaning. Life is no longer ashes in my mouth or bitter to the taste. It is all one great glorious whole, because God is holding it together! Faith~~,~~ that leap into the unknown, that venture into what lies ~~outside~~ BEYOND our ken~~, but~~ which brings untold rewards OF PEACE AND SERENITY. ~~Faith is my rock and my salvation.~~ Have I faith?

Meditation for the Day

Keep yourself like an empty vessel for God to fill. Keep pouring out yourself to help others, so that God can keep filling you up with His spirit. ~~Give constantly.~~ The more you give, the more you will have for yourself. God will see that you are kept filled, as long as you are giving to others. But if you selfishly try to keep all for yourself, you are soon blocked off from God YOUR SOURCE OF SUPPLY. And you WILL become stagnant. To ~~keep~~ BE clear, ~~water, a vessel~~ A LAKE must have ~~water coming in and going out.~~ AN INFLOW AND AN OUTFLOW.

Prayer for the Day

I pray that I may keep pouring out what I receive. I pray that I may keep the stream clear and flowing.

November 3 -- A. A. Thought for the Day

I have charity, which is another word for love. That right kind of love which is not selfish passion but an unselfish, outgoing desire to help my fellow man. To do what is best for the other person, to put what is best for him above ~~what I want.~~ MY OWN DESIRES. To put God first, the other fellow second and myself last. Charity that is gentle and kind and understanding and long-suffering and full of the desire to serve. A. A. has given me this. ~~Nothing else could.~~ What I do for myself is lost, what I do for others ~~is~~ MAY BE written somewhere in eternity. Have I charity?

Meditation for the Day

"Ask what ye will, and it shall be done unto you". God has unlimited power. There is no limit to what His power can do in human hearts. But we must will to have God's power and we must ask God for it. God's power is blocked off from us by our indifference to it. We can go along our own selfish way, without calling on God's help, and we get no power. But when we ~~believe~~ TRUST in God, ~~then~~ we can will to have ~~all~~ the power we need, ~~and~~ When we SINCERELY ask God for it, we get it abundantly.

Prayer for the Day

I pray that I may will to have God's power. I pray that I may ~~always ask Him for it.~~ KEEP PRAYING FOR THE STRENGTH I NEED.

311

November 4 -- A. A. Thought for the Day

I can do things that I never did before. Liquor took away my initiative and my ambition. I couldn't get up the steam to start anything. I let things slide. When I was drunk, I was too inert to even tie a loose shoelace. Now I can sit down and do something. I can write letters that need to be written. I can make telephone calls that should be made. I cam work in my garden. I can pursue my hobbies. I have the urge to create something, that creative urge that was completely stifled by alcohol. I am free to achieve again. Have I recovered my initiative?

Meditation for the Day

"In Thy presence is fullness of joy. At Thy right hand are pleasures forever". ~~You~~ WE cannot find TRUE happiness by looking for it. Seeking pleasure does not bring happiness IN THE LONG RUN, only disillusionment. Do not seek to ~~realize the~~ HAVE THIS fullness of joy by ~~effort.~~ SEEKING PLEASURE. It cannot be done that way. Happiness is a by-product of living the ~~abundant~~ RIGHT KIND OF A life. TRUE Happiness comes as a result of living IN ALL RESPECTS the way you believe God wants you to live~~, and of helping others.~~ WITH REGARD TO YOURSELF AND TO OTHER PEOPLE.

Prayer for the Day

I pray that I may not ALWAYS seek pleasure as a goal. I pray that I may be content with the happiness that comes ~~from doing~~ WHEN I DO the right thing.

312

November 5 -- A. A. Thought for the Day

~~Continuing~~ DURING our thoughts about the rewards that have come to us as a result of our new way of living, we have found that we have gained new KINDS OF homes, new relationships with our wives and children. ALSO Peace and contentment, hope, faith, charity, and new ambition. What are some of the things we have lost? Each one of us can answer this question in many ways. I have lost much of my fear. It used to control me, it was my master. It paralyzed my efforts. Fear always got me down. It made me an introvert, an ingrown person. When fear ~~turned into~~ WAS REPLACED BY faith, I got well. Have I lost some of my fears?

Meditation for the Day

The world would soon be brought CLOSER to God, His will would ~~soon~~ SOONER be done on earth, if all who acknowledge Him gave themselves unreservedly to being used by Him. God can use ~~each~~ EVERY human being as a channel for divine love and power. What delays the bringing of the world CLOSER to God is the backwardness of His followers. If each one lived each day for God and allowed God to work through him, then the world would soon be drawn MUCH CLOSER ~~to God~~, IT'S FOUNDER AND PRESERVER.

Prayer for the Day

I pray that I may be used as a channel to express the Divine Love. I pray that I may so live as to ~~express~~ BRING God's spirit CLOSER ~~to the world.~~

313

November 6 -- A. A. Thought for the Day

Fear and worry had me down. They were increased by my drinking. I worried about what I had done when I was drunk. I was afraid of what the consequences might be. I was afraid to face people because of the fear of being found out. Fear kept me in hot water all the time. I was a nervous wreck from fear and worry. I was a tied-up bundle of nerves. I had a fear of failure, of the future, of growing old, of sickness, of hangovers, of suicide. I had a wrong set of ideas and attitudes. When A. A. told me to surrender these fears and worries to a Higher Power, I did so. I now TRY TO think faith instead of fear. ~~Have I got rid of most of my fears?~~ HAVE I PUT FAITH IN PLACE OF FEAR?

Meditation for the Day

Spiritual power is God in action. God can only act through human beings. Whenever a man, however weak he may be, allows God to act through him, then all he THINKS AND SAYS AND does is spiritually powerful. It is not he ALONE WHO ~~that~~ produces a change in ~~someone's~~ THE LIVES OF OTHERS, ~~life~~, it is ALSO the Divine Spirit in him and working through him. Power is God in action. God can use you as a tool to accomplish miracles in people's lives.

Prayer for the Day

I pray that I may TRY TO let God's power act through me today. I pray that I may get rid of ~~the~~ THOSE blocks ~~that~~ WHICH keep His power from me.

314

November 7 -- A. A. Thought for the Day

I have lost many of my resentments. I have found that getting even with people doesn't ~~work.~~ DO ANY GOOD. When we try to get revenge, instead of making us feel better, it leaves us frustrated and cheated. Instead of punishing our enemies, we've only hurt our own peace of mind. It does not pay to nurse a grouch, it hurts us more than anyone else. Hate causes frustration, inner conflict and neurosis. If we give out hate, we will become hateful. If we are resentful, we will be resented. If ~~you~~ WE do not like people, ~~you~~ WE will not be liked by people. Revengefulness is a powerful poison ~~to~~ IN our systems. Have I lost ~~[illegible]~~ my resentments?

Meditation for the Day

It is not SO MUCH you, ~~but~~ AS the grace of God that is in you, that helps ~~other people~~ THOSE AROUND YOU. IF YOU WOULD HELP EVEN THOSE YOU DISLIKE, ~~All~~ you have to ~~do is to~~ see that there is nothing IN YOU to block the way, ~~so that~~ TO KEEP God's grace ~~can use~~ FROM USING you. Your own PRIDE AND selfishness ~~is~~ ARE the greatest blocks. Keep ~~that~~ THOSE out of the way, and God's grace will flow through you INTO THE LIVES OF ~~to~~ others. Then all who come in contact with you can be helped in some way. Keep the channel open, free from ~~self.~~ THOSE THINGS THAT MAKE YOUR LIFE FUTILE AND INEFFECTIVE.

Prayer for the Day

I pray that all who come in contact with me WILL FEEL BETTER FOR IT. ~~may be helped in some way~~. I pray that I may be ~~always eager to help.~~ CAREFUL NOT TO HARBOR THOSE THINGS IN MY HEART THAT PUT PEOPLE OFF

315

November 8 -- <u>A. A. Thought for the Day</u>

I have lost much of my inferiority complex. I was always trying to escape from life. I did not want to face reality. I was ~~full~~ FULL of self-pity. I was constantly sorry for myself. I tried to avoid all responsibilities. I did not feel that I could handle the responsibilities of my business or my home. ~~I resigned from business and was asked by my wife to leave home.~~ Owing to my inferiority complex, I was ~~glad at the time~~ EAGER to be free of all responsibilities. I wanted to drift, I wanted to be "on the beach". A. A. showed me how to get over my feeling of inferiority. It made me want to accept responsibility again. <u>Have I lost my inferiority complex</u>?

<u>Meditation for the Day</u>

"One thing I do, forgetting those things which are behind and reaching forth unto those things that are before, I press ONWARD toward the ~~mark~~ GOAL." ~~You must~~ WE SHOULD forget ~~the past~~ THOSE THINGS WHICH ARE BEHIND US AND PRESS ONWARD TOWARD SOMETHING BETTER. ~~That is all water over the dam.~~ WE CAN BELIEVE THAT God has forgiven ~~you~~ US for all ~~your~~ OUR past sins, provided ~~you~~ WE are honestly trying to live TODAY the way ~~you~~ WE believe He wants ~~you~~ US to live. ~~So~~ WE CAN wipe clean the slate of the past. WE CAN Start today with a clean slate, and go forward with confidence, TOWARD THE GOAL THAT HAS BEEN SET BEFORE US.

<u>Prayer for the Day</u>

I pray that I may drop off the load of the past. I pray that I may start today with a light heart, AND A NEW CONFIDENCE.

316

November 9 -- <u>A. A. Thought for the Day</u>

I have learned to be less negative and more positive. I used to take a negative view of ALMOST everything. Most people, IN MY ESTIMATION, were bluffing. There ~~was~~ SEEMED TO BE very little good in the world, but ~~there was~~ lots of hypocrisy and sham. People could not be trusted. They would "take you" if they could. All church-goers were PARTLY hypocrites. IT SEEMED I SHOULD Take everything with "a grain of salt". That was my GENERAL attitude TOWARD LIFE. Now I am more positive. I believe in people and in their capabilities. There is much love and truth and honesty in the world. ~~I no longer~~ I TRY NOT TO run people down. ~~I try to help them instead.~~ Life ~~is~~ NOW SEEMS worth while, AND It is good to live. <u>Am I less negative and more positive</u>?

<u>Meditation for the Day</u>

Think of God as a Great Friend and TRY TO realize the wonder of that friendship. ~~As soon as~~ WHEN you give God not only worship, obedience and allegiance, but also ~~loving understanding~~ CLOSE COMPANIONSHIP, then ~~God~~ HE becomes your friend, even as you are His. ~~God and you can work together.~~ YOU CAN FEEL THAT HE AND YOU ARE WORKING together. He can do things for you and you can do things for Him. Your ~~service becomes different~~ PRAYERS BECOME MORE REAL TO YOU, when you feel that God counts on your friendship ~~to do this or that for Him~~ AND YOU COUNT ON HIM.

<u>Prayer for the Day</u>

I pray that I may think of God as ~~a Great~~ MY Friend. I pray that I may ~~delight to work~~ FEEL THAT I AM WORKING for Him and with Him.

317

November 10 -- A. A. Thought for the Day

I am less self-centered. The world used to revolve around me at the center. I cared more about myself, my own needs and desires, my own pleasure, my own way, than I did about the whole rest of the world. What happened to me was more important than anything else I could think of. ~~Needless to say, I had no real friends, only drinking companions.~~ I was SELFISHLY TRYING ~~striving~~ to be happy, and therefore I was unhappy, most of the time. I HAVE FOUND THAT Selfishly seeking pleasure does not bring true happiness. Thinking of MYSELF ~~yourself~~ all the time cut~~s~~ ME ~~you~~ off from THE BEST IN life. A. A. taught me to care LESS ABOUT MYSELF AND more about the other fellow. Am I less self-centered?

Meditation for the Day

When something happens to upset you and you are discouraged, TRY TO FEEL THAT ~~remember~~ that life's difficulties and troubles are not intended to arrest your progress in the spiritual life, but TO TEST YOUR STRENGTH AND to increase your determination to keep going. Whatever it is that must be MET ~~surmounted~~, you are to EITHER overcome it OR USE IT. Nothing SHOULD ~~must~~ daunt you FOR LONG, nor SHOULD ~~must~~ any difficulty ENTIRELY OVERCOME OR conquer you. God's strength will always be there, waiting for you to use it. Nothing CAN BE ~~is~~ too great to be overcome, OR IF NOT OVERCOME, THEN USED.

Prayer for the Day

I pray that I may know that there can be no failure with God. I pray that WITH HIS HELP I may ~~tread the path of victory.~~ LIVE A MORE VICTORIOUS LIFE.

318

November 11 -- A. A. Thought for the Day

WHEN I THINK OF ALL WHO HAVE GONE BEFORE ME, I REALIZE THAT ~~I realize now that I am not the center of the universe.~~ I am only one, not very important, person. What happens to me is not so very important, after all. ~~I have learned to care more about what happens to the other fellow.~~ AND A. A. has taught me to be MORE out-going, to seek friendship by going at least halfway; to have a sincere desire to help. I have more self-respect now that I have less SENSITIVENESS ~~selfishness~~. I have found that the only way to live COMFORTABLY with myself is to take a real interest in others. ~~The good of A. A. is now my main interest. Have I lost some of my selfishness?~~ DO I REALIZE THAT I AM NOT SO IMPORTANT AFTER ALL?

Meditation for the Day

As you look back over your life, it is not TOO DIFFICULT ~~hard~~ to believe that what you went through was for a purpose, to prepare you for SOME VALUABLE WORK IN LIFE. ~~your real job in life, to help other alcoholics~~. Everything in your life may WELL have been planned by God to make you of some use in the world. Each person's life is like the pattern of a mosaic. Each thing that happened to you is like one TINY stone in the mosaic, and each TINY stone fits into the perfected pattern of the mosaic OF YOUR LIFE, WHICH HAS BEEN designed by God.

Prayer for the Day

I pray that I may not NEED ~~ask~~ to see the whole design OF MY LIFE. I pray that I may ~~only~~ trust the Designer.

319

November 12 -- A. A. Thought for the Day

I am less critical of other people, inside and outside of A. A. I used to run people down ~~constantly~~ ALL THE TIME. I realize now that it was because I wanted unconsciously to build myself up. I was envious of people who lived normal lives. I couldn't understand why I couldn't be like them. And so I ran them down. I called them sissies or hypocrites. I was always looking for faults in the other fellow. I loved to tear down what I liked to call "a stuffed shirt". I have found that I can never make a person ~~good~~ ANY BETTER by criticizing him. A. A. has taught me this. Am I less critical of people?

Meditation for the Day

You must admit your helplessness, before your ~~voiceless cry~~ PRAYER for help will be heard by God. Your own need must be recognized, before you can ask God for the strength to meet that need. But ~~that need~~ once THAT NEED IS recognized, your ~~voiceless cry~~ PRAYER is heard above all the music of heaven. It is not theological arguments that solve the problems of the questing soul, but the SINCERE cry of that soul to God FOR STRENGTH and the certainty ~~in~~ OF that soul that the cry ~~has been~~ WILL BE HEARD AND answered.

Prayer for the Day

I pray that I may send my VOICELESS cry for help out into the void. I pray that I may ~~be~~ FEEL certain that it will be heard somewhere, somehow.

320

November 13 -- A. A. Thought for the Day

Who am I to judge other people? Have I proved by my great success in life that I know all the answers? Exactly the opposite. Until I came into A. A., my life could be called a failure. I made all the mistakes a man could make. I took all the wrong roads there were to take. On the basis of my record, am I a fit person to be a judge of my fellow men? Hardly. In A. A. I have learned not to judge people. I am so often wrong. Let the results of what they do judge them. It's not up to me. Am I less harsh in my judgment of people?

Meditation for the Day IN OUR TIME OF MEDITATION, WE AGAIN SEEM TO HEAR:

"Come unto me, all ye that are weary and heavy laden, and I will give you rest." Again and again we SEEM TO hear God saying this to us. "Come unto me" for the solution of every problem, for the overcoming of every temptation, for the calming of every fear, for all ~~your~~ OUR need, physical ~~or~~ mental, OR SPIRITUAL, but mostly "Come unto me" for the strength we need to live ~~the abundant life,~~ WITH PEACE OF MIND and the power to ~~help other people.~~ BE USEFUL AND EFFECTIVE.

Prayer for the Day

I pray that I may go ~~unto~~ TO God TODAY FOR THOSE THINGS WHICH ~~for everything that~~ I need to help me live ~~a better life~~. I pray that ~~I may believe that God will never fail me.~~ I MAY FIND REAL PEACE OF MIND, THE RIGHT THING.

321

November 14 -- A. A. Thought for the Day

A better way than judging a man is to look for all the good you can find in him. If you look hard ENOUGH and LONG enough you ought to be able to find some good SOMEWHERE in every man. In A. A. I learned that my job was to try to bring out the good, not to criticize the bad. Every alcoholic is used to being judged and criticized. That has never helped him to get sober. In A. A. we tell him he can change. We TRY TO bring out the best in him. We encourage his good points and ignore his bad points as much as possible. Men are not converted by criticism. Do I look for the good in ~~all~~ people?

Meditation for the Day

There MUST BE ~~is~~ a design for the world ~~and for each person's life~~, in the mind of God. We CAN believe that ~~the~~ HIS design for the world is a universal brotherhood of men, under the fathership of God. The plan for your life ~~is one of honesty, purity, unselfishness and love, and a sincere desire to help your fellow man.~~ MUST ALSO BE IN THE MIND OF GOD. IN TIMES OF QUIET MEDITATION, YOU CAN SEEK FOR GOD'S GUIDANCE, FOR THE REVEALING OF GOD'S PLAN FOR YOUR DAY. THEN YOU CAN LIVE THIS DAY ACCORDING TO THAT GUIDANCE. Many people are not making of their lives what God meant them to be, and so they are unhappy. THEY HAVE MISSED THE DESIGN FOR THEIR LIVES.

Prayer for the Day

I pray that I may TRY TO follow ~~what I believe is~~ God's design for TODAY. ~~my life.~~ I pray that I may ~~leave the results to Him.~~ HAVE THE SENSE OF DIVINE INTENT IN WHAT I DO TODAY.

322

November 15 -- A. A. Thought for the Day

I am less sensitive and my feelings are less easily hurt. I no longer take myself so seriously. It didn't used to take much to insult me, to feel that I had been slighted or left on the outside. What happens to me now is not so important. One cause of our drinking was because we couldn't take it, so we escaped ~~into drunkenness.~~ THE UNPLEASANT SITUATION. We have to learn to take it on the chin, if necessary, and smile. A man that is wrapped up in A. A. will not notice the personal ~~hurts.~~ SLIGHTS SO MUCH. They do not SEEM TO matter so much. I have learned to laugh at self-pity, because it's so childish. Am I less sensitive?

Meditation for the Day

God's miracle-working power is as manifest today as it was in the past. It still works miracles of change~~d~~ IN lives and MIRACLES OF healing of twisted minds. Whenever a man trusts wholly in God and leaves to Him the choosing of the day and hour, there is God's miracle-working power SUDDENLY become manifest in that man's life. So WE CAN trust in God and have boundless faith in His power to make ~~you~~ US whole again, WHENEVER HE CHOOSES.

Prayer for the Day

I pray that I may ~~believe~~ FEEL SURE that there is nothing that God cannot accomplish in CHANGING my life. I pray that I may have faith in His miracle-working power.

November 16 -- A. A. Thought for the Day

I have got rid of most of my inner conflicts. I was always at war with myself. I was doing things that I did not want to do. I was waking up in strange places and wondering how I got there. I was full of recklessness when I was drunk and full of remorse when I was sober. My life didn't make sense. It was full of broken resolves and frustrated hopes and plans. I was "getting nowhere fast". No wonder my nerves were all shot. I was bumping up against a blank wall and I was dizzy from it. A. A. taught me how to get organized and to stop fighting against myself. Have I got rid of inner conflicts?

Meditation for the Day

"When two or three are gathered together in My name, there am I in the midst of them". The spirit of God comes upon his followers when they are all together at one time, in one place, AND with one accord. When ~~several alcoholics get~~ TWO OR THREE CONSECRATED SOULS ARE together at a meeting, PLACE, the ~~grace~~ SPIRIT of God is there, to help AND GUIDE them. Where any SINCERE group of people ~~get~~ ARE together, reverently seeking the help of God, His power, AND HIS SPIRIT is ~~always~~ there ~~for them.~~ TO INSPIRE THEM.

Prayer for the Day

I pray that I may ~~unite with others to serve God.~~ BE IN ACCORD WITH MY FELLOW MEN. I pray that I may feel the strength of a consecrated group.

November 17 -- A. A. Thought for the Day

Every man has two personalities, a good and a bad. We are all dual personalities to some extent. When we are drinking, the bad personality ~~is~~ WAS in control. We ~~do~~ DID things when we ~~are~~ WERE drunk that we would never do when we ~~are~~ WERE sober. When we sober up, we are different people. Then we wonder how we could have done the things we did. But we drink again, and again our bad side comes out. So we are back and forth, always in conflict with our other selves, always in a stew. This division of ourselves is not ~~natural~~ GOOD, we must somehow become unified. We do this by giving ourselves wholeheartedly to A. A. and TO sobriety. Have I become unified?

Meditation for the Day

"Well done, thou good and faithful servant. Enter into the joy of Thy Lord." These words are for many ORDINARY PEOPLE whom the world ~~would~~ MAY pass by, unrecognizing. Not to the world-famed, the proud, the wealthy, are these words spoken, but to the quiet followers who serve God unobtrusively yet faithfully, who bear their crosses bravely and put a smiling face to the world. "Enter into the joy of thy Lord." Pass into that fuller spiritual life, which is a life of joy, AND PEACE.

Prayer for the Day

I pray that I may not ~~care whether the world sees humble, patient, quiet service.~~ DESIRE THE WORLD'S APPLAUSE. I pray that ~~God may see it, and that I may leave the reward to Him.~~ I MAY NOT SEEK REWARDS ~~FROM THE WORLD~~ FOR DOING WHAT I BELIEVE IS RIGHT.

325

November 18 -- <u>A. A. Thought for the Day</u>

I have got over ~~some of~~ my procrastination. I was always putting things off till tomorrow and as a result they never got done. "There is always another day" was my motto instead of "Do it now". Under the influence of alcohol, I had grandiose plans. When I was sober I was too busy getting over my drunk to start anything. "Some day I'll do ~~this~~ [THAT]" - but I never did it. In A. A. I have learned that it's better to make a mistake once in a while than to never do anything at all. We learn by trial and error. But we must act now, and not put if off [UNTIL TOMORROW]. <u>Have I learned to do it now?</u>

<u>Meditation for the Day</u>

"Do not hide your light under a bushel. Arise and shine, for the light has come and the glory of the Lord is risen in thee." The glory of the Lord ~~is the~~ [SHINES IN THE] beauty of [A MAN'S] character. It is risen in you, even though you can realize it only in part. "Now you see as in a glass darkly, but later you will see face to face." The glory of the Lord is too dazzling for mortals to see fully on earth. But [SOME OF] this glory is risen in you, when you [TRY TO] reflect that light in your life.

<u>Prayer for the Day</u>

I pray that I may [TRY TO] be a reflection of the Divine Light. I pray that [SOME OF ITS RAYS] ~~its beam, however small,~~ may shine in ~~me.~~ [MY LIFE.]

326

November 19 -- <u>A. A. Thought for the Day</u>

In A. A. we do not speak much of sex. And yet putting sex, in its proper place in our lives is ~~a part~~ [ONE] of the rewards that have come to us as a result of our new way of living. The big book ~~"Alcoholics Anonymous"~~ says that many of us needed an overhauling there. It also says that we subjected each sex relation to this test - was it selfish or not? "We remembered always that our sex powers were God-given and therefore good, neither to be used lightly or selfishly nor to be despised and loathed." We ~~asked~~ [CAN ASK] God to mold our ideals and help us to live up to them. [WE CAN ACT ACCORDINGLY.] <u>Have I got my sex-life into proper control</u>?

<u>Meditation for the Day</u>

"I will lift up my eyes unto the heights, whence cometh my help." ~~Always~~ [TRY TO] raise ~~the eyes of your spirit~~ [YOUR THOUGHTS] from [THE DEPTHS OF] the sordid and mean and ~~false~~ [IMPURE THINGS] ~~of the earth~~ to the heights of goodness and ~~truth~~ [DECENCY] and beauty. Train your insight, by trying to take the ~~long~~ [HIGHER] view. Train it more and more, until distant heights [BECOME MORE] ~~seem~~ familiar. The heights of the Lord, whence cometh your help, will ~~seem~~ [BECOME] nearer ~~and dearer~~. [AND THE FALSE VALUES OF THE EARTH WILL SEEM FARTHER AWAY.]

<u>Prayer for the Day</u>

I pray that I may not keep my eyes [FOREVER] downcast. I pray that I may set my sights ~~high.~~ [ON HIGHER THINGS.]

327

November 20 -- <u>A. A. Thought for the Day</u>

I no longer try to escape life through alcoholism. Drinking built up an unreal world for me and I tried to live in it. But in the morning LIGHT the real life was back again and facing it was harder than ever, because I had less resources WITH WHICH to meet it. Each attempt at escape weakened my personality by the very attempt. Everyone knows that alcohol, by relaxing inhibitions, permits a flight from reality. Alcohol deadens the brain cells that preside over our highest faculties and we are off to the unreal world of drunkenness. A. A. taught me not to run away but to face reality. <u>Have I given up trying to escape ~~?~~ LIFE?</u>

<u>Meditation for the Day</u> IN THESE TIMES OF MEDITATION, TRY

More and more TO set your hopes on the ~~Lord~~ GRACE OF GOD. Know that whatever the future may hold, it will hold more and more of ~~God~~ GOOD. Do not set ALL your hopes and desires on material things. ~~but~~ THERE IS WEARINESS IN AN ABUNDANCE OF THINGS. Set your hopes on spiritual things, so that you may grow spiritually. Learn to ~~know~~ RELY ON God's power more and more, and in that ~~knowledge~~ RELIANCE you will have ~~all the answers that you need here on earth.~~ AN INSIGHT INTO THE GREATER VALUE OF THE THINGS OF THE SPIRIT.

<u>Prayer for the Day</u>

I pray that ~~all my answers to life may be found in God.~~ I MAY NOT BE OVERWHELMED BY MATERIAL THINGS. I pray that I may ~~seek His spirit more than knowledge about Him.~~ REALIZE THE HIGHER VALUE OF SPIRITUAL THINGS.

328

November 21 -- <u>A. A. Thought for the Day</u>

I no longer waste money, ~~I~~ BUT try to put it to a good use. Like all of us, when I was drunk I threw money around "like a drunken sailor". It gave me a feeling of importance, a "millionaire for a day". But the morning after with an empty wallet and perhaps some ~~bad~~ UNDECIPHERABLE checks to boot, was a sad awakening. One of the hardest things to face is the fact of wasted money. How could I have been such a fool? How will I ever make it up? Thoughts like these get you down. When we are sober, we spend our hard-earned money as it should be spent. ~~We give away a certain amount of it to help our fellow alcoholics. That makes us feel good.~~ ALTHOUGH PERHAPS SOME OF US COULD BE MORE GENEROUS IN OUR A.A. GIVING, AT LEAST WE DO NOT THROW IT AWAY. <u>Am I making good use of my money?</u>

<u>Meditation for the Day</u>

You were meant to be at home and comfortable in this world. ~~But~~ YET some people live a life of "quiet desperation". This is the opposite of being at home and at peace in the world. Let your peace of mind be ~~evidenced to everybody.~~ EVIDENT TO THOSE AROUND YOU. Men should see that you are comfortable, and seeing it, know that it springs from YOUR trust in ~~God.~~ A HIGHER POWER. The hard, dull way of resignation is not God's way. Faith takes the sting out of the winds of adversity, AND BRINGS PEACE EVEN IN THE MIDST OF STRUGGLE.

<u>Prayer for the Day</u>

I pray that I may be MORE comfortable in my way of ~~life.~~ LIVING. I pray that I may feel MORE at home and at peace, WITHIN MYSELF.

November 22 -- A. A. Thought for the Day

I have got rid of most of my boredom. One of the hardest things that a new member of A. A. has to understand is how he can stay sober and not be bored. Drinking was always the answer to all kinds of boring people or boring situations. There may well be a period of boredom when you are in the transition period of changing from an alcoholic to a sober ~~member of A. A.~~ [PERSON.] ~~We are not afraid to face a little boredom if we are going to get well.~~ But once you [HAVE] take~~n~~ up the interests of A. A., once you [HAVE] give~~n~~ it your time and enthusiasm, boredom ~~leaves you.~~ [SHOULD NOT BE A PROBLEM TO YOU.] ~~And~~ A new life opens up before you that can be ~~intensely~~ [ALWAYS] interesting. Sobriety ~~gives~~ [SHOULD GIVE] you so many new interests in life that you ~~don't~~ [SHOULDN'T] have time to be bored. Have I got rid of the fear of being bored?

Meditation for the Day [THE BEST WAY TO KEEP FROM BEING BORED IS TO FIND NEW INTERETS IN LIFE, AND ESPECIALLY IN DOING SOME CHARITABLE THING.]

"If I have not charity, I am become as sounding brass or a tinkling cymbal." ~~Only what is done in charity lasts.~~ Charity means to ~~love~~ [CARE ABOUT] your fellow ~~men~~ [MAN] enough to really want to ~~help them.~~ [DO SOMETHING FOR HIM.] A smile, a word of encouragement, a word of love, goes winged on its way, simple though it may seem, while the mighty words of an orator ~~may~~ fall on deaf ears. [USE UP THE ODD MOMENTS OF YOUR DAY IN TRYING TO DO SOME LITTLE THING TO CHEER UP YOUR FELLOW MAN. BOREDOM COMES FROM THINKING TOO MUCH ABOUT YOURSELF.]

Prayer for the Day

I pray that my ~~work may be done with true~~ [DAY MAY BE BRIGHTENED BY SOME LITTLE ACT OF] charity. I pray that I may [TRY TO ATONCE OVERCOME] ~~rid my heart~~ of [THE SELF-CENTEREDNESS THAT MAKES ME BORED.] ~~all that is not charitable.~~

November 23 -- A. A. Thought for the Day

I no longer refuse to do anything, because I cannot do it to perfection. Many of us alcoholics use the excuse of not being able to do something perfectly to enable us to do nothing at all. We pretend to be perfectionists. We are good at telling people how a thing should be done, but when we come to the effort of doing it ourselves, we balk. We say to ourselves: I might make a mistake, so I'd better let the whole thing slide. In A. A. we set our goals high, but that does not prevent us from trying. The mere fact that we will never fully reach these goals does not prevent us from doing the best we can. Have I stopped hiding behind ~~a~~ [THE] smoke-screen of perfectionism?

Meditation for the Day

"In the world ye shall have tribulation. But be of good cheer. I have overcome the world." Keep an undaunted spirit. Keep your spirit free and unconquered. You can be ~~unharmed~~ [UNDEFEATED] and untouched by ~~evil~~ [FAILURE] and all its power, by letting your spirit overcome the world, rise above earth's turmoil into the secret ~~place~~ [CHAMBER] of perfect peace [AND CONFIDENCE]. When ~~evil~~ challenges [COME TO] you, remember you ~~are on God's side~~ [HAVE GOD'S HELP], and nothing can ~~seriously harm~~ [WHOLLY DEFEAT] you.

Prayer for the Day

I pray that I may [HAVE CONFIDENCE AND] be of good cheer. I pray that I may not fear the power of ~~evil.~~ [FAILURE.]

331

November 24 -- A. A. Thought for the Day

Instead of being pretended perfectionists, in A. A. we are content if we are making progress. The main thing is to be growing. We realize that perfectionism is only a result of false pride and an excuse to save our faces. In A. A., we are willing to make mistakes and to stumble, provided we are always stumbling forward. We are not so interested in what we are as IN what we are becoming. We are on the way, not at the goal. And we will be on the way as long as we live. No A. A. has ever "arrived". But we are getting better. Am I making progress?

Meditation for the Day

Each new day brings an opportunity to do some little thing that will help to make a better world, that will bring God's Kingdom a little nearer to being realized on earth. Take each day's happenings as opportunities for something you can do for God. In that spirit, a blessing will attend all that you do. Offering ~~your~~ THIS day's service to God, you are sharing in ~~God's~~ HIS work. You do not have to do great things.

Prayer for the Day

I pray that TODAY I may do the ~~small~~ NEXT thing, ~~the honest thing, the pure thing~~, the unselfish thing, the loving thing. I pray that I may be content with ~~this.~~ DOING SMALL THINGS, AS LONG AS THEY ARE RIGHT.

334

November 25 -- A. A. Thought for the Day

I am not so envious of other people, nor am I so jealous of other people's possessions and talents. When I was drinking I was secretly full of jealousy and envy of people who could drink like gentlemen, who had the love and respect of their families, who lived a normal life and were accepted as equals by their fellows. I pretended to myself that I was as good as they were, but I knew it wasn't so. Now I don't have to be envious any more. I ~~do~~ TRY not TO want what I don't deserve. I'm content with what I have earned by my efforts to live the right way. More power to those who have what I have not. At least, I'm trying. Have I got rid of the poison of envy?

Meditation for the Day

"My soul is restless, till it finds its rest in Thee". A river flows on, until it loses itself in the sea. Our spirits long for REST IN the spirit of God. We yearn to realize a peace, a rest, a satisfaction that we have never found in the world or its pursuits. Some are not conscious of their need ~~of God~~ and so shut the doors of their spirits against the spirit of God. THEY ARE UNABLE TO HAVE TRUE PEACE.

Prayer for the Day

I pray that I may feel the divine unrest. I pray that my soul may find its rest in God.

333

November 26 -- A. A. Thought for the Day

Continuing our thoughts about the rewards that have come to us as a result of our new way of living; We have found that we have got rid of ~~most~~ MANY of our fears, resentments, inferiority complexes, negative points of view, self-centeredness, criticism of others, oversensitiveness, inner conflicts, the habits of procrastination, undisciplined sex, ~~drinking~~, wasting money, boredom, falsE perfectionism ~~and~~ jealousy and envy of others. We are glad to be rid of our drinking, ~~but~~ AND we are also very glad to be rid of ~~the~~ THESE other things. We can now go forward in the new way of life AS shown us by A. A. Am I ready to go forward in the new life?

Meditation for tha Day

"He that has eyes to see, let him see". To the seeing eye, the world is good. Pray for a seeing eye, to see the ~~hand~~ PURPOSE of God in everything good. Pray for enough faith to see ~~the beauty of~~ God's ~~love~~ CARE in His dealings with you. Try to see how He has brought you safely through YOUR past ~~experiences~~ LIFE, so that NOW you can now be of use in the world. With the eyes of faith you can see God's ~~love~~ CARE and purpose everywhere.

Prayer for the Day

I pray that I may have a seeing eye. I pray that WITH the eye of faith I may see ~~the world and find it good.~~ GOD'S PURPOSE EVERYWHERE.

334

November 27 -- A. A. Thought for the Day

The way of A. A. is the way of sobriety, fellowship, service and faith. Let us take up each one of these things and see if our feet are truly on the way. The first and greatest to us is sobriety. The others are built on sobriety as a foundation. We could not have the others if we did not have sobriety. We all come to A. A. to get sober, and we stay to help others get sober. We are looking for sobriety first, last and all the time. We cannot build any DECENT kind of a life unless we stay sober. Am I on the A. A. way?

Meditation for the Day

To truly desire to do God's will, therein lies happiness for a human being. We start out wanting our own way. We want our wills to be satisfied. We take and we do not give. Gradually we find that we are not happy when we are selfish, so we begin to make allowances for other people's wills. But this again does not give US full happiness, and we begin to see that the only way to be truly happy is to try to do God's will. IN THESE TIMES OF MEDITATION, WE SEEK TO GET GUIDANCE. SO THAT WE CAN FIND GOD'S WILL FOR US.

Prayer for the Day

I pray that I may subordinate my will to ~~the service of others.~~ THE WILL OF GOD. I pray that I may ~~give my will to the will of God.~~ BE GUIDED TODAY TO FIND HIS WILL FOR ME.

335

November 28 -- A. A. Thought for the Day

The A. A. way is the way of sobriety. ~~Everybody knows that.~~ A. A. is known everywhere as ~~the~~ A method that has been ~~most~~ VERY successful with alcoholics. Doctors, psychiatrists and clergymen have had some success. ~~But their success does not compare with the success of A. A.~~ AS THEY WILL TELL YOU, Some men AND WOMEN have got sober all by themselves~~, but they are very few, and far between~~. WE BELIEVE THAT A. A. is the most successful ~~and best~~ AND HAPPIEST way to sobriety. And yet ~~even~~ A. A. IS OF COURSE NOT WHOLLY ~~is not one hundred percent~~ successful. Some ~~we~~ are unable to ~~sober up~~ ACHIEVE SOBRIETY and some slip back ~~to~~ INTO alcoholism after they have had some measure of sobriety. ~~Have I got my sobriety the A. A. way?~~ AM I DEEPLY GRATEFUL TO HAVE FOUND A.A.?

Meditation for the Day

Gratitude to God is the ~~basis~~ THEME of Thanksgiving Day. The pilgrims gathered to give thanks TO GOD for their harvest, which was pitifully small. When we look around at all the things we have today, how can we help being grateful to God? Our families, our homes, our friends, our ~~work with~~ A. A. FELLOWSHIP, all these things are ~~a~~ free gifts of God to us. But for the grace of God, we would not have them.

Prayer for the Day

I pray that I may ~~not take credit to myself for anything I have.~~ BE VERY GRATEFUL TODAY. I pray that I may ~~remember always that I would have nothing worth while~~ NOT FORGET WHERE I MIGHT BE but for the grace of God.

336

November 29 -- A. A. Thought for the Day

The A. A. way is the way of sobriety, and yet ~~we have~~ THERE ARE slips. Why ~~do we have~~ THESE slips OCCUR? Why don't we all accept A. A. ~~at once~~ and stay sober from then on? ~~This is a sensible question,~~ THERE ARE MANY REASONS, ~~because~~ BUT it has been proved true without exception that once we have become alcoholics we can never drink ~~normally~~ SUCCESSFULLY again. This has never been disproved by ~~one single experiment in the history of A. A.~~ ANY CASE WE KNOW OF. Many ~~people~~ ALCOHOLICS have tried ~~the "noble experiment"~~ DRINKING after a period of sobriety from a few days to a few years and no one THAT WE KNOW OF has been successful in becoming a normal drinker. Could I be the only exception TO THIS RULE? ~~in the thousands of A. A.'s?~~ ~~ALCOHOLICS?~~

Meditation for the Day

"We are gathered together in Thy name." First, we are gathered together, bound by a common loyalty to God and to each other. Then, when this condition has been fulfilled, God is present WITH US. ~~too.~~ Then, when God is there and one with us, we voice ~~the same petitions to Him~~ A COMMON PRAYER. Then it follows that ~~the requests~~ OUR PRAYER will be ~~granted as God sees fit~~ ANSWERED ACCORDING TO GOD'S WILL. Then, when ~~the requests are granted, we live the abundant life and fulfill the purpose for which we were put on earth.~~ OUR PRAYER IS ANSWERED WE ARE BOUND TOGETHER IN A LASTING BROTHERHOOD OF THE SPIRIT.

Prayer for the Day

I pray that I may be loyal to God and to my fellow men. I pray that my life TODAY may be LIVED close to His and to theirs.

337

November 30 -- A. A. Thought for the Day

We have slips in A. A. It has been said these are not slips but premeditated drunks, because we have to think about taking a drink before we actually take one. The thought always comes before the act. It has been suggested that a man should always get in touch with an A. A. before taking that first drink. Their failure to do so makes it probable that they had decided to take a drink anyway. And yet the thoughts that come before taking that drink are often largely subconscious. The man doesn't know consciously what made him do it. Therefore, the common practice is to call these things slips. Am I on my guard against wrong thinking?

Meditation for the Day

"The Eternal God is thy refuge". He is a place to flee to, a sanctuary, an escape from the misunderstanding of others and also an escape from yourself. You can get away from others by retiring into the quiet of your own being. But from yourself, from a sense of your failures, your weakness, your shortcomings, whither can you flee? Only to the Eternal God, your refuge, until in the immensity of His spirit, your spirit loses its smallness and becomes one with His.

Prayer for the Day

I pray that I may lose my limitations in the immensity of God's love. I pray that my spirit may be absorbed by His spirit.

338

December 1 -- A. A. Thought for the Day

The thoughts that come before having a slip are often largely subconscious. It is a question whether our subconscious minds ever become entirely free from alcoholic thoughts as long as we live. For instance, some of us dream about being drunk when we are asleep, even after several years of sobriety in A. A. During the period of our drinking days, our subconscious minds have been thoroughly conditioned by our alcoholic way of thinking and it is doubtful if they ever become entirely free of such thoughts during our lifetime. But when our conscious minds are fully conditioned against drinking, we can stay sober and our subconscious minds do not often bother us. Do I ever have alcoholic dreams? Am I still conditioning my conscious mind?

Meditation for the Day

Having smypathy and compassion for all who are in the condition of temptation, which condition we are often in, we have a responsibility towards them, not only towards those who are close to us, but towards everybody. Sympathy always includes responsibility. Pity is useless, because it does not have a remedy for the need. Wherever your sympathy goes, our responsibility goes too. When we are moved with compassion, we go to the one in need and bind up his wounds as best we can.

Prayer for the Day

I pray that the needy may rely on me. I pray that they may know I am ready to help them. I may have compassion for others' trials.

339

December 2 -- <u>A. A. Thought for the Day</u>

The thoughts that come before having a slip ~~are~~ SEEM TO BE partly subconscious. And yet it is likely that at least a part of these thoughts get into our consciousness. An idle thought connected with drinking casually pops into our mind. That is the crucial moment. Will I harbor that thought even for one minute or will I banish it from my mind at once? If I let is stay, it may develop into a daydream. I may begin to see a cool glass of beer or a Manhattan cocktail in my mind's eye. If I allow the daydream to stay in my mind, it may lead to a decision, however unconscious, to take a drink. Then I am headed for a slip. <u>Do I let myself daydream</u>?

<u>Meditation for the Day</u>

~~Most~~ MANY of us have some sort of vision of what SORT OF MAN God ~~must be like.~~ WANTS US TO BE. We must be true to that vision, whatever it is, and we must try to live up to it, by living the way we believe we should live. We ~~may~~ CAN ALL believe that God has a vision of what He wants us to be like. ~~For~~ IN every man, there is the ~~ideal~~ GOOD man which God sees in him, the man he could be, the man God would like to have him be. ~~A~~ BUT MANY A man ~~often~~ fails to fulfill that promise and God's disappointments must be many.

<u>Prayer for the Day</u>

I pray that I may strive to be the kind of a person that God would have me be. I pray that I may try to fulfill God's vision of ~~me.~~ WHAT I COULD BE.

340

December 3 -- <u>A. A. Thought for the Day</u>

There is some alcoholic thought, conscious and unconscious, that comes before every slip. As long as we live, we must be on the lookout for such thoughts and guard against them. In fact, ~~most of~~ our A. A. training is MOSTLY to prepare us, to make us ready to recognize such thoughts at once and to reject them at once. The slip comes when we allow such thoughts to remain in our minds, even before we actually go through the motions of lifting the glass to our lips. The A. A. programme is largely one of mental training. <u>How well is my mind prepared</u>?

<u>Meditation for the Day</u>

Fret not your ~~soul~~ MIND with puzzles that you cannot solve. The solutions may never be shown to you, until you have left this life. The loss of dear ones, the inequality of life, the deformed and the maimed, and many other puzzling things may not be known to you until you reach the life beyond. "I have yet many things to say unto you, but ye cannot hear them now." Only step by step, stage by stage, can you proceed in your journey into greater knowledge and understanding.

<u>Prayer for the Day</u>

I pray that I may be content that things ~~that~~ WHICH I now see darkly will some day be made clear. I pray that I may have faith that someday I will see face to face.

341

December 4 -- A. A. Thought for the Day

If we allow an alcoholic thought to lodge in our minds for any length of time, we are in danger of having a slip. Therefore, we must dispel ~~them~~ SUCH THOUGHTS at once, by refusing their admittance and by immediately putting constructive thoughts in their place. Remember that alcohol is poison to you. Remember that it is impossible for you to drink normally. Remember that one drink will lead to others and you will eventually be drunk. Remember what happened to you in the past, as a result of your drinking. Think of every reason you have learned in A. A. for not taking that drink. Fill your mind with constructive thoughts. Am I keeping my thoughts constructive?

Meditation for the Day

Always seek to set aside the valuations of the world which seem wrong and try to judge only by ~~the~~ THOSE valuations ~~of the world~~ which seem right TO YOU. Do not seek too much the praise and notice of men. ~~By~~ BE one of those who, though sometimes scoffed at, have a ~~happiness~~ SERENITY and peace OF MIND which the scoffers never know. Be one of that band who feel the ~~majesty of God,~~ DIVINE PRINCIPLE IN THE UNIVERSE, though He be often rejected by men, BECAUSE HE CANNOT BE SEEN.

Prayer for the Day

I pray that I may not heed too much the judgment of men. I pray that I may test things by ~~the judgment of God.~~ WHAT SEEMS RIGHT TO ME.

342

December 5 -- A. A. Thought for the Day

In spite of all we have learned in A. A., our old way of thinking comes back on us, sometimes with overwhelming force, and ~~we do~~ OCCASIONALLY SOME OF US have slips. We forget or refuse to call on the Higher Power for help. We SEEM TO deliberately make out minds a blank ~~as~~ SO far as our A. A. training goes, and we take a drink. We eventually get drunk. We are TEMPORARILY right back where we started from. Those who have had slips say unanimously that they were no fun. They say A. A. had taken all the pleasure out of drinking. They ~~know~~ KNEW they ~~are~~ WERE doing the wrong thing. The old mental conflict ~~is~~ WAS back in full force. They ~~are~~ WERE disgusted with themselves. ~~Do I know~~ AM I CONVINCED that I can never ~~have any more fun with~~ GET ANYTHING MORE OUT OF drinking?

Meditation for the Day

Give something to ~~all you meet~~ THOSE WHO ARE HAVING TROUBLE, to ~~all~~ THOSE whose ~~lives touch yours~~ THOUGHTS ARE CONFUSED, something of your SYMPATHY, YOUR prayers, your time, ~~your self~~ YOUR SELF, your love, your thought. Then give of ~~this world's goods~~ YOUR OWN CONFIDENCE BY THE GRACE OF GOD as you have had ~~them~~ IT given to you. ~~To give money, without having given on a higher plane first, is wrong.~~ GIVE OF YOURSELF AND OF YOUR LOVING SYMPATHY. Give your best to ~~all~~ THOSE who need it and will accept it. ~~But give according to need, never according to deserts.~~ REMEMBER THAT THE GIVING OF ADVICE CAN NEVER TAKE THE PLACE OF GIVING OF YOURSELF.

Prayer for the Day

I pray that as I have received, so may I give. I pray that I may ~~try to meet the needs of those whom God brings to me.~~ HAVE THE RIGHT ANSWER FOR THOSE WHO ARE CONFUSED.

343

December 6 -- A. A. Thought for the Day

A man has had a slip. He is ashamed of himself. He is sometimes so ashamed that he fears to go back to A. A. He develops ~~that~~ THE old inferiority complex and sells himself the idea that he is no good, that he has let down his friends in A. A., that he is hopeless, AND that he can never make it. This state of mind is perhaps worse than it was originally. HE HAS PROBABLY BEEN SOMEWHAT WEAKENED BY HIS SLIP. ~~before he came into A. A. the first time.~~ But his A. A. training ~~is never~~ CANNOT EVER BE entirely lost. He ALWAYS knows he can go back if AGAIN he wants to. He knows there is still ~~salvation~~ GOD'S HELP for him, IF HE WILL ASK FOR IT. ~~in A. A. If he is too discouraged to go back, some member of A. A. can~~ MAY go and ~~persuade~~ INVITE ~~him to return.~~ Do I ~~know~~ BELIEVE that I can never entirely lose what I have learned in A. A.?

Meditation for the Day

Nobody ENTIRELY escapes temptation. You must expect it and be ready for it when it comes. NONE OF US IS ENTIRELY SAFE. You must try to keep your defenses up by daily thought and prayer. THAT IS WHY WE HAVE THESE DAILY MEDITATIONS. You must CLEARLY recognize temptation when it comes. The first step toward~~s~~ conquering temptation ALWAYS is to see it clearly as temptation and not to harbor it in your mind. Disassociate yourself from it, put it out of your mind as soon as it appears. Do not think of excuses for yielding to it. TURN AT ONCE TO THE HIGHER POWER FOR HELP.

Prayer for the Day

I pray that I may be prepared for whatever temptations MAY come to me. I pray that I may see it clearly and avoid it, WITH THE HELP OF GOD.

344

December 7 -- A. A. Thought for the Day

A man comes back to A. A. after having a slip. The temptation is strong to say nothing about it. No other A. A. member should force him to declare himself. It is entirely up to him. If he is well grounded in A. A., he will realize that it's up to him to get up on his feet in open meeting and tell about his slip. There is no possible evasion of this duty, if he is thoroughly honest and really desirous of living the A. A. way AGAIN. When he has done it, his old confidence returns. He is home again. His slip ~~is not~~ SHOULD NOT BE mentioned again by others. He is again a good member of A. A. ~~Have I honestly declared myself?~~ AM I TOLERANT OF OTHER PEOPLES' MISTAKES?

Meditation for the Day

It is in the union of a soul with God that strength, NEW life and spiritual power ~~pass.~~ COME. Bread sustains the body, but ~~you~~ WE cannot live by bread alone. To try to do the will of God is the ~~very strength~~ MEAT and support of true living. WE Feed on that spiritual food. Soul-starvation comes from failing to do so. The world talks about bodies that are undernourished. What of the souls that are undernourished? Strength and peace come from partaking of spiritual food.

Prayer for the Day

I pray that I may not try to live by bread alone. I pray that ~~I may also~~ MY SPIRIT MAY live by trying to do the will of God, AS I UNDERSTAND IT.

345

December 8 -- <u>A. A. Thought for the Day</u>

The length of time of our sobriety is not as important as the quality of it. A man who has been in A. A. for a number of years may not be in as good a mental condition as a man who has only been in a few ~~weeks~~ MONTHS. It is a great satisfaction to have been an A. A. member for a long time, and we often mention it. It MAY sometimes help~~s~~ the newer members, because they MAY say to themselves, if he can do it I can do it. And yet the older members must realize that as long as they live they are only one drink away from a drunk. <u>What is the quality of my sobriety</u>?

<u>Meditation for the Day</u>

"And greater works than this shall ye do." We can do greater works, when we have more ~~knowledge of the spirit of the universe~~ EXPERIENCE OF THE NEW WAY OF LIFE. We can have all the power ~~of~~ WE NEED FROM the Unseen God. We can have His grace, His spirit, to ~~help us~~ MAKE US EFFECTIVE AS WE GO ALONG EACH DAY. Opportunities for work for a better world are all around us. ~~We should work in the field where we can be most useful.~~ GREATER WORKS CAN WE DO. BUT WE DO NOT WORK ALONE. THE POWER OF GOD IS BEHIND ALL GOOD WORKS.

<u>Prayer for the Day</u>

I pray that I may find my RIGHTFUL place in the world. I pray that my work may be made MORE effective by the grace of God.

346

December 9 -- <u>A. A. Thought for the Day</u>

The way of A. A. is the way of fellowship. We have ~~said~~ READ a good deal about fellowship and yet it is such an important part of the A. A. programme that it does not seem that we can think too much about it. Man was not made to live alone. A hermit's life is not a normal or natural one. We all need to be by ourselves at times, but we cannot really live without the companionship of others. Our natures demand it. Our lives depend largely upon it. The fellowship of A. A. seems to us to be the best in the world. <u>Do I fully appreciate what the fellowship of A. A. means to me</u>?

<u>Meditation for the Day</u>

We are all seeking something, but many do not know what they want in life. They are seeking SOMETHING because they are RESTLESS AND dissatisfied, without realizing that faith IN GOD can give an objective AND PURPOSE for their ~~quest.~~ LIVES. ~~All~~ MANY men are at least subconsciously seeking for a ~~Higher~~ GREATER THAN THEMSELVES Power, because that ~~gives them a reason for their existence.~~ WOULD GIVE A MEANING TO THEIR EXISTENCE. If you have found that ~~Higger~~ HIGHER Power, you can be the means of leading men aright, by showing them that their search FOR A MEANING TO LIFE will end when they find faith AND TRUST in God as the answer. ~~to life.~~

<u>Prayer for the Day</u>

I pray that my soul will lose its restlessness BY FINDING REST in God. I pray that I may ~~rest in His peace.~~ FIND PEACE OF MIND IN THE THOUGHT OF GOD AND HIS PURPOSE FOR MY LIFE.

347

December 10 -- <u>A. A. Thought for the Day</u>

Our drinking fellowship was a substitute one, for lack of something better. At the time, we did not realize what real fellowship could be. Drinking fellowship has a fatal fault. It is not based on a firm foundation. Most of it is on the surface. It is based mostly on the desire to use your companions for your own pleasure, and ~~this~~ AMONG OTHERS is a false foundation. Drinking fellowship has been praised in song and story. The "cup that cheers" has become famous as a means of companionship. But we realize that the higher centers of our brain are dulled by alcohol and such fellowship ~~is not~~ CANNOT BE on the highest plane. It is at best only a substitute. <u>Do I see my drinking fellowship in its proper light?</u>

<u>Meditation for the Day</u>

Set yourself the task of growing daily more and more into the ~~knowledge~~ CONSCIOUSNESS of a Higher Power. WE MUST KEEP TRYING TO IMPROVE OUR CONSCIOUS CONTACT WITH GOD. This is done by prayer, quiet times and communion. Often, all you need do is to sit silent before God and let Him speak to you through your thoughts. TRY TO think God's thoughts after Him. When the guidance comes, you must not hesitate, but go out ~~and carry the message with you in all your work.~~ AND FOLLOW THAT GUIDANCE IN YOUR DAILY WORK, DOING WHAT YOU BELIEVE TO BE THE RIGHT THING.

<u>Prayer for the Day</u>

I pray that I may be still and know that God is ~~there.~~ WITH ME. I pray that I may open my mind to the leading of the Divine Mind.

348

December 11 -- <u>A. A. Thought for the Day</u>

Doctors think of the A. A. fellowship as group therapy. This is a very narrow conception of the depth of the A. A. fellowship. Looking at it purely as a means of acquiring and holding sobriety, ~~it~~ is right as far as it goes. But it doesn't go far enough. Group-therapy is directed toward the help that the individual receives from it. It is essentially selfish. ~~We~~ IT IS ~~use~~ USING the companionship of other alcoholics ONLY in order to stay sober ourselves. ~~This is all right as far as it goes, but it is~~ BUT THIS IS only the beginning of real A. A. fellowship. ~~Do I realize that group therapy is only the beginning?~~ ~~A PART OF TRUE FELLOWSHIP?~~ <u>DO I DEEPLY FEEL THE TRUE A.A. FELLOWSHIP?</u>

<u>Meditation for the Day</u>

Most of us have had to live through the dark part of our lives, the time of failure, the night-time of our lives, when we were full of struggle and care, worry and remorse, when we felt ~~all~~ DEEPLY the tragedy of life. But with our ~~new~~ DAILY surrender to a Higher Power, ~~came~~ COMES A peace and joy that ~~made~~ MAKES all things new. We can now take each day as a joyous sunrise-gift from God, to use for Him and for our fellow men. THE NIGHT OF THE PAST IS GONE, THIS DAY IS OURS.

<u>Prayer for the Day</u>

I pray that I may take this day as a gift from God. I pray that I may ~~use it to good advantage.~~ THANK GOD FOR THIS DAY AND BE GLAD IN IT.

349

December 12 -- A. A. Thought for the Day

Clergymen speak of spiritual fellowship of the church. This is much closer to ~~the~~ the A. A. ~~principles~~ way than ~~were~~ mere group therapy. Such a fellowship is based on a common belief in ~~a Higher Power,~~ God, and a common effort to live ~~the~~ a spiritual life. We certainly try to do this in A. A. But we do something more. Church members or religious groups theoretically help each other. But how often do they get down to the real problems in each others' lives? ~~and do something about it?~~ How much do they really open up to each other? How practical is their desire to be of real service to each other? Most ~~spiritual fellowships~~ members of church groups do not seem to go deep enough into the personal lives of its members. ~~Do I realize that spiritual fellowship is only part of it?~~ Do I appreciate the deep personal fellowship of A. A.?

Meditation for the Day

Love and fear cannot dwell together. By their very natures, they cannot exist side by side. Fear is a very strong force, and therefore a weak vacillating love can soon be routed by fear. But a ~~perfect~~ strong love, a love that trusts in God, is sure to eventually conquer fear. The only sure way to dispel ~~all~~ fear is to have the love of God more and more in your ~~life.~~ heart and soul.

Prayer for the Day

I pray that love will drive out the fear in my life. I pray that my fear will flee before the ~~sense of God's love.~~ power of the love of God.

350

December 13 -- A. A. Thought for the Day

We come now to A. A. fellowship. It is partly group therapy. ~~Yes.~~ It is partly spiritual fellowship. ~~Yes.~~ But it is even more. It is based on a common ~~disease~~ illness, a common failure, a common problem. It goes deep down into our personal ~~life~~ lives and our personal needs. It requires a full opening up to each other of our inmost thoughts and most secret problems. All barriers between us are swept aside. ~~They have to be.~~ Then we try to ~~help~~ each other ~~to get well~~. The A. A. fellowship is based on a sincere desire to help the other fellow. In A. A. we can be sure of sympathy, understanding and real help. ~~That makes~~ These things make the A. A. fellowship ~~deeper than anything else in the world, as far as we know.~~ the best that we know. Do I fully appreciate the ~~true value~~ depth of the A. A. fellowship?

Meditation for the Day

The Higher Power can guide us to the right decisions, if we pray about them. We can believe that ~~every~~ many details of our ~~spiritual life is~~ lives are planned by God and planned with a wealth of forgiving love for the mistakes we have made. We can ~~wait~~ pray today to be shown ~~God's way.~~ the right way. ~~When~~ We can when we choose it, we can feel that the ~~We~~ choose the good, the whole power of the universe is behind us. We can achieve a real harmony with God's purpose for our lives.

Prayer for the Day

I pray that I may choose aright today. I pray that I may be shown the right way to live, today.

351

December 14 -- A. A. Thought for the Day

The way of A. A. is the way of service. Without that, it would not work. We have been "on the wagon" and hated it. We have taken the pledge and waited for the time to be up. We have tried all manner of ways to help ourselves. But not until we begin to help other people, do we get full relief. It is an axiom that the A. A. programme has to be given away in order to be kept. A river flows into the Dead Sea and stops. A river flows into a clear pool and flows out again. We get and then we give. If we do not give, we do not keep. Have I given up all idea of holding A. A. for myself?

Meditation for the Day

Try to see the life of the spirit as a calm place, shut away from the turmoil of the world. Think of your spiritual life as a place full of peace, serenity and contentment. Go to this quiet, meditative place for the strength to carry you through all the daily duties and hardships of life. Keep coming back here for refreshment, when you are weary of the hubbub of the world.

Prayer for the Day

I pray that I may have a resting place where I can regain my strength. I pray that I may find refreshment in meditation on the Eternal.

352

December 15 -- A. A. Thought for the Day

Service of others makes the world go round. Civilization would cease if each man was for himself. We alcoholics have a wonderful opportunity to contribute to the well-being of the world. We have a problem. We find the answer. We are uniquely equipped to help others with that same problem. What a wonderful world it would be if everybody took their own greatest problem found the answer to it and spent the rest of their lives helping others with the same problem. Soon we would have the right kind of a world. Do I fully appreciate my unique opportunity?

Meditation for the Day

Each day can be lived in the consciousness of God's strength upholding you in all good thoughts, words and deeds. If sometimes there seems to be a shadow on your life and you feel out of sorts, remember that this is not the withdrawal of God's power, but only your own temporary unwillingness to make use of it. The quiet, gray days are the days for doing what you must do, but believe that God will return and be with you again.

Prayer for the Day

I pray that I face the dull days with courage. I pray that I may have faith that the bright days will return.

353

December 16 -- A. A. Thought for the Day

The way of A. A. is the way of faith. ~~This whole book is based on this premise.~~ ~~We just won't get well and stay well, We just~~ WE ~~won't~~ DON'T get the full benefit of the programme, until we surrender our lives to some ~~power~~ Power greater than ourselves and trust that Power to give us the strength we need. There is no ~~other~~ BETTER way ~~out~~ for us. ~~We can get sober without it, yes.~~ We can stay sober for some ~~time~~ without it, ~~yes.~~ But if we are going to truly live, we must take the way of faith in ~~God~~. That is the path ~~for us. We must follow it.~~ Have I taken the way of faith?

Meditation for the Day

Life is not a search for happiness. Happiness is a by-product of living the right kind of life, of doing the right thing. Do not ~~look~~ SEARCH for happiness, ~~look~~ SEARCH for right living and happiness will be ~~the~~ YOUR reward. Life is sometimes a march of duty during the dull, dark days. But happiness will come AGAIN, as God's smile of recognition of your faithfulness. ~~and true discipleship.~~ TRUE HAPPINESS IS ALWAYS THE BY-PRODUCT OF A LIFE WELL LIVED.

Prayer for the Day

I pray that I may not seek happiness ~~but~~ seek to do right. I pray that I may ~~be content with what happiness comes to me from the good life.~~ NOT SEEK PLEASURE SO MUCH AS THE THINGS THAT BRING TRUE HAPPINESS.

354

December 17 -- A. A. Thought for the Day

The way of faith is of course not confined to A. A. It is the way for everybody who wants to really live. But many people can go through life without much of it. Many are doing so, to their own sorrow. The world is full of lack of faith. Many people have lost confidence in ~~the~~ ANY meaning ~~of~~ IN the universe. ~~many~~ Many are wondering if it has any meaning at all. Many are at loose ends. Life has no goal for many. They are strangers in the land. They are not at home. But for us ~~in A. A.~~ IN A.A. the way of faith is the way of life. We have proved BY OUR PAST LIVES that we ~~cannot~~ COULD NOT HAPPILY live without it. Do I think I ~~can~~ COULD live HAPPILY without faith?

Meditation for the Day

"He maketh His sun to rise on the evil and the good, and sendeth rain on the just and the unjust." God does not interfere with the working of natural laws. The laws of nature are unchangeable, otherwise we could not depend on them. As far as natural laws ~~go~~ ARE CONCERNED, God makes no distinction between good and bad people. Sickness or death may strike anywhere. But spiritual laws are ALSO ~~different~~ MADE TO BE OBEYED. On ~~your~~ OUR choice of good or evil depends whether ~~you~~ WE go upward to ~~goodness~~ TRUE SUCCESS and ~~life~~ VICTORY IN LIFE or downward to ~~sin~~ LOSS and ~~death~~ DEFEAT.

Prayer for the Day

I pray that I may choose TODAY the way of the spiritual life. I pray that I may live TODAY with faith and hope and love.

355

December 18 -- A. A. Thought for the Day

Unless we have the key of faith to unlock the meaning of life, we are lost. We do not choose faith because it is one way for us; BUT BECAUSE it is the only way. ~~All others~~ MANY have failed and will fail. For we cannot live VICTORIOUSLY without faith; we are at sea without ~~it; no~~ A rudder, ~~no~~ OR AN anchor, drifting on the sea of life. Wayfarers without a home. Our souls are ~~lost~~ RESTLESS, until they find ~~themselves~~ REST in God. ~~Drinking has cut them off from God.~~ ~~They have been severed by a life of~~ WITHOUT FAITH, OUR LIVES ARE A MEANINGLESS SUCCESSION OF unrelated happenings, ~~with the background of an alcoholic haze~~ WITHOUT RHYME OR REASON. Have I come to rest in faith?

Meditation for the Day

This vast universe around us, including this ~~beautiful~~ WONDERFUL earth on which we live, ~~perhaps~~ was once PERHAPS only a thought in the mind of God. The nearer the astronomers and physicists get to the ultimate composition of all things, the ~~more it~~ NEARER THE UNIVERSE approaches a mathematical formula, which is thought. The universe may be the thought of the Great Thinker. We must try to think God's thoughts after Him. We must try to get guidance from the Divine Mind as to what is His intention for the world of men and what part we can have in carrying out that intention.

Prayer for the Day

I pray that I may not worry over the limitations of my human mind. I pray that I ~~be content to~~ live ~~and serve.~~ AS THOUGH MY MIND WERE A REFLECTION OF THE DIVINE MIND.

356

December 19 - A. A. Thought for the Day

The sceptic and the agnostic say it is impossible for us to find the answer to life. Many have tried and failed. But many more have put aside intellectual pride and have said TO THEMSELVES: "Who am I to say there is no God?" Who am I to say there is no meaning ~~to~~ IN life? The atheist makes a declaration: "The world originated in a cipher and aimlessly rushes nowhere". Others live for the moment and do not even think about why they are here or where they are going. They might as well be clams on the bottom of the ocean, protected by their hard shells of indifference. They are going nowhere and they do not care. Do I care where I am going?

Meditation for the Day

We may consider the material world as the clay ~~that~~ WHICH the artist works with, to make of it something beautiful or ugly. We need not fear material things, which are neither good nor bad IN THE MORAL SENSE. There seems to be no active force for evil -NO DEVIL- outside of man himself. The only thing we have to fear is the man of ill will. Man alone can have either evil intentions - resentments, malevolence, hate and revenge - or good intentions, love and good-will. He can make something ugly or something beautiful out of THE CLAY OF his life.

Prayer for the Day

I pray that I may make something good out of my life. I pray that I may be a good artisan, OF THE MATERIALS WHICH I HAVE BEEN GIVEN TO USE.

December 20 -- A. A. Thought for the Day

~~Our faith~~ OUR FAITH ~~must be everything~~ SHOULD BE ALL ~~or nothing~~. ~~It must~~ SHOULD control the whole of our life. ~~or none of it.~~ We ~~in A. A.~~ ALCOHOLICS were living a divided life. We ~~must~~ HAD TO find ~~the~~ A way to make it whole. When we were drinking, our lives were made up of a lot of scattered and unrelated pieces. We must pick up our lives and put them together again. We do it by A REORGANIZING faith in ~~the~~ A Divine Principle in the universe ~~that~~ WHICH holds us together and holds the whole universe together, ~~that~~ AND gives it meaning and purpose. We surrender our DISORGANIZED lives to that Power; we get into harmony with the Divine Spirit, and our lives are made whole again. Is my life whole again?

Meditation for the Day

Avoid fear as you would a plague. Fear, even the smallest fear, is a hacking at the cords of ~~love~~ FAITH that bind you to God. However small the fraying, in time those cords will wear thin, and then one disappointment or shock WILL MAKE THEM ~~and they~~ snap. But for the little fears, the cords of ~~love~~ FAITH would have held firm. Avoid depression, which is ~~caused by~~ ALLIED TO fear. Remember THAT all fear is disloyalty to God. IT IS A DENIAL OF HIS CARE AND PROTECTION.

Prayer for the Day

I pray that I may have such trust in God TODAY that I will not fear anything TOO GREATLY. I pray that I may have ~~faith~~ ASSURANCE that God will ~~always~~ take care of me, IN THE LONG RUN.

December 21 -- A. A. Thought for the Day

Have I ~~stopped~~ CEASED being inwardly defeated, at war with myself? Have I given myself freely to A. A. and to the Higher Power? Have I got over being sick inside? Am I still wandering mentally or am I "on the beam"? ~~You~~ I can face anything, if ~~you are~~ I AM sure ~~you are~~ I AM on the way. When ~~you are~~ I AM sure, ~~you~~ I should bet your ~~whole~~ life on A. A. ~~You~~ I have learned how the programme works. Now will ~~you~~ I follow it with all ~~you~~ I have, with all ~~you~~ I can give, with all ~~your~~ MY might, with all ~~your~~ MY life? ~~Where do I go from here?~~ AM I GOING TO LET A.A. PRINCIPLES GUIDE THE REST OF MY LIFE?

Meditation for the Day IN THIS TIME OF QUIET MEDITATION,

Follow the pressure of the Lord's leading. In all ~~things,~~ DECISIONS TO BE MADE TODAY, yield to the gentle pressure of YOUR CONSCIENCE. ~~God's leading.~~ Stay or go as that pressure indicates. Take the events of ~~each day~~ TODAY as A PART of God's planning and ordering. ~~He is the Lord of each day's happenings.~~ He may lead you TO A RIGHT DECISION. ~~to a man whom you can help.~~ Wait quietly until you have an inner urge, a leading, a thing A FEELING THAT ~~that seems~~ IS right ~~to do~~, a pressure on your ~~spirit~~ WILL by the ~~spirit~~ of God.

Prayer for the Day

I pray that TODAY I may try to follow the inner pressure of God's leading. I pray that I may ~~always try to do what seems right.~~ TRY TO FOLLOW MY CONSCIENCE AND DO WHAT SEEMS RIGHT TODAY.

359

December 22 -- A. A. Thought for the Day

As we look back over our drinking careers, we must realize that our lives were a mess because we were a mess inside. The trouble was in us, not in life itself. Life itself was ~~all right~~ GOOD ENOUGH, but we were looking at it in the wrong way. We were looking at life through the bottom of a whiskey glass, and it was distorted. We could not see all the beauty and goodness and purpose in the world, because our vision was ~~blocked~~ BLURRED. We were in a house with one-way glass in the windows. People could see us, but we could not look out and see them and see what life itself meant to them and should mean to us. We were blind then, but now we can see. Can I ~~see~~ NOW LOOK AT life as it really is?

Meditation for the Day

Fear no evil, because the ~~grace~~ POWER of God can conquer evil. Evil has power to SERIOUSLY hurt only those who do not place themselves under the protection of the Higher Power. This is not a question of feeling, it is an assured fact OF OUR EXPERIENCE. Say to yourself with assurance that whatever it is, no evil can SERIOUSLY harm you as long as you depend on the Higher Power. Be sure of ~~God's conquering power.~~ THE PROTECTION OF GOD'S GRACE.

Prayer for the Day

~~I pray that I may fear no evil. I pray that I may depend on the Higher Power to face all things.~~ I PRAY THAT THE FEAR OF EVIL WILL NOT GET ME DOWN. I PRAY THAT I MAY TRY TO PLACE MYSELF TODAY UNDER THE PROTECTION OF GOD'S GRACE.

360

December 23 -- A. A. Thought for the Day

We have definitely left that dream-world behind. It was only a sham. It was a world of our own making and it was not the real world. We are sorry for the past, yes, but we learned a lot from it. We can put it down to experience, valuable experience, as we see it now, because it has given us the knowledge necessary to ~~be of real use in the world.~~ FACE THE WORLD AS IT REALLY IS. We had to become alcoholics in order to ~~get the new life that we have now.~~ FIND THE A.A. PROGRAM. ~~But perhaps we~~ We would not have got it in any other way. In a way, it was worth it. Do I look at my past as valuable experience?

Meditation for the Day

Shed peace, not discord, wherever you go. ~~Be~~ TRY TO BE a part of the cure of every situation, not a part of the problem. TRY TO ~~ignore~~ IGNORE evil ~~more~~ RATHER than TO actively ~~combatting~~ TO COMBAT it. ~~Try to show~~ HELP ~~the person who has chosen the wrong way how to choose a better way. Never blame or scorn or ridicule.~~ Always try to be constructive, never destructive. Always try to build up, never to tear down. Show others by your example that happiness comes from living the right way. The power of your example is greater than the power of what you say.

Prayer for the Day

I pray that I may try to bring ~~peace~~ SOMETHING GOOD into every situation TODAY. I pray that I may ~~be calm, no matter what confusion surrounds me.~~ BE CONSTRUCTIVE IN THE WAY I THINK AND SPEAK AND ACT TODAY.

361

December 24 -- A. A. Thought for the Day

We have been given a new life, just because we happened to become alcoholics. We certainly don't deserve the new life that has been given us. There is nothing in our past to warrant the life we have now. Many people live good lives from their youth on, not getting into serious trouble, being well adjusted to life, and yet they have not found ALL THAT ~~what~~ we drunks have found. We had the good fortune to find Alcoholics Anonymous and with IT a new life. We are among the lucky few in the world who have LEARNED A NEW WAY TO LIVE. ~~really learned how to live.~~ ~~Have I learned how to live?~~ AM I DEEPLY GRATEFUL FOR THE NEW LIFE THAT I HAVE LEARNED IN A.A.?

Meditation for the Day

A deep gratitude to the Higher Power for all the blessings which WE ~~you~~ have and which WE ~~you~~ don't deserve HAS COME TO US. ~~is the first thing.~~ WE ~~Then~~ thank God and mean it. THEN ~~Next~~ comes service to OUR ~~your~~ fellow men, out of gratitude for what WE ~~you~~ have received. This entails some sacrifice of OURSELVES AND OUR ~~yourself and your~~ own affairs. BUT WE ARE GLAD TO DO IT. Gratitude, service and sacrifice are the steps that lead to GOOD A.A. WORK. ~~abundant living.~~ ~~They lead you into true usefulness.~~ THEY OPEN THE DOOR TO A NEW LIFE FOR US.

Prayer for the Day

I pray that I may GLADLY SERVE OTHERS, ~~serve my fellow men~~ out of deep gratitude for what I have received. I pray that I may KEEP A DEEP ~~never lose this~~ sense of obligation.

361

December 25 -- A. A. Thought for the Day

Many alcoholics will be saying today: "This is a good Christmas for me." They will be looking back over past Christmases which were not like this one. They will be thanking God for their sobriety and their new-found life. They will be thinking ABOUT how THEIR LIVES WERE CHANGED ~~they were born again~~ when they came into A. A. They will be thinking that perhaps God let them live through all the hazards of their drinking careers, when they were PERHAPS often close to death, in order that they might be USED BY HIM IN THE GREAT WORK OF A.A. ~~born again and used by Him to do their part in the great work of A. A.~~ Is this a happy Christmas for me?

Meditation for the Day

The Kingdom of heaven is ALSO for the lowly, the sinners, the repentant. "And they presented unto him gifts - gold, frankincense and myrrh". Bring your gifts of gold - your money and material possessions. Bring your frankincense - the consecration of your life to a worthy cause. Bring your myrrh - your sympathy and understanding and help. Lay these all at the feet of God and let Him have full use of them.

Prayer for the Day

~~I pray that I may use the new life that has been given to me for the glory of God. I pray that I may not hold back any of it for myself only.~~ I PRAY THAT I MAY BE TRULY THANKFUL ON THIS CHRISTMAS DAY. I PRAY THAT I MAY BRING MY GIFTS AND LAY THEM ON THE ALTAR.

363

December 26 -- A. A. Thought for the Day

I am glad to be a part of A. A., of that great fellowship that is spreading over the United States and ALL ~~will spread~~ over the world. I am only one of many A. A.'s, but I am one. I am grateful to be living at this time, when I can help A. A. to grow, when it needs me to put my shoulder to the wheel and HELP keep the ~~whole~~ movement going. I am ~~so~~ glad to be able to be useful, to have a reason for living, a purpose in life. I want to lose my life in this great cause and so find it again. Am I grateful to be an A.A.?

Meditation for the Day THESE MEDITATIONS CAN TEACH US HOW TO RELAX.

~~Make the purpose~~ MAIN of your ~~life to be of~~ ~~real~~ ~~service to your fellow man.~~ WE ~~You~~ can BE OF SERVICE TO OUR FELLOW MEN ~~do this~~ in a small way AT LEAST. ~~or in a big way.~~ AND WE CAN BE ~~But be~~ happy while doing it. ~~Take it easy.~~ ~~EASY DOES IT.~~ ~~Wear the world as a loose garment.~~ WE SHOULD ~~Do~~ not worry too much about people WE CANNOT HELP. WE CAN Make it a habit to LEAVE ~~learn~~ the outcome of THE THINGS WE DO ~~everything you do~~ to the Higher Power. WE CAN GO ~~Just go~~ along through life doing the best WE ~~you~~ can, but without A ~~any~~ feeling of urgency or strain. WE CAN Enjoy all the good things and the beauty of life, but, AT THE SAME TIME depend deeply on God.

Prayer for the Day

I pray that I may give my life to THIS WORTHWHILE CAUSE. ~~a great cause.~~ ~~I pray that I may take it easy and enjoy it as I go along.~~ I PRAY THAT I MAY ENJOY THE SATISFACTION THAT COMES FROM GOOD WORK WELL DONE.

364

December 27 -- A. A. Thought for the Day

I need the A. A. principles, for the development of the buried life within me, that good life, which I had misplaced, but which I found again in this fellowship. This life within me is developing slowly but surely, with many setbacks, many mistakes, many failures, but still developing. As long as I stick close to A. A., my life will go on developing, and I cannot see yet what it will be, but I know that it will be good. That's all I want to know. It will be good. Am I thanking God for A. A.?

Meditation for the Day

Build your life on the firm foundation of true gratitude to God for all His blessings and true humility because of your unworthiness of these blessings. Build the frame of your life out of self-discipline, never let yourself get selfish or lazy or contented, WITH YOURSELF. Build the walls of your life out of service to your fellow men, helping others to find the way to live. Build the roof of your life out of prayer and quiet times, waiting for God's guidance from above. Build a garden around your life out of peace of mind and serenity and a sure faith.

Prayer for the Day

I pray that I may BUILD MY LIFE ON ~~live by~~ A. A. principles. ~~I pray that these principles may guide my life.~~ I PRAY THAT IT MAY BE A GOOD BUILDING WHEN MY WORK IS FINISHED.

366

December 28 -- A. A. Thought for the Day

A. A. may be human in its organization, but it is divine in its purpose. The purpose is to point me toward God and the good life. My feet have been set upon the right path. I feel it in the depths of my being. I am going in the right direction. The future can safely be left to God. Whatever the future holds, it cannot be too much for me to bear. I have the Divine Power with me, to carry me through everything THAT MAY HAPPEN. Am I pointed toward God and the good life?

Meditation for the Day

Although unseen, the Lord is always near to those who believe in Him and trust Him and depend on Him for the strength to meet the challenges of life. Although veiled from MORTAL sight, the Higher Power is always available to us whenever we humbly ask for it. The feeling that God is with ~~you~~ US should not depend on any passing mood of ~~yours~~ OURS, but ~~you~~ WE should TRY TO be always conscious of His power AND LOVE in the background of ~~your life.~~ OUR LIVES.

Prayer for the Day

I pray that TODAY I may feel that God is ~~never~~ NOT too far away to depend on for help. ~~when I need it.~~ I pray that I may feel CONFIDENT ~~sure~~ OF HIS ~~secure in His availability.~~ READINESS TO GIVE ME THE POWER THAT I NEED.

366

December 29 -- A. A. Thought for the Day

Participating in the privileges of the movement, I shall share in the responsibilities, taking it upon myself to carry my fair share of the load, not grudgingly but joyfully. I am deeply grateful for the privileges I enjoy because of my membership in this great movement. They put an obligation upon me which I will not shirk. I will GLADY carry my fair share of the burdens. ~~with joy.~~ Because of the joy in doing them, they will no longer be burdens, but opportunities. Will I accept every opportunity gladly?

Meditation for the Day

Work and prayer are the two forces which are ~~slowly~~ GRADUALLY making a better world. We must work for the betterment of ourselves and our fellow men. Faith without works is dead. But all work with people ~~must~~ SHOULD be based on prayer. IF WE SAY A LITTLE PRAYER BEFORE WE SPEAK OR TRY TO HELP, IT WILL MAKE US MORE EFFECTIVE. Prayer is the force behind the work. Prayer is based on the faith that God is working with ~~you~~ US and through ~~you.~~ US. We can believe that nothing is impossible in human relationships, if we depend on the ~~grace~~ HELP of God.

Prayer for the Day

I pray that my life may be balanced between prayer and work. I pray that I may not work without prayer or pray without work.

367

December 30 -- A. A. Thought for the Day

To the extent that I fail in my responsibilities, A. A. fails. To the extent that I succeed, A. A. succeeds. Every failure of mine will set BACK A. A. ~~back~~ to that extent. Every success of mine will put A. A. ahead to that extent. I shall not wait to be drafted for service to my fellow men, but I shall volunteer. I shall accept every opportunity to work for A. A. as a challenge, and I shall do my best to accept every challenge and perform my task as best I can. Will I accept every challenge gladly?

Meditation for the Day

Men are always failures in the deepest sense when they seek to live without God's sustaining power. Many men try to be self-sufficient AND SEEK SELFISH PLEASURE and find that it does not work TOO WELL. No matter how much material wealth they acquire, nor how much fame and material power, the time of disillusionment AND FUTILITY USUALLY ~~always~~ comes. Death is ahead, and they cannot take any material thing with them WHEN THEY GO. What matters it if I ~~they~~ have gained the whole world, but lost ~~their own soul.~~ MY OWN SOUL?

Prayer for the Day

I pray that I will not come empty to the end of my life. I pray that I may so live that I will not be afraid to die.

368

December 31 -- A. A. Thought for the Day

I shall be loyal in my attendance, generous in my giving, kind in my criticism, creative in my suggestions, loving in my attitudes. I shall give A. A. my interest, my enthusiasm, my devotion, AND most of all, myself. The Lord's Prayer has become part of my A. A. thoughts for EACH ~~the~~ day: "Our Father who are in heaven, hallowed by thy name. Thy kingdom come. Thy will be done, on earth as it is in heaven. Give us this day our daily bread. And forgive us our trespasses as we forgive those who trespass against us. Lead us not into temptation, but deliver us from evil." Have I given myself?

Meditation for the Day

As we look back over the year just gone, it has been a good year to the extent that we have put good thoughts, good words and good deeds into it. None of what we have thought, said or done need be wasted. Both the good and the bad experiences can be profited by. In a sense, the past is not ENTIRELY gone. The results of it, for good or evil, are with us at the present moment. We only learn by experience and none of our experience is completely wasted. WE CAN HUMBLY THANK GOD FOR THE GOOD THINGS OF THE YEAR THAT HAS GONE.

Prayer for the Day

I pray that I may CARRY MANY GOOD THINGS INTO THE YEAR AHEAD. ~~live today, because there is no other time for me.~~ I pray that I may carry on with faith, WITH PRAYER, AND WITH HOPE.

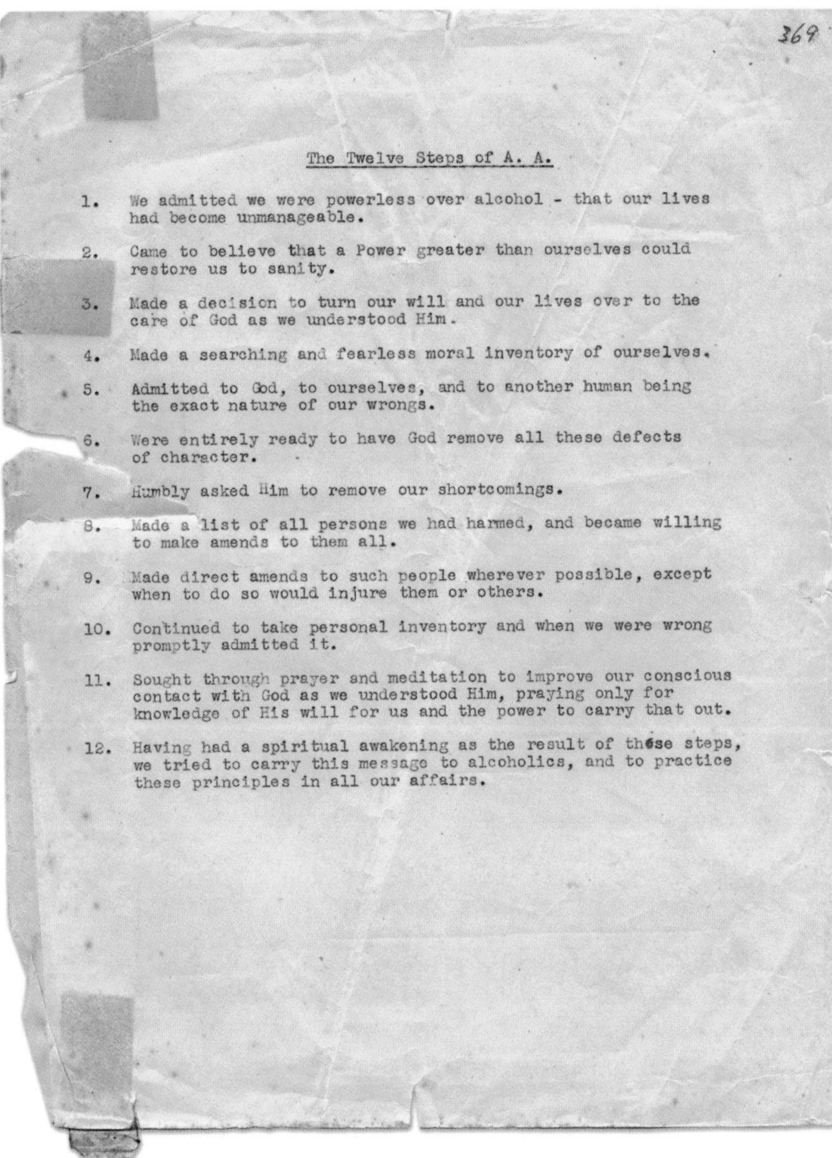

369

The Twelve Steps of A. A.

1. We admitted we were powerless over alcohol - that our lives had become unmanageable.
2. Came to believe that a Power greater than ourselves could restore us to sanity.
3. Made a decision to turn our will and our lives over to the care of God as we understood Him.
4. Made a searching and fearless moral inventory of ourselves.
5. Admitted to God, to ourselves, and to another human being the exact nature of our wrongs.
6. Were entirely ready to have God remove all these defects of character.
7. Humbly asked Him to remove our shortcomings.
8. Made a list of all persons we had harmed, and became willing to make amends to them all.
9. Made direct amends to such people wherever possible, except when to do so would injure them or others.
10. Continued to take personal inventory and when we were wrong promptly admitted it.
11. Sought through prayer and meditation to improve our conscious contact with God as we understood Him, praying only for knowledge of His will for us and the power to carry that out.
12. Having had a spiritual awakening as the result of these steps, we tried to carry this message to alcoholics, and to practice these principles in all our affairs.

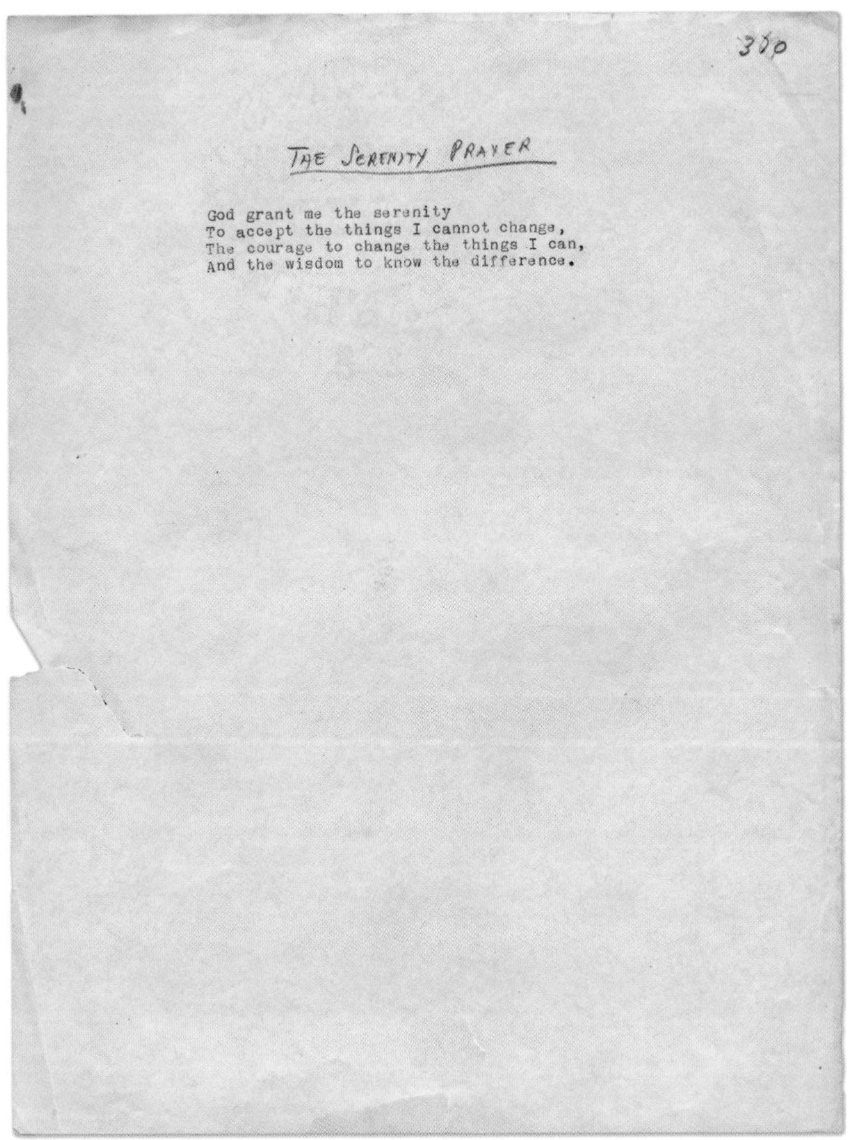

380

THE SERENITY PRAYER

God grant me the serenity
To accept the things I cannot change,
The courage to change the things I can,
And the wisdom to know the difference.

371

The Twelve Traditions of A.A.

1. Our common welfare should come first; personal recovery depenfs upon A.A. unity.

2. For our group purpose there is but one ultimate authority- a loving God as He may express Himself in our group conscience. Our leaders are but trusted servants - they do not govern.

3. The only requirement for A.A. membership is a desire to stop drinking.

4. Each group shall be autonomous, except in matters affecting other groups or A.A. as a whole.

5. Each group has but one primary purpose- to carry its message to the alcoholic who still suffers.

6. An A.A. group ought never endorse, finance or lend the A.A. name to any related facility or outside enterprise lest problems of money, property and prestige divert us from our primary spiritual aim.

7. Every A.A. group ought to be fully self-supporting, declining outside contributions.

8. Alcoholics Anonymous should remain forever non-professional, but our service centers may employ special workers.

9. A.A., as such, ought never to be organized, but we may create service boards or committees directly responsible to those they serve.

10. Alcoholics Anonymous has no opinion on outside issues, hence the A.A. name ought never be drawn into public controversy.

11. Our public relations policy is based on attraction rather than promotion; we need always maintain personal anonymity at the level of press, radio,television and films.

12. Anonymity is the spiritual foundation of all our traditions, ever reminding us to place principles above personalities.

372

FURTHER COPIES OF THIS BOOK MAY BE HAD

AT $1.00 APIECE BY WRITING TO

TWENTY-FOUR HOURS A DAY

BOX 2170

DAYTONA BEACH, FLORIDA

The Hidden Text

The Passages Under the Taped Scraps of Paper

The Hidden Text

In the working manuscript, readers will note several handwritten passages taped over earlier versions of the text: see January 2, 5, and 6, for example. Apparently Walker decided that the second day of the year warranted a firmer message about the turning points alcoholics face. So after drafting the new text, he slightly revised his original text for that date and moved it to May 29, where it now appears as a taped "patch." As for the original texts for January 5 and 6, Walker simply deleted them, apparently not satisfied with their quality or continuity. But he made another broader set of substitutions for the entire period June 5 through 19. What can we say about these in the context of Walker's creative process?

Having finished his A.A. Thoughts for the Day on May 30 based upon his work *For Drunks Only,* he then on the first of June started writing thoughts about the things that he did not miss since becoming dry—for example, his loss of memory, his cover-ups, and so on. There follows a paragraph (June 4) on what he likes since becoming dry.

Then suddenly there is an abrupt transition to an entirely new subject, from the very personal to a didactic presentation on the purpose and power of thought. These didactic texts on "thought" as the offshoot of our intellectual capacity stand in stark contrast to the "thoughts for the day" that serve as reflections for personal growth.

Walker provides no reason for his decision to go back and cover up what he had written (presumably he did not like the passages). It is only conjecture on my part, but either he himself saw that they were of a different genre than those of the previous five months, or others upon whom he relied for input felt that these new texts did not speak to them as poignantly and personally as did *For Drunks Only.* They seemed like a teacher's manual rather than thoughtful leads into meditation.

It took only a few weeks for Walker to realize that he had strayed from the basics of recovery and embarked upon a subject and style unappealing to his audience, who liked to remember what their lives "were like before, what happened, and what they were like now."

HIDDEN TEXT FOR JANUARY MEDITATIONS AND PRAYERS

January 2

Meditation for the Day

I will try to help others. I will never let a day pass without reaching out an arm of love to someone. Each day I will do something to lift another human being out of the sea of discouragement into which he or she has fallen. My helping hand is needed to raise the helpless to courage, to strength, to faith, to health. In my own lightheartedness, I will turn and help another alcoholic with the burden that is pressing too heavily upon him.

Prayer for the Day

I pray that I may be used by God to lighten many burdens in this new year. I pray that many souls will be helped through me.

January 5

Prayer for the Day

I pray that I may keep nothing for myself alone. I pray that I may hoard nothing, but only keep what I need and can use.

January 6

Prayer for the Day

I pray that I may not worry too much about others' lives at this time. I pray that I may perfect myself first in God's strength and then I will be ready to help others.

HIDDEN TEXT FOR JUNE THOUGHTS FOR THE DAY

June 5

"As a man thinketh in his heart, so is he." This really embraces the whole of a man's being and reaches out so as to embrace every condition and circumstance of his A.A. life. A man is literally "what he thinks" and his A.A. character is completely moulded by his thoughts. A plant springs from a seed. So every act of a man springs from the seed of thought, even those acts that are called spontaneous and unpremeditated, as well as those which are deliberately executed. <u>Am I thinking good A.A. thoughts?</u>

June 6

Man is a growth by law and not a creation by artifice. Therefore cause and effect are absolute. A good A.A. character is not a thing of chance, but is the result of continued effort in right thinking, the effect of long association with A.A. thoughts. On the other hand, an ignoble and bestial character, by the same process is the result of a continued harboring of the wrong kind of thoughts. Are my thoughts the right kind of thoughts?

June 7

A man can either make or unmake himself. By his thoughts, he forges the weapons by which he destroys himself and by the same process he fashions the A.A. tools which bring joy, strength and peace. By the right choice and true application of A.A. thoughts, man can ascend toward perfection and by wrong thoughts and the wrong application of thought he can descend below the level of the beast. Between the two extremes are all the different grades of A.A. character. What is the quality of my A.A. character?

June 8

Man is the master of thought, the molder of character and the maker and shaper of condition, environment and destiny. Man is a being of power, intelligence and love and the lord of his own A.A. thoughts. He holds the key to every situation and contains within himself that transforming and regenerative agency by which he may make himself that kind of A.A. member which he wills. What kind of an A.A. member am I making myself?

June 9

When man begins to reflect upon his condition and to search diligently for the law upon which his being is established, he then becomes the wise master, directing his energies with intelligence and fashioning his A.A. thoughts to fruitful issues. Man must discover within himself the correct laws of thought. This is done by application to the A.A. programme, self-analysis, and the help of God and A.A. experience. Am I applying myself fully to the A.A. programme?

June 10

Only by much searching and mining are gold and diamonds obtained and man can find every truth connected with A.A. if he will dig deep into the mine of the A.A. programme. He can prove to himself and the world that he is the maker of his character, the molder of his life and the builder of his destiny. "He that seeketh, findeth and to him that knocketh it shall be opened." Two things are essential in A.A., patience and practice. Am I patient in practicing the A.A. programme?

June 11

A man's mind may be likened to a garden, which may be intelligently cultivated or allowed to run wild, but whether it be cultivated or neglected, it must and will bring forth. If useless seeds are put into it, then an abundancy of useless weeds will appear. Just as a gardener cultivates his plot of ground, keeping it free from weeds and growing the flowers and fruit which he desires, so may a man tend the garden of his mind, weeding out all the wrong, useless and impure thoughts and cultivating the fruit and flowers of A.A. Am I doing a good job of A.A. cultivation?

June 12

Every man is where he is by the law of his thoughts. The thoughts which he has built into his character have brought him there and in the arrangement of his life there is no element of chance, but all is the result of those thoughts. This is true of both those who feel out of their harmony with their surroundings and those who are contented with them. Man must learn in order to grow and, as he learns the A.A. lessons, he progresses and makes a new better life. Am I progressing in A.A.?

June 13

Man is buffeted by circumstance just so long as he believes in himself to be the creature of outside conditions, but when he realizes that he is a creative power and that he may command the soil and seeds of his being out of which circumstances grow, then he becomes the rightful master of self. Any man who has practiced self-control and self-analysis through the A.A. programme, will note that the change in his circumstances is the exact ratio with the change from his old alcoholic thinking to his new A.A. thinking. Do I see the change in my circumstances?

June 14

How many people we know who sour their lives, who ruin all that is sweet and beautiful by explosive tempers, who destroy their poise and make "bad blood" by their resentments! Many people ruin their lives and mar their happiness by lack of self-control, as taught by A.A. How many A.A. members we come in contact with who are well-balanced and who have that poise which is characteristic of the true A.A.! Am I becoming well-balanced and am I developing poise?

June 15

Clean thoughts make clean habits. If you would improve your body, guard your mind. If you would renew your body, beautify your mind. Thoughts of malice, envy, disappointment and despondency rob the body of health. A sour body does not come by chance; it is made sour by sour thoughts. Wrinkles that mar the face are the result of folly, passion and pride. The serene look of a true A.A. comes from an inner peace of mind. Does my A.A. training show in my face?

June 16

To live continually in thoughts of ill will, cynicism, suspicion and envy is to confine yourself to a hell on earth. But to think well of all people, to be cheerful with all people, to patiently learn to find the good in all fellow members of A.A., to continually ask for God's help in living the A.A. programme, is to find yourself at the very portals of heaven. To dwell day by day in thoughts of peace towards every fellow man, will bring abounding peace to yourself. Do I look for the good in all people?

June 17

It's quite obvious in A.A. that we cannot transmit to someone else something which we haven't got ourselves. If our own house is not in order and if we are not really on this programme, our message to others will not carry the weight of conviction and we will not be able to portray convincingly what Alcoholics Anonymous can mean to the prospect we are calling on. Therefore, let us first put our own house in order. Have I taken a good square look at myself?

JUNE 18

If you are person of normal mentality, even though you may have some physical handicaps, it can be said that life is largely what you make it, in other words if you are normal mentally, you have the power to determine what your life shall be. That is, you can do so provided you ask for and receive God's help. What life means to you is determined not so much by what life brings to you as by the attitude you bring to life, and not so much by what happens to you as by the attitude you take to what happens. Is my A.A. attitude of the right kind?

JUNE 19

Circumstances and situations do color life, but with God's help you have the power to choose what the color shall be. Life is what you make it, because living is at least ninety percent attitude. If you will start each morning with a few moments of thought, meditation and prayer, asking for help to live the day at the highest and best that you know, life will become an art. Like all other arts, it requires patience and practice. Am I trying to live each day at its highest and best?

• • •

A Publishing History of *Twenty-Four Hours a Day*

With Photos of the Various Editions

A Publishing History

IN MEMORY OF

RICHMOND WALKER

1892–1965

AUTHOR OF

TWENTY-FOUR HOURS A DAY

"LET US THEREFORE

DO OUR BEST

TO LIVE BUT ONE DAY

AT A TIME."

JULY 31

— Plaque in the lobby of Richmond Walker Center
at Hazelden Foundation campus
Center City, Minnesota

When *Twenty-Four Hours a Day*, the first book of daily meditations for alcoholics, was published by Hazelden in 1954, no one dreamed that it would eventually sell close to ten million copies or be translated into eleven languages, from Spanish to Russian to Japanese. The publishing history of the Little Black Book began, however, on a much smaller scale.

Daytona Beach, Florida, which is perhaps best known for car races sponsored by major beer companies, marked the location where Richmond Walker began to self-publish and distribute copies of his anonymous work. When Alcoholics Anonymous World Services declined to publish the book, Walker approached Hazelden's Patrick Butler, who had expressed keen interest in becoming the publisher of record. Walker and Hazelden soon reached a congenial publishing agreement, and the rest is the story of millions of lives that were positively impacted each day of the year, beginning with the first line of the January 1 meditation ("When I came into A.A., was I a desperate person?") to the final sentence of December 31 ("I pray that I may carry on with faith, with prayer, and with hope").

It is in large part due to the enormous success of *Twenty-Four Hours a Day* that Hazelden has become the world's leading publisher of materials for people affected by addiction and professionals who treat them. In honor of the author who blazed the path, the building that houses Hazelden's publishing staff in Minnesota is named Richmond Walker Center. In harmony with the Little Black Book's theme of serenity and hope, the Richmond Walker building's façade of red bricks and windows opens to a vista of tall pines, woods, and farmland, all of which have not changed much over the years.

Nor has a great deal changed with the appearance and content of *Twenty-Four Hours a Day*. The popular hardcover edition has maintained the same handy "pocket" size over the years, measuring three inches wide and five and three-eighths inches deep. Whether one opens a copy of the book published in 1954 or 2012, the reader will find the same foreword

A visual history of *Twenty-Four Hours a Day*

FIRST EDITION, 1954

ORIGINAL TITLE PAGE

1956

25TH ANNIVERSARY EDITION, BOOK AND BOX, 1979

and Sanskrit proverb, followed by daily meditations, each one consisting of an A.A. Thought for the Day, Meditation for the Day, and Prayer for the Day. The book contained 365 daily passages until the mid-1990s, when Hazelden commissioned an anonymous author to write a February 29 meditation.

The wording of the meditations has not radically changed. Minor copyediting of the text occurred in 1975, mainly to correct slight grammatical and spelling errors and to render the text more inclusive of both genders.

The back pages of the Little Black Book have always included the Twelve Steps and Traditions of AA as well as the Serenity Prayer. A *Twenty-Four Hours a Day Index* brochure was published and sold by Hazelden in 1990. Several years later, the subject index was printed at the end of each book and is a useful point-of-reference tool for readers today.

PUBLISHING MILESTONES

When Hazelden first published the Little Black Book, its front cover color was green, which was soon changed to black when Walker expressed that he felt nostalgic about the book having a black cover, the way he had originally published it. The opening spread of the green-colored edition featured a promotion for Hazelden's treatment center, described as a "Country retreat for men with a drinking problem . . . Good food is a specialty . . . Reasonable Rates." The ad was removed when the book was printed with a black cover, showing a price of $1.50 at the bottom of the front title page.

The year 1975 was a special milestone for *Twenty-Four Hours a Day.* To commemorate the occasion, Hazelden published a limited edition with a gold-colored cover with black type. The opening page contained a personalized message to each recipient of the book:

SPANISH EDITION

DANISH EDITION

FRENCH EDITION

GERMAN EDITION

This special limited edition of *Twenty-Four Hours a Day* is dedicated to the memory of Richmond Walker. It is published to celebrate the sale of over one million copies of the book to alcoholics and other chemically dependent persons throughout the world. Hazelden Foundation, Inc. hereby presents this special copy of *Twenty-Four Hours a Day* to [person's name] whose loyalty, friendship and service have contributed to our prosperity and growth. This gift is a token of Hazelden's deep appreciation and gratitude to a very special person.

Other publishing milestones include the following:

- A twenty-fifth anniversary edition, printed in 1979, displayed a silver cover with a black foil stamp of the book's title, including a cloth crimson ribbon as a page marker.
- A large-print hardcover volume, with an expanded page size, was published in 1980 and is a popular item on the market today.
- In 1992, the first paperback edition was published, measuring four inches wide and six inches deep, with a four-color cover. In both a trade and an institutional edition, the paperback remains for sale today as an alternative to the hardcover.
- Another paperback edition subtitled *A Meditation Book and Journal for Daily Reflection* was released in 2001. The larger page size (seven inches wide by eight and one-half inches deep) allows room for readers to write their own thoughts for the day at the end of each daily meditation.
- 1994 marked the fortieth anniversary of the book. Hazelden published a special hardcover edition with a black cover, a foil stamp for the title, and an embossed *Twenty-Four Hours a Day* medallion as part of the cover design.

JAPANESE EDITION

POLISH EDITION

RUSSIAN EDITION

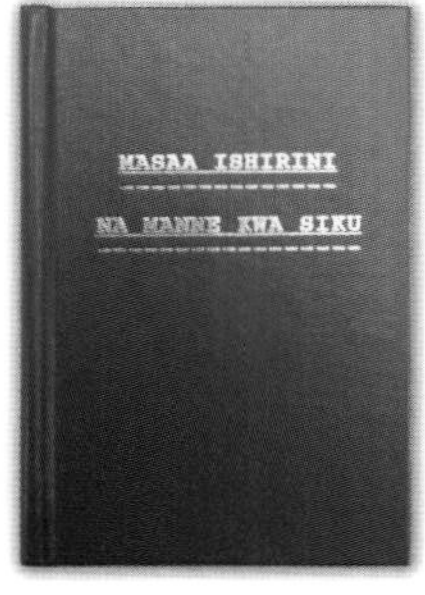

SWAHILI EDITION

- A leather volume, packaged in a gold-colored box, was printed in 2004 in celebration of the Little Black Book's fiftieth anniversary.
- As the publishing industry broadened to electronic dissemination of information, Hazelden released *Twenty-Four Hours a Day* as an e-book and mobile app in 2010.

Twenty-Four Hours a Day has been a perennial best seller for Hazelden over its entire publishing history. Publishing management was concerned that the release of an AA World Services book of daily meditations, *Daily Reflections,* in 1990 would negatively impact sales of the Little Black Book. The impact, however, was minimal. As Karen Casey, author of *Each Day a New Beginning* (the first book of daily meditations specifically for women), wrote about *Twenty-Four Hours a Day,* "How many books, other than the Bible, continue to be best sellers after fifty years and read on a daily basis?"

PRINTING AND BINDING

Midwest Editions, based in Minneapolis, has provided printing and binding for numerous reprints of *Twenty-Four Hours a Day* hardcover volumes over the years. The utilization of a high-quality binding technique known as Smyth sewing, which holds the pages together, has made for long-lasting copies of a book that is often opened and closed on a daily basis year after year.

The steady sales of the Little Black Book are demonstrated by the measure of job security it has helped to provide. Whenever there was downtime at the plant, management directed staff to bind together as many copies of the book as possible, even when no orders were pending. Management knew from experience that requests for replenishing stock were inevitable, so it was best to have boxes of books on hand ready to ship.

>>

SWEDISH EDITION

MILLION-COPY COMMEMORATION, 1975

LARGE-PRINT EDITION, 1980

40TH ANNIVERSARY EDITION, 1994

AN APPROPRIATE MISTAKE

The publishing history of *Twenty-Four Hours a Day* is far from perfect. There have been ups and downs. Take, for example, the story of a customer who opened his newly purchased book and found that all of the pages were printed upside down. He considered returning the book, but then thought otherwise. After all, hadn't his life as an alcoholic been quite the same way? The book served as a reminder, in more ways than one. Then, one day, he lost his special book. He called Hazelden to order a new copy, and made one small request. Days later, he received his book, and smiled when he opened the cover and saw the pages just as he wanted them: upside down again.

Don Freeman
Managing Editor, Hazelden Publishing

• • •

>>

INSTITUTIONAL EDITION, 1992

TRADE EDITION, 1992

50TH ANNIVERSARY EDITION, 2004

CURRENT HARDCOVER EDITION

The Richmond Walker and Patrick Butler Correspondence

Initially, Richmond Walker's relationship with Hazelden president Patrick Butler was purely business. Starting early in 1954, they discussed the details as Hazelden assumed the publication of *Twenty-Four Hours a Day.* But the relationship soon took on a more personal tone, as this sequence of letters shows. Later, in one of the last letters between the two, Walker wrote of a strong hope: "If we can do what will benefit just one person 50 years from now, it is worthwhile." More than fifty years have since elapsed, and his book has benefitted not one but millions worldwide.

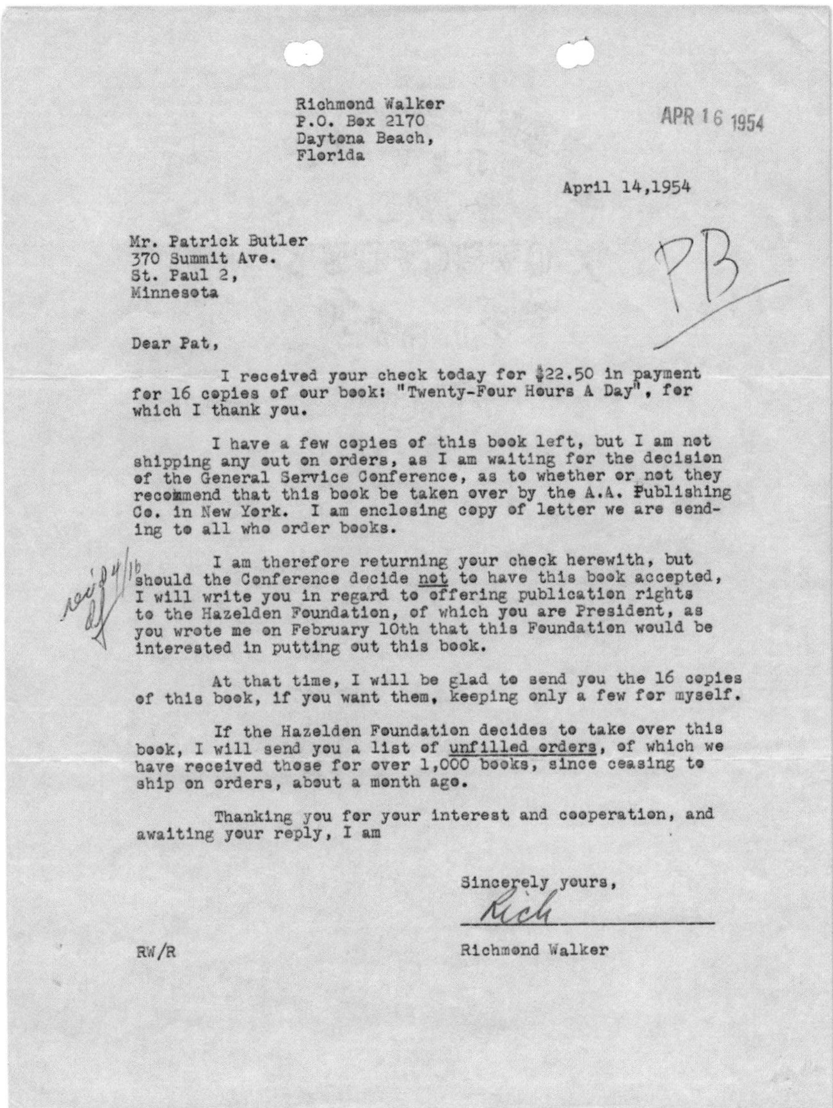

Richmond Walker
P.O. Box 2170
Daytona Beach,
Florida

APR 16 1954

April 14,1954

Mr. Patrick Butler
370 Summit Ave.
St. Paul 2,
Minnesota

PB

Dear Pat,

I received your check today for $22.50 in payment for 16 copies of our book: "Twenty-Four Hours A Day", for which I thank you.

I have a few copies of this book left, but I am not shipping any out on orders, as I am waiting for the decision of the General Service Conference, as to whether or not they recommend that this book be taken over by the A.A. Publishing Co. in New York. I am enclosing copy of letter we are sending to all who order books.

I am therefore returning your check herewith, but should the Conference decide <u>not</u> to have this book accepted, I will write you in regard to offering publication rights to the Hazelden Foundation, of which you are President, as you wrote me on February 10th that this Foundation would be interested in putting out this book.

At that time, I will be glad to send you the 16 copies of this book, if you want them, keeping only a few for myself.

If the Hazelden Foundation decides to take over this book, I will send you a list of <u>unfilled orders</u>, of which we have received those for over 1,000 books, since ceasing to ship on orders, about a month ago.

Thanking you for your interest and cooperation, and awaiting your reply, I am

Sincerely yours,
Rich
Richmond Walker

RW/R

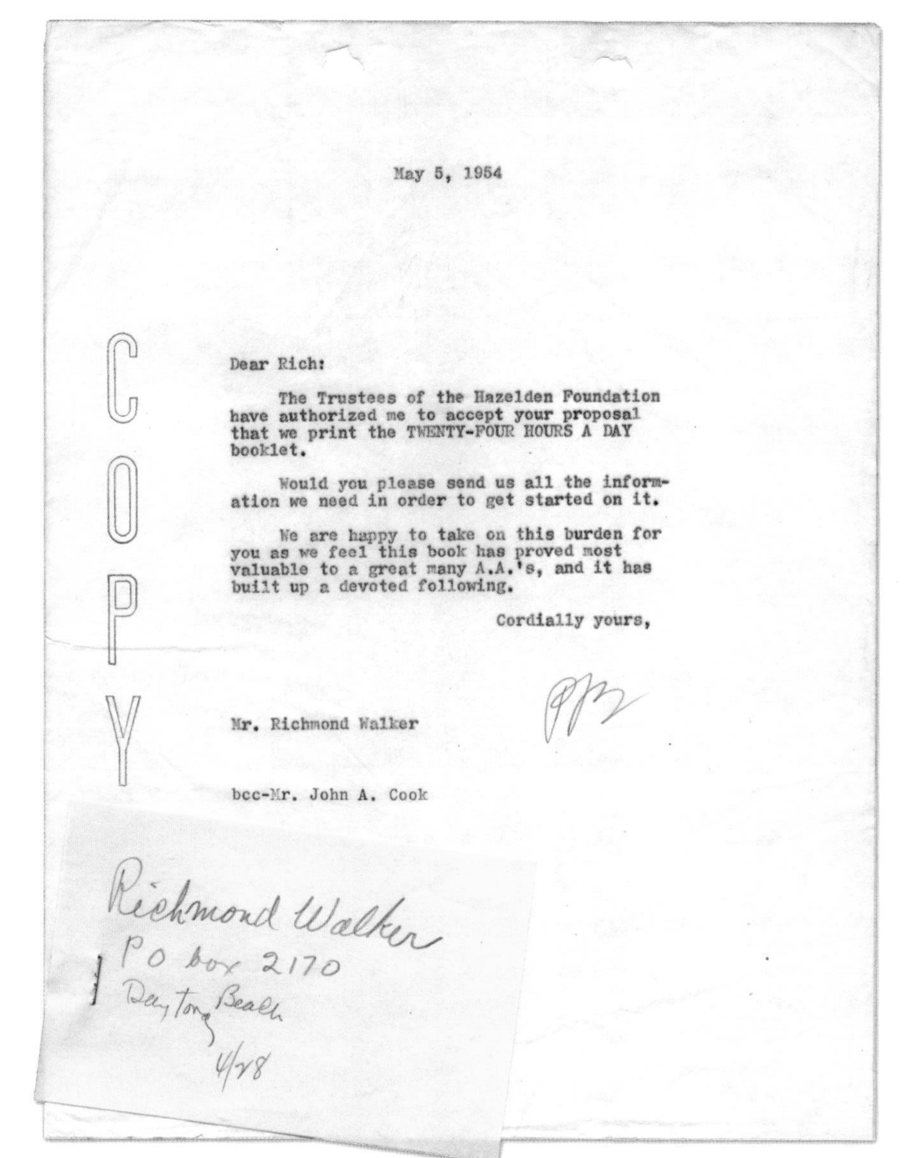

COPY

May 5, 1954

Dear Rich:

The Trustees of the Hazelden Foundation have authorized me to accept your proposal that we print the TWENTY-FOUR HOURS A DAY booklet.

Would you please send us all the information we need in order to get started on it.

We are happy to take on this burden for you as we feel this book has proved most valuable to a great many A.A.'s, and it has built up a devoted following.

Cordially yours,

Mr. Richmond Walker

bcc-Mr. John A. Cook

Richmond Walker
PO box 2170
Daytona Beach
4/28

Richmond Walker
P.O. Box 2170
Daytona Beach,
Florida

MAY 10 1954

May 7,1954

Mr. Patrick Butler
370 Summit Ave.
St. Paul 2,
Minnesota

PB

Dear Pat,

Since writing you today, I thought you might like to know more about where the book: "Twenty-Four Hours A Day" has been shipped, and also what some of the A.A. members around the country think about the book.

I am therefore sending you today my note book, containing this information, including 700 unsolicited endorsements of the book.

After you have had time to look this over (you probably know some of the A.A.s who have written me such nice things about the book), I would appreciate your returning it to me after May 15th to:

Richmond Walker
Box 78
Siasconset
Nantucket Island,
Mass.

With kind personal regards, I am

Sincerely yours,

Rich Walker

Richmond Walker

RW/R

Richmond Walter
Box 78 - Siasconset
Nantucket Island, Mass.

JUN 17 1954

June 15, 54

Mr. Patrick Butler
370 Summit Ave.
Saint Paul, Minn.

PB

Dear Pat - I haven't heard from you for some time, so I am writing to ask you if you received the 16 copies of "24 Hours a Day" which I sent you, also, if you are through with the <u>note book</u> I sent you, containing endorsements of the book, I would appreciate your sending it to me.

I have just returned from my 40th reunion with the class of 1914 at Williams College in Williamstown, Mass. and while there, I talked with my classmate, Bob Longyear, the geologist from St. Paul, and he said he knew you, and wanted me to give you his kind regards.

I received a letter from John Cook of the Hazelden Foundation, telling me that the book will be published in Minneapolis, and that he will send me a copy, when it is ready.

I would be glad to hear from you.

Best wishes.

Sincerely yours,

Richmond Walter

P.S. I hope to get out to Saint Paul this fall and am looking forward to meeting you.

Werham Chester 7, 6216 Richmond Walker
P.O. Box 78 - Siasconset
Nantucket Island, Mass. PB PB
JUN 23 1954
June 20, '54

Dear Pat -

Thanks for your letter and the literature, which I shall read with interest. I sincerely hope that the sales of "Twenty-Four Hours a Day" will help along the fine work being done by the Hazelden Foundation. I feel very glad that you made the suggestion of taking the book over. Did you know that on May 24th, I received a letter from Ed. A. Webster of "The Little Red Book" P.O. Box 564, Minneapolis, Minn., offering to take over my book. I wrote him that I had already given it to the Hazelden Foundation, and he wrote back that it was in good hands, and I'm sure of that!

Thanks for returning the note book. I hope you got some useful information from it. Also note that John Cook is sending check for the 16 books.

I do not remember meeting your wife's aunt and uncle - the Davis - here in Siasconset. We have been here on and off for a good many years. In my drinking days, I travelled with a pretty hard-drinking crowd here, mostly during prohibition. Things are very different now. Our children and grand-children come to visit us here, and we lead a quiet life. We have a small A.A. group here, with some of the local people as members, as well as quite a few summer people.

I hope to stop off at Saint Paul this fall, on my way to Los Angeles, where I have a married daughter. I will, if I can arrange it, as I would like to see your set-up.

With best wishes, I am

Sincerely yours,

Richmond Walker

(Age 6? - Sober 11 years)

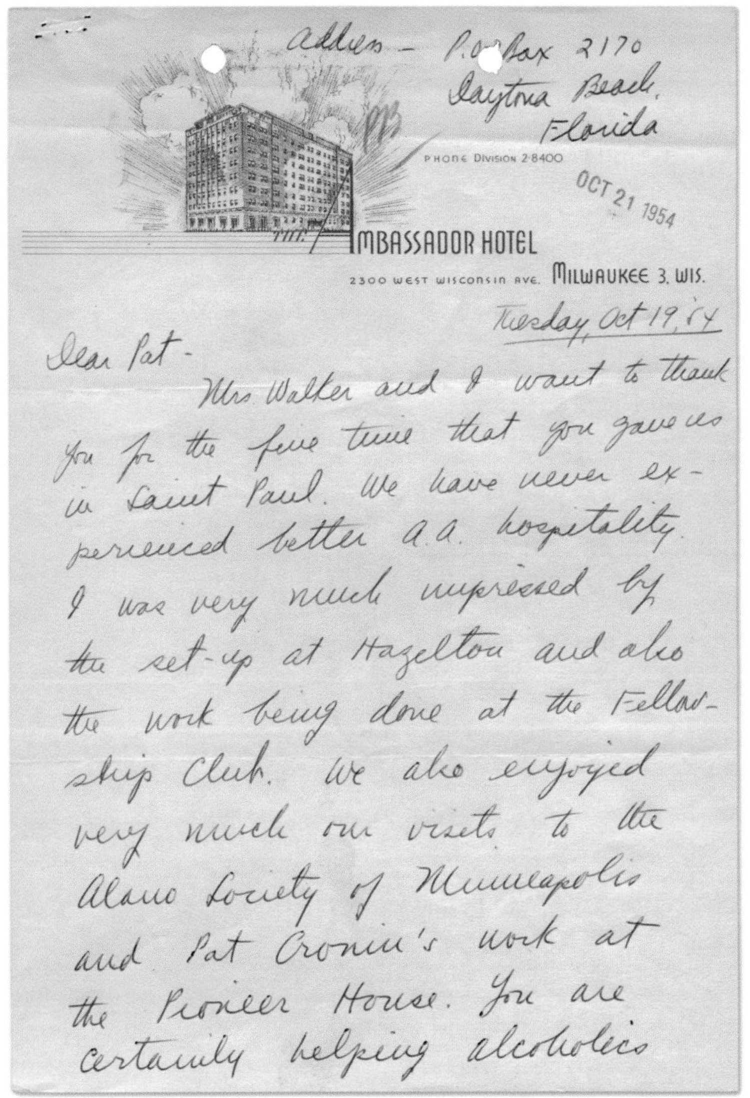

Address - P.O. Box 2170
Daytona Beach,
Florida

PHONE DIVISION 2-8400

OCT 21 1954

AMBASSADOR HOTEL
2300 WEST WISCONSIN AVE. MILWAUKEE 3, WIS.

Tuesday, Oct 19, 54

Dear Pat -

Mrs. Walker and I want to thank you for the fine time that you gave us in Saint Paul. We have never experienced better A.A. hospitality. I was very much impressed by the set-up at Hazelton and also the work being done at the Fellowship Club. We also enjoyed very much our visits to the Alano Society of Minneapolis and Pat Cronin's work at the Pioneer House. You are certainly helping alcoholics

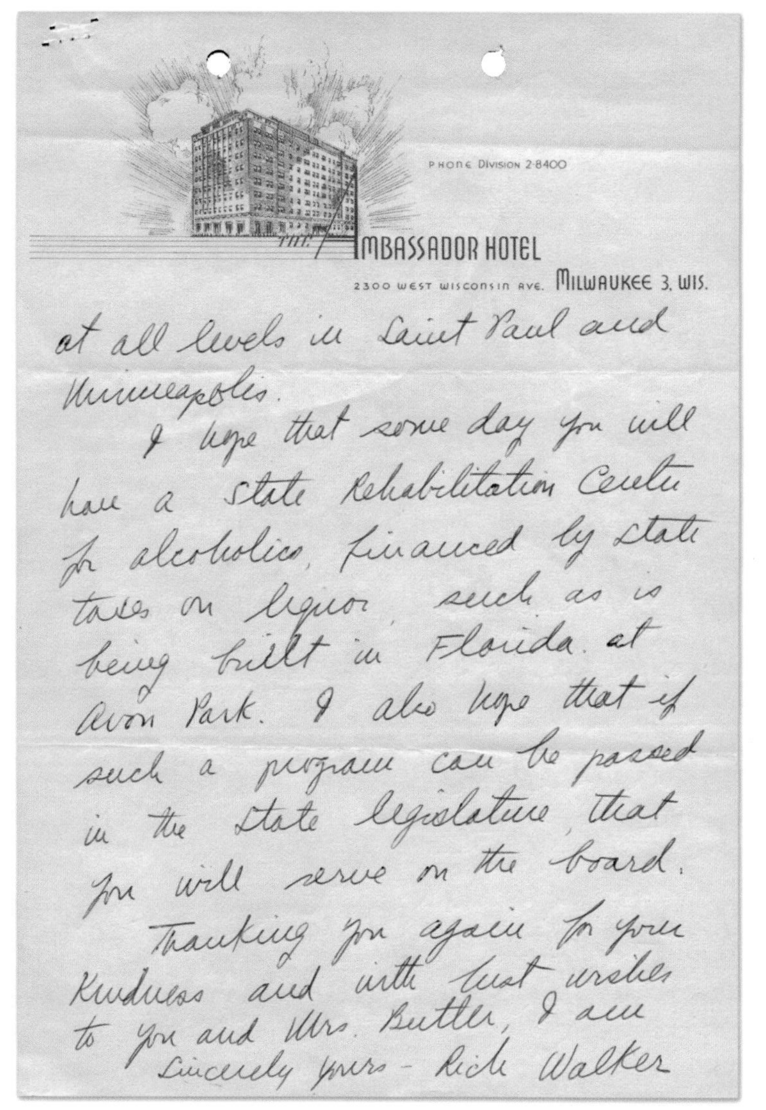

PHONE DIVISION 2-8400

AMBASSADOR HOTEL
2300 WEST WISCONSIN AVE. MILWAUKEE 3, WIS.

at all levels in Saint Paul and Minneapolis.

I hope that some day you will have a State Rehabilitation Center for alcoholics, financed by state taxes on liquor, such as is being built in Florida at Avon Park. I also hope that if such a program can be passed in the State legislature, that you will serve on the board.

Thanking you again for your kindness and with best wishes to you and Mrs. Butler, I am

Sincerely yours - Rich Walker

Selected Writings by Richmond Walker

Selected Writings by Richmond Walker

The following selections, from the Walker collections at Hazelden and Daytona Beach, have been chosen to capture more of the flavor and range of Walker's writings than were excerpted in the first essay in this book, "The Genesis of a Classic." We have retained the formatting of the originals—including underlining, punctuation, and capitalization—to better preserve the look of the typescripts themselves. All documents are drawn from Hazelden Archives and the four-volume Daytona Beach Archives, as noted below. A brief note at the end of each selection specifies the source in more detail.

Broadly, the selections reflect three main themes.

- **Walker's solid understanding of and commitment to AA:** "A Successful Group," "The Cause and Cure of Alcoholism," and "The Power to Overcome Drinking"
- **His spiritual grounding:** "Surrender," "Restitution," the poem "Meditation," and "Honesty"
- **His own story:** In the final selection, "Personal Witness," are Walker's notes for telling his story at an AA meeting on September 17, 1943.

In fact, we know that four of the selections—"The Cause and Cure of Alcoholism," "A Successful Group," and "The Power to Overcome Drinking," as well as "Personal Witness"—were notes for talks at AA meetings. The same could probably be said of some of the others—or they may simply have been personal reflections composed at various times for himself or to share with others. Their style and substance certainly are consistent with Walker's work. That fact, and their presence in the archives, give us every reason to believe they are from Walker's hand.

A Successful Group

I'm very glad to be here tonight. I know that this is a successful group, because it has the right purpose, to carry the A.A. message to alcoholics in Rutland, Proctor and other places in Vermont. That is the basis on which all A.A. groups should be formed, to carry the message to all we [who] need it and want it.

1. This group will be successful if it has a strong fellowship. A fellowship that is based on our common problem of alcoholism and our sincere desire to help each other. Keep your fellowship strong. Many a man and woman has stayed sober because of the good fellowship which he or she finds in an A.A. group. Pay particular attention to the newcomer. Be sure to make him welcome and make him feel a part of the group. Extend this fellowship to all alcoholics who ask for help.

2. This group will be successful if its members have a strong, steady faith in that Higher Power which gives us all the strength to stay sober. Do not make the mistake of soft-pedaling the spiritual part of the program. It's a spiritual program from start to finish. Members who try to live the way they believe God wants them to live, will be successful. They will surrender their lives to God. Not only their drink problem, but all parts of their lives. They will try to let God direct them in everything and try to do His will. With members like this, this group cannot help being successful.

3. This group will be successful if it has a strong sense of service. Encourage all members to do twelfth step work. Never refuse a twelfth step call. Be ready at all times to talk to anyone who needs and wants sobriety. Let an older member take a newer member with him, when he makes a call on a prospect. Carrying the message to others is what keeps an A.A. group alive and growing.

4. The newcomer is always the most important man at a meeting, because he is in the greatest need of A.A. Encourage him to find the strength he needs to stop drinking, by joining the fellowship. Take him into the group and into your hearts and make him feel at home. Encourage him to gain the strength he needs by getting off his chest the things that are bothering him. Encourage him to share his experiences. Encourage him to gain the strength he needs by turning to a Power greater than himself for help. Tell him to pray to God for the power he needs. Encourage him to gain the strength he needs by trying to carry this message to others. Put him to work and he'll stay sober.

5. This group will be successful if its members have true humility, which is based on gratitude. Each of us should be grateful to God and to A.A. that we have been given another chance to live. This attitude of gratitude should make us humble. If we are humble, if we have a true estimate of our own worth, we will be good A.A. members and the group will run smoothly.

6. Lastly, always remember that we are the lucky few. Out of all the alcoholics in the world, we are the lucky ones who through the grace of God and the help of A.A. have been given the gift of sobriety and a new and better way of life. There are thousands of alcoholics everywhere, including Rutland, who need your help. I'm sure that this group is doing a good job. May God bless you all and give you the strength to carry on.

Source: Hazelden's Pittman Archive (Hazelden I), Center City, Minnesota

• • •

SURRENDER

1. For a long time before I stopped drinking, I knew that eventually I would have to do something about it.

But toward the end of my drinking career I got more and more stubborn about it. I would not give in. No matter how much trouble I got into because of my drinking, I would not give it up. As long as I had that stubbornness, as long as I would not give up or admit that I was licked, as long as I would not surrender, there was no hope for me.

2. When I finally got to such a low point that I was forced to surrender, I began to get well.

When I admitted that I was powerless over alcohol, and turned to a Power greater than my own, I got the strength to stay sober. Giving up drinking is not a matter of will-power. It is the exact opposite of will-power. It is nothing less than surrender. It is not only admitting that we are licked; it is also going a step further and surrendering our lives to God. It's admitting that we can no longer run our own lives. It's putting our lives into the hands of God, and asking Him to run our lives for us.

3. We alcoholics have not got the A.A. program until we have surrendered our lives to God.

It is best if we can do this when we first come into A.A. But in some cases it takes a long time in A.A. before this complete surrender is made. In any case, we all have to reach it sooner or later if we are going to truly live the A.A. way of life. The essence of the program is to try to live in all respects the way you believe God wants you to live. Until we do this, we may be sober, but we have not got the A.A. program, whose second and third steps are to turn our will and our lives over to God as we understand Him.

4. This surrender of our lives to God is the crucial step.

It is the most important step that an alcoholic can take. And until he takes it, he does not have the necessary spiritual foundation under his life, which is the principal thing that makes A.A. work. There may be other ways to get sober and stay sober, but the A.A. way is to get the strength you need from a power greater than your own. We are essentially powerless until we turn to this Higher Power. Surrender to God is the basis of the A.A. program.

5. There is a hymn that ends: "We lay in dust life's glory dead and from the ground there blossoms red, life that shall endless be." We can say: "We lay in dust liquor's power dead and from that surrender blossoms red, life that shall sober be."

Source: Hazelden's Pittman Archive (Hazelden I), Center City, Minnesota

• • •

RESTITUTION

Study of the Twelve Steps

1. Every alcoholic has harmed someone by his drinking, the wife, the children, the relatives, the boss, the people he borrowed from and didn't pay back, the people he lied to, the people he injured, and so forth.

2. A man who says that just getting sober is enough amends for the harm he has done is like the farmer who came up out of his cyclone cellar to find his home ruined. To his wife he remarked: "Don't see anything the matter here, Ma. Ain't it grand the wind stopped blowin'?"

3. Just saying that we are sorry is not enough. We ought to sit down with the family and frankly analyze the past as we now see it. Those closest to us bore the brunt of our outrageous behavior. We should do our best to make amends in whatever way we can to our wife, daughter, son, or parents who, through no fault of their own, suffered physically, financially, and mentally the humiliation and embarrassment of going through life with a drunkard.

4. As we should consider the business associates who took on some of our work during our absence from the office or on those days when we had the shakes and our efficiency was low. Also consider our friends whose time we wasted with such very boring drunken blabber. Think of the effects of the bad example we were to others. We owe them all an explanation and an apology.

5. Then there are such things as the good we might have done but didn't, the contributions we were capable of making but didn't, the work and obligations which we shirked, the responsibilities we refused to take, the boost we might have given others but didn't. We harmed our fellow men largely by failing to do the things we could have done. We owe them all a debt for our omissions.

6. An explanation to those persons harmed of what we now believe to be the reasons for our past actions is the least we can do. Sometimes such an explanation will readjust our wrong personal relations with others. There are many things that will occur to us if we are sincere in trying to make amends, which we can try to do to make up to the ones we have hurt most, which usually are the ones we loved most. It is never too late to try.

7. Of course we should pay our just debts to the best of our ability. Unpaid debts cause feelings of guilt and often resentment towards the people we owe money to. We must get rid of these things by squaring our accounts with all men. Sometimes we can restore physical property to the rightful owners. We do not want past obligations hanging over us. We want to start out with a clean slate.

8. Perhaps the greatest amends are made by sincerely trying to live the A.A. way, by being very careful of our day-to-day conduct and our treatment of those closest to us. Sometimes we can restore the love and confidence and respect of our loved ones by the daily action of right living. We can at least try to redeem ourselves in their eyes by living the A.A. program day by day.

9. There are probably some wrongs that we never can make right. If so, and if we are sure that we can do nothing about them, we don't worry about them. They are out of our hands, if we can honestly say to ourselves that we would right them if we could. In any case, we can admit to ourselves and to God our past wrongs and humbly ask God's forgiveness, in lieu of making direct amends.

10. After we have honestly made all the amends we can, we should no longer carry a load of guilt. We should start over again with a clean slate. We can believe that God has forgiven us for our past sins, provided that we are honestly doing the best we can today to live the way we believe He wants us to live. Above all, we resolve to try not to hurt other people's feelings and to treat them with more consideration than we have in the past.

Source: Hazelden's Pittman Archive (Hazelden I), Center City, Minnesota

• • •

MEDITATION

God is the only Presence and the only Power
God is fully present here with me now
God is the only real Presence—all the rest is but shadow
God is perfect good—and God is the cause, only of perfect good
God never sends sickness, trouble, accident, temptation
Nor does he authorize these things
We bring them upon ourselves by our wrong thinking
God the good can cause only good

I am a child of God
In God I live and move and have my being
So I have no fear
I am surrounded by the peace of God
And all is well
I am not afraid of people—I am not afraid of things—
I am not afraid of circumstances—I am not afraid of sickness
For God is with me
The peace of God fills my soul
And I have no fear

I dwell in the presence of God
And no fear can touch me
I am not afraid of the past—I am not afraid of the present—
I am not afraid of the future
For God is with me

The Eternal God is my dwelling place
And underneath are the Everlasting Arms
Nothing can ever touch me but the direct action of God himself
And God is love
God is Life—I understand that and I express it
God is Truth—I understand that and I express it
God is Divine Love—I understand that and I express it

I send out thoughts of love and peace and healing
To the whole Universe—
To every man, woman, and child on earth—without any distinction

God is infinite Wisdom
And that wisdom is mine
That wisdom leads and guides me
God is a Lamp unto my feet—
Closer is He than breathing—nearer than hands and feet
In the presence of God I dwell forever
I thank God for perfect harmony with Him
And with my fellow men.

Source: Hazelden's Richmond Walker collection (Hazelden II), Center City, Minnesota

• • •

HONESTY

Be Honest with Yourself

It is better to ask a few questions than to know all the answers.

Every American applauds the honesty that storekeeper Abraham Lincoln practiced when he trudged miles to return a customer's change. This kind of honesty, toward others, cannot compare in importance to being honest with ourselves.

Lack of self-honesty can be profoundly damaging. Failures in self-honesty are at the root of almost every emotional and mental disturbance. Again and again, promising men and women ruin their careers because they are poor judges of their own abilities and aptitudes. On the other hand, the ability to look at yourself hard and honestly, admitting both the bad and the good, is the most powerful untapped source of human energy.

The emotional rewards of self-honesty are its most potent dividends. A mature self-knowledge greatly reduces the anxiety with which men live. People with emotional problems often have low opinions of themselves. But once they have experienced acceptance of themselves, exactly as they were, with all their shortcomings, a very positive change took place. Soon they were not only admitting their faults, but also their good points. From acceptance it was only a short step to emotional health.

Unfortunately, self-acceptance is rare. Analyzers of the national psyche have pictured millions of Americans as "OTHER DIRECTED"—looking to the goals, ideals, and ideas of others for guidance rather than inside themselves. This kind of thing distorts the individual and frustrates his inborn hunger for "personalization." He is forced constantly to dodge what he really thinks and feels—and yet in the end he cannot avoid it, because it is the deepest, most important concern of his life.

How can you check on your self-honesty?

1. Examine your sense of humor. Can you laugh at yourself—truly, genuinely laugh? If so, you probably have a good idea of what you are really like.

2. What is the last significant event in my life? A change of jobs? Marriage? Death of a loved one? Then ask yourself, "Have I ever sat down and thought this over and decided what it really meant to me?" If the answer is "No" you are rushing through life without reflecting on it and, the chances are not being completely honest with yourself.

3. It is also recommended that a thorough self-analysis be written, not as an end in

itself, but as a kind of check. A good friend should help you decide whether your list of traits and abilities is objective. If you do not have a friend from which you can ask such help —that—in itself could be a sign that you are not being honest with yourself.

Self-honesty is not easy to achieve, nor is it something that we win overnight. It is something toward which we must work slowly. Certainly, no one should spend all his time probing his inner motives, but we can at least try to be objective and honest about a selected set of goals. One important area is the 12 Steps to Recovery of the AA program. Sometimes failure, rather than success, can make us more honest about ourselves.

In searching for self-honesty, the greatest danger, is the human tendency to castigate oneself. Too many equate self-honesty with self-condemnation. Genuine self-honesty includes the appraisal of the good and the bad. We need to recognize our weaknesses; we must also recognize our potentialities so we can develop them. One of the worst mistakes is to deliberately suppress your true personality. The goal of self-honesty has been summed up as "THE OPEN SELF." The person who achieves mature self-knowledge is no longer afraid of life. He can accept all his experiences and feelings, whether of grief or happiness—of guilt or of love. He recognizes that it rests within himself to choose his way of living; the only question being,—"Is this a way that is deeply satisfying to me and which truly expresses me?"

Being honest with yourself is more than a formula for success. It is a WAY OF LIFE.

Source: Daytona Beach Archives, Vol. IV, South Daytona Beach, Florida

• • •

THE CAUSE AND CURE OF ALCOHOLISM

Richmond Walker, June 15, 1943

1. ALCOHOLISM IS A BODILY SICKNESS — Alcoholics are in the grip of a progressive sickness. Over any considerable period, they get worse, never better. There is no such thing as making a normal drinker out of an alcoholic. Once an alcoholic, always an alcoholic. The action of alcohol on alcoholics may be the manifestation of an allergy. These allergic types can never use alcohol safely in any form at all. This allergy sets these people apart as a distinct type. At some stage of his drinking career, an alcoholic begins to lose all control of his liquor consumption once he starts to drink. His disposition while drinking little resembles his normal nature. He is often perfectly sensible and well-balanced concerning everything except liquor. While an alcoholic keeps away from drink, he reacts much like other men, but once he takes any alcohol whatsoever into his system, something happens to him that makes it virtually impossible for him to stop.

2. ALCOHOLISM IS A MENTAL SICKNESS — The main problem of an alcoholic centers in his mind rather than in his body. Alcoholics are men and women who have lost the ability to control their drinking. No real alcoholic ever has recovered control. An alcoholic is absolutely unable to stop drinking on the basis of self-knowledge. He must admit he can do nothing about it himself. If he has an alcoholic mind, willpower and self-knowledge will not help in those strange mental blank spots. He has no effective mental defense against the first drink. He usually has no idea why he takes the first drink. There is also an obsession that somehow, someday he will beat the game. At a certain point in the drinking of every alcoholic he passes into a state where the most powerful desire to stop drinking is of absolutely no avail. The fact is will power becomes practically nonexistent. He is without defense against the first drink.

3. THE NEED OF A CHANGE IN THINKING — Unless an alcoholic can change his thinking, there is very little hope of his recovery. He must change his ideas, emotions, and attitudes, and a new set of motives must dominate him. The first step in recovery is to fully concede to his innermost self that he is an alcoholic. There must be no reservations of any kind, nor any lurking notion that some day he will be immune to alcohol. To get over drinking, a man must undergo a change of heart. This demands rigorous honesty. He must take stock of himself. His greatest enemies are resentments, jealousy, envy, pride, worldly desires, worry, self-pity, frustration, and fear. Once a change in thinking has taken place,

the very person who seemed doomed, who had so many problems that he despaired of ever solving them, suddenly finds himself able to control his desire for alcohol. He gains a sense of usefulness, where formerly there was utter futility. With a new outlook on life, he can look forward to each day with happiness because of the real enjoyment it is, to be sane, sober, and respectable.

4. HUMAN POWER IS NOT ENOUGH — But something more than human power is needed to produce this change in thinking. Alcoholic slaves can only be made free through the discovery of a power for good, found through a spiritual attitude toward life. They must believe in a power greater than themselves, if they are to recreate their lives. They are suffering from an illness which only a spiritual experience will conquer. They are doomed to an alcoholic death, or to live on a spiritual basis. They must accept a power greater than themselves—or else.

5. THE BELIEF IN A HIGHER POWER IS THE ANSWER — Nothing more is required to make a beginning. Lack of power had been our trouble. We have to find a power by which we can live, and it has to be a power greater than ourselves. As soon as we are willing to believe in this power, we begin to get results, even though it is impossible for us to fully define or comprehend this power. We need to ask ourselves but one question: Do I now believe, or am I willing to believe that there is a power greater than myself? As soon as a man can say that he does believe, he is on the way. It has been repeatedly proven that upon this simple cornerstone, a wonderful spiritual structure can be built. Each person has his or her own way of approaching and conceiving of this power, and each one must establish his own relationship to it. Deep down in every man and woman and child is the fundamental idea of God. It may be obscured by other things, but in some form or other it is there. We can find the Great Reality deep down within us, and when we have found it, it will revolutionize our whole attitude toward life, toward our fellows, and toward the world.

6. THE IDEA OF GOD WORKS — The spiritual life is not a theory; we have to live it. God can restore us all to our right minds. When we draw near to Him, He discloses Himself to us. We humbly offer ourselves to God, as we understand Him, to do with us as He will. We place ourselves unreservedly under His care and direction. We admit to ourselves that we are nothing; that without Him we are lost. We decide that hereafter God is going to be our Director. He is the principal, we are His agents. We abandon ourselves utterly to God. We give our lives to His care and direction, and we are willing to do anything necessary. This simple deal with God has to be continually renewed; we have to perpetually

keep the bargain. We place all our problems in God's hands. He can keep a man or woman sober if we will let Him. Say to God: Here I am and here are all my troubles. I've made a mess of things and I can't do anything about it. You take me and all my troubles and do anything You want with me. When we have done this, we find a new peace, happiness, and sense of direction. As we feel new power flow in, we get peace of mind, discover we can face life successfully, and lose our fear of today, tomorrow, or the hereafter. We feel that God has started to accomplish those things for us, which we could never do by ourselves. A new life has been given us, a design for living that really works. We feel we are on the broad highway, walking hand in hand with the Spirit of the universe.

7. STRENGTHENING FAITH THROUGH QUIET TIMES — A time of quiet meditation every morning before breakfast will help to strengthen our faith. We live one day at a time, twenty-four hours a day. On awakening, we think about the twenty-four hours ahead. We consider our plans for the day, but before we begin, we ask God to direct our thinking. We ask for strength to live that day with patience, tolerance, kindliness, and love. We ask for direction to do the right thing, no matter what the personal consequences may be. We ask God to keep us sober men and women for twenty-four hours. God will never let you down. As long as you seek God's help to the best of your ability, just so long will liquor never bother you. We conclude the period of meditation with a prayer that we be shown all through the day what our next step is to be. What we really have is a daily reprieve, but only if we maintain our relationship with God. Faith has to work in us and through us, or we perish.

8. THE PROGRAM OF ACTION — We have to take certain positive steps if we are going to live without alcohol. First is SURRENDER, we admit we are powerless over alcohol and that our lives have become unmanageable. Then comes COMMITMENT, we come to believe that a power greater than ourselves can restore us to sanity, and we make a decision to turn our will and our lives over to the care of God, as we understand Him. Then comes INVENTORY, we make a searching and fearless moral inventory of ourselves and admit to God, to ourselves, and to another person the exact nature of our wrongs, and we are entirely ready to have God remove all these defects of character, and we humbly ask Him to remove our shortcomings. Then comes RESTITUTION, we make a list of all the persons we have harmed, and are willing to make amends to such people whenever possible, except when to do so would injure them and others, and in all cases admit when we were wrong. Then comes QUIET TIMES, we seek through prayer and meditation to improve our

conscious contact with God as we understand Him, praying only for knowledge of His will for us and the power to carry it out. Then comes WITNESSING, we tell someone else all our life story and we are hard on ourselves, pocketing our pride and going to it, illuminating every twist of character, every dark cranny of the past, and withholding nothing. Then comes HELPING OTHERS, we try to carry this message to other alcoholics, and to practice these principles in all our affairs.

9. FELLOWSHIP — There exists among us a fellowship, a friendliness and an understanding which is indescribably wonderful. The tremendous fact for every one of us is that we have discovered a common solution. Frequent contact with each other is the bright spot of our lives. In the fellowship of A.A. we find release from care, boredom, and worry. Life means something at last, and we find that the most satisfactory years of our lives lie ahead. Among the fellows of A.A., you will make real friends. You will be bound to them with new and wonderful ties, for you will escape disaster together, and you will commence shoulder to shoulder your common journey. The expression on the faces, and the indefinable something in the eyes, the stimulating and electric atmosphere of the place all let you know that here is heaven at last. Social distinctions, petty rivalries and jealousies, these are laughed out of countenance. Being wrecked in the same vessel, being restored together with hearts attuned to each other's welfare, the things which matter too much to some people no longer signify much to them. There is a special atmosphere created by friendliness, sincerity, confidence, and good cheer.

10. WORKING WITH OTHERS — Practical experience shows that nothing will so much insure immunity from drinking as work with other alcoholics. Helping others is the foundation of our own recovery. Our very lives as alcoholics depend upon our constant thought of others and how we may help meet their needs. So carry this message to other alcoholics. You can help when no one else can. You can secure confidence, when others fail. Because of your own drinking experience, you can be uniquely useful to other alcoholics. The alcoholic who has found the solution, who is armed with the facts about himself, can generally win the confidence of another alcoholic. That you have had the same difficulty, that you obviously know what you are talking about, your whole deportment shouts at the new prospect that you are a man or woman with the real answer. You have no attitude of holier than thou, nothing whatever except the sincere desire to be helpful. You have that real tolerance of other people's shortcomings, which makes you useful to others. You discover the joy of helping others to face life again. No matter how far down the scale you have gone, you

will see how your experience can help others. The feeling of uselessness will disappear. Anyone can be the human agency, employed by God to bring another person into the new way of life. We have been given our experience so that we might understand and be of use in helping others to find a solution of their problems. We can find what it means to give of ourselves that others may survive and rediscover life. We can learn that full meaning of "love thy neighbor as thyself."

Source: Pittman Archive (Hazelden I).
This document is a commentary on *Alcoholics Anonymous,* the Big Book.

• • •

THE POWER TO OVERCOME DRINKING

Introduction—I want to say something about power. We're all looking for the power to overcome drinking. A fellow comes in here and his first question is: "How do I get the strength to quit?" At first, it seems to him that he will never get the necessary strength. He sees older members who have found the power he is looking for, but he doesn't know the process by which they got it. As we all know, the necessary strength comes in four ways:

1. FIRST, strength comes from the fellowship you find when you come in here. Just being with men and women who have found the way out, gives you a feeling of security. You listen to the speakers, you talk with other members, and you absorb the atmosphere of confidence and hope that you find in this place. So the first strength comes from fellowship.

2. SECOND, strength comes from honestly telling your own experiences with liquor. In religion they call it confession. We call it witnessing or sharing. You give a personal witness. You share your past experiences, the troubles you got into, the hospitals, the jails, the breakup of your home, the money wasted, the debts and all the foolish things you did when you were drinking. This personal witness lets out things you had kept hidden, brings them out into the open, and you find release and strength. So the second strength comes from personal witness.

3. THIRD, strength comes from gradually coming to believe in a Higher Power that can help you. You can't define this Higher Power, but you can see how it helps other alcoholics. You hear them talk about it, and you begin to get the idea yourself. You try praying in a quiet time each morning, and you begin to feel stronger, as though your prayers were heard. So you gradually come to believe there must be a Power in the world, outside of yourself, which is stronger than you, and to which you can turn for help. So the third strength comes from God.

4. FOURTH, strength comes from working with other alcoholics. When you are talking with a prospect and trying to help him, you are building up your own strength at the same time. One member expressed this by saying: "One look at that puss will keep me sober for a year." You see the other fellow in the condition you might be in and it makes your resolve to stay sober stronger than ever. Often you help yourself more than the other fellow, but if you do succeed in helping him to get sober, you are stronger from the experience of having helped another man. And, most important, you don't want to let him down. So the fourth strength comes from working with others.

CONCLUSION — So you get the power to overcome drinking through the fellowship of other alcoholics who have found the way out, by honestly sharing your past experiences by a personal witness, by gradually coming to believe in a Higher Power which can help you, and by working with other alcoholics and not letting them down. In these four ways, thousands of alcoholics have found all the power they need to overcome drinking. And we all know that this power is ready and waiting for any alcoholic who is ready and willing to accept it, and to work for it.

Source: Hazelden's Pittman Archive (Hazelden I), Center City, Minnesota

• • •

PERSONAL WITNESS

A.A. MEETING, September 17, 1943

Richmond Walker

1. I believe I was an alcoholic from the start. The first drink I had was when I was a freshman at Williams College. I drank champagne at a fraternity initiation, and passed out completely. When I woke up, I had names written in pencil, all over my white shirt front.

2. But I didn't drink much in college. I was in training for football a good deal of the time. The next time I was publicly drunk was after we won our big game with Amherst. The president of the college got quite a shock when he saw me hanging upside down on an old cannon in the public square of Northampton.

3. After I got out of college, I went into the wool business with my older brother. Neither of us was married and we lived together on Beacon Hill for eight years. I was becoming a heavy drinker.

4. War came and I enlisted as a private in the Army Medical Corps, and was sent to the Medical Supply Depot in New York City. A pal of mine and I managed to get drunk regularly in the New York hot spots. Through a pull with the Surgeon General's office, I was sent to an officer's training school, and got a commission as Second Lieutenant in the Sanitary Corps. I went south as Adjutant of an Evacuation hospital and continued drinking when off duty. I was in quarantine when the war ended.

5. I got married when I was thirty, and prohibition came along. We had a big house in Chestnut Hill with a private bar, and we had a lot of big parties. I remember once after a Harvard-Princeton football game, arguments led to a swell fight, which was won by the Princeton men.

6. We also had a cottage on Nantucket Island, where I traveled with a drinking crowd. There were cocktail parties morning, noon, and night. I flew down from Boston week-ends with a gallon of alcohol in my suitcase and plenty inside of me.

7. We took several trips with friends to Cuba and the West Indies. I tried to drink up all the Bacardi Rum in Cuba, so I don't remember much about it. I went to Bermuda with another fellow, and I don't remember anything about that trip to this day, except the money I spent.

8. During the depression I sold my house in Chestnut Hill, and we moved to Cohasset. We had three children by this time. Moving into a new town, I promised my wife I was through with liquor for good. But of course I wasn't.

9. I was soon frequenting the taverns around South Shore. Finally, it got so bad that I ended up in the Cohasset hospital. I had been in a hospital in Boston before this, with delirium from pneumonia or the D.T.s, I don't know which. While I was in the Cohasset hospital, my wife sent a lawyer to tell me she was through with me. And I didn't blame her. My drinking wasn't fair to her or the children.

10. I moved to Boston and took a room on Beacon Street, and stayed pretty drunk most of the time for the next six months, feeling sorry for myself. I traveled from one Boston barroom to another. There were lots of days I didn't get to work.

11. In the spring of last year my father died and I met my wife at the funeral. We became reconciled on the basis that I would never take another drink. I went back to my family in Cohasset.

12. I did pretty well for awhile, but soon I was sneaking out to the corner barroom, after my wife had gone to bed. I didn't get away with it, but my wife didn't say anything.

13. My last drink was this spring in the middle of May. I started with a few beers in Scituate, and was missing for a week. I came to in a Boston hotel room. I managed to get home somehow, and was in bed for three days and suffered the tortures of hell. I had come to the end of my rope. Thirty years had passed since my first drink at college. It had taken me that long to find out that liquor was poison to me.

14. My wife never said a thing, but of course I knew how she felt and how the children felt. When I was strong enough to get out of bed, I told my wife I would go to A.A. Evans Dick had told me about A.A. a year before this.

15. But I didn't go right away. A few days later, a friend of mine in the wool trade called me up at the office, and asked me to help him take care of another man we both knew, who was on a drunk. In the course of trying to help him, we called on the A.A. and Jack Priest came over to the Hotel Essex to help us. He asked me up to the A.A. meeting. And the next Wednesday I was there.

16. And I want to say that I've found a new life in A.A. As Nate Andrews said last Wednesday night, the A.A. is my whole life. If I ever drink again it will be the end of me.

Nobody who listened to Nate Andrews can doubt that the A.A. works. It worked in my case. I am more appreciative of my wife than every before and I'm very grateful to her. And my children and I get along fine.

17. The Higher Power can change any one of us from a drunkard to a sober person. He can give a new life, which is so much better than the old life that there is no comparison. All we have to do is to give God a chance.

Source: Hazelden's Pittman Archive (Hazelden I).

This selection shows a memory lapse when it comes to dates: In paragraph 11, Walker writes that his father died in the "spring of last year" [1942], when the actual date was the fall of 1941.

• • •

ABOUT THE AUTHOR

Before coming to Hazelden, Damian McElrath spent three decades as a Franciscan priest serving the spiritual needs of others in a variety of roles, including teaching, counseling, and administrative positions. He was president of St. Bonaventure University from 1972 to 1976. In that life, he wrote and edited a number of scholarly books and articles on historical and theological topics.

Damian arrived at Hazelden in 1977 to participate in its Clinical Pastoral Education program. Over the course of the next two decades, he served in a variety of administrative roles, including Executive Vice President of Recovery Services, as well as being chaplain to Hazelden's long-term care program for almost a decade. He has authored a number of books on Hazelden's history, including *Hazelden: A Spiritual Odyssey,* as well as biographies of its founders, Patrick Butler and Dan Anderson. His most recent book, *The Essence of Twelve Step Recovery,* is about the spiritual foundations of the Twelve Step Program.

He considers his introductory essays to this book as the culmination of a journey that began thirty-five years ago with his first encounter with the Little Black Book on the first morning he arrived at Hazelden, when he was asked to read the passage for that day.

• • •

Hazelden, a national nonprofit organization founded in 1949, helps people reclaim their lives from the disease of addiction. Built on decades of knowledge and experience, Hazelden offers a comprehensive approach to addiction that addresses the full range of patient, family, and professional needs, including treatment and continuing care for youth and adults, research, higher learning, public education and advocacy, and publishing.

A life of recovery is lived "one day at a time." Hazelden publications, both educational and inspirational, support and strengthen lifelong recovery. In 1954, Hazelden published *Twenty-Four Hours a Day,* the first daily meditation book for recovering alcoholics, and Hazelden continues to publish works to inspire and guide individuals in treatment and recovery, and their loved ones. Professionals who work to prevent and treat addiction also turn to Hazelden for evidence-based curricula, informational materials, and videos for use in schools, treatment programs, and correctional programs.

Through published works, Hazelden extends the reach of hope, encouragement, help, and support to individuals, families, and communities affected by addiction and related issues.